Oxford Islamic Studies Online

FREE 6-month subscription with the purchase of a new book– a $120 value!

Encompassing over 5,000 A–Z reference entries, chapters from scholarly and introductory works, Qur'anic materials, primary sources, images, maps, and timelines, *Oxford Islamic Studies Online* offers a multi-layered reference experience designed to provide a first stop for anyone needing information and context on Islam.

Online access to the finest scholarship in Islamic Studies includes...

• Content from *The Oxford Handbook of Islam and Politics, The Grove Encyclopedia of Islamic Art & Architecture, The Oxford Encyclopedia of the Islamic World*, and other scholarly works

• Two Oxford World's Classics versions of the Qur'an: M.A.S. Abdel Haleem's The Qur'an, a prose translation, and The Koran Interpreted, a renowned verse translation by A.J. Arberry

• Images, maps, and timelines

• Tools and resources to aid research at any level

To activate your FREE 6-month subscription to Oxford Islamic Studies Online, go to https://ams.oup.com/order/OISOITSPSCRIP and follow the instructions for entering your activation code.

SR16318041878718

For customers outside the Americas, please go to https://subscriberservices.sams.oup.com/views/access_token_1.html and enter the code.

Please note that your subscription will start as soon as the activation code is entered. This offer expires December 15, 2019.

http://www.oxfordislamicstudies.com

OXFORD
UNIVERSITY PRESS

Islam

Islam
The Straight Path

FIFTH EDITION
UPDATED

JOHN L. ESPOSITO
Georgetown University

New York   Oxford

OXFORD UNIVERSITY PRESS
2016

Oxford University Press is a department of the University of Oxford.
It furthers the University's objective of excellence in research,
scholarship, and education by publishing worldwide.

Oxford   New York
Auckland   Cape Town   Dar es Salaam   Hong Kong   Karachi
Kuala Lumpur   Madrid   Melbourne   Mexico City   Nairobi
New Delhi   Shanghai   Taipei   Toronto

With offices in
Argentina   Austria   Brazil   Chile   Czech Republic   France   Greece
Guatemala   Hungary   Italy   Japan   Poland   Portugal   Singapore
South Korea   Switzerland   Thailand   Turkey   Ukraine   Vietnam

For titles covered by Section 112 of the US Higher Education Opportunity
Act, please visit www.oup.com/us/he for the latest information about
pricing and alternate formats.

Published by Oxford University Press.
198 Madison Avenue, New York, NY 10016
http://www.oup.com

Oxford is a registered trademark of Oxford University Press

Library of Congress Cataloging-in-Publication Data
Names: Esposito, John L., author.
   Title: Islam : the straight path / John L. Esposito.
   Description: Fifth edition. | New York ; Oxford : Oxford University Press,
      2016. | Includes bibliographical references and index.
   Identifiers: LCCN 2016007043 (print) | LCCN 2016008506 (ebook) |
      ISBN 978–0–19–063215–1 | ISBN 978–0–19–938147–0 ()
   Subjects: LCSH: Islam.
   Classification: LCC BP161.2 .E85 2016 (print) | LCC BP161.2 (ebook) |
      DDC 297—dc23
   LC record available at http://lccn.loc.gov/2016007043

Printing number: 9 8 7 6 5 4 3 2

Printed in the United States of America
on acid-free paper

In memory of Ismail and Lois Al-Faruqi

CONTENTS

PREFACE

Islam: The Straight Path has enjoyed a broad audience as a textbook and as an introduction to Islam for educated readers not only in the English-speaking world, but also through translations from Europe to Southeast Asia. Earlier editions provided essential coverage of the origins, spread, and development of Islam and its roles in Muslim societies. This fifth edition has offered an occasion to reorganize the presentation of materials within some chapters significantly and to update and add materials in response to developments and events that have occurred since the publication of the fourth edition in 2009.

CHANGES TO THE FIFTH EDITION

In addition to updating the map of the Muslim world, chronological timeline, and bibliography and increasing the number of breakout boxes, a new feature has been added—discussion questions placed at the end of each chapter. More substantially, several chapters have been substantially reorganized and expanded. Chapter 2, "The Muslim Community in History," now includes extensive coverage of Islam in the West, a topic further developed in Chapter 6. Chapter 5, "The Resurgence of Religion in Politics," incorporates the unexpected and stunning Arab Spring: peoples' uprisings that overthrew entrenched authoritarian regimes in broad-based movements in Tunisia, Egypt, and Libya; popular revolts in Syria, Bahrain, and Yemen; and Islamic parties' (Egypt's Muslim Brotherhood and Tunisia's Ennahda) victories in presidential and parliamentary elections. Equally unexpected were the Egyptian military-led coup and restoration of authoritarianism and the emergence and rapid spread of ISIS, the Islamic State, with its victories in Iraq and Syria and vision of a restoration of a caliphate. However different, both the Arab Spring and ISIS underscore the need for and significance of Islamic reform, the subject of Chapter 6, "The Struggle for Islam in the Twenty-First Century." The chapter presents a selection of major religious scholars, intellectuals, and popular preachers who address critical questions and issues of Islamic reform. It surveys diverse and sometimes competing positions of traditionalist and more modernist Muslim reformers on issues of religious authority, violence and terrorism, Islam and democracy, Shariah reform, women's rights, human rights, and religious pluralism in Muslim countries and in the West. Finally, the chapter looks in detail at the American Muslim community, its challenges and accomplishments in becoming an integral part of the American mosaic as the exponential development of Islamophobia, anti-Islam and anti-Muslim bias, prejudice toward and discrimination against Muslims on the basis of their religion or religious identity, and the extent to which the actions of a small minority of Muslim extremists and terrorist American and European Muslims brushstroke the mainstream majority of Muslim citizens and affect their security, safety, and civil liberties.

ACKNOWLEDGMENTS

Many people have been supportive in the production of this book. At Oxford University Press the most important are my two editors: Cynthia Read, my longtime editor at Oxford who first contracted *Islam: The Straight Path*, and, in recent years, Robert Miller, with whom I have worked on subsequent editions.

I have been fortunate to have very talented and responsive senior research assistants: Melanie Trexler, Nathan Lean, Rahel Fishback, and especially Tasi Perkins, who assisted me at every stage in the writing and production process. I am indebted to Dalia Mogahed, with whom I co-authored *Who Speaks for Islam? What a Billion Muslims Really Think* and related articles, as well as my colleagues John Voll and Tamara Sonn, co-authors of *Islam and Democracy after the Arab Spring* and other works, who inform my writing and are always responsive when I ask for feedback. And last but most, special thanks to Jean Esposito, my wife and partner for fifty years, who, as with all my projects, has been always been my best editor and critic.

John L. Esposito
Washington, D.C.

INTRODUCTION

Few religions have had a greater impact as a faith and on world affairs, past and present, than Islam. Muslims, numbering 1.6 billion worldwide, account for one out of four people on our planet. Islam, the second largest of the world's religions, has a global presence. Muslims live in some fifty-seven Muslim countries, stretching from North Africa to the Middle East, to Central, South, and Southeast Asia. Muslims live as religious minorities from Europe and America to Asia and Australia. Islam in Europe and America in a matter of decades has gone from being invisible to being the second or third largest religion. Older Muslim minority communities extend from Africa to India—where the Muslim minority population of 160 million is the fourth largest Muslim population in the world—to the southern Philippines.

For more than fourteen centuries, Islam has grown and spread from the seventh-century Arabia of the Prophet Muhammad to a world religion with followers across the globe. It has spawned and informed Islamic empires and states as well as a great world civilization that stretched from North Africa to Southeast Asia. In the process, a great monotheistic tradition, sharing common roots with Judaism and Christianity, has guided and transformed the lives of millions of believers down through the ages. Characterized by an uncompromising belief in the one, true God—His revelation and Prophet—Islam developed a spiritual path with law, ethics, theology, and mysticism that have made it one of the fastest growing religions, both in the past and today.

Media images of Islam have often obscured the fact that Muslims, Jews, and Christians share much in common; they are indeed all children of Abraham. Like Jews and Christians, Muslims worship the God of Abraham and Moses, believe in God's revelation and prophets, and place a strong emphasis on moral responsibility and accountability. The vast majority of Muslims, like most members of other religious traditions, are pious, hardworking women and men, family and community oriented, who wish to live in peace and harmony rather than in warfare.

Despite Islam's global presence and rich faith, Islam and Muslims have been relatively invisible on the cognitive maps of most American and European citizens, educators, policymakers, and the media. All of this changed with the Iranian revolution and subsequent events in the Muslim world, in particular the impact of global terrorist attacks from Nigeria to Indonesia and in the United States, Europe, and elsewhere by al-Qaeda, ISIS, and other militant groups. However, too often interest in and coverage of Islam was driven by explosive headline events, acts of violence and terror that all but obscured the breadth and diversity of the Muslim experience and which were seen through the lens of a monolithic threat, commonly referred to as Islamic fundamentalism or Islamism, terms often signifying militant radicalism and violence. Thus Islam, a rich and dynamic religious tradition of the mainstream majority, became all but buried by menacing headlines and slogans, images of hostage takers and gun-toting mullahs.

In an increasingly globally interdependent world, understanding Islam as well as its multiple roles in Muslim politics and society is not only intellectually and religiously fruitful but also, as events in recent decades have demonstrated, politically important. This volume seeks to explain the faith, the belief, and the doctrines of Islam. It provides a guide to understanding how Islam has developed, spread, and informed the lives of Muslims, their faith, their politics, and their communities throughout the ages.

Islam: The Straight Path addresses a variety of questions that underscore the strength, vitality, and diversity of Islam as well as its role in Muslim history: What is Islam? Who are Muslims and what do they believe? How did Islam develop and spread throughout the world? How has Islam informed the faith and politics of Muslim life? Is Islam a particularly violent religion? Are Islam and democracy, gender, and human rights incompatible? Have Muslims, like religious believers throughout the world, wrestled with issues of change and reform to assure the continued relevance of Islam to modern Muslim life? What role did Islam play in the Arab Spring and in governments that emerged. What are the causes and impact of anti-Islam and anti-Muslim bias and discrimination (Islamophobia). The answers to these and other questions are concerns for all of us.

The foundation of Islamic belief and practice is the Quran, for Muslims the revealed literal word of God, and the example and teachings of the

Prophet Muhammad. Chapter 1, "Muhammad and the Quran: Messenger and Message," describes the emergence of Islam, focusing in particular on the life and role of the Prophet and the teachings of the Quran regarding God, prophecy, and revelation; the purpose and goal of human life; morality; and the afterlife. Where relevant, comparisons are drawn between Muslim, Jewish, and Christian teachings.

The Muslim community has been the central vehicle for the spread and actualization of Islam's universal message and mission. Chapter 2, "The Muslim Community in History," discusses the formation and development of the Muslim community, the phenomenal expansion of Islam, the creation of Islamic empires and states, the emergence of the Sunni and Shii branches of the Islamic community, and the florescence of Islam as a world civilization that made major contributions to the history of philosophy, theology, the sciences, literature, mathematics, astronomy, and medicine.

Muslim faith and practice are rooted in revelation but expressed in a variety of beliefs, attitudes, rituals, laws, and values. Chapter 3, "Religious Life: Belief and Practice," analyzes the development of Islamic theology, philosophy, law, and mysticism. In particular, it discusses the Five Pillars of Islam, those fundamental acts that provide the unity underlying the rich cultural diversity of Muslim life, as well as Muslim family law. As the Five Pillars are the core of a Muslim's duty to worship God, family law is central to social life, providing guidelines for marriage, divorce, and inheritance.

Like all great world religions, Islam has passed through many stages in its development. Throughout its long history, the community has had to respond to internal and external threats to its continued life and vitality. As a result, Islam has a long tradition of religious renewal and reform, extending from its earliest history to the present. The eighteenth century proved to be a turning point in Islamic history. The power, prosperity, and dynamic expansionism of imperial Islam went into decline. A previously ascendant and expanding community and civilization has had to struggle for its survival in the face of indigenous forces and the political and religiocultural threat of European colonialism. Chapter 4, "Modern Islamic Reform Movements," chronicles the rise of Islamic activist ("fundamentalist") movements, bent on the restoration of Islam, that sprang up across much of the Islamic world—the Wahhabi in Saudi Arabia, the Mahdi in the Sudan, the Sanusi in Libya—and that served as forerunners to twentieth-century revivalism. Most important, this chapter analyzes key individuals, movements, and organizations, such as the Islamic modernist movement, the Muslim Brotherhood, and the Jamaat-i-Islami, who have had a profound effect on twentieth- and twenty-first-century Islam, its faith, intellectual, and community life.

Although the Iranian revolution drew the attention of many to Islam and the Islamic resurgence, contemporary Islamic revivalism has had an impact on the personal and public lives of Muslims for the past two decades. Chapter 5, "The Resurgence of Religion in Politics," reviews the causes, worldview, and manifestations of Islamic revivalism. A series of case studies from Saudi Arabia, Libya, Iran, Lebanon, and Egypt is briefly presented to demonstrate the diversity of ways in which Islam has been used by governments and by mainstream and extremist opposition groups.

The events of September 11, 2001, signaled a watershed moment in global history and politics. Islam has been used to legitimate holy and unholy wars, movements of resistance and liberation, and violence and terror. In addition to the origins and growth of religious extremism: Chapter 5 deals with the relationship of Islam to violence and terrorism, the meaning of jihad, the origins of a global jihad ideology, the role of suicide bombing, and the political conditions and the influence of Wahhabi and of Salafi Islam, which are relevant to understanding Osama bin Laden and al-Qaeda as well as ISIS in Syria and Iraq. Finally, what role did religion and politics play in the Arab uprisings or Arab Spring, especially in Tunisia and Egypt, and what were the results?

Muslims today, like believers the world over, continue to grapple with the continued relevance of their faith to the realities of contemporary society. The adaptability of a religious tradition, its relevance to life in the twenty-first century, raises as many questions as it offers potential answers. The history of modern Islam has challenged many presuppositions and expectations—in particular, the notion that modernization results in the secularization of societies. Islamic revival and reform, the attempt to apply Islam to modern or postmodern life, have generated many questions and issues that are examined in Chapter 6, "The Struggle for Islam in the Twenty-First Century," which looks at the process of modern reform: Who are the reformers? What are the parameters and direction of Islamic reform—a restoration of the past or a process of reinterpretation and reconstruction? Is the future of Islam to be left in the hands of traditional religious leaders (ulama), Muslim rulers, or the laity? If change is to occur, how much is necessary or possible? What are the implications for democratization, pluralism, the rights of women and religious minorities, and interfaith relations?

Today, Islam is the religion of one quarter of the world's population. Muslims are truly global citizens, who are also part of the mosaic of Western societies; they are no longer foreign visitors but fellow citizens and colleagues. Increased recognition has led to an appreciation among many that Islam is an integral part of a theologically interconnected and historically intertwined Judeo-Christian-Islamic heritage.

As in the past, Islam is among the fastest growing religions in many parts of the world and has taken on diverse forms, depending on local political, social, and cultural contexts. The vast majority of mainstream Muslims, like many other global citizens of faith, lead constructive and productive lives informed by their faith. A very small but dangerous and deadly minority terrorize Muslim and Western societies alike. Relations between the Muslim world and the West will continue to require a joint effort, a process of constructive engagement, dialogue, self-criticism, and change. Regardless of religious and cultural differences, Muslims, Christians, Jews, and many other global citizens share common religious and civilizational principles, values, and aspirations: belief in God and His prophets, revelation, moral responsibility and accountability, the sanctity of life, the value of the family, a desire for economic prosperity, access to education, technology, peace and security, social justice, political participation, freedom, and human rights. The goal of *Islam: The Straight Path* is primarily to contribute to a better understanding of the faith of Islam, which, as in the past, inspires, guides, and motivates the vast majority of Muslims as believers and global citizens.

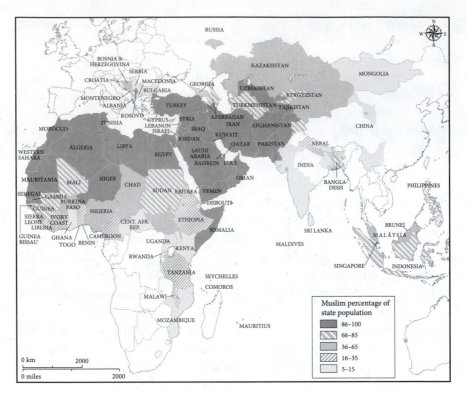

The Muslim world.

Chapter 1

Muhammad and the Quran: Messenger and Message

In the name of God, the Merciful and Compassionate:
praise belongs to God, the Lord of the Worlds, the
Merciful, the Compassionate; Master of the Day of
Judgment, You do we worship and You do we call on
for help; guide us on the Straight Path, the path of
those whom You have blessed, not of those who earn
your anger nor those who go astray.

(Quran 1:1–7)

Five times each day, hundreds of millions of Muslims face Mecca to pray. They are part of an Islamic community that spans the globe, numbers perhaps 1.6 billion adherents, and continues to spread its message successfully throughout Europe, Asia, Africa, and North America. The fifty-seven **Muslim** countries extend from Senegal to Indonesia, but the message of Islam and significant Muslim populations can be found in such diverse environments as the former Soviet republics, China, India, England, and the United States. Islam, the second largest of the world's religions, is indeed a world presence and force. If much of the Western world had missed that fact, events in the decades since the Iranian revolution have rectified this oversight. However, Muslim politics, from the Iranian revolution to the 9/11 attacks and subsequent terrorist attacks in the West and in Muslim countries, have often obscured or, at the very least, raised questions about the faith of Islam and its relationship to violence and terrorism.

Islam stands in a long line of Semitic, prophetic religious traditions that share an uncompromising monotheism and belief in God's revelation, His prophets, ethical responsibility and accountability, and the Day of Judgment. Indeed, Muslims, like Christians and Jews, are the **Children of Abraham**, because all trace their communities back to him: Islam's historic religious and political relationship to Christendom and Judaism has remained strong throughout history. This interaction has been the source of mutual benefit and borrowing as well as misunderstanding and conflict.

Although the followers of Islam belong to a single community of believers, there are two major historic divisions: **Sunni** and **Shii**. Sunni Muslims constitute 85 percent of the world's Muslims; Shii about 15 percent. Although this volume focuses on their common faith and belief, attention will also be given to differences in Muslim belief and practice. For although, as we shall see, all Muslims enjoy a unity of faith in **Allah**, the **Quran**, and the teachings of Muhammad, the interpretations and applications of Islam have varied in different cultural contexts and eras. Despite this recognition of diversity, the focus of this volume is the core of beliefs, practices, and institutions that unite and are integral to Muslim life, whatever the differences might be.

MUHAMMAD AND THE MUSLIM COMMUNITY

The Near East spawned and nurtured a rich variety of religious traditions: ancient Egyptian and Mesopotamian religions, Zoroastrianism, Judaism, and Christianity. However, given the nature of tribal society in seventh-century Arabia and the presence of the Roman (Byzantine) and Persian (Sasanid) empires as buffer states of the Arabian Peninsula, the rise of a new religious movement and the inauguration of a new stage in world history would have seemed unthinkable. Yet, this occurred with the revelation of the Quran and under the leadership of the Prophet Muhammad. Islamic religion and the activity of the Muslim community produced a new empire and a rich civilization that came to dominate much of Europe, the Middle East, Asia, and Africa. Because Islam developed in central Arabia, its religious and social milieu provides the context for Muhammad's reformist message and mission.

Arabia

Arabian religion and society reflected the tribal realities of the Peninsula. Arabia's 1 million square miles (nearly one third the size of the United States or Europe) were dominated by desert and steppe areas. Bedouin tribes pursuing a pastoral and nomadic lifestyle traveled from one area to another, seeking water and pasture for their flocks of sheep and camels. The landscape was dotted with oasis towns and cities. Among the more prominent was Mecca, a center of trade and commerce, and Yathrib (**Medina**), an important agricultural settlement. The principal sources of livelihood were herding, agriculture, trade, and raiding. Intertribal warfare was a long-established activity governed by clear guidelines and rules. For example, raiding was illegal during the four sacred months of pilgrimage. Its object was to capture livestock from enemy Bedouin tribes with a minimum of casualties. Its ultimate goal was to weaken and eventually absorb other tribes by reducing them to a dependent or "client" status.

Whether nomadic or sedentary, the peoples of Arabia lived in a Bedouin tribal society and culture. Social organization and identity were rooted in membership in an extended family. A grouping of several related families comprised a clan. A cluster of several clans constituted a tribe. Tribes were led by a chief (*shaykh*) who was selected by a consensus of his peers—that is, the heads of leading clans or families. These tribal elders formed an advisory council within which the tribal chief exercised his leadership and authority as the first among equals. Muhammad belonged to the Banu Hashim (sons of Hashim), a lesser clan of the powerful Quraysh tribe that dominated Meccan society.

The Arabs placed great emphasis on tribal ties, group loyalty, or solidarity as the source of power for a clan or tribe. The celebrated rugged individualism of the Bedouin Arab ethos was counterbalanced by subordination to tribal authority and tribal customs, the unwritten oral law of society. Tribal affiliation and law were the basis not only for identity but also for protection. The threat of family or group vendetta, the law of retaliation, was of vital importance in a society lacking a central political authority or law.

The religion of Arabia reflected its tribal nature and social structure. Gods and goddesses served as protectors of individual tribes, and their spirits were associated with sacred objects—trees, stones, springs, and wells. Local tribal deities were feared and respected rather than loved, the objects of cultic rituals (sacrifice, pilgrimage, prayer) and of supplication and propitiation celebrated at local shrines. Mecca possessed a central shrine of the gods, the **Kaba**, a cube-shaped building that housed the 360 idols of tribal patron deities and was the site of a great annual pilgrimage and fair. These deities were primary religious actors and objects of worship, but beyond this tribal polytheism was a shared belief in Allah (God). Allah, the supreme high god, was the creator and sustainer of life but remote from everyday concerns and thus not the object of cult or ritual. Associated with Allah were three goddesses who were the daughters of Allah: al-Lat, Manat, and al-Uzza.

The value system or ethical code of Arabia has been aptly termed a "tribal humanism," a way of life with origins that were not ascribed to God but were the product of tribal experience or tradition.[1] It was epitomized by its key virtue, manliness, which emphasized bravery in battle, loyalty to family and protection of its members, hospitality, patience, and persistence—in sum, the preservation of tribal and family honor. This was accompanied by a fatalism that saw no meaning or accountability beyond this life—no resurrection of the body, divine judgment, or eternal punishment or reward. Justice was guaranteed and administered not by God but by the threat of group vengeance or retaliation. Thus, Arabian religion had little sense of cosmic moral purpose or of individual or communal moral responsibility.

Although it is common to speak of Islam's origins in seventh-century Arabia, such a notion is historically inaccurate and, from a Muslim perspective, theologically false. Islam was not an isolated, totally new monotheistic religion. The monotheistic message of the Quran and the preaching of Muhammad did not occur in a vacuum. Monotheism had been flourishing in Semitic and Persian cultures for centuries preceding Muhammad's ministry. The scriptures and prophets of Judaism, Christianity, and Zoroastrianism had a long-established presence and roots in Irano-Semitic societies. Beyond their distinctive differences, all three religious traditions shared a monotheistic faith (the conviction that God is one), prophets, scriptures, beliefs in angels and devils, and a moral universe encompassing individual and communal accountability and responsibility. All were the product of primarily urban, not rural or desert, experiences and were institutionalized in commercial centers by scholarly elites, often supported by state patronage, who interpreted the early preaching of their prophets and apostles. Among their common themes were community, fidelity and infidelity, individual moral decision-making, social justice, final judgment, and reward and punishment. In contrast to Indian religious notions of cyclical history, rebirth, and personal perfection, the Judeo-Christian and Zoroastrian traditions affirmed a sacred history with a beginning and an end within which believers were to follow God's will and realize their eternal destiny in the next life. To differing degrees, all had become associated with political power; that is, all had become official state religions: Judaism in the kingdoms of Judea and Israel, Christianity in the Roman (Byzantine) empire, and Zoroastrianism in the Persian (Sasanid) empire.

Forms of monotheism did exist in Arabia alongside pre-Islamic tribal polytheism. Both Jewish and Christian Arab communities had been present in Arabia before Muhammad. Jewish communities in Khaybar, Tayma, and Yathrib (later called Medina) were successful in agriculture and trade. Although some Christians were settled in Mecca, most of the Christian communities were on the periphery of central Arabia (the Hijaz), along caravan routes in North and South Arabia. Particular contact with monotheism resulted from the caravan trade that brought Zoroastrian, Jewish, and Christian merchants to Mecca, a thriving commercial center, as well as from the travels of Meccan traders far and wide throughout the Middle East. Finally, in addition to biblical monotheism, native or pre-Islamic Arab monotheists, called *hanifs*, seem to have existed. The Quran (3:95) and Muslim tradition portray them as descendants of Abraham and his son **Ismail**.

Arabian tribal society, with its Bedouin, polytheistic ethos, provided the context for the rise of Islam. Of equal importance, this period was marked by the tensions and questioning that accompany change in a transitional society, for this was a period when cities like Mecca and Medina were prospering and attracting many from a nomadic to a more sedentary life. The emergence of Mecca as a major mercantile center precipitated the beginnings of a new political, social, and economic order. New wealth, the rise of a new commercial oligarchy from within the Quraysh tribe, greater division between social classes, and a growing disparity between rich and poor strained the traditional system of Arab tribal values and social security—its way of life. This was the time and social milieu in which Muhammad was born.

Muhammad: Prophet of God

History, legend, and Muslim belief portray Muhammad as a remarkable man and prophet. We know a good deal about Muhammad's life after his "call" to be God's messenger, but historical records tell us little about Muhammad's early years prior to becoming a prophet at the age of forty in 610 c.e. The Quran has served as a major source for information regarding the life of the Prophet. In addition, **hadiths** or Prophetic traditions (reports about what Muhammad said and did) and biographies give us a picture of his meaning and significance in early Islam, as do Islamic calligraphy and art, where the names of Allah and Muhammad often occur side by side—God and His Prophet. Muhammad serves both as God's human instrument in bearing His revelation and as the model or ideal all believers should emulate. Thus, understanding Muhammad and his role in the early Islamic community is crucial for an appreciation of the development of early Islam as well as the dynamics of contemporary Muslim belief and practice.

Muhammad ibn Abdullah (the son of Abd Allah) was born in 570 C.E. Tradition tells us that he was orphaned at a young age. His father was a trader who died before Muhammad was born; his mother, Amina, died when he was only six years old. As a young man, Muhammad was employed in Mecca's thriving caravan trade. The city was at the cross-roads of trade routes between the Indian Ocean and the Mediterranean. Central Arabia was emerging as a major commercial power, sitting astride important trade routes that extended from Africa across the Middle East to China and Malaysia. Muhammad became a steward or business man-ager for the caravans of a wealthy widow, **Khadija**, whom he subsequently married. Tradition tells us that at the time, Muhammad was twenty-five years old and Khadija was forty. During their fifteen years of marriage, they enjoyed a very close relationship and had three sons (who died in infancy) and four daughters. The most famous of Muhammad's surviving children was Fatima, who would marry **Ali**, the revered fourth **caliph** of Sunni Islam and the first legitimate **imam** (leader) of Shii Islam.

Mecca was a prosperous center of trade and commerce. Yet it was a society in which traditional tribal ways were strained by Mecca's transi-tion from a semi-Bedouin to a commercial, urban society. This process was accompanied by serious economic and social cleavages. Muhammad, who had become a successful member of Meccan society, was apparently profoundly affected by these changes. He enjoyed great respect for his judgment and trustworthiness, as was reflected by his nickname al-Amin, the trusted one. This rectitude was complemented by a reflective nature that led him to retreat regularly to a cave on Mt. Hira, a few miles north of Mecca. Here, in long periods of solitude, he contemplated his life and the ills of his society, seeking greater meaning and insight. Here, at the age of forty during the month of **Ramadan**, Muhammad the caravan leader became Muhammad the messenger of God. On the night Muslims call "The **Night of Power** and Excellence," he received the first of many revela-tions from God. A heavenly intermediary, later identified by tradition as the angel Gabriel, commanded, "Recite." Muhammad responded that he had nothing to recite. Twice the angel repeated the command, and each time a frightened and bewildered Muhammad pleaded that he did not know what to say. Finally, the words came to him:

> Recite in the name of your Lord who has created, Created man out of a germ-cell. Recite for your Lord is the Most Generous One Who has taught by the pen, Taught man what he did not know! (Quran, 96:1–5)

Mosque of the Prophet in Medina, Saudi Arabia, the first mosque in Islam, originally built by the Prophet Muhammad and the second-most sacred site in Islam.

With this revelation, Muhammad joined that group of individuals whom Semitic faiths acknowledge as divinely inspired messengers or prophets of God. Muhammad continued to receive divine revelations over a period of twenty-two years (610–632). These messages were finally collected and written down in the Quran ("The Recitation"), Islam's sacred scripture.

Muslim tradition reports that Muhammad reacted to his "call" following the pattern of the Hebrew prophets. He was both frightened and reluctant: frightened by the unknown—for surely he did not expect such an experience—and reluctant, at first, because he feared he was possessed and that others would dismiss his claims as inspired by spirits, or jinns. Despondent and confused, Muhammad resolved to kill himself but was stopped when he again heard the voice say, "O Muhammad! You are the messenger of God and I am Gabriel." Khadija, his wife, reinforced this message, reassuring him that he was neither mad nor possessed; the messenger was from God and not a demon. Interestingly, according to Muslim tradition a Christian played an important role as well. One of those to whom Khadija and Muhammad turned for advice was her Christian cousin, Waraqa ibn Qusayy. When he heard of Muhammad's experience, Waraqa reassured him:

> Surely, by Him in whose hand is Waraqa's soul, thou art the prophet of this people. There hath come unto thee the greatest Namus (angel or Gabriel) who came unto Moses. Like the Hebrew prophets, Thou wilt be called a liar, and they will use thee despitefully and cast thee out and fight against thee.[2]

For just such reasons, Muhammad, like many of the prophets before him, was initially reluctant to preach God's message. His fears were well founded.

The first ten years of Muhammad's preaching were difficult, marked by Meccan resistance and rejection. Although there was a trickle of converts, opposition to Muhammad was formidable. For the powerful and prosperous Meccan oligarchy, the monotheistic message of this would-be reformer, with its condemnation of Mecca's socioeconomic inequities, constituted a direct challenge not only to traditional polytheistic religion but also to the power and prestige of the establishment, threatening their economic, social, and political interests. The Prophet denounced false contracts, usury, and the neglect and exploitation of orphans and widows. He defended the rights of the poor and the oppressed, asserting that the rich had an obligation to the poor and dispossessed. This sense of social commitment and responsibility was institutionalized in the form of religious tithes or taxes on wealth and agricultural lands. Like Amos and Jeremiah before him, Muhammad was a "warner" from God who admonished his hearers to repent and obey God, for the final judgment was near:

> Say: "O men, I am only for you a warner." Those who believe, and do deeds of righteousness—theirs shall be forgiveness and generous provision. And those who strive against Our signs to avoid them—they shall be inhabitants of Hell. (Quran 22:49–50)

Muhammad's rejection of polytheism undermined the religious prestige of the Meccans (in particular, the Umayyad clan) as keepers of the Kaba, the religious shrine that housed the tribal idols. It threatened the considerable revenues that accrued from the annual pilgrimage and festival to this central sanctuary of Arabian tribal religion. This potential economic loss was coupled with the undermining of Meccan tribal political authority by Muhammad's claim to prophetic authority and leadership and his insistence that all true believers belonged to a single universal community (**umma**) that transcended tribal bonds.

Creation of the Islamic Community

For almost ten years, Muhammad struggled in Mecca, preaching God's message and gathering a small band of faithful followers. Among the early converts were Ali, his cousin and son-in-law, and Abu Bakr, his future father-in-law and the first caliph, or successor of the Prophet. The deaths of Khadija and his uncle and protector, Abu Talib, in 619 C.E. made life even more difficult. Meccan opposition escalated from derision and verbal attacks to active persecution. The core of the opposition came from the Umayyad clan of the Quraysh tribe. As we shall see, their descendants, even after their later conversion to Islam, would continue to challenge the family of the Prophet.

As conditions deteriorated in Mecca, Muhammad sent some of his followers to other areas, such as Christian Abyssinia, for safety. The situation changed significantly in 620. Muhammad was invited by a delegation from Yathrib (later called Medina), a city two hundred miles north of Mecca, to serve as a chief arbitrator or judge in a bitter feud between its Arab tribes. Muhammad and two hundred of his followers quietly emigrated, from July to September 622, to Medina. This migration (**hijra**) marked a turning point in Muhammad's fortunes and a new stage in the history of the Islamic movement. Islam took on political form with the establishment of an Islamic community-state at Medina. The importance of the *hijra* is reflected in its adoption as the beginning of the Islamic calendar. Muslims chose to date their history from neither Muhammad's birth nor his reception of the first revelation in 610, but from the creation of the Islamic Community (*umma*). The community, as much as the individual, was to be the vehicle for realizing God's will on earth.

Muhammad at Medina

At Medina, Muhammad had the opportunity to implement God's governance and message, for he was now the prophet-head of a religiopolitical community. He did this by establishing his leadership in Medina, subduing Mecca, and consolidating Muslim rule over the remainder of Arabia through diplomatic and military means.

Muhammad had come to Medina as the arbiter or judge for the entire community, Muslim and non-Muslim alike. In addition, he was the leader of all the Muslims, the commander of the faithful, both those who had emigrated from Mecca and those raised in Medina. Although the majority of the Arab tribes came to embrace Islam, the Jewish tribes (that is, those Arabs who had previously converted to Judaism) remained an important minority. Muhammad promulgated a charter, sometimes called the Constitution of Medina, that set out the rights and duties of all citizens and the relationship of the Muslim community to other communities. Muslims constituted a community whose primary identity and bond were no longer to be tribal ties but a common religious faith and commitment. Jews were recognized as a separate community allied to the Muslim *umma*, but with religious and cultural autonomy.

As the Medinan state was taking shape, Muhammad turned his attention to Mecca. Mecca was the religious, political, economic, and intellectual center of Arabia. Its importance was not diminished by its hostility to Muhammad's preaching. If anything, further revelations to Muhammad, which designated Mecca as the direction (*qibla*) for prayer and the site for Muslim pilgrimage (**hajj**), increased its religious significance. Muslim religious fervor was matched by the power of Meccan tribal mores that branded the Muslims as secessionists and traitors. All the ingredients were there for a formidable battle. Muhammad initiated a series of raids against Meccan caravans, threatening both the political authority and the economic power of the Quraysh. Several important battles ensued. In 624 at Badr, near Medina, Muslim forces, although greatly outnumbered, defeated the Meccan army. For Muslims, then and now, the Battle of Badr has special significance. It was the first and a most decisive victory for the forces of monotheism over those of polytheism, for the army of God over the followers of ignorance and unbelief. God had sanctioned and assisted His soldiers (Quran 3:123, 8:42ff) in victory. Quranic witness to divine guidance and intervention made Badr a sacred symbol, and it has been used throughout Muslim history, as evidenced most recently in the 1973 Arab-Israeli war, for which the Egyptian code name was "Operation Badr."

The elation after Badr dissipated when the Meccans defeated the Muslims in the Battle of Uhud in 625, in which Muhammad himself was wounded. Finally, in 627, frustrated by the growing strength of Muhammad, the Meccans mounted an all-out siege of Medina to crush their opposition once and for all. At the Battle of the "Ditch" (so named because the Muslims dug a trench to neutralize the Meccan cavalry), the Muslims held out so successfully against a coalition of Meccans and mercenary Bedouins that the coalition disintegrated. The Meccans withdrew. The failure of the Quraysh enhanced Muhammad's prestige and leadership among the tribes of Arabia, placing him in the ascendant position. He had consolidated his leadership in Medina, extended his influence over other tribal areas in the Hijaz, and asserted his independence of the dominant tribe in central Arabia. The balance of power had shifted. Muhammad would now initiate, and Mecca would respond.

The final phase in the struggle between Medina and Mecca highlights the method and political genius of Muhammad. He employed both military and diplomatic means, often preferring the latter. Instead of seeking to rout his Meccan opponents, Muhammad sought to gain submission to God and His messenger by incorporating them within the Islamic community-state. A truce was struck in 628 at Hudaybiyah to permit the Muslims to make their pilgrimage to Mecca the following year. In 629, Muhammad established Muslim control over the Hijaz and led the pilgrimage to Mecca, as had been scheduled. Then in 630, Muhammad accused the Quraysh of breaking the treaty, and the Muslims marched on Mecca, ten thousand strong. The Meccans capitulated. Eschewing vengeance and the plunder of conquest, the Prophet instead accepted a settlement, granting amnesty rather than wielding the sword toward his former enemies. For their part, the Meccans converted to Islam, accepted Muhammad's leadership, and were incorporated within the *umma*.

During the next two years, Muhammad established his authority over much of Arabia. The Bedouin who resisted were defeated militarily. At the same time, so many tribes in Arabia sent delegations to come to terms with the successor to the Quraysh that Muslim history remembers this period as the year of deputations. Alliances were forged. Although many converted to Islam, others did not. Representatives were sent from Medina

---

MUHAMMAD: THE FINAL MESSENGER

No prophet has played a greater role in a world religion and in world politics than Muhammad. He is viewed as the last or final prophet, who brought the final and complete revelation of God. Muhammad ibn Abdullah has served as the ideal model for Muslim life. Some Muslims have called him the "living Quran," that is, the embodiment or model of God's will as revealed in the Quran.

Muhammad is the "ideal" religious and political leader, statesman, merchant judge, soldier, and diplomat as well as ideal husband, father, and friend. Muslims look to his example for guidance in all aspects of life: eating, fasting, praying, the treatment of a spouse, parents, and children, the creation of contracts, the waging of war, and the conduct of diplomacy.

---

to teach the Quran and the duties and rituals of Islam and to collect the taxes due Medina. In the spring of 632, Muhammad led the pilgrimage to Mecca, where the sixty-two-year-old leader preached his farewell sermon, exhorting his followers:

> Know ye that every Moslem is a brother unto every other Moslem, and that ye are now one brotherhood. It is not legitimate for any one of you, therefore, to appropriate unto himself anything that belongs to his brother unless it is willingly given him by that brother.[3]

These words summarize both the nature of the Islamic community and the accomplishment of the Prophet Muhammad. When he died three months later in June 632, all Arabia was united under the banner of Islam.

Muhammad: Exemplar of Muslim Life and Piety

Muhammad was among those great religious figures, prophets and founders of religions, whose remarkable character and personality inspired uncommon confidence and commitment. His phenomenal success in attracting followers and creating a community-state that dominated Arabia could be attributed not only to the fact that he was a shrewd military strategist but also to the fact that he was an unusual man who elicited steadfast loyalty despite persecution and oppression. Muhammad's followers found him righteous, trustworthy, pious, compassionate, and honest. He was revered from earliest times: Muslims remembered and recounted what he said and did. Both during his lifetime and throughout the following centuries, Muhammad has served as the ideal model for Muslim life, providing the pattern that all believers are to emulate. He is, as some Muslims say, the "living Quran"—the witness whose behavior and words reveal God's will. Thus the practices of the Prophet became a material source of Islamic law alongside the Quran.

Muslims look to Muhammad's example for guidance in all aspects of life: how to treat friends as well as enemies, what to eat and drink, how to make love and war. Nowhere is this seen more clearly than in the growth of Prophetic traditions. For the tribes of Arabia, the ideals and norms of their way of life had been contained and preserved in their practices (Sunna, trodden path), the customs or oral laws handed down from previous generations by word and example. As Prophet and leader of the community, Muhammad reformed these practices. Old ways were modified, eliminated, or replaced by new regulations. His impact on Muslim life cannot be overestimated, as he served as both religious and political head of Medina: prophet of God, ruler, military commander, chief judge, lawgiver. As a result, the practice of the Prophet—his **Sunna,** or example—became the norm for community life. Muslims observed and remembered stories about what the Prophet said and did. These reports or traditions (**hadith**) were preserved and passed on in oral and written form. The corpus of hadith literature reveals the comprehensive scope of Muhammad's example; he is the ideal religiopolitical leader as well as the exemplary husband and father. Thus when many Muslims pray five times each day or make the pilgrimage to Mecca, they seek to pray as the Prophet prayed, without adding or subtracting from the way Muhammad is reported to have worshipped. Traditions of the Prophet provide guidance for personal hygiene, dress, eating, marriage, treatment of wives, diplomacy, and warfare.

Reformer

Muhammad was not the founder of Islam; he did not start a new religion. Like his prophetic predecessors, he came as a religious reformer. Muhammad maintained that he did not bring a new message from a new God but called people back to the one, true God and to a way of life that most of his contemporaries had forgotten or deviated from. Worship of Allah was not the evolutionary emergence of monotheism from polytheism but a return to a forgotten past, to the faith of the first monotheist, Abraham. The Prophet brought a revolution in Arabian life, a reformation that sought to purify and redefine its way of life. False, superstitious practices such as polytheism and idolatry were suppressed. Such beliefs were viewed as the worst forms of ingratitude or unbelief, for they contradicted and denied the unity or oneness (**tawhid**) of God. Polytheism, or association (**shirk**) of anything with Allah, was denounced as the worst

of sins, idolatry. For Muhammad, the majority of Arabs lived in ignorance (*jahiliyya*) of Allah and His will as revealed to the prophets Adam,
Abraham, Moses, and Jesus. Moreover, he believed that both the Jewish
and the Christian communities had distorted God's original revelation to
Moses and later to Jesus.

Thus, Islam brought a reformation; it was the call once again to total
surrender or submission (***islam***) to Allah and the implementation of His
will as revealed in its complete form one final time to Muhammad, the
last, or "seal," of the prophets. For Muhammad, Islam was not a new faith
but the restoration of the true faith (***iman***), a process that required the
reformation of an ignorant, deviant society. Repentance, or the heeding
of God's warning, required turning away from the path of unbelief and
turning toward or returning to the straight path (*sharia*) or law of God.
This conversion required both individual and group submission to God.
Muslims were not only individuals but also a community or brotherhood
of believers. They were bound by a common faith and committed to the
re-establishment of a socially just society through the implementation of
God's will—the establishment of the rule or kingdom of God on earth.

The example of the Prophet offers a basis for the interdependence of
religious and political authority and, in modern times, one that Islamic
activist movements have interpreted as the basis for a paradigm or ideology for the fusion of religion and state. The early Islamic worldview
provides a model both for the formation of a political community-state
and for protest and revolution. The world is seen as divided between the
believers or the friends of God, who represent the forces of good, and the
Meccan unbelievers, who are the allies of evil, the followers of Satan:

> God is the Protector of the believers; He brings them forth from dark-
> ness to the light. And the unbelievers—their protectors are the idols,
> that bring them forth from the light into the shadows; those are the
> inhabitants of the Fire, therein dwelling forever. (Quran 2:257–59)
>
> The believers fight in the way of God, and the unbelievers fight in the
> idols' way. Fight you therefore against the friends of Satan. (4:76)

The Muslims in Mecca were the oppressed and disinherited, struggling in an unbelieving society. The Quran compares their plight with that
of Moses and the Israelites before them (Quran 28:4–5). Muslims were
reminded that God is their refuge and helper:

> And remember when you were few and abased in the land, and were
> fearful that the people would snatch you away; but He gave you refuge,
> and confirmed you with His help. (Quran 8:26)

Faced with persecution, Muslims, like Muhammad at Mecca, had two choices: emigration (*hijra*) and armed resistance (**jihad**). First, the true believers were expected to leave a godless society and establish a community of believers under God and His Prophet. Second, Muslims were permitted, indeed exhorted, to struggle against the forces of evil and unbelief, and, if necessary, sacrifice their lives, to establish God's rule:

> So let them fight in the way of God who sell the present life for the world
> to come; and whosoever fights in the way of God and is slain, or con-
> quers, We shall bring him a mighty wage. (4:74)

God's preference is made even clearer a few verses later: "God has preferred in rank those who struggle [jihad] with their possessions and their selves over the ones who sit at home" (4:95).

Those who wage war engage in this armed struggle for God, engage in a religiopolitical act. The God who commands this struggle (jihad) against oppression and unbelief will assist His Muslim holy warriors as He did at the Battle of Badr, where, the Quran states, an unseen army of angels aided the Muslim army. These warriors (*mujahidin*, those who participate in the jihad) will be rewarded in this life with victory and the spoils of war. Those who fall in battle will be rewarded with eternal life as martyrs (*shahid*, witness) for the faith. The Arabic term for martyr comes from the same root ("witness") as the word for the confession or profession of faith, indicating that willingness to sacrifice all, even life itself, is the ultimate profession or eternal witness of faith. In this way, early Islamic history provides Muslims with a model and ideology for protest, resistance, and revolutionary change.

The reformist spirit of Islam affected religious ritual as well as politics and society. This process of adaptation or Islamization would characterize much of the development of Islam. While Islam rejected some beliefs and institutions and introduced others, the more common method was to reformulate or adapt existing practices to Islamic norms and values. Rituals such as the annual pilgrimage (*hajj*) and prayer (**salat**) were reinterpreted. The Kaba remained the sacred center, but it was no longer associated with the tribal idols that had been destroyed when Muhammad conquered Mecca. Instead, he rededicated it to Allah, for whom, Muslims believe, Abraham and Ismail had originally built the Kaba. Similarly, Arab pagan and Jewish prayer practices were adapted rather than totally replaced. Muslims, too, were to pray at fixed times each day. However, they would pray facing Mecca and reciting the Quran. Initially, Muslims, like the Jews of Arabia, faced Jerusalem to pray. However, when the Jews did not accept Muhammad's prophetic claims, a new revelation directed Muhammad to shift the center of prayer to Mecca.

Muhammad introduced a new moral order in which the origin and end of all actions was not self or tribal interest but God's will. Belief in the Day of Judgment and resurrection of the body added a dimension of human responsibility and accountability that had been absent in Arabian religion. Tribal vengeance and retaliation were subordinated to a belief in a just and merciful creator and judge. A religiously bonded community (*umma*) governed by God's law replaced a society based on tribal affiliation and tribal law or custom. Specific reforms addressed social injustices of Meccan society, such as banning female infanticide and usury, and encouraged the freeing of slaves; the empowerment of the poor, women, and other less privileged groups; and the institutionalization of charity.

MUHAMMAD AND THE WEST

Talk of Islam's new moral order and the normative nature that Muhammad's life had for Muslims seems to clash with Western perceptions of Islam. If Muslim tradition exalted the Prophet, Western tradition too often has denigrated and vilified his memory. Two issues in particular—Muhammad's treatment of the Jews and his (polygynous) marriages—have proven popular stumbling blocks, or perhaps more accurately whipping posts, for Western critics and polemics.

In his early preaching, Muhammad had looked to the Jews and Christians of Arabia as natural allies whose faiths had much in common with Islam. He anticipated their acceptance and approval. When the Islamic community was established at Medina, Muslims, like the Jews, had faced Jerusalem to pray. However, the Jewish tribes, which had long lived in Medina and had political ties with the Quraysh, tended to resist both religious and political cooperation with the Muslims. They denied Muhammad's prophethood and message and cooperated with his Meccan enemies. Although the constitution of Medina had granted them autonomy in internal religious affairs, political loyalty and allegiance were expected. Yet the Quran accuses the Jewish tribes of regularly breaking such pacts: "Why is it that whenever they make pacts, a group among them casts it aside unilaterally?" (2:100).

After each major battle, one of the Jewish tribes was accused and punished for such acts. Muslim perception of distrust, intrigue, and rejection on the part of the Jews led first to exile and later to warfare. After Badr, the Banu Qainuqa tribe and after the Battle of Uhud, the Banu Nadir, with their families and possessions, were expelled from Medina. After the

Battle of the Ditch in 627, the Jews of the Banu Qurayza were denounced as traitors who had consorted with the Meccans. As was common in Arab (and, indeed, Semitic) practice, the men were massacred; the women and children were spared but enslaved. However, it is important to note that the motivation for such actions was political rather than racial or theological. Although the Banu Qurayza had remained neutral, they had also negotiated with the Quraysh. Moreover, the exiled Jewish clans had actively supported the Meccans. Muhammad moved decisively to crush the Jews who remained in Medina, viewing them as a continued political threat to the consolidation of Muslim dominance and rule in Arabia.

One final point should be made. Muhammad's use of warfare in general was alien neither to Arab custom nor to that of the Hebrew prophets. Both believed that God had sanctioned battle with the enemies of the Lord. Biblical stories about the exploits of kings and prophets such as Moses, Joshua, Elijah, Samuel, Jehu, Saul, and David recount the struggles of a community called by God and the permissibility, indeed requirement, to take up arms when necessary against those who had defied God and to fight "in the name of the Lord of hosts, the God of the armies of Israel."[4] Similarly, in speaking of the Israelite conquests, Moses recalls: "And I commanded you at that time, saying, 'The Lord your God has given you this land to possess . You shall not fear them; for it is the Lord your God who fights for you'" (Deuteronomy 3:18–22).

Muhammad's marriages have long provided another source of Western criticism of the moral character of the Prophet. A noted British author has observed:

> No great religious leader has been so maligned as Muhammad. Attacked in the past as a heretic, an imposter, or a sensualist, it is still possible to find him referred to as "the false prophet." A modern German writer accuses Muhammad of sensuality, surrounding himself with young women. This man was not married until he was twenty-five years of age, then he and his wife lived in happiness and fidelity for twenty-four years, until her death when he was forty-nine. Only between the age of fifty and his death at sixty-two did Muhammad take other wives, only one of whom was a virgin, and most of them were taken for dynastic and political reasons. Certainly the Prophet's record was better than that head of the Church of England, Henry VIII.[5]

In addressing the issue of Muhammad's polygynous marriages, it is important to remember several points. First, Semitic culture in general and Arab practice in particular permitted polygyny. It was common practice in Arabian society, especially among nobles and leaders. Although

Page from an eleventh- to twelfth-century Quran manuscript on paper in stylized Kufic script with gold illumination, made in eastern Islamic lands (Metropolitan Museum of Art, New York accession # 18.26.4).

less common, polygyny was also permitted in biblical and even in post-biblical Judaism. From Abraham, David, and Solomon down to comparatively modern times polygyny was practiced by some Jews. Jewish law changed after the Middle Ages due to the influence of Christian rule, but for Jews under Islamic rule, polygyny remained licit, although it was not extensively practiced.[6] Second, during the prime of his life, Muhammad remained married to one woman, Khadija. Third, it was only after her death that he took a number of wives; all with the exception of Aisha were widows. Fourth, Muhammad's use of the special dispensation from God to exceed the limit of four wives imposed by the Quran occurred only after the death of Khadija.

Most of the eleven marriages had political and social motives. As was customary for Arab chiefs, many were political marriages to cement alliances. Others were marriages to the widows of his companions who had fallen in combat and were in need of protection. Remarriage was difficult in a society that emphasized virgin marriages. Aisha was the only virgin that Muhammad married and the wife with whom he had the closest relationship. Fifth, as we shall see later, Muhammad's teachings and actions, as well as the Quranic message, improved the status of all women—wives, daughters, mothers, widows, and orphans.

Talk of the political and social motives behind many of the Prophet's marriages should not obscure the fact that Muhammad was attracted to women and enjoyed his wives. To deny this would contradict the Islamic outlook on marriage and sexuality, found in both revelation and Prophetic traditions, which emphasizes the importance of family and views sex as a gift from God to be enjoyed within the bonds of marriage. The many stories about Muhammad's concern and care for his wives reflect these values.

God's word, as revealed in the Quran, is the centerpiece of Muslim faith. Copying the Quran was the noblest of arts and luxury manuscripts were produced at all times. This copy, transcribed in 1491 by the noted Ottoman calligrapher Shaykh Hamdullah and lavishly decorated with arabesque designs, is a worthy testament to Muslim faith.

THE QURAN: THE WORD OF GOD

For Muslims, God's revelation was not given only to Jews and Christians and then Muslims but, according to the Quran, given universally to all peoples: "For every community, there is a messenger" (10:47) and "We sent messengers before you; among them are those We have told you of, and those about whom we have not told you" (40:78). The Quran is the final and complete, eternal, uncreated, literal word of God, revealed one final time to the Prophet Muhammad as a guide for humankind (2:185). The Quran consists of 114 chapters of six thousand verses, originally revealed to Muhammad over a period of twenty-two years. It is approximately four-fifths the size of the New Testament, and its chapters are arranged according to length,

---

THE QURAN

For Muslims, God's word, as revealed in the Quran, is the final and complete revelation. It provides the primary and ultimate source of guidance, the basis for belief and practice in Islam. Study, memorization of the entire text, and copying (calligraphy) of the Quran have been central acts of piety. Recitation or chanting of the Quran is a major art form as well as an act of worship. Muslims gather in stadiums and auditoriums around the world to attend international Quran recitation competitions as many in the West might attend an opera.

---

not chronology. The longer chapters, representing the later Medinan revelations, precede the shorter, earlier Meccan revelations to Muhammad.

Islam teaches that God's revelation has occurred in several forms: in nature, history, and scripture. God's existence can be known through creation; nature contains pointers or "signs" of God, its creator and sustainer (3:26–27). The history of the rise and fall of nations, victory and defeat, provides clear signs and lessons of God's sovereignty and intervention in history (30:2–9). In addition, God in His mercy determined to reveal His will for humankind through a series of messengers: "Indeed, We sent forth among every nation a Messenger, saying: 'Serve your God, and shun false gods'" (16:36; see also 13:7, 15:10, 35:24). The verses of revelation are also called signs of God. Thus, throughout history, human beings could not only know that there is a God but also know what God desires and commands

If scripture is a sign from God sent to previous generations, what can be said about these scriptures and prophets? Why was the Quran subsequently revealed, and what is the relationship of the Quran and Muhammad to previous revelations?

Although God had revealed His will to Moses and the Hebrew prophets and later to Jesus, Muslims believe that the scriptures of the Jewish community (Torah) and that of the Christian church (the Evangel or Gospel) were corrupted. The current texts of the Torah and the New Testament are regarded as a composite of human fabrications mixed with divine revelation. Of God's revelation to the Jews, the Quran declares:

> Surely We sent down the Torah, wherein is guidance and light; thereby
> the Prophets who had surrendered themselves gave judgment for those
> of Jewry, as did the masters and rabbis, following that portion of God's
> book as they were given to keep and were witness to. (5:47)

Muslims believe that after the deaths of the prophets, extraneous, nonbiblical beliefs infiltrated the texts and thus altered and distorted the original, pure revelation. The Jews, and later the Christians, are portrayed as having distorted their mission to witness into a doctrine of their divine election as a chosen people:

> And the Jews and Christians say, "We are the sons of God, and His beloved ones." Say: "Why then does He chastise you for your sins? No; you are mortals, of His creating; He forgives whom He will, and He chastises whom He will." (5:20)

The Quran teaches that a similar degeneration or perversion of scripture occurred in Christianity. God sent Jesus as a prophet: "He [God] will teach him [Jesus] the Book, the Wisdom, the Torah, the Gospel, to be a messenger to the Children of Israel" (3:48–49). Yet, the Quran declares that after his death, Jesus's message was altered by those who made him into a god:

> The Christians say, "The Messiah is the Son of God."   God assail them! How they are perverted!   They were commanded to serve but One God; There is no God but He. (9:30–31)

A Muslims believe that God in His mercy, after the falsification of the revelation given to the Jews and the Christians, sent down His word one final time. The Quran does not nullify, but rather corrects, the versions preserved by the Jewish and Christian communities: "**People of the Book**, now there has come to you Our messenger making clear to you many things you have been concealing of the Book, and effacing many things" (5:16).

Thus, Islam is not a new religion with a new scripture. Instead of being the youngest of the major monotheistic world religions, from a Muslim viewpoint it is the oldest. Islam represents the "original" as well as the final revelation of the God of Abraham, Moses, Jesus, and Muhammad. The Quran, like the Torah and the Evangel, is based on a preexisting heavenly tablet, the source or mother of scripture. It is a book written in Arabic that exists in heaven with God; from it, the discourses or teachings of the three scriptures are revealed at different stages in history: "Every term has a book   and with Him is the essence of the Book" (13:38–39).

Because Muslims believe that the Quran's Arabic language and character are revealed (26:195, 41:44), Muslims, regardless of their national language, memorize and recite the Quran in Arabic whether they fully understand it or not. Arabic is the sacred language of Islam because, in a very real sense, it is the language of God. In contrast to Judaism and

Christianity, whose scriptures were not only translated into Greek and Latin at an early date but also disseminated in vernacular languages, in Islam Arabic has remained the language of the Quran and of religious learning. Until modern times, the Quran was printed only in Arabic; it could not be translated in Muslim countries. Even now, translations are often accompanied by the Arabic text.

Because the Quran is God's book, the text of the Quran, like its author, is regarded as perfect, eternal, and unchangeable. This belief is the basis for the doctrine of the miracle of inimitability of the Quran, which asserts that the ideas, language, and style of the Quran cannot be reproduced. The Quran proclaims that even the combined efforts of human beings and jinns could not produce a comparable text (17:88). The Quran is regarded as the only miracle brought by the Prophet. Muslim tradition is replete with stories of those who converted to Islam on hearing its inimitable message and of those pagan poets who failed the Quranic challenge (10:37–38) to create verses comparable with those contained in the Quran. Indeed, throughout history, many Arab Christians as well have regarded it as the perfection of Arabic language and literature.

In addition to its place as a religious text, the Quran was central to the development of Arabic linguistics and provided the basis for the development of Arabic grammar, vocabulary, and syntax. As Philip K. Hitti observed:

> In length the Koran is no more than four-fifths that of the New Testament, but in use it far exceeds it. Not only is it the basis of the religion, the canon of ethical and moral life, but also the textbook in which the Moslem begins his study of language, science, theology, and jurisprudence. Its literary influence has been incalculable and enduring. The first prose book in Arabic, it set the style for future products. It kept the language uniform. So that whereas today a Moroccan uses a dialect different from that used by an Arabian or an Iraqi, all write in the same style.[7]

Today, crowds fill stadiums and auditoriums throughout the Islamic world for public Quran recitation contests. Chanting of the Quran is an art form. Reciters or chanters are held in an esteem comparable to that of opera stars in the West. Memorization of the entire Quran brings great prestige as well as merit. Recordings of the Quran are enjoyed for their aesthetic as well as their religious value.

Revelation and Prophecy
While sharing a belief in revelation and prophecy, Islam's doctrine of prophecy is broader than that of Judaism and Christianity. In addition to prophets, there are messengers from God. Both are divinely inspired,

sinless recipients of God's revelation. However, messengers are given a message for a community in book form and, unlike prophets, are assured success by God. Whereas all messengers are prophets, all prophets are not messengers. The word "prophet" is applied far more inclusively in Islam than in the Judeo-Christian traditions. It is applied to Abraham, Noah, Joseph, and John the Baptist as well as nonbiblical prophets of Arabia like Hud and Salih. "Messenger" is limited to men like Abraham, Moses, Jesus, and Muhammad, who are both prophets and messengers.

The Quran, like the Bible, is a history of prophecy and God's revelation but with fundamental differences. Muslims trace their heritage back to Abraham, or Ibrahim. Thus, Jews, Christians, and Muslims are not only "People of the Book," but also Children of Abraham. However, they belong to different branches of the same family. Whereas Jews and Christians are descendants of Abraham and his wife Sarah through their son Isaac, Muslims trace their lineage back to Ismail, Abraham's first-born son by his Egyptian bondswoman, Hagar. Islamic tradition teaches that Abraham, pressured by Sarah who feared that Ismail, as firstborn, would overshadow Isaac, took Hagar and Ismail to the vicinity of Mecca, where he left them on their own. Ismail became the progenitor of the Arabs in northern Arabia. When Abraham later returned, Ismail helped his father build the Kaba as the first shrine to the one true God. Muslim tradition also holds that it was here at the Kaba that Abraham was to sacrifice his son. In contrast to the biblical tradition (Genesis 22), the Quran designates Ismail rather than Isaac as the intended victim, spared by divine intervention.

Islam's doctrine of revelation (*wahy*) also contrasts with that of modern biblical criticism. The form and the content, as well as the message and the actual words, of revelation are attributed to an external source, God. Muhammad is merely an instrument or a conduit. He is neither author nor editor of the Quran, but God's intermediary. Traditional teachings, emphasizing that the Prophet was illiterate, that he received the revelation from God through the angel Gabriel, and that even the order of the chapters of the Quran was revealed, can be seen as underscoring the belief that in every sense the Quran is the *literal* word of God with no input from Muhammad.

In Islam, God is transcendent. Revelation of His will or guidance occurs through the direct inspiration of prophets or through angelic intercession:

> God speaks to no human except through revelation [*wahy*] or from behind a veil or He sends a messenger [angel] and reveals whatever he wills   a straight path, the path of God. (42:51–53)

Many Muslim theologians, and even more so, the **Sufis**, have often maintained that God does reveal Himself in a limited way through his signs (*ayat*) in the Quran, in nature, and in the souls and intellect of human beings. Moreover, the Quran not only reveals God's will but also details something of His nature, through repeated mention of His Attributes, which are not other than His Essence, according to Muslim theology, as well His Acts, which again reveal aspects of who He is. As Vincent Cornell argues, "the Qur'an is not only didactic but 'autobiographical,' because God is often depicted as speaking about God's own divine nature."[8]

The Quran was initially preserved in oral and written form during the lifetime of the Prophet. The companions of the Prophet committed to memory portions of the revelation as they were received, or they were written down by his secretaries. The entire text of the Quran was finally collected in an official authorized version during the rule of the third **Caliph**, Uthman ibn Affan (r. 644–56). The Quran was collected, not edited or organized thematically. This format has long proved frustrating to many non-Muslims who find the text disjointed or disorganized, as the topic or theme often changes from one paragraph to the next. However, many Muslims believe that the ordering of the chapters and verses was itself divinely inspired. Moreover, this format enables a believer, however brief one's schedule, to simply open the text at random and start reciting at the beginning of any paragraph, as each bears a truth to be learned and remembered.

Major Teachings of the Quran

Whereas the Muslim sees but one divine source for the Quran, the non-Muslim will search out human sources and explanations. This is particularly true where parallels exist between Quranic and biblical stories. Christian and Jewish communities did exist in Arabia. Muhammad's travels as a caravan trader brought him into contact with other People of the Book. He would have known and been aware of these forms of monotheism. However, determining the movement from social and mercantile contacts to religious influences and causal connections is difficult. Muslims offer a simple and direct solution. Similarities in revelation and practice are due to their common divine source; differences occur where Judaism and Christianity departed from their original revelation.

If there is a statement of the core doctrines of Islam, it occurs in the fourth chapter of the Quran:

> O believers, believe in God and His Messenger and the Book He has sent down on His Messenger and the Book which He sent down before.

Whoever disbelieves in God and His angels and His Books, and His messengers, and the Last Day, has surely gone astray into far error. (4:136)

Allah

At the center and foundation of Islam is Allah, the God, whose name appears more than 2,500 times in the Quran. In a polytheistic, pagan society Muhammad declared the sole existence of Allah, the transcendent, all-powerful and all-knowing Creator, Sustainer, Ordainer, and Judge of the universe. Although God is concerned about humanity, knows people intimately, and can act in history, He is and remains transcendent: "No vision can grasp Him, but His grasp is over all vision. He is above all comprehension, yet is acquainted with all things" (6:103).

The transcendence of God is a central theme in scholastic Islamic theology (*ilm al-kalam*), but the Quran as well as some theologians and many Sufis also emphasize God's "immanence" in that God is omnipresent and as the Quran reminds human beings, with God speaking in the first person, "We are nearer to him than the jugular vein" (50:16).

The transcendent God is the one God, and He is the only God: "And your God is One God. There is no god but He" (2:163). God is not a Trinity (5:76); He has not taken a son (2:116) nor daughters nor consorts (6:100–101); and finally, unlike the religion of pre-Islamic Arabia, God has no partners or associate deities (6:22–24).

When Muslims worship five times each day, they declare Islam's absolute or radical monotheism: "I witness that there is no god but the God (Allah)." Throughout the Quran, God reminds His people that He alone exists and is to be worshipped. This radical monotheism and the consequent iconoclasm of Islam were vividly demonstrated when Muhammad entered the Kaba on his triumphant return to Mecca and destroyed the tribal idols. Its central theological significance is underscored by the Quran's condemnation of associationism or idolatry (associating or allowing anything to usurp God's place) as the great sin (31:13). Indeed it is the one unforgivable sin: "God forgives not that aught should be associated with Him. . . . Whoso associates with God anything, has indeed forged a mighty sin" (4:48).

Culturally, this concern not to compromise the unity and transcendence of God led to an absolute ban on any image or representation of God and of Muhammad in many Muslim cultures. Many Arab Muslims extended this ban to any representation in art of the human form for fear that such statues and paintings might lead to idol worship. This attitude resulted in the use of calligraphy (Arabic script) and arabesque (geometric and floral design) as dominant forms in Islamic art.

The absolute monotheism of Islam is preserved in the doctrine of the unity and sovereignty of God that dominates Islamic belief and practice. Allah is the one, true God. As God is one, His rule and will or law are comprehensive, extending to all creatures and to all aspects of life. As we shall see, this belief affected early Muslim conceptions and institutions so that religion was viewed as integral to state, law, and society.

The overwhelming sense of God's sovereignty and power is epitomized in the declaration "God is Most Great" (**Allahu Akbar**), which has served as a preface to the call to prayer and as the traditional battle cry of God's fighters or holy warriors throughout Islamic history, from Muhammad's early battles to contemporary struggles in Iran and Afghanistan.

If God is the Lord, then the **Muslim** is His servant before whom submission (*Islam*) or obedience is the most natural and appropriate response. The term "Muslim" means "one who submits" or surrenders to God; it includes everyone who follows His guidance and performs His will. All the great monotheistic prophets are regarded as true Muslims. Thus, Abraham is not a Jew or a Christian but a follower of the true religion, one who submitted (*muslim*) to God (3:67). Is this submission that of a slave before a powerful and fearsome master? Many non-Muslim commentators portray Allah in this way. A careful reading of the Quran and a look at Muslim practice indicate otherwise.

Although the Quran, like the Bible, underscores the awesome power and majesty of God and the Day of Judgment, the verses of the Quran reveal a merciful and just judge. Opening the Quran to its initial chapter, one reads, "In the name of God, the Merciful and Compassionate." All but one of its chapters begins with this appellation, keeping before the believer a reminder of the nature of the God of this revelation. The terms "merciful" and "compassionate" are from the same Arabic root (*r-h-m*), which signifies beneficence. This quality or attribute includes the idea not only of forgiveness but also of a bounteous mercy that sustains, protects, and rewards people. "Mercy" includes such meanings as the beneficence, compassion, and graciousness of God.

God's mercy permeates the entire life and milieu of the believer. It is reflected in nature, which serves as the theater for the human realization of God's will in history and creation, and reaches its zenith in God's merciful gift to humankind, His revelation.

The Quran declares that everyone experiences the signs of God's mercy in the activities of nature:

It is He who sends the winds like heralds of glad tidings, going before His Mercy: when they have carried the heavy-laden clouds, We drive them to a land that is dead, make rain to descend thereon, and produce every kind of harvest therewith. (7:57)

The Quran teems with references to the many wonders of nature that God's mercy provides: "Night and Day that you may rest therein" (28:73); the "sun and moon follow courses [exactly] computed" (55:5); God provides animals such as cattle and "from them you derive warmth, and numerous benefits, and of them ye eat   for your Lord is indeed Most Kind, Most Merciful" (16:5–7); and God created man and made all the earth subject to him (22:65).

Creation and God's dealings with His creatures reflect His Mercy, but His beneficence is supremely manifest in His revelation to humankind through the prophets, culminating in the final revelation of the Quran. Its author is the Most Merciful (36:5), in it is mercy (29:51), and its motivation is the mercy of God: "We sent it down during a blessed night for We (ever) wish to warn (against evil) .... For We (ever) send (revelation) as a Mercy from your Lord: for He hears and knows (all things)" (44:3–6). Similarly, the sending of Muhammad was a sign of God's mercy: "We sent you not, but as a Mercy for all creatures" (21:107).

The lesson of God's mercy proclaimed by the Quran has been institutionalized and reinforced by the Muslim practice of beginning important matters such as a letter, public speech, lecture, article, or book with the phrase, "In the name of God, the Merciful and Compassionate." No wonder Muslims take exception to those who describe Muslim faith as primarily based on fear of a terrible God.

Strong emphasis on God's mercy should not conjure up a permissive deity. God's mercy exists in dialectical tension with His justice. The Quran gives the sobering warning, "Your Lord is quick in retribution, but He is also oft forgiving, Most Merciful" (7:167). Even here, justice is tempered by mercy toward the repentant sinner. However, sinners, such as those who fall away from the faith, can expect "the curse of Allah and the angels and of men combined" (3:86–87). The absolute justice of God and the sinner's inability to escape His retribution (save for repentance) are declared time and again:

As to those who reject faith, if they had everything on earth, and twice repeated, to give as ransom for the penalty of the Day of Judgment, it would never be accepted of them. Theirs will be to get out therefrom: Their penalty will be one that endures. (5:39–40)

Yet, if the sinner repents of wrongdoing, the Quran assures that "Allah is Forgiving and Merciful" (5:42).

God's justice is based on the belief that He knows and sees all and that individuals are responsible for each and every action. Reward and punishment follow from individual, ethical responsibility and accountability before an all-knowing and just judge. Thus, Islamic ethics follow from mankind's special status and responsibility on earth.

The Quranic Universe

The Quranic universe consists of three realms: heaven, earth, and hell. Governed by its creator-judge, the world is inhabited by human beings and spirits (angels, jinns, and devils) who are called to obedience to the one, true Allah, the Lord of the Universe. Angels serve as the link between God and human beings. Created out of light, immortal and sexless, they function as guardians, recorders, and messengers from God. They are transmitters of God's message, communicating divine revelation to the prophets. Thus, Gabriel (Jibril) brought down the Quran from heaven to Muhammad. Among the more prominent angels are Michael, Israfel, and Azrael. Somewhere between angels and humans are the invisible, intelligent spirits called jinn. In contrast to human beings, the jinn were created from fire instead of earth (7:12, 55:14–15). They have the ability to assume visible form and, like humans, can be good or bad, sin as well as be saved (46:29–31). They will be judged on the Last Day and consigned to paradise or hell.

Folktales such as *The Thousand and One Nights* ascribe magical powers to the jinn, who became known in the West as genies. Finally, at the opposite end of the spectrum from God, the principle of good, is Satan (**shaytan**, adversary), the principle of evil. The origin of Satan goes back to the Garden, where, as will be discussed, one of the angels (**Iblis** or Satan, the devil), sometimes also referred to as a jinn, refused to pay homage to Adam. Satan is the leader of other fallen angels and jinn, disobedient servants of God who tempt human beings in their moral struggle on earth. It was Iblis who tempted Adam and Eve (20:116–22). Although permitted by God to engage in their evil ways, Iblis and his followers will be consigned to hell on Judgment Day.

Of all creation, man enjoys a unique relationship with God, for after creating Adam, God breathed into him His spirit (15:29). Moreover, the Quran declares that God created human beings in "the best of molds or stature" (95:4) to be His representatives on earth. This special selection and status led to Satan's rebellion, a story that strikingly conveys the cosmic significance of humankind.

Informed by God of mankind's special status, the angels initially protested, "Will You set therein one who will do corruption there, and shed blood, while we proclaim your praise and call You Holy?" (2:30). Adam proved the uniqueness of humankind by demonstrating a God-given knowledge of creation that the angels did not possess. However, when God commanded the angels to prostrate themselves before Adam, Satan or Iblis refused (2:34, 7:11ff). It was Satan's refusal to accept man's unique status in the hierarchy of the universe that caused his rebellion and expulsion from heaven and led to the Fall and to the age-long moral struggle of human beings, torn between the forces of good (God) and those of evil (Satan).

> Then the angels bowed all together, except for Iblis who refused to be among those bowing. God said: Iblis, why are you not among those who bow down on their knees? He said: I am not going to kneel before a human being that you have made from clay, from molded mud. God said: Get out of here; you are an outcast. My curse will be on you until the Day of Judgment! He said: My Lord, let me wait until the Day of Resurrection. God said: You shall be allowed to wait until the appointed time. He said: My Lord, since you have led me astray, I shall make things on the earth attractive to them and lead them astray, except for your sincere servants. God said: This will be a straight path to me. You shall have no authority except over those who are perverse and follow you. Hell shall be their promised place. (15:30–42)

The essence of human uniqueness lies in one's vocation as God's representative on earth. God has given people the earth as a divine trust (33:72); they are thus His vicegerents or agents on earth (2:30, 35:39) to whom God has made all creation subservient (16:12–14). It is on the basis of how this vicegerency is executed, or how God's will in history is realized or actualized, that a person will be rewarded or punished:

> It is He who had made you (His) agents, inheritors of the earth. He hath raised you in ranks, some above others that He may try you. For thy Lord is quick in punishment, yet He is indeed Oft Forgiving, Most Merciful. (6:165)

It is here that we see the roots of Islamic ethics. God ordains; humankind is to implement His will. Human responsibility and mission are of cosmic proportion, and people will be judged on the cosmic consequences of their acts. As God's representatives, the measure of human actions, and indeed life, is the extent to which the Muslim contributes to the realization of God's will on earth. This responsibility lies squarely on each individual's shoulders, as no one can bear another's responsibility or suffer for another:

> Nor can a bearer of burdens bear another's burden. If one heavily laden should call another to (bear) his load, not the least portion of it can be carried (by the other), even though he be nearly related.... And whosoever purifies himself does so for the benefit of his own soul. (35:18)
> And whatever good you do, you shall not be denied the just reward of it.... As for the unbelievers, their riches shall not avail them, neither their children against God; those are the inhabitants of the Fire, dwelling therein forever. (3:115–16)

Although it is not a prominent theme in the Quran, Muslim tradition did come to accept the intercession of Muhammad on behalf of individuals. However, unlike Christianity, there is no vicarious suffering or atonement for humankind. Such actions are unnecessary, because Islam has no doctrine of original sin.

The story of the Fall in the Quran differs from that in the Bible in its teaching regarding personal responsibility. It is Adam, not Eve, who is tempted by the devil. Woman is not portrayed as the cause of the Fall, as in the Judeo-Christian traditions. Moreover, the sin of Adam and Eve is just that—their own personal sin. It is an act of disobedience for which they, and they alone, are responsible. Unlike Christianity, there is no notion of an inherited "original" sin, committed by the progenitors of the human race, for which all humanity suffers. Sin is not a state of being; it is the result of an act of disobedience, failure to do or not to do what God commands or prohibits. Human beings are not sinful by nature; as they are created or finite creatures, they are naturally limited, weak, and subject to temptation. Similarly, death follows from the human condition and is not due to sin or the Fall. The consequences of sin, like human responsibility, belong solely to those who commit sin.

The biblical and Quranic stories about the consequences of the Fall reveal the basis for the divergent doctrines of Christianity and Islam. The former views the Fall as the cause of man's flawed nature and existence; the latter finds here the story of sin, God's mercy, and repentance. In the Bible, the Fall brings a life of shame, disgrace, and hardship:

> To the woman He said, "I will greatly multiply your pain in childbearing; in pain you shall bring forth children, yet your desire shall be your husband, and he shall rule over you." And to Adam He said, "Because you have listened to the voice of your wife, and have eaten of the tree of which I commanded you, you shall not eat of it, cursed is the ground

because of you; in toil you shall eat of it all the days of your life; thorns and thistles it shall bring forth to you." (Genesis 3:16–18)

In sharp contrast, the Quran teaches that after Adam disobeys God but repents, God extends to Adam His mercy and guidance: "But his Lord chose him. He turned to him and gave him guidance" (20:122). Adam turned away from Satan and sin and turned back to God; Adam repented, and God forgave. This is the paradigm for sin and repentance in Islam. If the Muslim is one who is to submit to God by following His will, sin is disobedience or refusal to submit. It is the arrogance and ingratitude of creatures who forget or turn away from their creator and sustainer. Repentance is simply remembering or returning to God's path, the straight path of Islam. There is little or no emphasis on feelings of shame and disgrace or guilt. What God commands, and what His awesome character engenders, is fear of God (*taqwa*): "The most honored of you in the sight of God is the most righteous or God fearing of you" (49:13).

Taqwa means self-protection or fear of God. This attitude or disposition follows from belief in an all-powerful, omnipresent God (an ever-present God who is as near as one's jugular vein; 50:16), who has commanded submission or obedience to His will and before whom the Muslim is morally responsible and accountable. It is the response of the believer who knows what he or she must do and who lives life ever mindful of the eternal consequences that await on the Last Day. The duties and obligations of Muslim life, as well as its rewards and punishments, fall equally on men and women:

> The believers, men and women, are guardians of one another; they enjoin good and prohibit evil, perform the prayer, give alms, and obey God and His Prophet. (9:71)   Whoever does a righteous deed, whether man or woman, and has faith, we will give a good life; and we shall reward them according to the best of their actions. (16:97)

The Muslim Community

The Muslim mission to be servants of God and to spread God's rule is both an individual and a community obligation. The Quran emphasizes the social dimension of service to God, for it is on earth and in society that God's will is to govern and prevail. As humankind came from a single pair of parents, so, too, God "made you into nations and tribes" (49:13). Similarly, as God had sent His prophets and revelation to the Jews and then to the Christians, He declares in the Quran that the Muslims now constitute the new community of believers who are to be an example to other nations: "Thus We made you an *umma* justly balanced, that ye might be witness over the nations" (2:143).

Guided by the word of God and the Prophet, the Muslim community has a mission to create a moral social order: "You are the best community evolved for mankind, enjoining what is right and forbidding what is wrong" (3:110). This command has influenced Muslim practice throughout the centuries, providing a rationale for political and moral activism. Government regulations, Islamic laws, and the activities of piety-minded policers of public behavior have all been justified as expressions of this moral mission to command the good and prohibit evil. Again, Muhammad and the first Muslim community are seen as exemplifying this ideal, implementing the socially just society envisioned by the Quran.

While recognizing differences in status, wealth, and tribal origin, the Quran teaches the ultimate supratribal (transnational) unity and equality of all believers before God. Common faith, not tribal or family ties, binds the community together. The Quran envisions a society based on the unity and equality of believers, a society in which moral and social justice will counterbalance oppression of the weak and economic exploitation. Belief and action are to be joined; Muslims are not only to know and believe, but also to act and implement. Worship and devotion to God embrace both private and public life, affecting not only prayer, fasting, and pilgrimage, but social behavior as well. Like his prophetic predecessors, Muhammad brought a revelation that challenged the established order. The message of the Quran was reformist, if not revolutionary. Quranic prescriptions would provide the basis for the later development of Islamic law to chart this new social order. The scope of Quranic concerns reflects the comprehensiveness of Islam. It includes rules concerning modesty, marriage, divorce, inheritance, feuding, intoxicants, gambling, diet, theft, murder, fornication, and adultery.

The socioeconomic reforms of the Quran are among its most striking features. Exploitation of the poor, weak, widows, women, orphans (4:2, 12), and slaves is vividly condemned:

> Those who live off orphans' property without having any right to do so will only suck up fire into their bellies, and they will roast in the fires (of hell). (4:10)

False contracts, bribery, abuse of women, hoarding of wealth to the exclusion of its subordination to higher ends, and usury are denounced. The Quran demands that Muslims pursue a path of social justice, rooted in the recognition that the earth belongs ultimately to God and that human beings are its caretakers. Although wealth is seen as good, a sign of hard work and God's pleasure, God's law limited its pursuit and accumulation. Its rewards are subject to social responsibility toward other members of the community, in particular the poor and needy:

> The alms [**zakat**] are for the poor and needy, those who work to collect them, those whose hearts are to be reconciled, the ransoming of slaves and debtors, and for the cause of God, and for travelers. (9:60)

Social justice was institutionalized by Quranic decrees that required the payment of an alms tax (*zakat*) and a voluntary charity for the poor, stipulations of fixed shares of inheritance for women and children, and a host of regulations regarding the just treatment of debtors, widows, the poor, orphans (90:13–16), and slaves (24:33). Those who practice usury are sternly rebuked and warned that they face "war from God and His prophet" (2:279).

The Last Day

Muslims are exhorted to follow God's will out of obedience and gratitude to their creator, but the specter of the Last Judgment, with its eternal reward and punishment, remains a constant reminder of the ultimate consequences of each life. It underscores the Quran's strong and repeated emphasis on the ultimate moral responsibility and accountability of each believer. At a moment known only to God, all will be called to judgment in a great cosmic cataclysmic event (81:114), also referred to as the Day of Decision or the Day of Reckoning. Each community will be judged by the standards brought by its prophets and Book. Humans and jinn (spirits) alike will stand before the throne of God. All are responsible for their own actions and will be judged according to the record found in the Book of Deeds (45:29–30).

As discussed previously, there is no redemption, atonement, or intercession through an intermediary. Allah, who is a merciful but all-powerful judge, consigns all either to heaven or to hell as He wills (5:43). Although the Quran teaches that intercession belongs to God alone (39:44, 6:54, 70), belief in Muhammad's role as a divinely designated intercessor did develop and was justified by the text, "There is no intercessor [with God] unless He gives permission" (10:3).

The Quranic vision of the afterlife is both spiritual and physical. Because the Last Day will be accompanied by bodily resurrection (41:39–40,), the pleasures of heaven and the pain of hell will be fully experienced. The Garden of Paradise is a heavenly mansion of perpetual peace and bliss with flowing rivers, beautiful gardens, and the enjoyment of one's spouses and beautiful, dark-eyed female companions (*houris*). Descriptions of heavenly bliss follow from the general tenor of the Quran, which is life-affirming, emphasizing the beauty of creation and enjoyment of its pleasures within the limits set by God. This more integral, comprehensive view of life stands in sharp contrast to the Christian tendency to compartmentalize life into the sacred and the profane, body and soul, sensual and spiritual. In contrast to the "spiritual" images of a more somber, celibate Paradise predominant in Christianity, the Quran offers vivid descriptions of the delights and pleasures of Paradise, seeing no contradiction between enjoyment of both the beatific vision and the fruits of creation:

> in gardens of bliss   a multitude will be seated on couches set close together.... Immortal youths will serve them with goblets, pitchers and cups filled with water from a spring which will not upset them or dull their senses; and they may choose fruit of any kind and whatever fowl they desire and chaste companions with eyes of a beauty like pearls hidden in shells.... We formed them perfectly and made them spotless virgins, chastely amorous and of the same age. (56:12–37)

In sharp contrast, the damned will be banished to hell, separated from God. Anguish and despair will be coupled with physical torment, for they will experience:

> a fire whose sheets encompass them. If they should ask for relief, then water like molten copper shall be showered upon them to scald their faces. How awful is such a drink and how evil a resting place. (18:29)

CONCLUSION

For Muslims throughout the centuries, the message of the Quran and example of the Prophet Muhammad constitute the formative and enduring foundation of faith and belief. They have served as the basic sources of Islamic law and the reference points for daily life. Muslims today, as in the past, continue to affirm that the Quran is the literal word of God, the Creator's immutable guidance for an otherwise transient world. This transhistorical significance is rooted in the belief that the Book and the Prophet provide eternal principles and norms on which Muslim life, both individual and collective, is to be patterned. The challenge for each generation of believers has been the continued formulation, appropriation, and implementation of Islam in history. Islamic history and civilization provide the record of that struggle to interpret and to follow the straight path.

KEY TERMS

Ali

Allah

Allahu Akbar

caliph

Children of Abraham

hadith

hajj

hijra

Medina

Iblis

imam

iman

Ismail

jihad

Kaba

Khadija

Muslim

Night of Power

People of the Book

Quran

Ramadan

salat

shaytan

Shii

shirk

Sufis

Sunna

Sunni

tawhid

umma

zakat

QUESTIONS

1. Describe the environment in which historical Islam emerged relative to other "Semitic monotheisms."

2. How has the West typically understood Muhammad's involvements with violence and polygyny? How were they understood in his day and age?

3. What roles have the Quran and the Prophet Muhammad played in shaping the Islamic worldview?

4. Is Islam better described as a social system or an individual piety?

5. How do sin, the Last Day, and the afterlife function in the Islamic schema? Contrast this with Jewish or Christian notions.

6. Why can Islam be described as "the Straight Path"? What does this say about the Islamic approach to daily living?

NOTES

1. W. Montgomery Watt. *Muhammad at Mecca* (Oxford: Oxford University Press, 1953), p. 24.
2. *The Life of Muhammad*, A. Guillaume, trans. (London: Oxford University Press, 1955), p. 107.
3. Ibn Hisham, as quoted in Philip K. Hitti, *History of the Arabs*, 9th ed. (New York: St. Martin's Press, 1966), p. 120.
4. 1 Samuel 17:45, *The Oxford Annotated Bible: Revised Standard Version* (New York: Oxford University Press, 1962). See also Exodus 14:14, Deuteronomy 20:4, 1 Samuel 15:33, 1 Kings 18:36–40, and 2 Kings 10:25–31.
5. Geoffrey Parrinder, *Mysticism in the World's Religions* (New York: Oxford University Press, 1976), p. 121.
6. Rachel Biale, *Women and Jewish Law* (New York: Schocken Books, 1984), pp. 49–51.
7. Philip K. Hitti, *Islam: A Way of Life* (New York: Henry Regnery, 1971), p. 27.
8. Vincent Cornell, "Fruit of the Tree of Knowledge," in *The Oxford History of Islam*, John L. Esposito, ed. (New York: Oxford University Press, 2000), p. 71.

Chapter 2

The Muslim Community in History

The history of Islam has often been linked to the existence of an Islamic state, empire, or sultanate. From its beginnings, Islam existed and spread as a community-state; it was both a faith and a political order. Within centuries after his death, Muhammad's local Arabian polity became a vast empire, extending from North Africa to Southeast Asia. The development of Islam and Muslim institutions (the caliphate, law, education, the military, social services) were intertwined. Again, the Prophetic period provided the paradigm for later generations. For it was in Medina that the Quranic mandate took on form and substance under the guidance and direction of the Prophet.

The Medinan community formed a total framework for state, society, and culture. It epitomized the Quranic mandate for Muslims as individuals and as a community "to transform the world itself through action in the world."[1] This aspiration and ideal has constituted the challenge for the Islamic community throughout much of its history. It inspired Muhammad to transform a local sheikdom into a trans-tribal state.

MUHAMMAD AND THE MEDINAN STATE

Two great empires, the Byzantine (Christian), or Eastern Roman, empire and the Sasanian Persian (Zoroastrian) empire, dominated seventh-century Arabia. In the middle was the Arabian Peninsula, composed of apparently weak and divided tribal societies. Within one hundred years, both empires would fall before the armies of Allah as Muhammad and his successors united Arabia under the umbrella of Islam, which provided a principle of organization and motivation. In time, a vast empire and a commonwealth of Islamic states would come to dominate much of the world. Its missionaries would be soldiers, merchants, and mystics. Islam would provide the basis of community identity and the rationale or legitimacy for rulers and their policies of expansion and conquest. Thus, for example, the wars of expansion were termed *fath*, "opening" or "conquest" of the way for Islam.

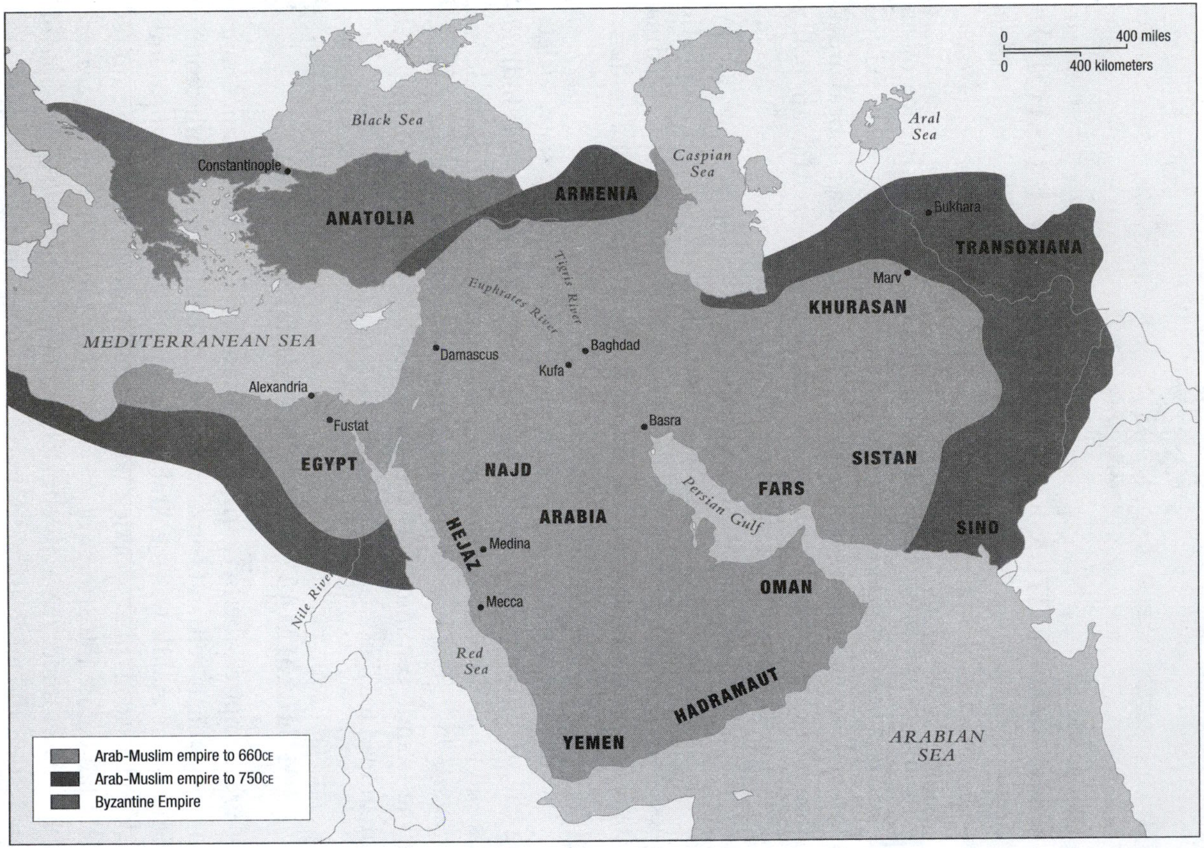
0
400 miles
0
400 kilometers
Black Sea
Aral Sea
Caspian Sea
Constantinople
ARMENIA
ANATOLIA
Bukhara
TRANSOXIANA
Marv
KHURASAN
Tigris River
Euphrates River
MEDITERRANEAN SEA
Damascus
Baghdad
Kufa
Alexandria
Fustat
Basra
EGYPT
NAJD
SISTAN
FARS
Persian Gulf
ARABIA
HEJAZ
Medina
SIND
Nile River
Mecca
OMAN
Red Sea
HADRAMAUT
YEMEN
ARABIAN SEA
Arab-Muslim empire to 660CE
Arab-Muslim empire to 750CE
Byzantine Empire

The Muslim Empire to 750 C.E.

As Muhammad governed a trans-tribal state in the name of Islam, so, too, the Islamic community became associated with an expansive empire. Why and how did this come to pass?

Shortly after the surrender of Mecca, Muhammad turned his attention to the extension and consolidation of his authority over Arabia. Envoys were sent and alliances were forged with surrounding tribes and rulers. The fiercely independent Bedouin tribes of Arabia were united behind the Prophet of Islam through a combination of force and diplomacy. As Muhammad was both head of state and messenger of God, so, too, were the envoys and soldiers of the state the envoys and soldiers of Islam, its first missionaries. Along with their treaties and armies, they brought the Quran and the teachings of their faith. They spread a way of life that affected the political and social order as well as individual life and worship. Islam encompassed both a faith and a sociopolitical system. Ideally, this new order was to be a community of believers, acknowledging the ultimate sovereignty of God, living according to His law, obeying His Prophet, and dedicating their lives to spreading God's rule and law. This was the message and vision that accompanied Arab armies as they burst out of Arabia and established their supremacy throughout the Middle East.

The Muslim Empire to 750 C.E.

What is most striking about the early expansion of Islam is its rapidity and success. Western scholars have marveled at it. Muslim tradition has viewed the conquests as a miraculous proof or historic validation of the truth of Islam's claims and a sign of God's guidance. Within a decade, Arab forces overran the Byzantine and Persian armies, exhausted by years of warfare, and conquered Iraq, Syria, Palestine, Persia, and Egypt.

The momentum of these early victories was extended to a series of brilliant battles under great generals like Khalid ibn al-Walid and Amr ibn al-As, which extended the boundaries of the Muslim empire to Morocco and Spain in the west and across Central Asia to India in the east. Driven by the economic rewards from conquest of richer, more developed areas and united and inspired by their new faith, Muslim armies proved to be formidable conquerors and effective rulers, builders rather than destroyers. They replaced the indigenous rulers and armies of the conquered countries but preserved much of their government, bureaucracy, and culture. For many in the conquered territories, it was no more than an exchange of masters, one that brought peace to peoples demoralized and disaffected by the casualties and heavy taxation that resulted from the years of Byzantine–Persian warfare. Local communities were free to continue to follow their own way of life in internal, domestic affairs. In many ways, local populations found Muslim rule more flexible and tolerant than that of Byzantium and Persia. Religious communities were free to practice their faith—to worship and be governed by their religious leaders and laws in such areas as marriage, divorce, and inheritance. In exchange, they were required to pay tribute, a poll tax (*jizya*) that entitled them to Muslim protection from outside aggression and exempted them from military service. They were therefore called the "protected ones" (**dhimmi**). In effect, this often meant lower taxes, greater local autonomy, rule by fellow Semites with closer linguistic and cultural ties than the Hellenized, Greco-Roman elites of Byzantium, and greater religious freedom for Jews and indigenous Christians. Most of the Christian churches, such as the Nestorians, Monophysites, Jacobites, and Copts, had been persecuted as heretics and schismatics by Christian orthodoxy. For these reasons, some Jewish and Christian communities aided the invading armies, regarding them as less oppressive than their imperial masters. In many ways, the conquests brought a Pax Islamica to an embattled area:

> The conquests destroyed little: what they did suppress were imperial rivalries and sectarian bloodletting among the newly subjected population. The Muslims tolerated Christianity, but they disestablished it; henceforward Christian life and liturgy, its endowments, politics and theology, would be a private and not a public affair. By an exquisite irony, Islam reduced the status of Christians to that which the Christians had earlier thrust upon the Jews, with one difference. The reduction in Christian status was merely judicial; it was unaccompanied by either systematic persecution or a blood lust, and generally, though not everywhere and at all times, unmarred by vexatious behavior.[2]

A common issue associated with the spread of Islam is the role of **jihad**, or so-called holy war. Whereas Westerners are quick to characterize Islam as a religion spread by the sword, modern Muslim apologists sometimes explain jihad as simply defensive in nature. In its most general sense, jihad in the Quran and in Muslim practice refers to the obligation of all Muslims to strive (jihad, self-exertion) or struggle to follow God's will. This includes both the struggle to lead a virtuous life and the universal mission of the Muslim community to spread God's rule and law through teaching, preaching, and, where necessary, armed struggle. Contrary to popular belief, the early conquests sought not to

JIHAD: THE STRUGGLE FOR GOD

Jihad, "to strive or struggle," is sometimes referred to as the sixth pillar of Islam, although it has no such official status. In its most general meaning, jihad refers to the obligation incumbent on all Muslims, as individuals and as a community, to exert (jihad) themselves to realize God's will, to lead a virtuous life, to fulfill the universal mission of Islam, and to spread the Islamic community through preaching Islam to convert others or writing religious tracts ("jihad of the tongue" and "jihad of the pen"). Thus, today it can be used to describe the personal struggle to keep the fast of Ramadan, to lead a good life, and to fulfill family responsibilities. Popularly, it is used to describe the struggle for educational or social reform—to establish good schools, to clean up a neighborhood, to fight drugs, or to work for social justice. However, it also includes the struggle for or defense of Islam, holy war. Although jihad is not supposed to include aggressive warfare, this tactic has been invoked by early extremists such as the Kharijites, by rulers to justify their wars of conquest and expansion, and by contemporary extremists such as Osama bin Laden and his jihad against America as well as jihadi organizations in Lebanon, the Persian Gulf, and Indonesia.

spread the faith through forced conversion but to spread Muslim rule. In fact, Islamic empires were inhabited by large numbers of Christians, Jews, and members of other religions; many contributed significantly to their administration and cultural development. Moreover, as Richard Bulliet notes in his *Conversion to Islam in the Medieval Period: An Essay in Quantitative History*,[3] it took centuries for some major areas to become majority Muslim.

Many early Muslims regarded Islam solely as an Arab religion. Moreover, from an economic perspective, increase in the size of the community through conversion diminished Arab Muslims' share in the spoils of conquest. As Islam penetrated new areas, people were offered three options: (1) conversion, that is, full membership in the Muslim community, with its rights and duties; (2) acceptance of Muslim rule as "protected" people and payment of a poll tax; (3) battle or the sword if neither the first nor the second option was accepted. The astonishing expansion of Islam resulted not only from armed conquest but also from these two peaceful options. In later centuries, in many areas of Africa, the Indian subcontinent, and Southeast Asia, the effective spread of Islam would be due primarily to Muslim traders and Sufi (mystic) missionaries who won converts by their example and their preaching.

THE CALIPHATE (632–1258)

Given Muhammad's formative and pivotal role, his death (632) threatened to radically destabilize the community. Who was to lead? What was to happen to the community? The companions of the Prophet moved quickly to steady and reassure the community. Abu Bakr, an early follower of Muhammad, announced the death of the Prophet to the assembled faithful: "Muslims! If any of you has worshipped Muhammad, let me tell you that Muhammad is dead. But if you worship God, then know that God is living and will never die!" Nevertheless, the Prophet's death did plunge the Islamic community into a series of political crises revolving around leadership and authority. Issues of succession and secession were to plague the early community.

The caliphate period (632–1258) traditionally has been divided into three periods: the "Rightly Guided Caliphs" (632–661), the Umayyad empire (661–750), and the Abbasid empire (750–1258). During these eras, a vast empire was created with successive capitals in Medina, Kufa, Damascus, and Baghdad. Stunning political success was complemented by a cultural florescence in law, theology, philosophy, literature, medicine, mathematics, science, and art.

The Rightly Guided Caliphs

The caliphate began in 632 with the selection of Muhammad's successor. The first four caliphs were all companions of the Prophet: Abu Bakr (r. 632–634), Umar ibn al-Khattab (634–644), Uthman ibn Affan (644–656), and Ali ibn Abi Talib (656–661). Their rule is especially significant not only for what they actually did but also because the period of Muhammad and the Rightly Guided Caliphs came to be regarded in Sunni Islam as the normative period. It provides the idealized past to which Muslims have looked back for inspiration and guidance, a time to be remembered and emulated.

The vast majority of Muslims (Sunni) believe that Muhammad died without designating his replacement or establishing a system for the selection of his successor. After an initial period of uncertainty, the Prophet's companions, the elders or leaders of Medina, selected or acknowledged Abu Bakr, an early convert and the Prophet's father-in-law, as caliph (*khalifa*, successor or deputy). Abu Bakr's designation as leader was symbolized by the offering of *baya* (oath), a handclasp used by the Arabs to seal a contract, in this case an oath of obedience and allegiance. Abu Bakr had been a close companion and a trusted adviser of Muhammad; he was a man respected for his sagacity and piety. Muhammad had appointed him to lead the Friday community prayer in his absence. As caliph, Abu Bakr was the political and military leader of the community. Although not a prophet, the caliph enjoyed religious prestige as head of the community of believers. This was symbolized in later history by the caliph's right to lead the Friday prayer and the inclusion of his name in its prayers.

Having resolved the question of political leadership and succession, Abu Bakr turned to the consolidation of Muslim rule in Arabia. Muhammad's death had precipitated a series of tribal rebellions. Many tribal chiefs claimed that their allegiance had been based on a political pact with Medina that ceased with the Prophet's death. Tribal independence and factionalism, long a part of Arab history, once more threatened the unity and identity of the new Islamic state. Abu Bakr countered that the unity of the community was based on the interconnectedness of faith and politics and undertook a series of battles that later Muslim historians would call the wars of apostasy. Relying on Khalid ibn al-Walid, whom Muhammad had dubbed "the sword of Allah," he crushed the tribal revolt, consolidating Muslim rule over the entire Arabian Peninsula, and thus preserved the unity and solidarity of the Islamic community-state.

Abu Bakr's successor, Umar, initiated the great period of expansion and conquest. One of the great military leaders of his time, he added the title "Commander of the Faithful" to that of "Successor" or "Deputy" of the Prophet of God. He also introduced a new method for the selection of his successor. On his deathbed, Umar appointed an "election committee" to select the next caliph. After due consultation, the council of electors chose Uthman ibn Affan from the Umayyad clan, a leading Meccan family, using the traditional sign or oath of allegiance, the clasping of hands. Thus, based on the practice of the first three caliphs, a pattern was established for selecting the caliph from the Quraysh tribe through a process characterized by consultation and an oath of allegiance.

Before long, tribal factionalism and the threat of rebellion resurfaced in the community. Uthman's family had been among the strongest foes of the Prophet. Many of the Medinan elite, who had been among the early supporters of Muhammad, resented Uthman's accession to power and the increased prominence and wealth of his family. Although personally pious, Uthman lacked the presence and leadership skills of his predecessors. Accusations that the caliph was weak and guilty of nepotism fueled political intrigue. In 656, Uthman was assassinated by a group of mutineers from Egypt. The caliph's murder was the first in a series of Muslim rebellions and tribal fratricides that would plague the Islamic community's political development.

The Caliph Ali and the First Civil Wars

Ali, the cousin and son-in-law of the Prophet, succeeded Uthman as the fourth caliph. Ali was devoted to Muhammad and among the first to embrace Islam. He had married Fatima, the only surviving child of Muhammad and Khadija, with whom he had two sons, Hasan and **Husayn**. Ali was a charismatic figure who inspired fierce loyalty and commitment. Many of Ali's supporters (Alids) believed that leadership of the Islamic community should remain within the family of the Prophet and that, indeed, Muhammad had designated Ali as his rightful successor and heir. For these partisans of Ali, later to be called Shii (*shiat-u-Ali*, party of Ali), the first three caliphs were interlopers who had denied Ali his rightful inheritance. However, their satisfaction and expectations were to be short-lived. Within the few short years that Ali ruled, the caliphate was racked by two civil wars. Ali's authority was challenged by two opposition movements: first, by a coalition headed by Muhammad's widow, Aisha (the daughter of Abu Bakr), and second, by the forces of Muawiyah, the governor of Syria and a relative of Uthman. Ali's failure to find and prosecute Uthman's murderers became the pretext for both revolts. In the first, Ali crushed a triumvirate led by Aisha, the youngest wife of Muhammad. The "Battle of the Camel," so named because it took place around the camel on which Aisha was mounted, marked the first time a caliph had led his army against another Muslim army.

Of greater long-range significance was Muawiyah's challenge to Ali's authority. Securely established in Damascus with a strong army, Muawiyah, the nephew of Uthman, had refused to step down and accept Ali's appointment of a replacement. In 657, at Siffin (in modern-day Syria), Ali led his army against his rebellious governor. Faced with defeat, Muawiyah's men raised Qurans on the tips of their spears and called for arbitration according to the Quran, crying out, "Let God decide." Although the arbitration proved inconclusive, it yielded two results that would have lasting effects. A splinter group of Alids, the Kharijites or "seceders," broke with Ali for having failed to subdue Muawiyah. Muawiyah walked away from Siffin and continued to govern Syria, extending his rule to Egypt as well. When the Kharijites assassinated Ali in 661, Muawiyah laid successful claim to the caliphate, moving its capital to Damascus and frustrating the belief of Ali's followeers that leadership of the Muslim community should be restricted to Ali's descendants. With the establishment of the Umayyad dynasty, the "golden age" of Muhammad and the Rightly Guided Caliphs came to an end and the caliphate became an absolute monarchy.

Despite the turmoil during the early caliphal years, Muslims regard the period of Muhammad and the first generation of companions or elders as normative for a variety of reasons. First, God sent down His final and complete revelation in the Quran and the last of His prophets, Muhammad. Second, the Islamic community-state was created, bonded by a common religious identity and purpose. Third, the sources of Islamic law, the Quran and the example of the Prophet, originated at this time. Fourth, this period of the early companions serves as the reference point for all Islamic revival and reform, both traditionalist and modernist. Fifth, the success and power that resulted from the near-miraculous victories and geographic expansion of Islam constitute, in the eyes of believers, historical validation of the message of Islam.

Muslim Organization and Institutions

The early caliphate established the pattern for the organization and administration of the government. Islam provided the basic identity and ideology of the state, a source of unity and solidarity. The caliph's authority and leadership were rooted in his claim to be the successor of the Prophet as head of the community. Muhammad's practice provided the model for governance. The caliph exercised direct political, military, judicial, and fiscal control of the Muslim community. He was chosen through a process of consultation, nomination, and selection by a small group of electors who, after pledging their allegiance, presented the caliph to the people for acceptance by public acclamation. The caliph was the protector and defender of the faith; he was to assure the following of God's law and spread the rule of God through expansion and conquest. The community was a brotherhood of believers, a society based on religious rather than tribal solidarity.

In general, the Arabs did not occupy conquered cities but established garrison towns nearby, such as Basra and Kufa in Iraq, Fustat (Cairo) in Egypt, and Qairawan in North Africa. From these towns, conquered territories were governed and expeditions launched. They were centered around a mosque, which served as the religious and public focal point of the towns. Conquered territories were divided into provinces, each of which was administered by a governor, who was usually a military commander. The internal civil and religious administration remained in the hands of local officials. An agent of the caliph oversaw the collection of taxes and other administrative activities. Revenue for the state came from the captured lands and taxes.

The Islamic system of taxes took several forms: the tithe or wealth tax to benefit the poor and a land tax paid by Muslims; and the poll tax and tribute, later a land tax, paid by non-Muslims. All revenue was owned, collected, and administered by the state. The distribution of revenue was managed by the registry at Medina through a system of payments and pensions based on priority in accepting Islam. The Muslims at Medina and the family of the Prophet enjoyed a special place of honor because of their closeness to Muhammad and their fidelity to God's call.

Muslim society was divided into four major social classes. The elites of society were the Arab Muslims, with special status given to the companions of the Prophet because of their early support and role in establishing the community. Next came the non-Arab converts to Islam. Although in theory all Muslims were equal before God, in fact, practice varied. Under the Umayyads, non-Arab Muslims were clearly second-class citizens. They continued to pay those taxes levied on non-Muslims even after their conversion. The *dhimmi*, or non-Muslim People of the Book (those who possessed a revealed scripture, Jews and Christians), constituted communities within and subject to the wider Islamic community-state. In time, this protected status was extended to Zoroastrians, Sikhs, Hindus, and Buddhists. Finally, there were the slaves. As in much of the Near East, slavery had long existed among the Arabs. Although the Quran commanded the just and humane treatment of slaves (16:71) and regarded their emancipation as a meritorious act (90:13, 58:3), the system of slavery was adopted in a modified form. Only captives in battle could be taken as slaves. Neither Muslims nor Jews and Christians could be enslaved in early Islam. Thus, religion played an important role in the government, law, taxation, and social organization of society.

The Umayyad Empire: Creation of an Arab Kingdom

The advent of Umayyad rule set in motion a process of continued expansion and centralization of authority that would transform the Islamic community from an Arab shaykhdom into an Islamic empire with rulers who were dependent on religion for legitimacy and the military for power and stability.

In 661, Muawiyah (r. 661–80) laid claim to the caliphate and ushered in the Umayyad era (661–750): imperial, dynastic, and dominated by an Arab military aristocracy. The capital was moved to Damascus. This permanent shift from the less sophisticated Arabian heartland to the established, cosmopolitan Greco-Roman Byzantine city symbolized the new imperial age. From this new center, the Umayyads completed the conquest of the entire Persian and half the Roman (Byzantine) empire. When Muawiyah seized power, Islam had already spread to Egypt, Libya, the Fertile Crescent, Syria, Iraq, and Persia across Armenia to the borders of Afghanistan. Under the Umayyads, Muslims captured the Maghreb (North Africa), Spain, and Portugal, marched across Europe (before being halted in the heart of France by Charles Martel at the Battle of Tours in 732), and extended the empire's borders to the Indian subcontinent. The accomplishments of the Umayyads were indeed remarkable. Damascus became an even greater imperial capital than it had been under Byzantine rule. Umayyad rulers developed a strong centralized dynastic kingdom, an Arab empire. The more advanced government, institutions, and bureaucracy of Byzantium were adopted and adapted to Arab Muslim needs. Civil servants and ministers were retained to guide and train their Muslim masters. In time, through a process of conversion and assimilation, language and culture, state and society were Arabized and Islamized. Arabic became the language of government as well as the lingua franca of what today constitutes North Africa and much of the Middle East. Islamic belief and values constituted the official norm and reference point for personal and public life.

Umayyad rulers relied on Islam for legitimacy and as a rationale for their conquests. Caliphs were the protectors and defenders of the faith charged with extending the rule of Islam. The basis of Umayyad unity and stability was the establishment of an Arab monarchy and reliance on Arab, in particular Syrian, warriors. Contrary to previous practice, hereditary succession, not selection or election, restricted the caliphate to the Umayyad house. This innovation, or departure from early Islamic practice, became the pretext for later Muslim historians, writing with Abbasid patronage, to denounce Umayyad rule as kingship and thus un-Islamic. In fact, a form of hereditary succession and dynastic rule became standard practice for the remainder of the caliphal period. Centralization and militarization of the state resulted in an increasingly autocratic and absolutist government supported and protected by its military.

Umayyad society was based on the creation and perpetuation of an Arab military aristocracy that constituted a hereditary social caste. Syrian troops were the heart of the caliphs' powerful military. As the source of caliphal power and security, they were amply rewarded from the booty and tribute that poured into Damascus as a result of the conquests. Arab Muslims enjoyed special tax privileges, exempted from the more substantial taxes levied on non-Arab Muslims and non-Muslims. This preferential treatment became a source of contention, especially among non-Arab Muslims, who regarded their lesser status as a violation of Islamic egalitarianism. Their alienation contributed to the eventual downfall of the Umayyad dynasty.

Divisions within the Islamic Community
As had been done from the time of the Prophet, critics and opponents used an "Islamic yardstick" to judge or condemn the Umayyads and

legitimate their own actions and aspirations. Political, social, economic, and religious grievances were viewed through the prism of an Islamic ideal relevant to all areas of life. Thus, Umayyad practice incurred an opposition that ranged from Kharijites, Alids (Shii), and disgruntled non-Arab Muslims to the early legal scholars and mystics of Islam.

The Kharijites

The Kharijites originated in the time of the caliphs Uthman and Ali. They were radical revolutionaries who combined a rigorous puritanism and religious fundamentalism with an "exclusivist egalitarianism." As previously noted, the occasion for the Kharijite secession from the main body of the community was Ali's submission to arbitration in his struggle with Muawiyah. For the Kharijites the situation was simple. Muawiyah had challenged the legitimate authority of the caliph; this grave sin rendered him an apostate or infidel, and thus Ali, and all true Muslims, had an obligation to wage jihad until Muawiyah desisted or was subdued. When the arbitration was announced, the Kharijites shouted, "Only God can decide." It was not the job of human beings to counter God's command and sit as judge. As a result, the Kharijites believed that Ali too was now guilty of a grave sin and no longer the legitimate head of the community. This early incident illustrates the basic Khariji beliefs. They were very pious believers who interpreted the Quran and Sunna (example) of the Prophet literally and absolutely. Therefore, they believed that the Quranic mandate to "command the good and prohibit evil" must be applied rigorously and without compromise. Acts were either good or bad, permitted or forbidden. Similarly, their world was divided sharply into the realms of belief and unbelief, Muslim (followers of God) and non-Muslim (enemies of God), peace and warfare. Faith must be informed by action; public behavior must rigorously conform to their version of Islamic principles if one was to be a Muslim. Therefore, any action contrary to the letter of the law constituted a grave sin that rendered a person a non-Muslim, subject to excommunication (exclusion), warfare, and death unless the person repented. Sinners were not simply backsliders but apostates who were guilty of treason against the community-state. All true believers were obliged to fight and subdue these nominal or self-styled Muslims.

Within their exclusivist view of the world and the nature of the Muslim community, the Kharijites incorporated an egalitarian spirit that maintained that any good Muslim, even a slave, could be the leader, or imam, of the community, provided he had community support. Their puritan absolutism demanded that a leader guilty of sin be deposed.

When the Kharijites broke with Ali, they went about establishing their vision of the true charismatic community based strictly and literally on the Quran and Sunna. Modeling themselves on the example of the Prophet, they first withdrew (hijra) to live together in a bonded community. From their encampments, they waged battle (jihad) against their enemies, seeing themselves as the instruments of God's justice. They were the people of God (paradise) fighting against the people of evil (hell). Because they were God's army struggling in a heavenly crusade against the forces of evil, violence, guerrilla warfare, and revolution were not only legitimate but obligatory in their battle against the sinful usurpers of God's rule. Defeated by Ali at Nahrawan in 658, they continued to lead uprisings and join in revolts against Muawiyah's Umayyad descendants and engaged in guerrilla warfare against subsequent Abbasid caliphs. A moderate branch of the Kharijites, known as the Ibadiyya, followers of Abd Allah ibn Ibad, founded Ibadi imamates in North (Tripolitania and Tahert) and East (Zanzibar) Africa, Yemen, and Oman. Their descendants still exist in small numbers in North Africa and are a plurality in Oman. Despite their seeming lack of success in their own times, their outlook has informed contemporary radical groups from Egypt's Takfir wal Hijra and Jamaat al-Jihad to al-Qaeda and ISIS.

Shii Islam

The first civil war between Ali and Muawiyah, which had resulted in the secession of the Kharijites and the alienation of Ali's supporters, came back to haunt the Umayyads. During the reign of Muawiyah's son, Yazid, a second round of civil wars broke out. One of these, the revolt of Ali's son Husayn, would lead to the division of the Islamic community into its two major branches, Sunni and Shii, and shape the worldview of Shii Islam.

When Yazid came to power in 680, Husayn, the son of Ali, was persuaded by a group of Alids in Kufa (Iraq) to lead a rebellion. However, when popular support failed to materialize, Husayn and his small band of followers were slaughtered by an Umayyad army at Karbala. The memory of this tragedy, the "martyrdom" of Alid forces, provided the paradigm of suffering and protest that has guided and inspired Shii Islam. For these partisans (shia) of Ali, the original injustice that had denied Ali his succession to Muhammad had been repeated, thwarting the rightful rule of the Prophet's family. Thus, the Shii developed their own distinctive vision of leadership and of history, centered on the martyred family of the Prophet and based on a belief that leadership of the Muslim community belonged to the descendants of Muhammad.

The fundamental difference between Sunni and Shii Muslims is the Shii doctrine of the imamate as distinct from the Sunni caliphate. As we have seen, the caliph was the selected or elected successor of the Prophet. He succeeded to political and military leadership but not to Muhammad's religious authority. By contrast, for the Shii, leadership of the Muslim community is vested in the imam (leader), who, although not a prophet, is the divinely inspired, sinless, infallible, religiopolitical leader of the community. He must be a direct descendant of the Prophet Muhammad and Ali, the first imam. He is both political leader and religious guide, the final authoritative interpreter of God's will as formulated in Islamic law. Whereas after the death of Muhammad, Sunni Islam came to place final religious authority for interpreting Islam in the consensus (*iima*) or collective judgment of the community (the consensus of the **ulama**, the traditional religious scholars), the Shii believe in continued divine guidance through their divinely inspired guide, the imam.

Sunni and Shii Muslims also developed differing doctrines concerning the meaning of history. For Sunni historians, early Islamic success and power were signs of God's guidance and rewards to a faithful community as well as validation of Muslim belief and claims. For the Shii, history was the theater for the struggle of an oppressed and disinherited minority community to restore God's rule on earth over the entire community under the imam. A righteous remnant was to persist in God's way against the forces of evil (Satan), as had Ali against Muawiyah and Husayn against the army of Yazid, to reestablish the righteous rule of the imam. The lives of the suffering imams, like that of Husayn, were seen as embodying the oppression and injustice experienced by a persecuted minority community. Realization of a just social order under the imam was to remain a frustrated hope and expectation for centuries as the Islamic community remained under Sunni caliphal governments.

The imam's rule over the entire Muslim community was frustrated not only by "usurper" Sunni caliphs but also by disagreements within the Shii community over succession. This led to three major divisions: Zaydi, Ismaili, and Ithna Ashari or Imami. The Zaydis claimed that Zayd ibn Ali, a grandson of Husayn, was the fifth imam. The majority of the Shii recognized Muhammad al-Baqir and his son Jafar al-Sadiq as rightful heirs to the imamate. Unlike other Shii, who restricted the imamate to the descendants of Ali by his wife Fatima, the Prophet's daughter, Zaydis believed that any descendant of Ali could become imam. They were political activists who, like the Kharijites, believed that the duty to enjoin the good and prohibit evil was incumbent on all Muslims at all times. They, too, rebelled against both Umayyad and Abbasid rule. The Zaydis were the first Shii to gain independence when Hasan ibn Zayd founded a Zaydi dynasty in Tabaristan, on the Caspian, in 864. Another Zaydi state was established in Yemen in 893, where it continued to exist until 1963.

In the eighth century, the majority of the Shii community split again into its two major branches in a dispute over succession to the sixth imam, Jafar al-Sadiq (d. 765). Most accepted his younger son, Musa al-Kazim, but some followed Ismail, the elder son. This resulted in the two major Shii communities, the Ithna Asharis, or Twelvers, and the Ismailis (sometimes called the Seveners). The numerical designation of each group stems from a crisis caused by the death or disappearance of their imam and thus the disruption of hereditary succession. For the Twelvers, or Ithna Asharis, the end of imamate succession occurred in 874 with the disappearance of the twelfth imam, the child Muhammad al-Muntazar (Muhammad, the awaited one). Shii theology resolved this dilemma with its doctrines of the absence or **occultation of the imam** and his return in the future as the **Mahdi** (the expected one).

For these Shii, the imam had not died but had disappeared and gone into hiding or seclusion. He would return as a messianic figure, the Mahdi, at the end of the world to vindicate his loyal followers, restore the community to its rightful place, and usher in a perfect Islamic society in which truth and justice will prevail. During the absence of the **hidden imam**, the community was to await his return and be guided by its religious experts, *mujtahids, ulama* (religious scholars) who interpret God's will, Islamic law, for the community. The Ismaili split into a number of subdivisions. For a major group of Ismailis, the line of imams ended in 760 when Ismail, the designated seventh imam, died before his father. Another group believed that Ismail had not died but was in seclusion and would return as the Mahdi. Others accepted Ismail's son, Muhammad, as imam.

The Ismailis

The image of the Ismaili today as a prosperous merchant community, led by the Aga Khan, belies their early revolutionary origins.[4] The early Ismaili were a revolutionary missionary movement. They attacked and assassinated Sunni political and religious leaders, seized power, and at their peak, ruled an area that extended from Egypt to the Sind province of India. For the Ismaili, as for Shii in general, the Quran had two meanings, an exoteric, literal meaning and an esoteric, inner teaching. This secret knowledge was given to the Imam and through a process of initiation to his representatives and missionaries. The followers of the imam, as distinguished from the majority of Muslims, constituted a religious elite who possessed the true guidance necessary for salvation and a mission to spread or propagate, by force if necessary, the message and rule of the Imam. Often functioning as secret organizations to avoid the Abbasid police, Ismaili also used *taqiyya* (to shield or guard), a common Shii practice that permits concealment of one's belief for self-protection or survival as a persecuted minority.

The Fatimid Dynasty

The Ismaili consisted of a variety of missionary communities or movements. During the early tenth century, one branch, the Qarmatians, attacked Syria, Palestine, and southern Mesopotamia and set up their own state in Bahrain. Other groups spread to North Africa and India. It was in North Africa and Egypt that the Ismaili Fatimid dynasty (named for Fatima, the Prophet's daughter, from whom the ruler claimed descent) was created. After an abortive attempt to conquer Syria, Ubayd Allah had fled to Qairawan (Tunisia), where he successfully seized power in 909, declaring himself the Mahdi and establishing a line of Fatimid Imams. In 969, Egypt was conquered and a new capital, Cairo (al-Qahira, the victorious), was built outside the older city of Fustat to celebrate the conquest of Egypt. The Fatimids established an absolute hereditary monarchy. The infallible Imam ruled over a strong, centralized monarchy that relied on its military and religious missionaries. From the tenth to the twelfth centuries, the Fatimids successfully competed with a weakened, fragmented Abbasid empire, spreading their influence and rule across North Africa, Egypt, Sicily, Syria, Persia, and western Arabia to the Sind province of India. Although the state was Fatimid, the majority of the population remained Sunni. During this period, the Fatimid caliphate flourished culturally and commercially as well as militarily. Among its most enduring monuments was its religious center, the al-Azhar mosque in Cairo, which served as a training center for its missionary propagandists. Reputed to be one of the world's oldest universities, al-Azhar has remained an internationally recognized center of (Sunni) Islamic learning, training students from all over the Islamic world and issuing authoritative religious judgments on major issues and questions.

Although the Fatimids even managed to briefly capture Baghdad, their attempt to rule all of the *dar al-Islam* (abode of Islam) came to an abrupt end in 1171 when Salah al-Din (Saladin) conquered Egypt and restored the Sunni rule of the (Seljuq) Abbasid caliphate. However, the Ismaili persist through several offshoots. The Nizari Ismaili began as a Persian-based sect under Hasan al-Sabah that broke away from the Fatimids in 1094. Called the assassins and guided by a series of Grand Masters who ruled from a stronghold on Mt. Alamut in northern Persia (thus each becoming known as the Old Man of the Mountain), they were particularly effective in murdering Abbasid princes, generals, and leading *ulama* in the name of their hidden imam.[5] They struck such terror in the hearts of their Muslim and Crusader enemies that their exploits in Persia and Syria earned them a name and memory in history long after they were overrun and driven underground by the Mongols in 1258. A descendant of Hasan al-Sabah, Hasan Ali Shah, received the honorary title Aga Khan ("chief ruler") through marriage to the daughter of the shah. He fled to India in 1840 after a failed revolt in Persia. Centered in Bombay, these Nizari (Khoja) Ismailis were led by a series of imams, known as the Aga Khan, whose personal fortunes have been matched by the wealth of remarkably successful and thriving Ismaili communities in East Africa, South Asia, Britain, and Canada. Currently, the Aga Khan oversees the spiritual and cultural life of the community. As its living imam, he has been able to reinterpret Islam to respond to modern life. At the same time, he oversees extensive commercial and industrial Ismaili investments and supervises the many educational, medical, and social welfare projects of its philanthropic foundation.

The Druze

Among the sectarian offshoots of Ismailism were the Druze of Lebanon. The Druze date back to two Fatimid missionaries named Darazi (d. 1019) and Hamza ibn Ali, who had been encouraged by the Fatimid caliph al-Hakim (r. 996–1021) to spread the Ismaili faith in southern Lebanon. Al-Hakim was an eccentric ruler who took the title Imam and progressively came to believe that he was not only the divinely appointed religio-political leader but also the cosmic intellect, linking God with creation. Darazi and Hamza became leaders of a movement centered on recognition of al-Hakim as a divine incarnation, the highest or first cosmic intellect. This supernatural status became the excuse for his erratic, authoritarian behavior, which at times included the persecution of Ismaili, Sunni, and Christian leaders alike.

When al-Hakim disappeared or was killed, they maintained that he had gone into seclusion to test the faith of his followers and would return to restore justice in the world. After Darazi's death, Hamza, now claiming to be the leader (imam) in Hakim's absence, organized and developed Hakim's cult into what became a separate religion. Hamza then disappeared, and was expected to return as the Mahdi at a later date with al-Hakim. In the interim, Baha al-Din al-Muktana served as the earthly link between Hamza and the community.

The Druze call themselves the unitarians, followers of al-Hakim who embodied and revealed the one true God. Forming a distinct religion, the Druze possess their own scripture, the *Rasail al-Hikma* (the Books of Wisdom), and law. The Books of Wisdom are a collection of letters from al-Muktana, al-Hamza, and al-Hakim. Druze law, places of prayer, and religious leadership replace the Sharia, mosque, and *ulama*. The community is hierarchically organized. The two major divisions are the majority of ordinary members, the so-called ignorant, and the wise, those men and women who are initiated and as such can read the scriptures and are expected to lead an exemplary life of regular prayer and abstention from wine, tobacco, and other stimulants. They can be recognized by the quality of their lives and their special dress or white turbans. Among the wise are a group of religious leaders called shaykhs, noted for their learning and piety, who preside over meetings, weddings, and funerals. The *rais* (chief), who is selected from one of the leading families, is the head of the community.

Historically, the Druze have been a secretive and closed community. They have steadfastly kept their texts, beliefs, and practices secret, carefully guarding them from outsiders. Regarded by both Sunni and Shii as heretics and living in a Sunni-dominated world, they too have followed the Shii doctrine of *taqiyya*, with its double meaning of caution and dissimulation for survival in a hostile world. Thus, although they do not observe the fast of Ramadan or pilgrimage to Mecca, when necessary they have outwardly followed the prevailing Sunni faith and a modified form of Hanafi (Islamic) law. Druze beliefs and practices emphasize solidarity; they neither accept converts nor marry outside the faith. They practice monogamy and endogamy (marrying within their group) and discourage divorce. The seven pillars or basic religious obligations reinforce a strong sense of community. They include speaking the truth to other members (although not necessarily to nonbelievers), mutual defense, and living separately from unbelievers. Unlike other monotheistic faiths, the Druze believe in the transmigration of souls until perfected souls cease to be reborn and ascend to the stars. At the end of time, when Hakim and Hamza return to establish a reign of justice, God will reward the faithful by being placed close to Him. The Druze have survived in Syria, Israel, and especially Lebanon, where they number several hundred thousand.

Law and Mysticism

Dissatisfaction with Umayyad rule also resulted in the development of nonrevolutionary reform movements within society. The rapid geographic expansion and conquests brought the rise of new centers of power and wealth, an influx of "foreign" ways, and greater social stratification. The very success of the Umayyad empire contained the seeds of its downfall. With wealth and power came corruption and abuse of power, symbolized by the new lifestyle of its flourishing, cosmopolitan capital and the growth of new cities. This was accompanied by the infiltration of new ideas and practices. The strengths that came with acculturation were offset, in the eyes of some, by innovations that were seen as undermining the older Arab way of life. In addition to the disaffected Kharijites and Alids, a host of other critics sprang up who contrasted an idealized Medinan Islamic community with the realities of Umayyad life. This gave rise, in particular, to the growth of two Islamic movements or institutions, the *ulama* (religious scholars) and the Sufis (mystics).

For a growing number of pious Muslims, who would become a religious and social class in the Muslim community known as the *ulama* (plural of *alim*, "learned" or scholar), Arab power and wealth, not Islamic commitment and ideals, inspired and unified the empire. The behavior of many caliphs, the intrigues of court life, and the privileged status of new elites were regarded as having little to do with Islam. What the Umayyads had done was pragmatically necessary, because the Arabs had not had the institutions and trained personnel required for empire building.

Their critics, however, believed that the Umayyad system produced a society based more on the command of the caliph than the command of God. They emphasized the need to understand and consolidate a life and society informed by revelation. God's law, they argued, should provide the blueprint or pattern for an Islamic society. Believing that Umayyad institutions and law should be brought into line with Islamic principles, they wanted to consolidate Islamic law and make it the central guiding principle of Islamic society.

The outcome of this movement was a burst of activity that would result in the development of Islamic religious sciences. Pious Muslims from all walks of life devoted themselves to the study of the Quran, Arabic language and linguistics, and the collection and examination of Prophetic traditions. In particular, to safeguard their beliefs and limit the power of the caliph, many devoted themselves to the formulation and explication of Islamic law. They also incorporated local customs or customary laws; non-Arab customs or precedents not in conflict with Islamic norms were considered normative. In this way, elements from Roman Byzantine (including Roman provincial) law, Talmudic law, the canon law of the Eastern churches, and Persian Sāsānian law entered Islamic law during its formative period. By the late Umayyad period, centers of law could be found in many cities of the empire.

Reaction to the worldly excesses of empire contributed to the development of mysticism as well as law. Luxury, the pursuit of conquest and
wealth, the transformation of the caliphate into a dynastic monarchy with
the trappings of imperial court life, and the doubtful moral character of
some of the Umayyad caliphs struck some pious Muslims as standing in
sharp contrast to the early example of Muhammad and the Rightly Guided
Caliphs and the relative simplicity of life in Medina. They believed that
Umayyad goals of power and wealth conflicted with and distracted from
the true center and goal of Muslim life, Allah. Therefore, the early mystics
preached a message stressing renunciation and detachment from worldly
concerns and attachments for the pursuit of the "real" God. As we shall
see, mysticism or Sufism became a major popular force within Islam that
swept across the Muslim world, spreading its spirit of love and devotion.

Growth of "Islamic" Revolt

Despite the accomplishments of Umayyad rule, by the eighth century
(720) anti-Umayyad sentiment had spread and intensified. It encompassed
a variety of disaffected factions: non-Arab Muslims who denounced their
second-class status vis-à-vis Arab Muslims as contrary to Islamic egalitarianism; Kharijites and Shii who continued to regard the Umayyads as
usurpers; Arab Muslims in Mecca, Medina, and Iraq who resented the
privileged status of Syrian families; and, finally, pious Muslims, Arab and
non-Arab alike, who viewed the new cosmopolitan lifestyle of luxury and
social privilege as foreign and an unwarranted innovation or departure
from their established, Islamic way of life.

Opposition forces shared a discontent with Umayyad rule as well as
a tendency to legitimate their own claims and agenda Islamically; they
condemned Umayyad practice and policies as un-Islamic innovations and
called for a return to the Quran and the practices of the Prophet and the
early Medinan community:

> The ideology of a restoration of primitive Islam, with variants reflect-
> ing different trends, had conquered the masses, and, with the support
> of the majority of the learned men, became part of the programme of
> all, or nearly all, the leaders of parties. It triumphed when the Abbasids
> adopted it as their slogan.[6]

By 747, an opposition movement, with substantial Shii support, rallied
behind a Persian named Abu Muslim. In 750, the Umayyads fell, and Abu
al-Abbas, a descendant of the Prophet's uncle al-Abbas, was proclaimed
caliph. Islam's capital was moved from Damascus to the newly created
Baghdad, known in Arabic as the City of Peace. Under Abbasid rule, the

Islamic community would become an empire remembered not only for its wealth and political power but also for its extraordinary cultural activity and accomplishments.

The Abbasid Caliphate: The Flowering of Islamic Civilization

Abbasid rule of the Islamic community ushered in an era of strong centralized government, great economic prosperity, and a remarkable civilization. Abbasid caliphs could be as autocratic and ruthless as many of their Umayyad predecessors. Indeed, Abu al-Abbas did not hesitate to take the title "the blood shedder" (al-saffah); he came to be remembered as Abu Abbas al-Saffah. The Abbasid caliphs consolidated their power by crushing their Shii supporters as well as their opponents. This betrayal further alienated the Shii from the Sunni majority. The name "Sunni" comes from their self-designation as ahl al-sunna wal jamaa, those who follow the Prophet's example and thus belong to his society or community.

The Abbasids came to power under the banner of Islam, legitimating their seizure of power and dynastic reign Islamically. They became the great patrons of an emerging religious class, the ulama (religious scholars). They supported the development of Islamic scholarship and disciplines, built mosques, and established schools.

The Abbasids refined Umayyad practice, borrowing heavily from Persian culture, with its divinely ordained system of government. The caliph's claim to rule by divine mandate was symbolized by the transformation of his title from Successor or Deputy of the Prophet to Deputy of God and by the appropriation of the Persian-inspired title, Shadow of God on Earth. The ruler's exalted status was further reinforced by his magnificent palace, his retinue of attendants, and the introduction of a court etiquette appropriate for an emperor. Thus, subjects were required to bow before the caliph, kissing the ground, a symbol of the caliph's absolute power. Persian influence was especially evident in the government and military. Preempting critics of the previous regime, the Arab Syrian-dominated military aristocracy was replaced by a salaried army and bureaucracy in which non-Arab Muslims, especially Persians, played a major role. The Abbasids explained this change in terms of Islamic egalitarianism. More often than not, however, it was royal favor and fear, symbolized by the royal executioner who stood by the side of the caliph that brought him prestige and motivated obedience.

The early centuries of Abbasid rule were marked by an unparalleled splendor and economic prosperity whose magnificence came to be immortalized in the Arabian Nights (The Thousand and One Nights), with its legendary exploits of the exemplary caliph, Harun al-Rashid (r. 786–809).

In a departure from the past, Abbasid success was based not on conquest but on trade, commerce, industry, and agriculture. The enormous wealth and resources of the caliphs enabled them to become great patrons of art and culture and thus create the more significant and lasting legacy of the Abbasid period, Islamic civilization. The development of Islamic law, the Sharia, constitutes their greatest contribution to Islam. Because part of the indictment of the Umayyads had been their failure to implement an effective Islamic legal system, the Abbasids gave substantial support to legal development. The early law schools, which had begun only during the late Umayyad period (c. 720), flourished under caliphal patronage of the *ulama*. Although Islam has no clergy or priesthood, by the eighth century the *ulama* had become a professional elite of religious leaders, a distinct social class within Muslim society. Their prestige and authority rested on a reputation for learning in Islamic studies: the Quran, traditions of the Prophet, law. Because of their expertise, they became the jurists, theologians, and educators in Muslim society, the interpreters and guardians of Islamic law and tradition. The judge (*qadi*) administered the law, as it was developed by the early jurists, firmly establishing the Islamic court system.

In addition to law, the Abbasids were also committed patrons of culture and the arts. The process of Arabization, begun during the late Umayyad period, was completed by the end of the ninth century. Arabic language and tradition penetrated and modified the cultures of conquered territories. Arabic displaced local languages—Syriac, Aramaic, Coptic, and Greek—becoming the language of common discourse, government, and culture throughout much of the empire. Arabic was no longer solely the language of Muslims from Arabia but the language of literature and public discourse for the multiethnic group of new Arabic-speaking peoples, especially the large number of non-Arab converts, many of whom were Persian. Translation centers were created. From the seventh to the ninth centuries, manuscripts were obtained from the far reaches of the empire and beyond and translated from their original languages (Sanskrit, Greek, Latin, Syriac, Coptic, and Persian) into Arabic. Thus, the best works of Hellenistic literature, philosophy, and the sciences were made accessible: Aristotle, Plato, Galen, Hippocrates, Euclid, and Ptolemy. The genesis of Islamic civilization was indeed a collaborative effort, incorporating the learning and wisdom of many cultures and languages.

As in government administration, Christians and Jews, who had been the intellectual and bureaucratic backbone of the Persian and Byzantine empires, participated in the process as well as Muslims. This "ecumenical" effort was evident at the Caliph al-Mamun's (r. 813–33) House of Wisdom and at the translation center headed by the renowned scholar Hunayn ibn Ishaq, a Nestorian Christian. This period of translation and assimilation was followed by one of Muslim intellectual and artistic creativity. Muslims ceased to be merely disciples and became masters, in the process producing Islamic civilization, dominated by the Arabic language and Islam's view of life: "It was these two things, their language and their faith, which were the great contribution of the Arab invaders to the new and original civilization which developed under their aegis."[7] Major contributions were made in many fields: literature and philosophy, algebra and geometry, science and medicine, art and architecture. Towering intellectual giants dominated this period: al-Razi (865–925), al-Farabi (d. 950), ibn Sina (known as Avicenna, 980–1037), ibn Rushd (known as Averroes, d. 1198), al-Biruni (973–1048), and al-Ghazali (d. 1111). Islam had challenged the world politically; it now did so culturally. Great urban cultural centers in Cordoba, Baghdad, Cairo, Nishapur, and Palermo emerged and eclipsed Christian Europe, mired in the Dark Ages. The activities of these centers are reflected in the development of philosophy and science.

Islamic philosophy was the product of a successful transplant from Greek to Islamic soil, where it flourished from the ninth to the twelfth centuries. Muslim philosophers appropriated Hellenistic thought (Aristotle, Plato, Plotinus), wrote commentaries, and extended the teachings and insights of Greek philosophy within an Islamic context and worldview. The result was Islamic philosophy, indebted to Hellenism but with its own Islamic character. Its contribution was of equal importance to the West. Islamic philosophy became the primary vehicle for the transmission of Greek philosophy to medieval Europe. The West reappropriated its lost heritage as European scholars traveled to major centers of Islamic learning, retranslating the Greek philosophers and learning from the writings of their great Muslim disciples: men like al-Farabi, who had come to be known as "the second teacher or master" (the first being Aristotle), ibn Sina (Avicenna), and Ibn Rush (Averroes), remembered as "the great commentator" on Aristotle. Thus we find many of the great medieval Christian philosophers and theologians (Albert the Great, Thomas Aquinas, Peter Abelard, Roger Bacon, John Duns Scotus) acknowledging their intellectual debt to their Muslim predecessors.

The enormous accomplishments of Islamic philosophy and science were the product of men of genius, multitalented intellectuals (who often mastered the major disciplines of medicine, mathematics, astronomy, and philosophy). They were the "renaissance" men of classical Islam. Avicenna's reflections on his own training typify the backgrounds of many of the great intellectuals of this period:

> I busied myself with the study of the *Fusus al-Hikam* [a treatise by al-Farabi] and other commentaries on physics and mathematics, and the doors of knowledge opened before me. Then I took up medicine. Medicine is not one of the difficult sciences, and in a very short time I undoubtedly excelled in it, so that physicians of merit studied under me. I also attended the sick, and the doors of medical treatments based on experience opened before me to an extent that cannot be described. At the same time I carried on debates and controversies in jurisprudence. At this point I was sixteen years old.
>
> Then, for a year and a half, I devoted myself to study. I resumed the study of logic and all parts of philosophy. During this time I never slept the whole night through and did nothing but study all day long. Whenever I was puzzled by a problem I would go to the mosque, pray, and beg the Creator of All to reveal to me that which was hidden from me and to make easy for me that which was difficult. Then at night I would return home, put a lamp in front of me, and set to work reading and writing.... I went on like this until I was firmly grounded in all sciences and mastered them as far as was humanly possible.... Thus I mastered logic, physics, and mathematics.
>
> The **Sultan** of Bukhara was stricken by an illness which baffled the physicians.... I appeared before him and joined them in treating him and distinguished myself in his service.
>
> One day I asked his permission to go into their library, look at their books, and read the medical ones.... I went into a palace of many rooms, each with trunks full of books, back-to-back. In one room there were books on Arabic and poetry, in another books on jurisprudence, and similarly in each room books on a single subject. I asked for those I needed read these books, made use of them, and thus knew the rank of every author in his own subject.... When I reached the age of eighteen, I had completed the study of all these sciences. At that point my memory was better, whereas today my learning is riper.[8]

Islamic science was an integrated and synthetic area of knowledge. It was integrated in that Muslim scientists, who were often philosophers or mystics as well, viewed the physical universe from within their Islamic worldview and context as a manifestation of the presence of God, the Creator and source of unity and harmony in nature.[9] Islamic science was also a grand synthesis informed by indigenous and foreign sources (Arab, Persian, Hellenistic, Indian) and transformed by scholars and scientists in urban centers throughout the world of Islam. Thus, it constituted a major component of Islamic civilization and, in the eyes of many Muslims, a worthy complement to Islam's international political order. As one Muslim intellectual observed:

> Islamic science came into being from a wedding between the spirit that issued from the Quranic revelation and the existing sciences of various civilizations which Islam inherited and which it transmuted through its spiritual power into a new substance, at once different from and continuous with what had existed before it. The international and cosmopolitan nature of Islamic civilization, derived from the universal character of the Islamic revelation and reflected in the geographical spread of the Islamic world, enabled it to create the first science of a truly international nature in human history.[10]

The legacy of Islamic civilization was that of a brilliant, rich culture. Its contributions proved to be as significant for the West, which in subsequent centuries appropriated and incorporated its knowledge and wisdom.

Thus during the Abbasid period, the comprehensiveness of Islam was clearly manifested and delineated:

> Islam—the offspring of Arabia and the Arabian Prophet—was not only a system of belief and cult. It was also a system of state, society, law, thought and art—a civilization with religion as its unifying, eventually dominating factor.[11]

For Muslim and non-Muslim alike, the political and cultural life of a vast empire, consisting of many tribal, ethnic, and religious groups, was brought within the framework of the Arabic language and Islamic faith.[12] Islamic civilization was the result of a dynamic, creative process as Muslims borrowed freely from other cultures. It proceeded from a sense of mission, power, and superiority. Muslims were the dominant force—masters not victims, colonizers not the colonized. The new ideas and practices were Arabized and Islamized. It was a process of change characterized by continuity with the faith and practice of Muhammad. Unlike the modern period, Muslims controlled the process of assimilation and acculturation. Their autonomy and identity were not seriously threatened by the specter of political and cultural domination. As with the early conquests and expansion of Islam, Muslims then (and now) regarded this brilliant period as a sign of God's favor and a validation of Islam's message and the Muslim community's universal mission.

The extraordinary spread and development of Islam was not without its religious conflicts. The same concern that had motivated the attempt by the *ulama* to preserve Islam in the face of caliphal whim and uncritical adoption of foreign, un-Islamic practices led to conflicts between the *ulama* and those whom they sometimes regarded as their competitors, the Sufis, philosophers, Shiites, and political establishment. The *ulama* delineation of law as the embodiment of the straight path of Islam set the criteria for belief and behavior in intellectual, social, and moral life and the pattern for orthodoxy (correct belief) or, perhaps more accurately, orthopraxy (correct practice). This vision of Muslim life as the observance of God's law did not always coincide comfortably with the Sufi emphasis on the interior path of contemplation and personal religious experience or the tendency of philosophy to give primacy to reason over the unquestioned acceptance of revelation. The tension between religious scholars on the one hand and philosophers and Sufis on the other was reflected in the life and work of a towering giant in the history of Islam, indeed in the history of religions, Abu Hamid al-Ghazali.

Ironically, the golden age of Islamic civilization paralleled the progressive political fragmentation of the universal caliphate. The relative peace, prosperity, and unity of the Islamic community, epitomized during the rule of Harun al-Rashid, was challenged internally by competing groups and externally by the Fatimids and the **Crusades**.

Governing a vast empire extending from the Atlantic to central Asia proved impossible. Abbasid political unity deteriorated rapidly from 861 to 945 as religious (Khariji and Shii) and regional differences, and particularly competing political aspirations, precipitated a series of revolts and secessionist movements. In Morocco, Tunisia, Iran, Syria, and Iraq itself, local governors, who were often army commanders, asserted their independence as heads of semiautonomous states. These regional rulers (amirs, or commanders), while continuing to give formal, nominal allegiance to the caliph, exercised actual rule over their territories, establishing their own hereditary dynasties. By 945, the disintegration of the universal caliphate was evident when the Buyids (Buwayhids), a Shii dynasty from western Persia, invaded Baghdad and seized power, and their leader assumed the title commander-in-chief or commander of the commanders. Although Shii, they did not change the Sunni orientation of the empire and left the caliph on his throne as a titular leader of a fictionally unified empire. The Abbasids continued to reign but not rule. With an Abbasid on the throne as a symbol of legitimate government and Muslim unity, real power passed to a series of Persian (Buyid) and Turkic (Seljuq) military dynasties or sultanates. The sultan ("power," ruler), as chief of the commanders, governed a politically fragmented empire as the caliph helplessly stood by.

Sunni Islam was also threatened by two other developments during the Abbasid caliphate—the rise of the Fatimid dynasty and the Crusades. The Ismaili rebellion in Tunisia and subsequent establishment of a Shii imamate in Egypt constituted a serious religiopolitical challenge. The Fatimid rulers claimed to be Imams and were not content to simply govern Egypt but, as we have seen, followed other Ismaili groups in sending their missionaries to spread their Shii doctrine. This Shii challenge elicited a religious as well as a military response as Sunni *ulama* moved to protect their version of orthodoxy in the face of Shii innovations. They were supported in their endeavors by the royal court, which wished to counter Shii anticaliphal sentiments. This contributed to a growing tendency among the Sunni *ulama* to preserve the unity of Islam through greater self-definition and standardization. In the face of the internal breakup of the central empire, this meant achieving a consensus on the corpus of Islamic law to protect and maintain the sociopolitical order.

ISLAM AND THE WEST: THE CRUSADES AND MUSLIM RESPONSE TO MILITANT CHRISTIANITY

Despite their common monotheistic roots, the history of Christianity and Islam has more often than not been marked by confrontation rather than peaceful coexistence and dialogue. For the Christian West, Islam is the religion of the sword; for Muslims, the Christian West is epitomized by the armies of the Crusades. From the earliest decades of Islamic history, Christianity and Islam have been locked in a political and theological struggle, because Islam, unlike other world religions, has threatened the political and religious ascendancy of Christianity. Muslim armies overran the Eastern Roman empire, Spain, and the Mediterranean from Sicily to Anatolia. At the same time, Islam challenged Christian religious claims and authority. Coming after Christianity, Islam claimed to supersede Christian revelation. Although acknowledging God's revelation and revering God's messengers, from Adam through Jesus, as prophets, Islam rejected the doctrine of Christ's divinity, the finality of Christian revelation, and the authority of the church. Instead, it called on all, Jews and Christians as well, to accept the finality of revelation and prophecy in Islam, to join the Islamic community, and to live under Islamic rule. Islam's universal mission had resulted in the spread of Muslim rule over Christian territories and Christian hearts. Conversions were initially slow, but by the eleventh century large numbers of Christians living under Muslim rule were converting to Islam. Even those who had remained Christian were becoming Arabized, adopting Arabic language and manners. The European Christian response was, with few exceptions, hostile, intolerant, and belligerent. Muhammad was vilified as an imposter and

Courtyard of the Lions, Alhambra Palace, the fourteenth-century residence of the Nasrid dynasty in Granada, Spain, one of the remarkable monuments remaining from the several centuries of Muslim rule in Andalusia, when Muslims, Jews, and Christians coexisted and produced a high culture.

identified as the anti-Christ. Islam was dismissed as a religion of the sword led by an infidel driven by a lust for power and women. This attitude was preserved and perpetuated in literature such as the *Divine Comedy*, where Dante consigned Muhammad to the lowest level of hell. Christian fears were fully realized as Islam became a world power and civilization while Christianity staggered and stagnated in its Dark Ages.

By the eleventh century, Christendom's response to Islam took two forms: the struggle to reconquer (the ***Reconquista***) Spain (1000–1492) and Italy and Sicily (1061), and the undertaking of another series of Christian holy wars—the Crusades (1095–1453). Two myths pervade Western perceptions of the Crusades: first, that the Crusades were simply motivated by a religious desire to liberate **Jerusalem**, and second, that Christendom ultimately triumphed.

Jerusalem was a sacred city for all three Abrahamic faiths. When the Arab armies took Jerusalem in 638, they occupied a center whose shrines had made it a major pilgrimage site in Christendom. Churches and the Christian population were left unmolested. Jews, long banned from living there by Christian rulers, were permitted to return, live, and worship in the city of David and Solomon. Muslims proceeded to build a shrine, the **Dome of the Rock**, and a mosque, the al-Aqsa, near the area formerly

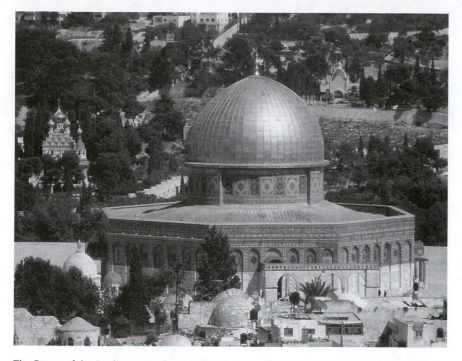

The Dome of the Rock in Jerusalem is part of a complex that includes the Masjid al-Aqsa, or Farthest Mosque, in the third holiest city for Muslims. Built in the Umayyad period, the shrine encloses the rock said to be the place where Muhammad ascended to heaven during the miraculous Night Journey.

occupied by Herod's Temple and close by the Wailing Wall, the last remnant of Solomon's temple.

The Dome of the Rock in Jerusalem, a major holy site and a place of pilgrimage erected by the Umayyad caliph Abd al-Malik, was completed in 692. The famous shrine is built on the spot from which Muslims believe Muhammad ascended to God and then returned to the world. In this story, one of the grand themes of Islamic scholarship and popular piety, the Prophet, in the company of the angel Gabriel, was transported at night from the Kaba in Mecca to Jerusalem. From there, he ascended to the heavens and the presence of God.

Five centuries of peaceful coexistence elapsed before political events and an imperial-papal power play led to centuries-long series of so-called holy wars that pitted Christendom against Islam and left an enduring legacy of misunderstanding and distrust.

In 1071, a Seljuq (Abbasid) army decisively defeated the Byzantine army. The Byzantine emperor, Alexius I, fearing that all Asia Minor would be overrun, called on fellow Christian rulers and the pope to come to the aid of Constantinople by undertaking a "pilgrimage" or crusade to free Jerusalem and its environs from Muslim rule. For Pope Urban II, the "defense" of Jerusalem provided an opportunity to gain recognition for papal authority and its role in legitimating the actions of temporal rulers. A divided Christendom rallied as warriors from France and other parts of Western Europe (called "Franks" by Muslims) united against the "infidel" in a holy war whose ostensible goal was the holy city. This was ironic because, as one scholar has observed, "God may indeed have wished it, but there is certainly no evidence that the Christians of Jerusalem did, or that anything extraordinary was occurring to pilgrims there to prompt such a response at that moment in history."[13] In fact, Christian rulers, knights, and merchants were driven primarily by political and military ambitions and the promise of the economic and commercial (trade and banking) rewards that would accompany the establishment of a Latin kingdom in the Middle East. However, the appeal to religion captured the popular mind and gained its support.

The contrast between the behavior of the Christian and Muslim armies in the First Crusade has been etched deeply in the collective memory of Muslims. In 1099, the Crusaders stormed Jerusalem and established Christian sovereignty over the Holy Land. They left no Muslim survivors; women and children were massacred. The Noble Sanctuary, the Haram al-Sharif, was desecrated as the Dome of the Rock was converted into a church and the al-Aqsa mosque, renamed the Temple of Solomon, became a residence for the king. Latin principalities were established in Antioch, Edessa, Tripoli, and Tyre. The Latin Kingdom of Jerusalem lasted less than a century. In 1187, Salah al-Din (Saladin), having reestablished Abbasid rule over Fatimid Egypt, led his army in a fierce battle and recaptured Jerusalem. The Muslim army was as magnanimous in victory as it had been tenacious in battle. Civilians were spared; churches and shrines were generally left untouched. The striking differences in military conduct were epitomized by the two dominant figures of the Crusades: Saladin and Richard the Lion-Hearted. The chivalrous Saladin was faithful to his word and compassionate toward noncombatants. Richard accepted the surrender of Acre and then proceeded to massacre all its inhabitants, including women and children, despite promises to the contrary.

By the thirteenth century the Crusades degenerated into intra-Christian wars, papal wars against its Christian enemies who were denounced as heretics and schismatics. The result was a weakening, rather than a strengthening, of Christendom. As Roger Savory has observed:

> An ironical but undeniable result of the Crusades was the deterioration of the position of Christian minorities in the Holy Land. Formerly

these minorities had been accorded rights and privileges under Muslim rule, but, after the establishment of the Latin Kingdom, they found themselves treated as "loathsome schismatics." In an effort to obtain relief from persecution by their fellow Christians, many abandoned their Nestorian or Monophysite beliefs, and adopted either Roman Catholicism, or—the supreme irony—Islam.[14]

By the fifteenth century, the Crusades had spent their force. Although they were initially launched to unite Christendom and turn back the Muslim armies, the opposite had occurred. Amid a bitterly divided Christendom, Constantinople fell in 1453 before Turkish Muslim conquerors. This Byzantine capital was renamed Istanbul and became the seat of the Ottoman empire.

THE SULTANATE PERIOD: MEDIEVAL MUSLIM EMPIRES

By the thirteenth century, the Abbasid empire was a sprawling, fragmented, deteriorating commonwealth of semiautonomous states, sultanates, governed by military commanders. It was an empire in name only. The fictional unity of a united Islamic community symbolized by the caliph in Baghdad stood in sharp contrast to the underlying reality of its political and religious divisions. Invaded and ruled successively by the Buyids and then the Seljuks, Baghdad was completely overrun in the thirteenth century by the Mongols. Pouring out of Central Asia, the armies of Genghis Khan had subjugated much of Central Asia, China, Russia, and the Near East. In 1258, the Mongol army under Hulagu Khan, the grandson of Genghis Khan, captured Baghdad, burned and pillaged the city, slaughtered its Muslim inhabitants, and executed the caliph and his family. Only Egypt and Syria escaped the Mongol conquest of the Muslim empire. In Egypt, the Mamluks ("the owned ones"), Turkish slave soldiers who served as a sort of praetorian guard, seized power from their Ayyubid masters. The Mamluk sultanate successfully resisted the Mongols and ruled until 1517.

Although the destruction of Baghdad and the abolition of the Abbasid caliphate brought an end to the caliphal period and seemed to many an irreversible blow to Muslim power, by the fifteenth century Muslim fortunes had been reversed. The central caliphate was replaced by a chain of dynamic Muslim sultanates or states, each ruled by a sultan, which eventually extended from Africa to Southeast Asia, from Timbuktu to Mindanao, as Islam penetrated Africa, Central and Southeast Asia, and Eastern Europe. Among the principal missionaries of Islam were traders and Sufi brotherhoods.

Muslim power peaked in the sixteenth century. Three major Muslim empires emerged in the midst of the many sultanates: the Ottoman Turkish empire, centered in Istanbul but encompassing major portions of North Africa, the Arab world, and Eastern Europe; the Persian Safavid empire, with its capital in Isfahan, which effectively established Twelver Shii Islam as the state's religion; and the Mughal empire, centered in Delhi and embracing most of the Indian subcontinent (modern-day Pakistan, India, and Bangladesh).[15] Baghdad's successors were the imperial capitals of Istanbul, Isfahan, and Delhi. Political ascendancy was accompanied by a cultural florescence. As in Abbasid times, great sultans, such as the Ottoman Sulayman the Magnificent (r. 1520–66), Shah Abbas in Persia (r, 1587–1629), and the Mughal emperor Akbar (r. 1556–1605) in India, were patrons of learning and the arts.

The Ottoman Empire

The Ottoman empire was the heir to the Mongol-Turkish legacy of Ghengis Khan and his successors. The fall of Constantinople (Istanbul) in 1453 to the Ottoman sultan Mehmet II and the conquest of Byzantium realized the cherished dream of Muslim rulers and armies since the seventh century. The acknowledgment of Mehmet as "The Conqueror" throughout the Islamic world and his cosmopolitan capital at Istanbul, which sat astride both Europe and Asia, symbolized the power and mission of an emerging imperial giant.

The Ottomans drew on their Mongol-Turkish and Islamic roots and traditions, combining a warrior heritage with an Islamic tradition that believed in Islam's universal mission and sacred struggle (jihad), to establish themselves as worldwide propagators and defenders of Islam. They became the great warriors of Islamic expansion through military conquest. The titles taken by Ottoman sultans, such as "Warrior of the Faith" and "Defender of the Sharia," reflected this religiopolitical justification and rationale. Ottoman suzerainty was extended to the Arab Middle East and North Africa, incorporating such major Islamic cities as Mecca, Medina, Cairo, Damascus, and Tunis along with great centers of Islamic learning like Egypt's Al-Azhar and Tunisia's Zaytouna Mosque-University. Greece, Malta, Cyprus, Tripoli, the Balkans, and much of Eastern Europe were also absorbed. A besieged Europe struggled for its existence. After two centuries of confrontation, Ottoman forces were decisively turned back by the navies of Christian Europe at the Battle of Lepanto in 1571. The Ottoman defeat and the truce of 1580 in the Mediterranean "confirmed the frontier between Christian and Muslim civilizations that has lasted to the present day." In 1683 Ottoman expansion in Eastern Europe was checked by the failure of the siege of Vienna.

During the 1600s the Ottoman empire fully evolved. Istanbul, whose population of 500,000 was more than twice the size of any European capital, became once again an international but now Islamized center of power and culture. Scholars, artists, and architects from all over the Islamic world and Europe were commissioned, as Muslim conquerors also proved to be great builders of civilization. Istanbul's skyline was transformed by palaces and mosques with their distinctive cupolas. The royal family lived in splendor in the Topkapi palace, preserved today as a great museum. An imperial monarchy governed subjects of many tribal, ethnic, linguistic, and religious backgrounds from the Mediterranean to Iran.

Both Byzantine and Turkish-Muslim influences informed the development of the political, legal, economic, and social institutions of the state. The ruling class comprised the Ottoman family and a special cadre of Balkan slaves who had been Turkified and Islamized through a sophisticated educational system so that they might serve as government administrators and members of the elite military, the Janissaries. Ottoman sultans relied on a strong military of slave-soldiers supported by gunpowder technology; the empire was governed by means of a centralized administration and a well-organized bureaucracy. Alongside the political establishment was a structured religious establishment. The *ulama*, schools, and the courts were brought within the state's bureaucracy. Through royal patronage, the empire developed a hierarchy of Islamic institutions: local Quran schools, mosque-universities (**madrasas**), and courts. The **shaykh al-Islam** was at the apex of the state's religious bureaucracy; like the chief **qadi** (judge), was appointed by the sultan. Thus, Ottoman *ulama* families became a religious aristocracy.

A distinctive feature of the Ottoman sultanate was the millet system, a variation on the earlier Islamic institution of the *dhimmi*, or protected non-Muslim peoples, which recognized and regulated the rights and duties of religious communities. (Whatever the Ottoman desire was to forge a broader identity, the basic units of society were the empire's religious communities, which provided the primary source of identity and loyalty.) Leaders of religious communities (Christian patriarchs and chief rabbis) were appointed by the sultan to collect the taxes due the royal household and to rule over their communities. Religious communities enjoyed limited autonomy. They could operate their own churches and synagogues, schools, and domestic religious courts, train and govern their clergy, and oversee their charitable institutions.

As the Ottoman empire prospered in its imperial fortunes, new rival Muslim empires were emerging in the sixteenth century: the Safavid dynasty (1501–1722) in Iran and the Mughal empire (1520–1857) in the Indian subcontinent. The Safavids had begun as a revivalist Sufi brotherhood in the thirteenth century, calling for a restoration of a purified Islam. By the fifteenth century, the brotherhood was transformed into a religiopolitical movement, combining Shii messianism and a call for armed struggle (jihad) against other Muslim regimes, which it denounced as un-Islamic. In 1501, Ismail (1487–1524), head of the Safavid family, invaded and occupied Tabriz, proclaiming himself shah of Iran. Within a decade he had conquered the rest of Iran, rapidly building an empire east of the Ottoman frontier. The creation of the Safavid dynasty made Shii Islam the official religion of an Islamic empire.

The Safavid Empire

Shii Islam was effectively imposed in Iran through a process of persecution and doctrinal interpretation. Shah Ismail imposed Twelver Shii Islam upon Iran's Sunni majority to unify his rule. He sought religious legitimacy and leadership by asserting that he was a descendant of the twelfth (hidden) imam and a **mahdi**, or divinely guided reformer. Thus, the shah was both temporal and spiritual ruler, emperor and messianic messenger. The religious pretensions of Safavid rulers were symbolized by their title, "Shadow of God on Earth." Rival Islamic groups or interpretations of Islam (Sunni and Sufi) as well as non-Muslim communities were suppressed. The Safavids enforced their own brand of Twelver religiopolitical ideology and identity in an attempt to legitimate their political authority and to forge a new Safavid Shii Iranian bond of solidarity. A full-blown Shii alternative to Sunni Islam was skillfully developed. Sufi ideas, philosophical doctrines, and popular religious practices such as saint veneration were selectively appropriated. Emphasis was placed on the veneration of sacred "Shii" persons: Husayn, the imams, and their families. Visits to their shrines replaced popular Sufi village shrines. Sunni persecution of Ali and his family was commemorated, and the first three caliphs were ritually cursed as usurpers. Karbala, the scene of the original massacre of Husayn and his followers by Sunni forces, became a central religious symbol, ritually reenacted during the sacred month of Muharram in passion plays that emphasized mourning, self-sacrifice, and atonement. Karbala served as an alternative pilgrimage site to Mecca, which was under Ottoman control. Shii *ulama* from Iraq, southern Lebanon, and Bahrain were brought to Iran as missionaries and became part of the state-created and controlled Shii religious establishment, responsible for preaching Shii doctrine and manning the schools, universities, seminaries, and courts.

The Safavid empire reached its zenith guided by the genius of its most celebrated sultan, Shah Abbas (1588–1629). From his capital in Isfahan, he oversaw an ambitious program of state building, implementing administrative, military, economic, and religious reforms. Generous religious endowments supported the building of major religious monuments, schools, mosques, and hospitals. As with the Ottomans, the *ulama* and their educational and judicial institutions were brought within the Safavid state bureaucracy.

The Mughal Empire

India's Mughal dynasty matched splendor and accomplishments of the Ottomans in the Arab Middle East and Eastern Europe and of the Safavids in Iran. North India had long been the scene of Muslim penetration and conquest, with the invasions of Arab soldiers in the seventh century and the establishment of the Turkish and Afghan dynasties of the Delhi sultanate (1211–1556). Muslims in the Indian subcontinent were a minority ruling a vast Hindu majority. In fact, Muslims never actually ruled all of India.

The Emperor Akbar (1565–1605) made the Mughal empire a reality. During his long reign, through conquest and diplomacy he significantly extended Muslim rule into major areas of the subcontinent. The emperor initiated policies to foster greater political centralization and the social integration of his Muslim and Hindu subjects. Religious learning, tolerance, harmony, and syncretism were hallmarks of Akbar's reign. Royal patronage sponsored the building of schools and libraries. A policy of universal tolerance and abolition of the poll tax as well as a tax on Hindu pilgrims fostered loyalty among Hindus, who constituted the majority of his subjects. Akbar encouraged the study of comparative religions and built a House of Worship, where religious scholars from various faiths engaged in theological discussion and debate. Sufi brotherhoods followed a more flexible, eclectic approach in their encounter with other faiths enjoyed court favor. Their emphasis on religious synthesis, which stressed similarities rather than religious differences, was preferred to the rigid legalism of the more conservative *ulama*. The power of the *ulama* was circumscribed, and their ire incurred by a state-sponsored religious cult, the religion of God or divine religion (***din illahi***), which emphasized the truth to be found in all religions. They took special offense at the Infallibility Decree of 1579, which recognized the emperor, rather than the *ulama,* as the final authority in religious matters.

Ulama opposition to Akbar's eclectic religious approach and legacy was joined to that of religious reformers such as Shaykh Ahmad Sirhindi (1564–1624), a member of the Naqshbandi Sufi brotherhood, who rejected religious assimilation and advocated a more pronounced emphasis on the Islamic basis and character of state and society. However, it was the emperor Aurangzeb (1658–1707), who dismantled Akbar's pluralistic system of governance and theological syncretism. Aurangzeb implemented the *ulama's* more exclusive (rather than Akbar's inclusive) religiopolitical order. He introduced the institution of moral policemen (**muhtasib**) who could enforce implementation of Islamic laws prohibiting alcohol, gambling, and other objectionable or "un-Islamic" practices and reintroduced a more subordinate political and social status for non-Muslims, reimposing the poll (**jizya**) tax, which required that his Hindu subjects pay a property tax levied on all non-Muslims.

The political and religious accomplishments of Akbar and his successors were accompanied by the florescence of Mughal art. Mughal painting and architecture reflected both Persian and Ottoman influences. As with its Safavid and Ottoman counterparts, Mughal art reached great heights in manuscript illustration and miniature paintings as well as the design and building of religious and public monuments—grand mosques, forts, and palaces. Perhaps the most famous product of this period is the Taj Mahal, built in Agra by Shah Jahan, a grandson of Akbar, as a memorial to his beloved wife.

Despite the division of the Muslim world into separate sultanates, a Muslim traveler across this vast area could experience an international Islamic order that transcended state boundaries, particularly in the urban/intellectual culture of cities and towns. All Muslim citizens were members of a transnational community of believers, citizens of the **dar al-Islam** (abode of Islam) who, despite differences of interpretation, professed faith in one God, His Prophet, and revelation. All were bound by the Sharia, Islamic law, and obligated to observe the Five traditional Pillars of Sunnī Islam. The Islamic city reflected this common framework and culture in its organization and institutions (mosques, legal codes and courts, schools and universities, Sufi convents, religious endowments, a political establishment of sultans, military commanders, and soldiers as well as a religious establishment of *ulama* and Sufi shaykhs or pirs—scholars and mystics).

Despite variations and the individual policies of some rulers, the imperial Ottoman, Safavid, and Mughal sultanates demonstrated a somewhat common Islamic ideological outlook and approach to state organization, support, and use of Islam. Rulers bore the title "sultan" (the one who possesses power or authority). Their rule was based on a blend of

The Taj Mahal, the mausoleum built (1631–47) by the grief-stricken emperor Shah Jahan for his beloved wife Mumtaz Mahal, who died in childbirth. Situated in a 42-acre garden, it is flanked by two perfectly proportioned mosque complexes. This crowning achievement, a landmark of world architecture, symbolizes the wealth and splendor of the Mughal empire. The project brought together craftsmen and calligraphers from the Islamic world, who worked with Muslim and Hindu craftsmen from the empire.

military strength and religious legitimacy. The sultan appropriated the caliph's charge as defender and protector of the faith. Islamic law continued to enjoy pride of place as the official law of the state. Religion not only supported the state but also was itself supported by state patronage. In particular, many of the *ulama* became part of a prosperous religious establishment that assisted the sultan's attempt to centralize and control the educational, legal, and social systems. They educated the military, bureaucratic, and religious elites in their schools, supervised and guided the interpretation and application of Islamic law in the Sharia courts, and oversaw the disbursement of funds from religious endowments (**waqf**) for educational and social services from the building of mosques and schools to hospitals and lodges for travelers. During this time, a number of the nonofficial *ulama* in particular developed strong international linkages. Many people came from far and wide to study at Mecca and Medina or at the renowned al-Azhar University in Cairo. After years of study and interchange, they returned to their home territories or took up residence in other parts of the Islamic world. Scholars, in particular, often traveled throughout the Muslim world to study with great masters and collect

Prophetic traditions and reports about the Prophet's words and deeds. Islamic learning and interpretation possessed truly international character due to the sacrifice and commitment of these learned men.

As the *ulama* developed and prospered, so too did the Sufis. Their eclectic, syncretistic tendencies enabled Islam to adapt to new environments and absorb local religious beliefs and customs. This complemented and enhanced the general process of adaptation pursued by the sultans and attracted droves of converts as Islam spread at an astonishing rate in Africa, India, and Southeast Asia. Established Sufi orders, like the Naqshbandi, spread from the Indian subcontinent to the Mediterranean, becoming vast international networks, and new orders sprang up and prospered.

Within the diversity of states and cultures, Islamic faith and civilization provided an underlying unity, epitomized by a common profession of faith and acceptance of the Sharia, Islamic law. Islam provided the basic ideological framework for political and social life, a source of identity, legitimacy, and guidance. A sense of continuity with past history and institutions was maintained. The world was divided into Islamic (**dar al-Islam**, the abode of Islam) and non-Islamic (*dar al-harb*, the abode of warfare). All Muslims were to strive to extend Islam wherever possible. Thus, merchants and traders as well as soldiers and mystics were the early missionaries of Islam. The sultan was the protector and defender of the faith charged with extending the Islamic domain. Citizenship, taxation, law, education, social welfare, defense, and warfare were based on Islam. The *ulama* for their part successfully asserted their role as protectors and interpreters of the tradition. Thus, both the political and the religious authorities, the "men of the sword" and the "men of the pen," appealed to Islam to legitimate their authority. For the majority of believers, there was a continuum of guidance, power, and success that transcended the contradictions and vicissitudes of Muslim life, and validated and reinforced the sense of a divinely mandated and guided community with a purpose and mission.

By the turn of the eighteenth century, the power and prosperity of the imperial sultanates were in serious decline. The decline of the great Muslim gunpowder empires coincided with the Industrial Revolution and modernization in the West. The emergence of modern Europe as a major military, economic, and political power ushered in the dawn of European colonialism. Internal political disintegration (the rise of semi-autonomous regional and provincial governments), military losses, a deteriorating economy affected by European competition in trade and manufacturing, and social disruption signaled the dénouement of Muslim imperial ascendancy. The Safavid empire fell in 1736; dynastic rule would not be reestablished until the end of the century under the relatively weak Qajar dynasty. The Mughal empire lingered on in name only, subservient to Britain, until 1857, when India was formally declared a British colony. Only the Ottoman empire survived into the twentieth century, when it collapsed and was dismembered by the British and the French during the post–World War I Mandate period. As we shall see, the social and moral decline of these great Muslim empires would contribute to a wave of Islamic revivalist movements throughout much of the Muslim world.

ISLAM IN THE WEST

In a matter of only decades, Islam has gone from being invisible in the West to the second or third largest religion in Western Europe and third largest in America. In the 1960s and 1970s, most Europeans and Americans knew nothing or little about Islam and Muslims, and Islam was seen as a religion of peoples that lived way out there in the Arab world and beyond. Today Muslims and mosques and Islamic centers are visible on the streets of major cities and many towns and villages. Thus, the capitals and major cities where Muslims live are not only Cairo, Khartoum, Tunis, Rabat, Istanbul, Mecca, Amman, Damascus, Islamabad, Kuala Lumpur, and Jakarta but also in Paris, Marseilles, London, Oslo, Vienna, New York, Boston, Chicago, Detroit, and Los Angeles. Old worlds are giving way to new realities and a predominantly Judeo-Christian mindset needs to be expanded to recognize a common Judeo-Christian-Islamic tradition.

Most Muslims in Europe and many in America, which already had an indigenous African American Muslim community, came as immigrants. Many wished to fit into their new societies, to be accepted, gain employment, raise families, and live quietly in newly adopted countries. Others came as workers who came to obtain jobs, earn money to send back, or have a nest egg when they went back home. They often lived apart and avoided any prospect of integration or assimilation.

The Muslims of Western Europe

The presence of Muslims in European areas is not a new phenomenon. It is important to recall that from the eighth to the fifteenth centuries, Muslims ruled Spain and some areas of southern Italy and southern France. From the eleventh century, Muslims also existed as a minority under Christian rulers who, having ceased to execute their Muslim captives, sold them as slaves, a practice that continued until the nineteenth century.[16] Although many have been taught that in 1492 Queen Isabella sent Christopher Columbus off to the New World, few are equally aware that 1492 also marks both the expulsion of Jews from the Iberian peninsula and the fall of Granada, the latter of which greatly furthered a campaign to drive the Muslims (Moors) out of Spain and seemingly out of Western Europe. By the seventeenth century, most Muslims, along with Jews, who were also persecuted as heretics, had fled to North Africa.

The Muslim Community in the West Today
Today, several centuries later, Islam has returned. More than 46 million Muslims can be found in Europe, including the more than 20 million Muslims in European Union countries. Because many, although certainly not all, wish to retain their religion, culture, and values, the presence and citizenship of Muslims in Europe, as in America, have made assimilation, acculturation, and multiculturalism major religious, social, and political issues.

Muslims can be found in significant numbers in most Western European countries, but particularly in Britain, France, Germany, and the Netherlands. The largest Muslim population in Western Europe is in France, with 4.7 million[17] Muslims (70 percent of whom come from North Africa),[18] followed by Germany (4.3 million), the United Kingdom (2.9 million), and Italy (2.4 million).[19] The Muslims of France, comprising almost 7.5 percent[20] of the population, now exceed Protestants and Jews in number and are second only to France's Catholic community. There are grand mosques in Paris and Lyons and more than a thousand mosques and prayer rooms throughout the country. The majority of Germany's 4.3 million Muslims are of Turkish origin (63 percent);[21] Britain's 2.9 million[22] Muslims come primarily from the Indian subcontinent.

Migration to Britain and France began before World War II, but the major waves of Muslim migration occurred afterward. In contrast to America, whose Muslim population is heavily indebted to family or village-based immigration, educational migration, and the growth of Islam among the African American community, the Muslim presence in Europe is due in large part to laborer and family immigration and vestigial colonial connections.[23] At independence, many Muslims who had cooperated with European colonizers chose to emigrate. France gave asylum to hundreds of thousands of Algerians who had fought with French forces during Algeria's war of independence (1954–62). Many, in particular professionals and skilled laborers, from former European colonies in Africa, South Asia, and the Arab world immigrated to Europe seeking a better life. In the 1960s and 1970s, unskilled laborers flooded into a Europe with growing economies that were in need of cheap labor. More than a million Muslims, many from France's former North African and West African colonies, were admitted. At the same time, increasing numbers of Muslim students went to Europe, as they did to America, to study. Although many returned home as trained physicians, engineers, scientists, and teachers, others—for political or economic reasons—chose to stay.

However different Muslim experiences in Europe might be, Muslims there, like many in America, have shared common concerns regarding the practice of their faith, the retention of Islamic identity (in particular for their children), and the preservation of family life and values. Specific religious concerns revolve around the ability to take time out from work to pray daily, to attend mosque on Friday, to have two major feasts of Islam (Id al-Adha and Id al-Fitra) recognized as official holidays for Muslim nationally or locally, to have halal foods available in schools and the military, and to wear a headscarf (**hijab**) in society/public square (schools, employment, etc.). Some, like many conservative Christians, are concerned about sex education and secularism in the schools.

The Muslim experience in Europe has been affected negatively by the rise of right-wing nationalism with its anti-immigrant and Islamophobic (discrimination based on Muslim religion or culture) rhetoric, policies, and actions. A foreign labor force once welcomed during a period of economic expansion has become a convenient scapegoat, charged with stealing "jobs" amidst growing unemployment.[24] Moreover, Muslim terrorist attacks in the United Kingdom and Spain, the murder of anti-immigrant politicians in the Netherlands and in France, and the arrest and prosecution of suspected Muslim terrorists in many European countries have intensified concern among European as they have among American Muslims.

The Muslims of America

Islam is the fastest growing religion in the United States. Estimates of the number of American Muslims vary significantly, from 4 to 6 million. Many believe that in the first half of the twenty-first century, Islam will become the second largest religion in America after Christianity. Muslims were present in America before the nineteenth century. Perhaps 20 percent of the African slaves brought to America from the sixteenth to the nineteenth centuries were Muslim. However, most were forced to convert to Christianity.

African American Islam

African American Islam emerged in the early twentieth century when a number of black Americans converted to Islam, as a return to more authentic spiritual and cultural roots. Islam was seen as part of an original (African) identity, whereas many converts saw Christianity as the religion of white supremacy and oppression, subjugating black Americans from the days of slavery to the present as second-class citizens denied full civil rights. In contrast, Islam's egalitarian ideal in which all Muslims belong to a brotherhood of believers, transcending race and ethnic ties, was very attractive. As a result, quasi-Islamic or "proto-Islamic" groups that combined a selective use of Islamic symbols with Black Nationalism emerged.

Elijah Muhammad (formerly Elijah Poole, 1897–1975) founded the most prominent and lasting movement in the 1930s. Elijah Muhammad had been the follower of Wallace D. Fard Muhammad, who began preaching in the black ghetto of Detroit in the early 1930s.

After Fard mysteriously disappeared in 1934, Elijah Muhammad became the leader of the Nation of Islam. Elijah Muhammad announced that Fard was Allah, and thus God was a black man. Adopting the title of the Honorable Elijah Muhammad, he identified himself as the messenger of God. Under his leadership, the Nation of Islam, whose adherents were popularly known as Black Muslims, was redefined and turned into an effective national movement. Elijah Muhammad's message of self-transformation and self-reliance encompassed the physical and the spiritual needs of black Americans as addressed in his *Message to the Blackman in America* and *How to Eat to Live*.

Elijah Muhammad denounced the political and economic oppression of blacks by white society, past and present, and its results: black self-hatred, poverty, and dependency. He gave to an often alienated and marginalized people, many of them poor and unemployed, a religious message that offered a sense of identity and community as well as a program of survival, self-improvement, and empowerment in a society and culture that many perceived as hostile, racist, and oppressive.

The Nation of Islam offered an apocalyptic, millenarian message whose promise was the ultimate fall of the oppressor, white, racist America, and the future restoration of a righteous black community, a "Chosen People." Its black separatist nationalism was based on withdrawal from white society with no political allegiance or participation; black people constituted a separate community or nation. Because the "white man is the devil," Elijah Muhammad taught that life is a war between the forces of good (blacks) and the forces of evil (the white devil), which will culminate in a future battle from which blacks will emerge triumphant and reestablish their global rule under Allah.

Elijah Muhammad preached black pride and identity, strength and self-sufficiency, black racial supremacy, and strong family values. The spirit and ethic of the Nation of Islam was embodied in the phrase, "Do for Self," a doctrine of economic independence based on "a kind of African-American puritanism," which emphasized self-improvement and responsibility for self through hard work, discipline, thrift, and abstention from gambling, alcohol, drugs, and eating pork."[25]

Under Elijah Muhammad's leadership, hundreds of temples as well as small businesses (grocery stores, restaurants, bakeries) were established nationally. The message of black pride, self-respect, and militancy proved particularly attractive to black youth, many of whom were recruited from ghetto streets and prisons. By the 1970s, the Nation of Islam would claim more than 100,000 members.

The Black Muslim movement diverged significantly from mainstream Islam with respect to a number of basic beliefs. Black Muslims claimed that Allah (God) was human, a black man named Wallace D. Fard, and that Elijah Muhammad (not the Prophet Muhammad) was the last messenger of God. The Nation taught black supremacy and black separatism, whereas Islam teaches the brotherhood of all believers in a community that transcends racial, tribal, and ethnic boundaries. The Nation did not follow the Five Pillars of Islam.

Three individuals epitomized the transition and transformation of Elijah Muhammad's Black Muslim movement: Malcolm X, Wallace D. Muhammad (who later took the name Warith Deen Muhammad), and Louis Farrakhan.

Malcolm X (1925–65), born Malcolm Little, was the product of the very social conditions (white racism, poverty, broken families, drugs, and crime) that Elijah Muhammad denounced and combated. His life exemplified the personal and religious transformation for which the Nation of Islam was noted.

Born in Omaha, Nebraska, Malcolm blamed white, racist society for the murder of his father (a Baptist minister and follower of Marcus Garvey), the mental breakdown and institutionalization of his mother, and the breakup of the family's eight children, scattered in separate foster homes. Although Malcolm was a gifted student in primary school, his experience of racism and prejudice led to his alienation and rejection of American society. He became a pimp and a hustler, whose life of drugs and crime in the ghettos of Roxbury, Massachusetts, and later New York City's Harlem led to his imprisonment.[26] During his incarceration (1946–52) he educated himself, reading widely in history, politics, and religion. He became convinced that Christianity was the "white man's religion" and that the Bible "[in the] white man's hands and his interpretation of it, has been the greatest single ideological weapon for enslaving millions of non-white human beings."[27]

In 1948 Malcolm formally accepted the teachings of the Nation of Islam, attracted by its black nationalism and militant denunciation of American racism as well as by Elijah Muhammad's program of self-help. Malcolm Little became Malcolm X, the "X" symbolizing what he had become: ex-smoker, ex-drinker, ex-Christian, and ex-slave.[28] A gifted speaker, dynamic and articulate, with a charismatic personality, Malcolm X rose quickly through the ranks of the Nation of Islam to national prominence. He organized many of the Nation's temples, started its newspaper *Muhammad Speaks*, and became an effective and militant proponent for the Nation of Islam at a time when America was in the midst of the civil rights movement. Elijah Muhammad recognized the talents and accomplishments of Malcolm, appointing him minister of major temples of the Nation in Boston and then Temple 7 in Harlem in mid-1954. Malcolm was named "national representative" of the Nation, second only to Elijah Muhammad.[29]

By the early 1960s, Malcolm was receiving widespread media coverage. His increased involvement in domestic and international politics, as well as his contacts with Sunni Muslims in America and in the Muslim world, led to a gradual shift in his religious/ideological worldview, a development that at times put him at odds with some of the teachings of Elijah Muhammad.

During the same period, Wallace D. Muhammad, a son of Elijah Muhammad, greatly influenced by Malcolm, was also encountering problems as he questioned some of his father's teachings. Although it was not apparent at the time, this questioning was the beginning of Malcolm's and Wallace's gradual transition (and later the transition of the majority of the Nation of Islam itself) from the community and teachings of the Nation to that of mainstream Islam, or the global Islamic community.

Whereas Elijah Muhammad advocated a separation and self-sufficiency that excluded involvement in "white man's politics," Malcolm came to believe that "the Nation of Islam could be even a greater force in the American Black man's overall struggle if we engaged in more action."[30] He spoke out forcefully on a variety of issues: the civil rights movement, the Vietnam War, and solidarity with liberation struggles in colonial Africa. His public comment in November 1963 that the assassination of President John F. Kennedy was "a case of chickens [coming] home to roost" provided the occasion for Elijah Muhammad to silence Malcolm for ninety days.[31]

In March 1964 Malcolm X left the Nation of Islam to start his own organization and a month later went on pilgrimage to Mecca. There Malcolm underwent a second conversion—to mainstream Sunni Islam.

The pilgrimage brought Malcolm and the religious teachings of the Nation face to face with those of the global Islamic community, vividly exposing their contradictions. Malcolm did not know how to perform Islam's daily prayers (*salat*), nor had he observed the other prescribed practices of the Five Pillars of Islam. Malcolm observed and experienced the pilgrimage with its emphasis on the equality of all believers regardless of race, tribe, or nation and came to realize that "We were truly all the same (brothers)—because their belief in one God removed the 'white' from their minds, the 'white' from their behavior, and the 'white' from their attitude."[32] He returned a Muslim rather than a Black Muslim, changing his name to El Hajj Malik El-Shabazz.

On February 21, 1965, El Hajj Malik El-Shabazz (formerly Malcolm X) was assassinated as he spoke to an audience in New York. Two members of the Nation of Islam were convicted of the murder. Subsequently Temple No. 7 as well as schools and streets were given his name.

The 1960s was a major transitional period for the Nation of Islam. Malcolm X and Wallace D. Muhammad, each in his own way, questioned and challenged some of the teachings and strategy of Elijah Muhammad. As a result, both Wallace and his brother Akbar Muhammad, a scholar of Islam who studied in Egypt and Scotland, were excommunicated by their father. But, toward the end of his life Elijah Muhammad himself made the pilgrimage to Mecca and began to modify some of his teachings. By the time of his death, however controversial Elijah Muhammad and the Nation might have been, mayors of many major American cities publicly acknowledged the constructive contributions of the Nation to their inner cities and communities.

Upon the death of Elijah Muhammad in February 1975, Wallace D. Muhammad (1933–2008) succeeded his father as Supreme Minister. Despite their disagreements, Elijah Muhammad had designated Wallace as his successor, and Wallace won the support of his family and others in the leadership as well as that of Elijah Muhammad's most prominent disciple, Muhammad Ali, the former world heavyweight boxing champion, revered not only in America but also throughout the Muslim world. Wallace set about reforming the doctrines of the Nation and its organizational structure, simultaneously integrating the Nation within the American Muslim community, the broader American society, and the global Islamic community. The Nation's political and economic programs were redefined and subordinated to its new religious identity and mission. Throughout the 1970s and 1980s, the doctrines of the Nation, and indeed the Nation itself, were brought into conformity with the teachings of orthodox Sunni Islam. The name of Nation was initially changed to the World Community of al-Islam in the West (WCIW); *Muhammad Speaks* became the *Bilalian News*, named after the first black convert to Islam. Wallace Fard was identified as the founder of the Nation and Elijah Muhammad as the leader who brought black Americans to the Quran; Wallace Muhammad made the pilgrimage to Mecca and encouraged his followers to study Arabic to better understand Islam; temples were renamed masjids or mosques and their leaders were called imams rather than ministers; the community observed the Five Pillars of Islam (profession of faith, prayer, fasting, almsgiving, and pilgrimage) in union with the worldwide Islamic community of which they were now members Black separatist doctrines were dropped as the community began to participate within the political process and system; and the equality of men and women believers was reaffirmed and women were given more responsible positions in the ministry of the community.

Wallace continued to champion the plight of the urban poor not only as a critic of racism and the failures of the system but also as one who worked within the system for change. He quickly emerged as a major Muslim religious leader internationally and at home. In 1977, he met with President Jimmy Carter and subsequently met with other major political and religious leaders in the United States and the Muslim world.

In 1978, the WCIW (World Community of Islam in the West) was reorganized as Wallace transferred organizational leadership to an elected council of six imams (leaders) and focused on his role as a religious and spiritual leader. In 1980, as if to signal his and the community's new religious identity and mission, Wallace changed his name to Warith Deen Muhammad, he renamed the WCIW the American Muslim Mission, and the *Bilalian News* became the *American Muslim Journal* (later renamed *Muslim Journal*).[33]

The integration of the American Muslim Mission within the country at large did not lessen its concern with issues of racism and injustice. However, its critique of racism has been articulated within its primary function as a religious community, framed within its twin foci, black identity and following the straight path of Islam:

> You can't live in America without hearing the message. The message of white supremacy is everywhere. You are conscious that Jesus is in a white body even if you don't go to church…. Every American knows that apostles and saints and angels are made European by Church society…. We are not to see God in a racial image. As long as white (Caucasian) people think that their physical image is in the world as the image of God, and as long as non-white people see and know that the Caucasian image is in the world as the purported image of God, there

will be no real coming together and no peaceful meeting of the minds of Caucasians and non-Caucasians.[34]

The transformation of the Nation of Islam under Warith Deen Muhammad did not occur without dissent. Although the majority of the Nation's temples and ministers accepted Wallace and his reforms, a minority under the leadership of Louis Farrakhan (b. 1933) did not. A bitter foe of the reform of both Malcolm and Wallace, Farrakhan broke with Wallace and the WCIW in March 1978. Maintaining that he and his followers had remained faithful to the message and mission of Elijah Muhammad, he claimed the mantle of leadership of the Nation of Islam. Minister Louis Farrakhan retained the name and organizational structure of the Nation of Islam as well as its black nationalist and separatist doctrines. However, from 1986 onward, while retaining much of the political and economic teachings and program of Elijah Muhammad, he moved the Nation closer to more orthodox Islamic practices and pursued ties with leaders in the Muslim world, including controversial ties with Libya's Muammar Qaddafi.

The militancy and anti-Semitic statements of Farrakhan and some of his lieutenants brought condemnation and criticism, but the effectiveness of the Nation in fighting crime and drugs in ghettos and in rehabilitating prisoners won the Nation praise from many who otherwise disagreed with Minister Farrakhan. A charismatic leader, Farrakhan denounced the many causes of racism and poverty and articulated the grievances of African Americans and other minorities, often enhancing his stature even among those who chose not to join his organization. Farrakhan's leadership of the 1995 Million Man March on Washington received widespread media coverage and support among Christian as well as Muslim leaders and organizations.

At the same time, Farrakhan remained controversial for what is regarded as his strident, separatist message and international connections with militant leaders such as those of Libya and Iran. Although the Nation of Islam had many fewer members than Warith Deen Muhammad's American Muslim Mission, Farrakhan's persona and actions have given him and the Nation a disproportionate amount of visibility and media coverage.

Muslim Immigration to America

It was not until the late nineteenth and especially the mid-twentieth century that significant numbers of Muslims first became a visible presence in America. Waves of immigrant laborers initially came from the Arab world (Syria, Lebanon, and Jordan). Palestinian refugees, forced to flee their homes, followed after the creation of Israel in 1948. In recent decades many more Muslims have come from the Middle East and South Asia, leaving their home countries for political or economic reasons. In contrast to Europe, where large numbers of Muslims were immigrant laborers needed by the booming economies of the 1960s and 1970s, in America, many who came were well-educated professionals and intellectuals.

Who Are American Muslims?

Muslims come from more than 68 countries as well as African American, and Hispanic, Caucasian (28 percent). They are one of most diverse religious groups racially, economically and politically. They range from immigrants coming to America for political, religious, or economic freedom and subsequent generations to native-born African Americans, many of whom are the descendants of slaves, and Caucasian and Hispanic converts. The identity of immigrants has been shaped by the Muslim societies from which they came and their subsequent experience in American society, including contact with Muslims from other countries.

The Muslims of America, as in Europe, are far from homogeneous. They come from more than sixty-eight countries. Thus, Islam in America, like Christianity, is a mosaic of many ethnic, racial, and national groups: African American, Arab, Iranian, South Asian, and Southeast Asian. American Muslim issues, like those of other religious minorities, center on their identity: their integration into a new society, the preservation and practice of their Islamic faith in an American society based on Judeo-Christian or secular values and, finally, their empowerment in American politics and culture. This is exacerbated by difficulties Muslims encounter in an American society in which Islam and Muslims are often characterized by stereotypes, brush-stroked by the acts of extremists regarded with fear and distrust. The situation is exacerbated by the rise of **Islamophobia** in America as in Europe, with its anti-Islam and anti-Muslim rhetoric, hate speech, and hate crimes.

Living as minorities in a dominant culture often ignorant of or hostile to Islam, many Muslims have experienced a sense of marginalization and powerlessness. The tendency of some in America, as in Europe, to facilely contrast a "Judeo-Christian national culture and values" with "Islamic culture and values" further complicates Muslim efforts to integrate. Finally, media depictions of Islam as the principal global threat in the post–Cold War period, or equations of Islam with extremism and terrorism with al-Qaeda or ISIL, coupled with American foreign policies. As major polls by Gallup, PEW, and others have long reported, the United States is often perceived as pursuing a double standard in its espousal of but failure to promote self-determination, democracy, and human rights in the Israeli–Palestinian conflict and the Middle East with its long time support for authoritarian and repressive regimes and invasion and occupation of Iraq.

Many Muslims have grappled with question of national identity: Are they Muslims in America or American Muslims? Is it possible to be fully American in a society often characterized as Judeo-Christian or secular? Like American Jews before them, can they simultaneously retain their distinctive religious values while also becoming part of the majority culture, part of the fabric of American society? Today, the vast majority of American Muslims are in fact educationally, economically, and increasingly politically and religiously integrated in American society.

After American Jews, American Muslims are the most educated religious community in America. Forty percent have college degrees vs. 29 percent of Americans overall. Muslim women, unlike their Jewish counterparts, are statistically as likely as Muslim men to hold college or postgraduate degrees.

American Muslims span the socioeconomic spectrum. Many are economically as successful as other Americans and tend to believe in the American dream. They are professionals (doctors, lawyers, engineers, and educators, corporate execs, small business owners, or blue-collar workers and laborers. Among nonworking Muslims, 31 percent are full-time students compared to 10 percent in the general population. Muslims are family oriented: 78 percent are married; of those, 83 percent have one or more children.

Religiously, 77 percent of Muslims believe they worship the same God as Christians and Jews. Eighty-four percent said Muslims should strongly emphasize shared values with Christians and Jews.[35]

In response to what American Islamic scholar Abdulaziz Sachedina has called the "acid test of pluralism"—whether a religion is willing to recognize members of other religions as potential citizens in the world to come—a minority (33 percent) of those polled responded, "My religion is the one, true faith leading to eternal life," while a majority (56 percent) believed, "Many religions can lead to eternal life."[36]

At the same time, Muslims (48 percent) are more likely than Americans of other major religious groups to say they, personally, have experienced racial or religious discrimination. Muslim Americans are more than twice as likely as U.S. Jews, Catholics, and Protestants to say they experienced such discrimination in the past year. And about half of the surveyed Americans from major religious groups agreed, stating their belief that most Americans are prejudiced toward Muslim Americans.[37]

Today, Muslims are increasingly involved in national government and local politics and government. The U.S. Congress has two Muslim members in the House of Representatives, are mayors and members of city councils. However, Muslim representation in senior national government positions continues to be almost nonexistent.

Issues of Religious Identity and Integration

Muslim communities, like Christian and Jewish communities initially before them, have been dependent on foreign-born and trained religious leaders. Many imams in America (and in Europe), in the past especially, had little desire to integrate, fearing assimilation and loss of faith and identity. They were ill-equipped to respond rather than react to the challenges of life in America, reinforcing a "ghetto mentality," living, acting, and teaching as if they were still in Cairo, Mecca, or Islamabad rather than in New York, Detroit, or Des Moines.

In recent years, many have addressed these issues. American (and European) Muslims have created *fiqh* (law) councils and other locally based and staffed Islamic institutions to train imams and scholars. Rather than continuing to be solely dependent on foreign-born *muftis* who might be out of touch with the local conditions and circumstances in North America, Muslims often seek new interpretations of Islamic law needed to cope with many modern problems raised by life in American society. The thinking of educated members of the American Muslim community as well as advice from Islamic legal scholars around the world are brought to bear in formulating fresh legal opinions (*fatwas*) on such matters as the legality of business projects under Sharia law, the propriety of Muslims voting in a non-Muslim society or for non-Muslim candidates, and the acceptability of Muslims observing *juma* (community) prayer on Sunday instead of Friday. In this way the dynamism of Islamic law, its historic ability to provide answers appropriate to changing and diverse sociohistorical contexts, is preserved.

If some religious leaders continue to view living in non-Muslim territories as less than ideal, something to be tolerated, many American Muslims, like other ethnic and religious groups (such as Jews and Christians) before them, have defined and embraced the conditions under which Muslims can live permanently as loyal citizens in their newfound homes as well as preserve their faith and identity. They have encouraged integration and engagement, emphasized common religious, civic, and social interests and values with other faiths, and pursued economic, political, and social integration to establish Islam as part of the American religious and cultural landscape. African American Muslims have long been highly visible and active in asserting their Muslim identity, many focusing on the issues facing inner-city America. The diversity of American Muslims among and within communities has raised issues of interpretation, law, and cultural identity.

Muslim leaders have offered the prayer for the opening of Congress, and Muslim chaplains now exist in the military and prison system and at colleges and universities. Hartford Seminary created the first academically accredited Chaplain Program in 1999, which over the years has trained chaplains for the military, prisons, and educational institutions.

The Army appointed its first Muslim chaplain in 1993, but it was not until 2009 that the Marines and National Guard followed suit. The first full-time Muslim chaplain in America was appointed by Georgetown University in 1999; this began a slow trend in the first decade of the twenty-first century, which included universities like Brown (2006) and Princeton (2009). Mosques and mosque leaders (imams) have been transformed by the American experience. In contrast to many parts of the Muslim world, mosques in America serve not only as places of worship but also as community centers. Sunday at the mosque or Islamic center is a long day of congregational prayer, bake sales, socializing, and education. Influenced by the American Christian custom of Sunday school, children receive religious instruction. Similarly, imams in America are not only responsible for the upkeep of mosques and leading of prayers but often take on the activities of their fellow clergy of other faiths, ranging from counseling to hospital visits.

In North America, as in France and other parts of Europe, the hijab (headscarf) has symbolized the debate over Muslim integration or assimilation as a legal and religious issue. Although Muslims are theoretically equal members of the societies in which they live—societies that protect freedom of religion—in fact as minorities their rights are often compromised or denied.

In France, for example, the primary focus has been on Muslim students; France banned religious symbols and apparel in public schools on September 2, 2004. Although the ban includes all overtly religious dress and signs (including Muslim headscarves, Sikh turbans, Jewish skullcaps, and large Christian crosses), the furor over the ban has focused mainly on banning Muslim hijabs. In 2012, a similar government rule extended women escorting their children on school outings. Workers at the Paris Opera in 2014 ejected a woman wearing a full-face veil, or niqab, which Paris outlawed in 2011.

In America women wearing a headscarf have experienced discrimination in the workplace and other social settings. For example, despite the guarantees of freedom of religion, some employers (corporations and smaller businesses, police and fire departments, the military) have refused to hire women who wear a headscarf. Some have voluntarily changed their policies, and others have been involved in litigation. Muslim women wearing a hijab have been disproportionately profiled and searched at airports and are harassed in public. For many Muslims, this raises profound questions about Muslim identity, civil rights, and equality of citizenship in America.

In recent years, American Muslims have increasingly sought to respond rather than simply react to life in America. Like Jews and other religious and ethnic minorities before them, they have developed their own civic organizations and institutions. Muslim educational associations monitor textbooks and teaching about Islam to ensure accuracy and objectivity; public affairs organizations monitor and educate the media, legislators, and the general public; Islamic information services develop and distribute films, videos, and print publications on Islam and Muslims in America to further better understanding; in some communities Islamic schools (primary and secondary) have been created; and teaching materials and syllabi on Islam and Muslim life have been created to be used in classes for children and adults at mosques and in schools. Great headway has been made, but the resources, numbers, and impact of such projects remain relatively small. Whether Muslim communities in America will be able to supply the financial and human resources necessary to build a strong self-sustaining community in the twenty-first century remains an important unanswered question.

The religious situation of immigrant American Muslims has at times been especially difficult for the younger generation. Many parents raised in overseas Muslim societies tend to equate cultural practices with the principles of Islam. Thus, their children face the challenge of both fitting into American society and retaining their Islamic identity, of distinguishing between what is mandated by religion and the "foreign" cultural baggage of their parents. Religiously, educationally, and socially, they are sometimes caught between the religious interpretations and cultural practices of their parents and an American society that is Judeo-Christian or secular in its mores and activities. Participation in school and society requires a response to an American society in which drinking alcohol, dating, and co-ed activities, from gym classes and sports to dances and other social events, are common and the participation of all is expected. However, increasingly, like other religious groups, many Muslims have accommodated their faith within American culture while others, just as in other faiths, cease to practice their religion.

While Muslims are defining their roles as religious and ethnic minorities, non-Muslims in the West have been equally challenged to accept a religious as well as a demographic reality. Today, Islam is a major and fast-growing religion in the West, and Muslims are increasingly an integral part of the mosaic of Western societies.

KEY TERMS

Ali

Crusades (1095–1453)

dhimmi

Dome of the Rock

hidden imam

hijab

Husayn

Islamophobia

Jerusalem

jihad

jizya

madrasa

Mahdi

mujtahid

occultation of the imam

qadi

Reconquista (1000–1492)

sultan

taqiyya

ulama

waqf

QUESTIONS

1. Contrast Muslim political structures in the Medinan, Caliphate, and Sultanate periods.

2. What are the origins of the Nation of Islam? What impact have Elijah Muhammad, Malcom X, and Louis Farrakhan had on the American civil rights movement?

3. Are "Islam" and "the West" mutually exclusive categories? Can one be a "Western" Muslim?

4. What effects have the Crusades had on Muslim collective consciousness?

5. Contrast law and the *ulama* with mysticism and the Sufis.

6. Describe some non-Sunni Islamic offshoots. What (if anything) makes a Muslim a Muslim?

NOTES

1. Marshall S. G. Hodgson, *The Venture of Islam* (Chicago: University of Chicago Press, 1974), vol. 1, p. 185.
2. Francis E. Peters, "The Early Muslim Empires: Umayyads, Abbasids, Fatimids," in *Islam: The Religious and Political Life of a World Community*, Marjorie Kelly, ed. (New York: Praeger, 1984), p. 79.

3. Richard Bulliet, *Conversion to Islam in the Medieval Period: An Essay in Quantitative History* (Cambridge, MA: Harvard University Press, 1979).

4. See Bernard Lewis, *The Origins of Ismailism* (Cambridge: Cambridge University Press, 1940); W. Madelung, "Ismailiyya," in *The Encyclopedia of Islam*, 2nd ed., vol. 4, H. A. R. Gibb et al., eds. (Leiden, Netherlands: E. J. Brill, 1960); S. M. Stern, "Ismailis and Qarmatians," in *L'Elaboration de l'Islam*, Claude Cahen, ed. (Paris: Paul Geuthner, 1961), pp. 99–108.

5. Bernard Lewis, *The Arabs in History* (New York: Harper & Row, 1966), p. 149.

6. Laura Vecca Vaglieri, "The Patriarchal and Umayyad Caliphates," in *The Cambridge History of Islam*, P. M. Holt, Ann K. S. Lambton, and Bernard Lewis, eds. (Cambridge: Cambridge University Press, 1977), 1A, p. 103.

7. Lewis, *Arabs in History,* p. 131.

8. *Islam: From the Prophet Muhammad to the Capture of Constantinople*, Bernard Lewis, ed. and trans. (New York: Harper & Row, 1974), pp. 179–81.

9. Bernard G. Weiss and Arnold H. Green, *A Survey of Arab History* (Cairo: The American University in Cairo Press, 1985), p. 187.

10. Seyyed Hossein Nasr, as quoted in Weiss and Green, p. 187.

11. Lewis, *Arabs in History*, p. 133.

12. Hodgson, *Venture of Islam*, vol. 1, p. 236.

13. Peters, "Early Muslim Empires," p. 85.

14. Roger Savory, "Christendom vs. Islam: Interaction and Co-existence," in *Introduction to Islamic Civilization*, Roger Savory, ed. (Cambridge: Cambridge University Press, 1976), p. 133.

15. Ira Lapidus, *A History of Islamic Societies* (Cambridge: Cambridge University Press, 1988), p. 315. For an authoritative discussion of the Ottoman, Safavid, and Mughal empires, see Lapidus, chap. 17–19.

16. P. S. van Koningsveld, "Islam in Europe." *The Oxford Encyclopedia of the Modern Islamic World* (New York: Oxford University Press, 1995), vol. 2, p. 290.

17. "The Future of the Global Muslim Population, Region: Europe" *Pew Research Religion and Public Life Project*, January 27, 2011: http://www.pewforum.org/2011/01/27/future-of-the-global-muslim-population-regional-europe/.

18. *l'Islam dans la République* (Haut Conseil à l'intégration, November 2000, p. 26).

19. Haug et al. (2009): Muslimisches Leben in Deutschland [Muslim Life in Germany] (published by the Federal Office for Migration and Refugees on behalf of the German Islam Conference), available online at: http://www.bmi.bund.de/cae/servlet/contentblob/566008/publicationFile/31710/vollversion_studie_muslim_leben_deutschland_.pdf.

20. "The Future of the Global Muslim Population, Region: Europe" *Pew Research Religion and Public Life Project*, January 27, 2011: http://www.pewforum.org/2011/01/27/future-of-the-global-muslim-population-regional-europe/.

21. Haug et al. (2009): Muslimisches Leben in Deutschland [Muslim Life in Germany] (published by the Federal Office for Migration and Refugees on behalf of the German Islam Conference), available online at: http://www.bmi.bund.de/cae/servlet/contentblob/566008/publicationFile/31710/vollversion_studie_muslim_leben_deutschland_.pdf.

22. "The Future of the Global Muslim Population, Region: Europe" *Pew Research Religion and Public Life Project*, January 27, 2011: http://www.pewforum.org/2011/01/27/future-of-the-global-muslim-population-regional-europe/.

23. I am indebted to Muqtedar Khan, my graduate research assistant, for assistance in the compilation of information on the Muslims of the West.

24. "The Muslims in France: Rejecting Their Ancestors the Gauls," *The Economist* November 16, 1996, p. 93.

25. Lawrence H. Mamiva, "Nation of Islam." *The Oxford Encyclopedia of the Modern Islamic World* (New York: Oxford University Press, 1995), vol. 3, p. 236.

26. Akbar Muhammad, "Malcolm X." *Oxford Encyclopedia of the Modern Islamic World* (New York: Oxford University Press, 1995), vol. 3, p. 38.

27. Malcolm X with Alex Haley, *The Autobiography of Malcolm X* (New York: Ballantine Books, 1973), pp. 241–42.

28. Lawrence H. Mamiya, "Malcom X." *The Encyclopedia of Religion* (New York: Macmillan, 1987), vol. 9, p. 145.

29. Ibid.

30. As quoted in Clifton E. Marsh, *From Black Muslims to Muslims: The Transition from Separatism to Islam, 1930–1980* (Metuchen, NJ: Scarecrow Press, 1984), p. 76.

31. *The New York Times,* December 2, 1963, p. 21.

32. *Autobiography of Malcolm X,* pp. 316–17.

33. Martha F. Lee, *The Nation of Islam: An American Millenarian Movement* (Syracuse, NY: Syracuse University Press, 1996), p. 72.

34. Ibid., p. 74.

35. CAIR Survey of Attitudes Released: October 24, 2006. http://pa.cair.com/annreport/AmericanMuslimVoters.pdf

36. Islam and religious pluralism in a PEW February 2008 survey. http://www.pewforum.org/files/2013/05/report-religious-landscape-study-full.pdf

37. http://www.gallup.com/poll/157082/islamophobia-understanding-anti-muslim-sentiment-west.aspx#2.

Chapter 3

Religious Life: Belief and Practice

For Christianity, the appropriate question is, "What do Christians believe?" In contrast, for Islam (as for Judaism), the correct question is, "What do Muslims *do*?" Whereas in Christianity theology was the "queen of the sciences," in Islam, as in Judaism, law enjoyed pride of place, for "to accept or conform to the laws of God is *Islam*, which means to surrender to God's law."[1]

Because Islam means surrender or submission to the will of God, Muslims have tended to place primary emphasis on obeying or following God's will as set forth in Islamic law. For this reason, many commentators have distinguished between Christianity's emphasis on orthodoxy, or correct doctrine or belief, and Islam's insistence on orthopraxy, or correct action. However, the emphasis on practice has not precluded the importance of faith or belief. Faith (**iman**) and right action or practice are intertwined.

THEOLOGY

As the confession of faith or basic creed ("There is no god but God and Muhammad is the messenger of God") illustrates, faith in God and the Prophet is the basis of Muslim belief and practice. As discussed in Chapter 1, the Quran established a set of basic beliefs that are the foundation of its worldview and the criterion for belief versus unbelief: belief in God and His Prophet, previous prophets and revealed scripture, angels, and the Day of Judgment (4:136). Acceptance of these beliefs renders one a believer (**mumin**); to reject them is to be an unbeliever (**kafir**). Faith places the Muslim on the straight path; acts demonstrate commitment and faithfulness. In Islam, the purpose of life is not simply to affirm but to actualize; not simply to profess belief in God but to realize God's will in one's life, community, and the world. Thus, faith implies and is connected to works; indeed, it is the Book of Deeds that will be the basis for divine judgment. Thus, law has had primacy over theology in Islam.

Kalam: Dialectical Theology

Islamic theology, unlike Christian theology, was not developed systematically, nor was it the product of theoretical reflection or speculation. Theology (**kalam**, "speech" or discourse) emerged as a reaction to specific debates or issues that grew out of early Islam's sociopolitical context, for example, the Kharijite split with Ali, early Christian–Muslim polemics, and the penetration of Greek thought during the Abbasid period. Although theological issues and discourse began during the early caliphal years, theology developed as an Islamic discipline during Abbasid times under royal patronage. Its scope reflected the mixing of faith and politics: questions of belief, sin, eschatology, and legitimate governance. Among the key theological issues were the relationship of faith to works, the nature of God and the Quran, predestination, and free will.

The relationship of faith to works was the first major theological issue confronting the early community. It involved both the question of grave sin and its effect on membership in the community (Does a Muslim guilty of a grave sin remain a Muslim?) and the legitimacy of its ruler or caliph. The occasion was the Kharijite rejection of the third caliph, Uthman, and of Ali's agreement to arbitration with Muawiyah. The Kharijites insisted on total commitment and observance of God's will. They equated faith with works. There could be no compromise, no middle ground. A Muslim was either rigorously observant, a true believer, or not a Muslim at all. Their worldview admitted of only two categories: believer and unbeliever, or infidel. For the Kharijites, Uthman had sinned seriously in his favoritism toward members of his family. Muawiyah, an Umayyad relative of Uthman, was an infidel due to his rebellion against the authority of Uthman's successor, the Caliph Ali. However, Ali's acceptance of arbitration, and thus failure to move decisively against the enemy of God, was also a grave sin. He, too, ceased to be a true Muslim and forfeited his right to rule. The Kharijites regarded these leaders as renegade Muslims (apostates), whose grave sin rendered them infidels and illegitimate rulers, against whom jihad was mandatory.

The majority of the community steered away from the extremism of the Kharijites and followed the more moderate position of the Murjites, who refused to judge, maintaining that only God on the Last Day could judge sinners and determine whether they were excluded from the community and from paradise. This attitude came to prevail in mainstream Islam. Faith, not specific acts, determined membership in the Islamic community. Except for obvious acts of apostasy, sinners remained Muslims. Non-Muslims were the object of Islam's universal mission to call (**dawa**, "the call," propagation of the faith) all humanity to the worship and service of the one true God.

The Murjia position also provided a justification for Umayyad legitimacy and rule. The caliphs had asserted that, whatever sins and injustices they might have committed, they remained Muslims and that they ruled by a divine decree predetermined by God. This belief gave rise to a second theological issue, determinism versus free will. The opposition to the Umayyads maintained that it was not God but human beings who committed injustices and thus were responsible for their acts. The theological question was, "Does an omnipotent and omniscient God predetermine all acts and events and thus constitute the source of evil and injustice; or are human beings free to act and therefore responsible for sin?" The determinists argued that to attribute free will to human beings limited an omnipotent God. The advocates of free will countered that to deny free will ran counter to the sense of human accountability implicit in the notion of the Last Day and Judgment. Both sides were able to utilize Quranic texts to justify their positions. On the one hand, human freedom is affirmed in such passages as, "Truth comes from your Lord. Let anyone who will, believe, and let anyone who wishes, disbelieve" (18:29). On the other hand, many verses portray an all-powerful God who is responsible for all events: "God lets anyone He wishes go astray while He guides whomever He wishes" (35:8). The issue of free will versus predestination became a major theological issue, with the majority accepting a divinely determined universe. Among the chief advocates of free will were the Mutazila, who developed into a major theological movement.

The Mutazila

The origins of the Mutazila have often been traced back to the early discussion and debate over the status of a grave sinner during the Umayyad dynasty. The word *mutazila,* "those who stand aloof," may well refer to those who espoused a middle or intermediate position, regarding the grave sinner as neither a Muslim nor a non-Muslim. In any case, the Mutazila emerged as a formal school of theology during the Abbasid period. The Mutazila were especially strong during the reign of the Caliph Mamun (r. 813–33), who attempted in vain to force their theological position on the majority, initiating an inquisition that persecuted and imprisoned its opposition. One of its most famous victims was Ahmad ibn Hanbal, the traditionist leader and legal scholar.

The Mutazila called themselves "the people of (divine) justice and unity," the defenders of divine unity (monotheism) and justice. Influenced by the influx of Greek philosophical and scientific thought during the

Abbasid period, with its emphasis on reason, logical argumentation, and study of the laws of nature, they relied on reason and rational deduction as tools in Quranic interpretation and theological reflection. Reason and revelation were regarded as complementary sources of guidance from a just and reasonable God.

The Mutazila took issue with the majority of **ulama** over the doctrines of God's attributes or names and the eternal, uncreated nature of the Quran. Both beliefs were seen as contradictory and as compromising God's unity (Islam's absolute monotheism). How could the one, transcendent God have many divine attributes (sight, hearing, power, knowledge, will)? The Mutazila maintained that the Quranic passages that affirmed God's attributes were to be understood metaphorically or allegorically, not literally. Not to do so was to fall into anthropomorphism, or worse, *shirk*, idolatry or polytheism. Similarly, the Islamic doctrine that the Quran is the speech or word of God should not be taken literally, for how could both God and His word be eternal and uncreated? The result would be two divinities. The Mutazila interpreted metaphorically those Quranic texts that spoke of the Quran as preexisting in heaven. Contrary to majority opinion, they taught that the Quran is the *created* word of God, who is its uncreated source. The Caliph Mamun in a letter to his governor in Baghdad Mutazila summarized the critique of those scholars like Ahmad ibn Hanbal, who believed in the eternity of the Quran:

> Everything apart from Him is a creature from His creation—a new thing which He has brought into existence. [This perverted opinion they hold] though the Koran speaks clearly of God's creating all things, and proves to the exclusion of all differences of opinion. They are, thus, like the Christians when they claim that Isa bin Maryam [Jesus, the son of Mary] was not created because he was the word of God. But God says, "Verily We have made it a Koran in the Arabic language," and the explanation of that is, "Verily, We have created it," just as the Koran says, "And He made from it His mate that he might dwell with her."[2]

For the Mutazila, belief in God's justice required free will and responsibility. How could God be a just judge if people were not free, if human action was predetermined? How could there be divine justice if God was solely responsible for all acts, including evil and injustice? They rejected the image of an all-powerful divinity, who arbitrarily and unpredictably determined good and evil, and instead declared that a just God could command only that which is just and good. His creatures bore the responsibility for acts of injustice. Thus, the Mutazila provided a counterweight to the Murjia; Mutazila teachings provided a rationale for critics of Umayyad policies and rule.

The Mutazila also had a strong influence on Shii Islam, particularly through Muhammad ibn al-Hasan **Tusi** (d. 1067). A foundational figure in Shii theology. Shii theologian, jurist, traditionist, bibliographer, and Quran commentator , he compiled two of the four canonical books of Twelver Shii *hadith* collections. Tusi was a major influence on the markedly rationalist bent of Shii theology, drawing strongly on Mutazili ideas.

The Asharite Response

Muslim theology was pulled in two seemingly irreconcilable directions by those who asserted the unqualified, absolute power of God and by their adversaries, the Mutazila, who maintained that God's actions followed from His just and reasonable nature and that all people were free and morally responsible. Once again, someone arose to bring about a new synthesis. Ironically, it was Abu al-Hasan Ali al-Ashari (d. 935), one of the great Mutazila thinkers of his time, who was the father of the Asharite school of theology, which came to dominate Sunni Islam.

Al-Ashari used the rational dialectic of the Mutazila to expose the deficiencies of their system and to defend the non-rational aspects of belief, which, he maintained, transcended human categories and experience. A critique of the Mutazila tendency to rationalize God and theology is contained in the story of al-Ashari's break with his Mutazila teacher, al-Jubbai, which underscores the limits of human reason and human concepts of justice in explaining divine justice. Al-Ashari is reported to have said:

> Let us imagine a child and a grown-up person in Heaven who both died in the True Faith. The grown-up one, however, has a higher place in Heaven than the child. The child shall ask God: "Why did you give that man a higher place?" "He has done many good works," God shall reply. Then the child shall say, "Why did you let me die so soon that I was prevented from doing good?" God will answer, "I knew that you would grow up into a sinner; therefore, it was better that you should die a child." Thereupon a cry shall rise from those condemned to the depths of Hell, "Why, O Lord! did You not let us die before we became sinners?"[3]

Al-Ashari, like al-Shafii in law and al-Ghazali in theology, undertook a synthesis of contending positions. He staked a middle ground between the extremes of ibn Hanbal's literalism and the Mutazila's logical rationalism. He reasserted the doctrines of the omnipotence of God, His attributes, the uncreatedness of the Quran, and predestination. However, he did this with some reinterpretation, drawing on the language and categories of Greek thought that had now become an integral part of Muslim theological discourse. Al-Ashari used reason to provide a rational defense for that which transcended, and at times seemed contrary to, reason. Thus, although reason and logic might be used to explain and defend belief, revelation was not subordinate to the requirements of reason. The stark divinity of the Mutazila's attributeless God was countered by a reaffirmation of God's eternal attributes, which, al-Ashari maintained, were neither His essence nor accidents.

Al-Ashari's universe was controlled by a transcendent, omnipotent God, who could intervene in every place and at every moment. Yet he maintained a qualified law of causality by stating that God customarily allowed many events to follow from certain causes. Although al-Ashari's God decreed (willed and created) all actions and events, this determinism was accompanied by a theory of "acquisition," which maintained that people acquire responsibility and thus accountability by their actions.

Al-Ashari and his successors produced a school of theology that by the eleventh century had attracted many adherents, including followers of the Shafii law school, and had become a major stream of Muslim learning. Despite this success, for many, in particular Ahmad ibn Hanbal, al-Ashari and scholastic theology in general remained suspect. Whatever the accomplishments of theology, its use of reason, even if subordinated to revelation, was unacceptable. However, in time the followers of al-Ashari came to be regarded as the dominant school of Sunni theology, including among its members perhaps the most influential Muslim scholar, Abu Hamid Muhammad ibn Muhammad al-Ghazali (1056–1111)

Mutazila fortunes were more limited. Always a small minority, they failed to attract a substantial following. Their association with the excesses of Caliph Mamun's attempt to impose Mutazila theology as orthodoxy and their use of a rational dialectic struck the majority of *ulama* as a blasphemous attempt to limit God's power. However, much of their thought continued to influence Shii Islam, and many of the issues they raised remain influential today.

At the same time that Greek philosophy and science influenced the development of scholastic theology, philosophy developed as a separate Muslim discipline. Because of the movement to translate classical texts into Arabic, Muslim thinkers were able to appropriate Aristotle, Plato, Plotinus, and the Stoics and rework these materials within their own context, producing an extraordinarily rich contribution to Islamic civilization. Men like the Arabs Abu Yusuf al-Kindi (d. 873) and al-Farabi (d. 950), the Persian Ibn Sina (Avicenna, d. 1037), and the Spaniard Ibn Rushd (Averroes, d. 1198) were among the intellectual giants of their times. Their ideas challenged their Muslim contemporaries.

Ironically, despite the genius of Muslim philosophers, their impact on Islamic thought was suspect and limited. If the use of reason in scholastic theology had been suspect, how much more was philosophy, which, in contrast to theology, took reason and not revelation as its starting point and method. The *ulama* (scholars of tradition, law, and theology alike) viewed philosophy as embodying the conflict between reason and revelation, a direct threat to faith. Talk of creation through a process of emanation, reason as the surest means to the truth, and philosophy as the superior path to the real drove a wedge between the philosophers and the bulk of orthodoxy. Al-Ghazali, the great theologian, legal scholar, and mystic, mastered philosophy to refute the philosophers in his *Incoherence of the Philosophers*. It became a standard work. Ibn Rushd countered with his ringing defense *The Incoherence of the Incoherence*, in which he argued that the differences between philosophy and religion were only apparent, as both pursued the real, the former relying on the language of reason and science and the latter on the metaphorical language of revelation. The measure of the gulf between the philosophers and the community could be seen in the response to Ibn Rushd and the philosophical tradition. Despite the accomplishments of many great philosophers, not only in philosophy but also in medicine and the sciences (for they were truly renaissance men), more often than not they were viewed as rationalists and nonbelievers. Philosophy never established itself as a major discipline. In contrast, Muslim philosophy had a major impact on the West. By transmitting Greek philosophy to medieval Europe, it influenced the curriculum of its universities and the work of such scholars as Albertus Magnus (Albert the Great), Thomas Aquinas, John Duns Scotus, and Roger Bacon.

Philosophy continued to develop, even though the Peripatetic or Aristotelian tradition of philosophy ceased to develop. The Illuminationist school, which was more Neoplatonic but also more amenable to synthesis with revelation and with mysticism, was established and hugely influential in Iran. It produced Mulla Sadra (1571–1636), the Shia Islamic philosopher and theologian. Mulla Sadra's synthesis of philosophy, theology, and mysticism led the Iranian cultural renaissance in the seventeenth century and he was regarded by many as the most influential philosopher in Iran and in the Muslim world in the last four hundred years. The philosophical tradition also continued to be influential in Sunni Muslim India, in the works of the reformer Shah Wali Allah (1703–62), the most prominent and influential eighteenth-century Islamic scholar and reformer in South Asia, which are replete with philosophical arguments and discussions of philosophical issues, and the Ottoman Empire.

ISLAMIC LAW

Law is the primary religious science in Islam. Once committed to Islam, the believer's overriding concern and question is: "What do I do; what is God's will/law?" Law is essentially religious, the concrete expression of God's guidance (*sharia,* path or way) for humanity. Throughout history, Islamic law has remained central to Muslim identity and practice, for it constitutes the ideal social blueprint, the moral compass, for the "good society." The **Sharia** has been a source of law and moral guidance, the basis for both law and ethics. Despite vast cultural differences, Islamic law has provided an underlying sense of identity, a common code of behavior, for Muslim societies. As a result, the role of Islamic law in Muslim society has been and continues to be a central issue for the community of believers.

Historical Development

For the early Muslim community, following the Sharia of God meant obedience to God's revelation and to His Prophet. Issues of worship, family relations, criminal justice, and warfare could be referred to Muhammad for guidance and adjudication. Both Quranic teaching and Prophetic example guided and governed the early Islamic state. With the death of Muhammad, divine revelation ceased; however, the Muslim vocation to follow God's will did not. Knowledge and enforcement of God's law were continuing concerns. The first four caliphs, assisted by their advisers, carried on, rendering decisions as new problems and questions arose. With the advent of the Umayyad dynasty, an Islamic legal system began gradually to take shape, replacing this ad hoc approach. Part of the new administrative structure established by the Umayyads was the office of the *qadi*, or judge.

The *qadi* was originally an official appointed by the caliph as his delegate to provincial governors. He was to see that government decrees were carried out and to settle disputes. In rendering a decision, judges relied on the prevailing Arab customary laws of the particular province and the Quran as well as their own personal judgment. A rudimentary legal code developed, consisting of administrative decrees and judicial decisions. The result was a body of laws that differed from one locale to another, given the cultural diversity of the empire's provinces and the independent judgment exercised by judges.

Growing dissatisfaction with Umayyad practice led to a new page in the history of Islamic law. Critics of the Umayyads charged that the development of law had become too subjective a process and resulted in a confused and often contradictory body of laws. They argued that if all

Muslims were bound to submit to and carry out God's law, then Islamic law ought to be defined clearly and more uniformly. By the eighth century, such critics, eager to limit the autonomy of Muslim rulers and to standardize the law, could be found in major cities: Medina, Damascus, Basra, Kufa, and Baghdad. In time, these great early legal scholars, such as Abu Hanifa (d. 767), Malik ibn Anas (d. 796), Muhammad al-Shafii (d. 819), and Ahmad ibn Hanbal (d. 855), who came to be viewed respectively as the founders or leaders of the Hanifa, Maliki, Shafii, and Hanbali law schools, attracted followers. They began systematically to review Umayyad law and customs in light of Quranic teachings. Maintaining that Islam offered a comprehensive way of life, they sought to apply Islam to all aspects of life. These loosely organized endeavors were the beginnings of early law centers or schools.

The major development of Islamic law and jurisprudence took place during the Abbasid caliphate. Having justified their revolution in the name of Islam, the Abbasid caliphs became the great patrons of Islamic learning. Study of the Quran, traditions of the Prophet, and law excelled in the hands of a new class of scholars (*ulama*), who sought to discover, interpret, and apply God's will to life's situations. Islamic law was not the product of government decrees or judges' decisions but the work of jurists or scholars who struggled from 750 to 900 C.E. to set out a religious ideal, to develop a comprehensive law based on the Quran. Jurists interpreted and formulated Islamic law, and judges were restricted to the application of the law. The consensus of jurists during this period produced the binding legal formulations that were to govern Muslim life down through the centuries.

Despite their common purpose and goals, differences soon arose during Abbasid times, pitting one law school against another and causing divisions within the law schools themselves. This divergence resulted from a combination of factors. The Quran is not a law book. About six hundred of the six thousand verses in the Quran are concerned with law, many of them covering matters of prayer and ritual. Approximately eighty verses treat legal topics in the strict sense of the term: crime and punishment, contracts, and family laws.[4] Therefore, in many instances the doctrines of the law schools remained dependent on the interpretation or opinion of jurists who were, in turn, influenced by the differing customs of their respective social milieux.

Medina and Kufa provide instructive examples of this stage in the process of legal development. The legal interpretations in both cities shared a common starting point—the Quran was interpreted in light of the precedents of the Prophet and the early caliphs. However, where the

Quran was silent, jurists in each city relied on local practice in elaborating the law. The older Arab patrilineal system of Medina contrasted with the more recently established, cosmopolitan Arab and non-Arab urban society of Kufa. Legal scholars who lived in Medina tended to identify their way of life with that of the Prophet and his early companions. Thus, customary tribal law (*sunna*, trodden path or practice) became associated or equated with the practice of the Prophet (what the Prophet said, did, or permitted) and his companions.

For the Medinans, law in Islam was based on the Quran and the Prophetically informed practice or local consensus of the Medinan community. This perspective was epitomized by Malik ibn Anas, who wrote the first compendium of Islamic law. Malik was a scholar of both tradition (*hadith*, written reports about the practice or Sunna of Muhammad and his companions) and law. His treatise, the *Muwatta*, is a collection of traditions and laws. Legal arguments and conclusions are justified or supported by citations from the Quran and traditions. Where differences existed, the local consensus of Medina remained authoritative.

In contrast, legal scholars in the much younger community of Kufa, followers of Abu Hanifa and al-Shaybani (d. 804), relied on jurist opinion and local law. The law of equality in marriage is a clear example of the differences that followed from this approach. Because Kufa was a far more diverse and class-conscious society, influenced by Persian practice, a husband was required to be the equal of his wife's family in terms of lineage, financial status, and so forth. However, no such law developed in the more homogeneous society at Medina.

By the end of the eighth century, Muslims again found that despite their best efforts to bring uniformity to the law, significant differences in their legal doctrines continued to exist, given the number of law schools, differences of cultural milieu, and the diversity of legal techniques or criteria employed by jurists (personal opinion, tradition, equity, public welfare). Two contending camps emerged: those who wished to bring uniformity to the law by restricting the use of reason and relying primarily on the traditions of the Prophet versus those who vigorously asserted their right to reason for themselves in the light of such criteria as equity or public interest. Into the fray stepped Muhammad ibn Idris al-Shafii (d. 819), the father of Islamic jurisprudence.

Born in Mecca, al-Shafii studied with Malik ibn Anas at Medina. He spent the early part of his career traveling through Syria and Iraq, thoroughly familiarizing himself with the legal schools and the thinking of his time before settling in Egypt. It was here that his thought crystallized, and he emerged as the champion of those who sought to curb the diversity of legal practice. Al-Shafii was primarily responsible for the formulation that, after great resistance and debate, became the classical doctrine of Islamic jurisprudence, establishing a fixed, common methodology for all law schools. According to al-Shafii, there are four sources of law (*usul al-fiqh*, roots or sources of law): the Quran, the example (Sunna) of the Prophet, consensus (*ijma*) of the community, and analogical reasoning or deduction (*qiyas*).

Al-Shafii taught that there were only two material sources of law: the Quran and the Sunna of the Prophet, as preserved in the *hadith*. He maintained that Muhammad was divinely inspired, and thus his example was normative for the community. He restricted the use of the term *Sunna* to the Prophet. Henceforth, it came to be identified solely with the divinely inspired practice of Muhammad and no longer with tribal custom or the consensus of law schools. Al-Shafii also transferred the authority for legal interpretation from individual law schools to the consensus of the community. Basing his opinion on a tradition of the Prophet—"My community will not agree upon an error"—the agreed-on practice of the community (*ijma*) became the third infallible source of law. Finally, the role of personal reasoning in the formulation of law was restricted. Where no explicit revealed text or community consensus existed, jurists were no longer free to rely on their own judgment to solve new problems. Instead, they were to use deductive reasoning (*qiyas*) to seek a similar or analogous situation in the revealed sources (Quran and Sunna), from which they were to derive a new regulation. Reasoning by analogy would eliminate what al-Shafii regarded as the arbitrary nature of legal reasoning prevalent in the more inductive approach of those who relied on their own judgment.

The Sources of Law

The literal meaning of Sharia is "the road to the watering hole," the clear, right, or straight path to be followed. In Islam, it came to mean the divinely mandated path, the straight path of Islam, Muslims were to follow, God's will or law. However, because the Quran does not provide an exhaustive body of laws, the desire to discover and delineate Islamic law in a comprehensive and consistent fashion led to the development of the science of law, or jurisprudence (*fiqh*). *Fiqh*, "understanding," is that science or discipline that sought to ascertain, interpret, and apply God's will or guidance (Sharia) as found in the Quran to all aspects of life. As a result of al-Shafii's efforts, classical Islamic jurisprudence recognized four official sources, as well as other subsidiary sources.

Quran

As the primary source of God's revelation and law, the Quran is the sourcebook of Islamic principles and values. Although the Quran declares, "Here is a plain statement to men, a guidance and instruction to those who fear God," it does not constitute a comprehensive code of laws. Although it does contain legal prescriptions, the bulk of the Quran consists of broad, general moral directives—what Muslims ought to do. It replaced, modified, or supplemented earlier tribal laws. Practices such as female infanticide, exploitation of the poor, usury, murder, false contracts, fornication, adultery, and theft were condemned. In other cases, Arab customs were gradually replaced by Islamic standards. Quranic prescriptions governing alcohol and gambling illustrate this process. At first, the use of alcohol and gambling had not been expressly prohibited. However, over a period of years, a series of revelations progressively discouraged their use. The first prescription against the old custom is given in the form of advice: "They ask thee concerning wine and gambling. Say: in them is great sin and some use for man; but the sin is greater than the usefulness" (2:219). Then, Muslims were prohibited from praying under the influence of alcohol: "Approach not prayer with a mind befogged until you can understand all that you say" (4:43). Finally, liquor and gambling were prohibited: "Satan's plan is to incite enmity and hatred between you with intoxicants and gambling, and hinder you from the remembrance of God and from prayer: Will you not then abstain?" (5:93).

Much of the Quran's reforms consist of regulations or moral guidance that limit or redefine rather than prohibit or replace existing practices. Slavery and women's status are two striking examples. Although slavery was not abolished, slave owners were encouraged to emancipate their slaves, to permit them to earn their freedom, and to "give them some of God's wealth which He has given you" (24:33). Forcing female slaves into prostitution was condemned. Women and the family were the subjects of more wide-ranging reforms affecting marriage, divorce, and inheritance. Marriage was a contract, with women entitled to their dower (4:4). Polygamy was restricted (4:3), and men were commanded to treat their wives fairly and equally (4:129). Women were given inheritance rights in a patriarchal society that had previously restricted inheritance to male relatives.

Sunna of the Prophet

Quranic principles and values were concretized and interpreted by the second and complementary source of law, the Sunna of the Prophet, the normative model behavior of Muhammad. The importance of the Sunna is rooted in such Quranic injunctions as "obey God and obey the Messenger.... If you should quarrel over anything refer it to God and the Messenger" (4:59) and "In God's messenger you have a fine model for anyone whose hope is in God and the Last Day" (33:21). Belief that Muhammad was inspired by God to act wisely, in accordance with God's will, led to the acceptance of his example, or Sunna, as a supplement to the Quran, and thus, a material or textual source of the law. Sunna includes what the Prophet said, what he did, and those actions that he permitted or allowed.

The record of Prophetic deeds transmitted and preserved in tradition reports (*hadith*, pl. *ahadith*) proliferated. By the ninth century, the number of traditions had mushroomed into the hundreds of thousands. They included pious fabrications by those who believed that their practices were in conformity with Islam and forgeries by factions involved in political and theological disputes. Recognition that many of these traditions were fabricated led to the development of the science of tradition criticism and the compilation of authoritative compendia. The evaluation of traditions focused on the chain of narrators and the subject matter. Criteria were established for judging the trustworthiness of narrators—moral character, reputation for piety, intelligence, and good memory. Then a link-by-link examination of each of the narrators was conducted to trace the continuity of a tradition back to the Prophet. The process required detailed biographical information about narrators: where and when they were born, where they lived and traveled, and so forth. Such information might support or refute the authenticity of a narrator. For example, it might be shown that a reputed narrator could not have received a *hadith* from his predecessor because they did not live at the same time or because they neither lived nor traveled near each other. Alternatively, it might be discovered that someone in the chain of transmission was known for immorality and thus could not be trusted to pass along traditions without embellishing them.

The second criteria, evaluation of a tradition's subject matter, entailed an examination to determine whether, for example, a tradition contradicted the Quran, an already verified tradition, or reason. After traditions had been subjected to both external (narrators) and internal (subject matter) examination, they were categorized according to the degree of their authenticity (authority) or strength as sound, good or acceptable, and weak.

Throughout the ninth and tenth centuries, scholars traveled throughout the Muslim world collecting traditions and gathering information on their narrators or transmitters. Faced with the enormous corpus of traditions that had grown up, they sought to study and sift through them to authenticate and compile those traditions worthy of being conserved and followed by the Muslim community. Six collections came to be accepted as authoritative: those of **Ismail al-Bukhari** (d. 870), **Muslim ibn al-Hajjaj** (d. 875), Abu Dawud (d. 888), al-Nisai (d. 915), al-Tirmidhi (d. 892), and Ibn Maja (d. 896). Among these, the collections of al-Bukhari and Muslim have enjoyed an especially high status as authoritative sources.

Shii *hadith* developed separately but along similar lines to Sunni *hadith*. The principal differences between the two are: (1) in addition to traditions of the Prophet, reliance on narrative reports or traditions of Muhammad's family and descendants (*ahl al-bayt*), regarded as the true successors and leaders, Imams, of the community; and (2) an emphasis on *hadith* related to Shii doctrines, particularly those concerning the family of the Prophet. Four major books or collections of *hadith* became authoritative for Shii.

Authenticity of Tradition Literature

Orientalist Western scholarship has seriously questioned the historicity and authenticity of the *hadith*, maintaining that the bulk of traditions attributed to the Prophet Muhammad were actually written much later.[5] Joseph Schacht, the most influential modern Western authority on Islamic law, building on the work of his European predecessors, concluded that the term "Sunna of the Prophet" developed for the first time in the eighth century due to the influence of the Traditionist movement and under the aegis of al-Shafii, and that this usage gave legal authority to later customary practices and traditions. On the basis of his research, Schacht found no evidence of legal traditions before 722, one hundred years after the death of Muhammad. Thus, he concluded that the Sunna of the Prophet is not the words and deeds of the Prophet, but apocryphal material originating from customary practice that was projected back to the eighth century to more authoritative sources—first the Successors, then the Companions, and finally the Prophet himself.

Many Muslim scholars, although critical of some Prophetic traditions, take exception to Schacht's conclusions.[6] To state that no tradition goes back prior to 722 creates an unwarranted vacuum in Islamic history. Schacht's "first century vacuum" with regard to the existence of Prophetic traditions is a theory or conclusion that completely overlooks or dismisses the Muslim science of tradition criticism and verification and does violence to the deeply ingrained sense of tradition in Arab culture, which all scholars, Muslim and non-Muslim, have acknowledged. As Fazlur Rahman notes:

> The Arabs, who memorized and handed down the poetry of their poets, sayings of their soothsayers and statements of their judges and tribal leaders, cannot be expected to fail to notice and narrate deeds and sayings of one whom they acknowledged as the Prophet of God.[7]

Accepting Schacht's conclusion regarding the many traditions he did examine does not warrant its automatic extension to all the traditions. To consider all Prophetic traditions apocryphal until proven otherwise is to reverse the burden of proof. Moreover, even where differences of opinion exist regarding the authenticity of the chain of narrators, they need not detract from the authenticity of a tradition's content and common acceptance of the importance of tradition literature as a record of the early history and development of Islamic belief and practice. As H. A. R. Gibb observed regarding the significance of tradition literature:

> It serves as a mirror in which the growth and development of Islam as a way of life and the larger Islamic community are truly reflected .... [It] is possible to trace in *hadiths* the struggle between the supporters of the Umayyads and the Medinan opposition, the growth of Shiism and the divisions between its sects   the rise of theological controversies, and the beginnings of the mystical doctrines of the Sufis.[8]

Analogical Reasoning

Throughout the development of Islamic law, reason had played an important role as caliphs, judges, and, finally, jurists or legal scholars interpreted law where no clear, explicit revealed text or general consensus existed. The general term for legal reasoning or interpretation was **ijtihad** (to strive or struggle intellectually). It comes from the same root as jihad (to strive or struggle in God's path), which included the notion of holy war. The use of reason (legal reasoning or interpretation) had taken a number of forms and been described by various terms: personal opinion, jurist preference, and analogical reasoning (*qiyas*). Reasoning by analogy was a more restricted, systematic form of *ijtihad*. When faced with new situations or problems, scholars sought a similar situation in the Quran and Sunna. The key is the discovery of the effective cause or reason behind a Sharia rule. If a similar reason could be identified in a new situation or case, then the Sharia judgment was extended to resolve the case. The determination of the minimum rate of dower offers a good example of analogical deduction. Jurists saw a similarity between the bride's loss of virginity in marriage and the Quranic penalty for theft, which was amputation. Thus, the minimum dower was set at the same rate that stolen goods had to be worth before amputation was applicable.

Consensus of the Community

The authority for consensus (*ijma*) as a fourth source of law is usually derived from a saying of the Prophet, "My community will never agree on an error." Consensus did not develop as a source of law until after the death of Muhammad, with the consequent loss of his direct guidance in legislative matters. It began as a natural process for solving problems and making decisions; one followed the majority opinion or consensus of the early community as a check on individual opinions. However, two kinds of consensus came to be recognized. The consensus of the entire community was applied to those religious duties, such as the pilgrimage to Mecca, practiced by all Muslims. But despite al-Shafii's attempt to define the fourth source of law as this general consensus, classical Islamic jurisprudence defined the community in a more restricted sense as the community of legal scholars or religious authorities who act in behalf of and guide the entire Muslim community.

Consensus played a pivotal role in the development of Islamic law and contributed significantly to the corpus of law or legal interpretation. If

The Kaaba is a simple stone building in Makkah, toward which all Muslims pray each day. According to the Quran, it was first built by Abraham with his son Ishmael (Isma'il). The stones are visible underneath the gold-embroidered covering called the kiswa.

questions arose about the meaning of a Quranic text or tradition or if revelation and early Muslim practice were silent, jurists applied their own reasoning (*ijtihad*) to interpret the law. Often this process resulted in a number of differing legal opinions. Over time, perhaps several generations, certain interpretations were accepted by more and more scholars and endured the test of time, whereas others disappeared. Looking back on the evolving consensus of scholars, it was concluded that an authoritative consensus had been reached on the issue. Thus, consensus served as a brake on the vast array of individual interpretations of legal scholars and contributed to the creation of a relatively fixed body of laws.

Although all came to accept the four sources of law, Islamic jurisprudence recognized other influences, designating them subsidiary principles of law. Among these were custom, public interest, and jurist preference or equity. In this way, some remnant of the inductive, human input that had characterized the actual methods of the law schools in their attempt to realize the Sharia's primary concern with human welfare, justice, and equity was acknowledged. However, the ultimate effect of the acceptance of al-Shafii's formulation of the four sources of law, with its tendency to deny independent interpretation and derive all laws directly from revelation, the inspired practice of Muhammad, or the infallible consensus of the community, was the gradual replacement of the real by the ideal. The actual, historical development of the law was forgotten.

By the tenth century, the basic development of Islamic law was completed. The general consensus (*ijma*) of Muslim jurists was that Islamic law (Islam's way of life) had been satisfactorily and comprehensively delineated in its essential principles and preserved in the regulations of the law books or legal manuals produced by the law schools.

This attitude led many to conclude that individual, independent interpretation (*ijtihad*) of the law was no longer necessary or desirable. Instead, Muslims were simply to follow or imitate (**taqlid**) the past, God's law as elaborated by the early jurists. Jurists were no longer to seek new solutions or produce new regulations and law books but instead study the established legal manuals and write their commentaries. Islamic law, the product of an essentially dynamic and creative process, now tended to become institutionalized. While individual scholars like Ibn Taymiyya (d. 1328) and al-Suyuti (d. 1505) demurred, the majority position resulted in traditional belief prohibiting substantive legal development. This is commonly referred to as the closing of the gate or door of *ijtihad*.

Belief that the work of the law schools had definitively resulted in the transformation of the Sharia into a legal blueprint for society reinforced the sacrosanct nature of tradition; change or innovation came to be viewed as an unwarranted deviation (*bida*) from established sacred norms. To be accused of innovation—deviation from the law and practice of the community—was equivalent to the charge of heresy in Christianity.

There is a danger in overemphasizing the unity and fixed nature of Islamic law. First, although an overall unity or common consensus existed among the law schools with regard to essential practices such as the confession of faith, fasting, and pilgrimage to Mecca, the divergent character of the law schools was preserved by differences in such areas as the grounds for divorce, the levying of taxes, and inheritance rights. Acknowledgment of this diversity within the unity of law was sanctioned by the saying of the Prophet, "Difference of opinion within my community is a sign of the bounty of Allah." This diversity continued in practice as judges applied the laws of the various law schools in their courts. Second, legal development and change did occur where scholars interpreted and clarified details of legal doctrine. This was especially true as regards the activity of the **mufti**, a legal expert or consultant. These experts advised both judges and litigants on matters of law. Their formal, written legal opinions (*fatwa*), based on their interpretation of the law, were often relied on in judicial matters. Many of the more important opinions became part of collections of *fatwas*, which became authoritative in their own right.

Schools of Law

Although there had been many law schools, by the thirteenth century the number became stabilized. For Sunni Islam, four major schools predominated: the Hanafi, Hanbali, Maliki, and Shafii. Today, they are dominant in different parts of the Islamic world. The Hanafi predominate in Syria, Iraq, South Asia, Central Asia, Turkey, and Eastern Europe. Due to the legacy of the Ottoman empire, where Hanafi law was official, it remained the official law in many Arab states despite the fact that the majority of the population are Shafii as is also true for the peoples of East Africa, southern Arabia, and Southeast Asia. The Maliki remain a major school in North, Central, and West Africa; and the Hanbali in Saudi Arabia and Qatar.

Shii Islam also generated its own schools, the most important of which is the Jafari, named for Jafar al-Sadiq (699–765), considered by Twelver Shii, who comprise the majority of Shii, as their sixth **imam** and the founder of its most prominent Shii school of law.

Jafar was a scholar of *hadith* and *fiqh* whose influence extended well beyond the confines of the Shii community. He counted many important Sunni scholars among his students, including two of the founders of the four schools of Sunni law, Abu Hanifa and Malik ibn Anas. Jafar was also a major Sufi and spiritual teacher whose name appears in practically all Sufi "chains of transmission." Traditional Sufi orders or schools trace their origins or "chains of transmission" back to the Prophet

Muhammad, either through his cousin and son-in-law Imam Ali ibn Abi Talib or through his early companion and the first caliph, Abu Bakr. Jafar's prominence in the Sunni tradition also indicates that in the early formative Islamic period, divisions between Sunni and Shii developed only gradually and were not as apparent as they would later become.

The Shii doctrine of the imamate resulted in fundamental differences in Islamic jurisprudence. Although both Sunni and Shii accept the Quran and Sunna of the Prophet as inspired authoritative textual sources, the Shii have maintained their own collections of traditions that include not only the Sunna of the Prophet but also that of Ali and the Imams. In addition, the Shii reject analogy and consensus as legal sources, because they regard the Imam as the supreme legal interpreter and authority. In his absence, qualified religious scholars serve as his agents or representatives, interpreters (*mujtahids*) of the law. Their consensus guides the community and is binding during the interim between the seclusion of the Imam and his return as the Mahdi.

In contrast to Sunni Islam, Shii Islam did not attempt to curb the use of *ijtihad*. However, in practice, Shii religious leaders, although not formally accepting the Sunni doctrine of imitation (*taqlid*), tended to follow their medieval legal manuals as well. In the eighteenth century, the right to *ijtihad* was challenged in the conflict between the Akhbari and Usuli schools over the question of religious authority. Were the sacred texts sufficient, or was there still need for jurist interpretation of the law? The Akhbari (a synonym for tradition, or *hadith*) took a more rigid approach and maintained that the sacred texts were sufficient. Therefore, they sought to curb the authority of jurists by maintaining that independent interpretation was not necessary. The Usuli, defending the right and authority of jurists to interpret the law, asserted the need for *mujtahids*. In the end, the Usuli school won out. Moreover, Shii Islam also developed its own distinctive doctrine of emulation or imitation. This was the belief that in the absence of the Imam, leading *mujtahids,* those publicly acknowledged for their learning, piety, and justice, should serve as a religious guide whose example and teachings believers should follow.

Courts of Law

The application of Islamic law was the task of the Sharia courts and their judges (*qadis*). The judiciary was not independent, for judges were appointed by the government and were paid and served at the pleasure of the caliph. Although originally judges had been interpreters and makers of law, their role came to be restricted to the application of law—that body of laws developed by the jurists and enshrined in the law books. Sharia judges were not to interpret or add to the law. Thus, Islamic law does not recognize a case law system of legally binding precedents. This reflected the belief that jurists, not judges, were to interpret the law. Judges served under a chief judge appointed by the caliph. They were assisted in their work by experts or legal consultants, muftis. Among the notable judicial procedures were rules of evidence that required an oath sworn before God in the absence of two adult male Muslim witnesses to a crime, the exclusion of circumstantial evidence, and the absence of cross-examination of witnesses. Legal decisions were final. There was no system of judicial appeal. In reality, however, the caliph or his provincial governor could review all decisions. The *ulama* were the backbone of the legal system. These scholars were experts in a number of fields, but many specialized in law. A specialist in law, or jurist, was called a ***faqih*** (pl. *fuqaha*). They dominated the Sharia system, serving as lawyers, teachers, judges, and muftis.

In addition to the Sharia courts, a class of officials or religious police were charged with the supervision and enforcement of public morals. The office of *muhtasib* (ombudsman) originally referred to a market inspector who was to regulate business transactions and practices in the marketplaces or bazaars. However, the office was extended to ensuring public morality in general: the observance of prayer times, fasting, modesty between the sexes. Islamic justification for his activities was rooted in the Quranic command to the Muslim community to encourage good and prohibit evil (3:104, 9:71). The *muhtasib* was empowered to impose penalties for violation of Islamic laws, flogging for public drunkenness, and amputation for theft. The institution continues to exist in a number of Muslim countries like Saudi Arabia, Kenya, Iran, Pakistan, and the Taliban's Afghanistan. However, its functions vary from monitoring economic transactions to public dress and behavior.

Although the Sharia system remained integral to state and society, it was not the sole system of law. Although in theory the Sharia was the only officially recognized system of law, in practice a parallel system of caliphal laws and courts existed from earliest times. Legal idealism and imperial absolutism contributed to the development of an alternative or, rather, supplementary system. An idealism that accepted in good faith an oath sworn before God and excluded circumstantial evidence and cross-examination of witnesses proved cumbersome. More important, the Sharia system limited the powers of strong and often autocratic rulers. The caliph's desire to exercise absolute power clashed with the belief that God was the only lawmaker. An Islamic rationale was created to circumvent the problem. Citing the caliph's obligation to uphold and ensure governance according to the Sharia, the Umayyads asserted broad discretionary legislative and judicial powers. They issued administrative ordinances and created Grievance courts, ostensibly to enhance the proper administration and implementation of the Sharia in society. Carefully avoiding the term "law," government regulations were called ordinances; the only requirement was that they not be contrary to the Sharia. The Grievance courts were initially established to permit the caliph or his representative to hear complaints against senior officials whose status or power might have inhibited the judges. They soon became a system of courts with scope and function that were determined by the ruler.

As a result, Islamic society possessed a dual system of laws and courts (Sharia and Grievance), religious and secular, with complementary jurisdictions. Sharia courts were increasingly restricted to the enforcement of family laws (marriage, divorce, inheritance) and the handling of religious endowments. The Grievance courts dealt with public law, especially criminal law, taxation, and commercial regulations. This approach continued throughout Islamic history. In modern times, it has been employed in countries like Saudi Arabia to provide the rationale for the introduction of a series of modern ordinances, such as the Mining Code (1963) and the Civil Service Law (1971), that supplement the Sharia. Similarly, the creation of Grievance courts made possible the broadening of the judicial system and the introduction of a hierarchy of courts.

Despite the differences between the ideal and the reality, Islamic law endured as the officially recognized cornerstone of the state. When Sunni Muslim jurists and theologians faced the issue of what to do about tyrants and despots, they concluded that it was not the moral character of the caliph but the ruler's acknowledgment of the Sharia as official state law that preserved the unity of the community and determined the Islamic nature and acceptability of a state.

The Content of Law

Law in Islam is both universal and egalitarian. The Sharia is believed to be God's law for the entire Islamic community. Non-Muslims were not expected to follow Islamic laws unless they interfered with the function of the state. Other religious communities (*dhimmi*), particularly Jews and Christians, were to be guided by their religious laws.

In the final analysis, God is the sovereign ruler of the world, and Islamic law is as much a system of ethics as it is law, for it is concerned with what a Muslim ought to do or ought not to do. All acts are ethically categorized as: (1) obligatory; (2) recommended; (3) indifferent or permissible; (4) reprehensible but not forbidden; or (5) forbidden. To break the law is a transgression against God and society, a crime and a sin; the guilty are subject to punishment in this life and the next.

The idealism of the law can be seen in the fact that ethical categories such as recommended and reprehensible were not subject to civil penalties. Islamic law is also egalitarian; it transcends regional, family, tribal, and ethnic boundaries. It does not recognize social class or caste differences. As members of a single transnational community of believers, all Muslims—Arab and non-Arab, rich and poor, black and white, caliph and craftsman, male and female—are bound by Islamic law.

The belief that Islamic law was a comprehensive social blueprint was reflected in the organization and content of law. Legal rights and duties are divided into two major categories: (1) duties to God (ritual observances), such as prayer, almsgiving, and fasting; and (2) duties to others (social trans-actions), which include penal, commercial, and family laws. The heart of the former is the so-called Five Pillars of Islam; that of the latter is family law.

The Five Pillars

Despite the rich diversity in Islamic practice, as previously discussed, the Five Pillars of Islam remain the core and common denominator. They are essential and obligatory practices all Muslims accept and follow: the Profession of Faith, prayer (*salat*) five times each day, almsgiving (*zakat*), the Fast of Ramadan, and pilgrimage (*hajj*) to Mecca.

1. The Profession of Faith. A Muslim is one who proclaims (*shahada*, wit-ness or testimony): "There is no god but the God [*Allah*] and Muhammad is the messenger of God." This acknowledgment of and commitment to Allah and His Prophet is the rather simple means by which a person professes his or her faith and becomes a Muslim, and a testimony that is given throughout the day when the muezzin calls the faithful to prayer. It affirms Islam's absolute monotheism, an unshakable and uncompromis-ing faith in the oneness or unity (*tawhid*) of God. As such, it also serves as a reminder to the faithful that polytheism, the association of anything else with God, is forbidden and is the one unforgivable sin:

> God does not forgive anyone for associating something with Him, while He does forgive whomever He wishes to for anything else. Anyone who gives God associates [partners] has invented an awful sin. (4:48)

The second part of the confession of faith is the affirmation of Muhammad as the messenger of God, the last and final prophet, who serves as a model for the Muslim community. Molding individuals into an Islamic society requires activities that recall, reinforce, and realize the word of God and the example of the Prophet. The praxis orientation of Islam is witnessed by the remaining four pillars or duties.

2. Prayer. Five times each day, Muslims are called to worship God by the muezzin (caller to prayer) from atop a mosque's minaret:

Across Muslim lands, the call to prayer is given before each of the five prayers. This young muezzin calls worshippers to the dawn prayer in central Kabul at 5:30 a.m. Today, calls to prayer issue from loudspeakers on minarets across the city, and the muezzin no longer climb the towers.

> God is most great (Allahu Akbar), God is most great, God is most great, God is most great, I witness that there is no god but Allah (the God); I witness that there is no god but Allah. I witness that Muhammad is His messenger. I witness that Muhammad is His messenger. Come to prayer, come to prayer. Come to prosperity, come to prosperity. God is most great. God is most great. There is no god but Allah.

Facing Mecca, the holy city and center of Islam, Muslims, individually or in a group, can perform their prayers (*salat*, or in Persian, *namaz*) wherever they may be—in a mosque (*masjid*, place of prostration), at home, at work, or on the road. Recited when standing in the direction of Mecca, they both recall the revelation of the Quran and reinforce a sense of belonging to a single worldwide community of believers. Although the times for prayer and the ritual actions were not specified in the Quran, they were established by Muhammad. The times are daybreak, noon, midafternoon, sunset, and evening. Ritually, prayer is preceded by ablutions that cleanse the body (hands, mouth, face, and feet) and spirit and bestow the ritual purity necessary for divine worship. The prayers themselves consist of two to four prostrations, depending on the time of day.

Five times each day across the Muslim world, the faithful are called to prayer in Arabic by a muezzin.

Each act of worship begins with the declaration, "God is most great," and consists of bows, prostrations, and the recitation of fixed prayers that include the opening verse of the Quran (the *Fatihah*) and other passages from the Quran:

> In the name of God, the Merciful and Compassionate. Praise be to God, Lord of the Universe, the Merciful and Compassionate. Ruler on the Day of Judgment. You do we worship and call upon for help. Guide us along the Straight Path, the road of those whom You have favored, those with whom You are not angry, who are not lost. (1:1–7)

At the end of the prayer, the *shahada* is again recited, and the "peace greeting"—"Peace be upon all of you and the mercy and blessings of God"—is repeated twice.

On Friday, the noon prayer is a congregational prayer and should be recited preferably at the official central mosque, designated for the Friday prayer. The congregation lines up in straight rows, side by side, and is led in prayer by its leader (*imam*), who stands in front, facing the niche (*mihrab*) that indicates the direction (*qibla*) of Mecca. A special feature of the Friday prayer is a sermon (*khutba*) preached from a pulpit (*minbar*). The preacher begins with a verse from the Quran and then gives a brief exhortation based on its message. Only men are required to attend the Friday congregational prayer. If women attend, for reasons of modesty due to the prostrations, they stand at the back, often separated by a curtain, or in a side room. Unlike the Sabbath in Judaism and Christianity, Friday was not traditionally a day of rest. However, in many Muslim countries today, it has replaced the Sunday holiday, usually instituted by colonial powers and therefore often regarded as a Western, Christian legacy.

3. *Almsgiving (zakat)*. Just as the performance of the *salat* (prayer) is both an individual and a communal obligation, so payment of the *zakat* instills a sense of communal identity and responsibility. As all Muslims share equally in their obligation to worship God, so they all are duty-bound to attend to the social welfare of their community by redressing economic inequalities through payment of an alms tax or poor tithe. It is an act both of worship or thanksgiving to God and of service to the community. All adult Muslims who are able to do so are obliged to pay a wealth tax annually. It is a tithe or percentage (usually 2.5 percent) of their accumulated wealth and assets, not just their income. This is not regarded as charity because it is not really voluntary but instead is owed, by those who have received their wealth as a trust from God's bounty, to the poor. The Quran (9:60) and Islamic law stipulate that alms are to be used to support the poor, orphans, and widows, to free slaves and debtors, and to assist in the spread of Islam. Although initially collected and then redistributed by the government, payment of the *zakat* later was left to the individual. In recent years, a number of governments (Pakistan, the Sudan, Libya) have asserted the government's right to a *zakat* tax.

4. *The Fast of Ramadan*. Once each year, Islam prescribes a rigorous, month-long fast during the month of Ramadan, the ninth month of the Islamic calendar. From dawn to sunset, all adult Muslims whose health permits are to abstain completely from food, drink, and sexual activity. Ramadan is a time for reflection and spiritual discipline, for expressing gratitude for God's guidance and atoning for past sins, for awareness of human frailty and dependence

Muslims are required to abstain from food and drink from dawn to dusk during the month of Ramadan. At dusk each day during Ramadan, families gather to break the fast and share a meal. This practice is called "breakfast."

on God, as well as for remembering and responding to the needs of the poor and hungry. The rigors of the fast of Ramadan are experienced during the long daylight hours of summer, when the severe heat in many parts of the Muslim world proves even more taxing for those who must fast while they work. Some relief comes at dusk, when the fast is broken for the day by a light meal (popularly referred to as breakfast). Evening activities contrast with those of the daylight hours as families exchange visits and share a special late evening meal together. In some parts of the Muslim world, there are special foods and sweets that are served only at this time of the year. Many will go to the mosque for the evening prayer, followed by a special prayer recited only during Ramadan. Other special acts of piety, such as the recitation of the entire Quran (one thirtieth each night of the month) and public recitation of the Quran or Sufi chantings, may be heard throughout the evening. After a short evening's sleep, families rise before sunrise to take their first meal of the day, which must sustain them until sunset. As the end of Ramadan nears (on the twenty-seventh day), Muslims commemorate the "Night of Power" when Muhammad first received God's revelation. The month of Ramadan comes to an end with a great celebration, the Feast of the Breaking of the Fast, *Id al-Fitr*. The spirit and joyousness remind one of the celebration of Christmas. Family members come from near and far to feast and exchange gifts in a celebration that lasts for three days. In many Muslim countries, it is a national holiday. The meaning of Ramadan is not lost for those who attend mosque and pay the special alms for the poor (alms for the breaking of the fast) required by Islamic law.

5. Pilgrimage: The Hajj. Ramadan is followed by the beginning of the pilgrimage season. Every adult Muslim physically and financially able is expected to perform the annual pilgrimage (*hajj*) to Mecca at least once in his or her lifetime. The focus of the pilgrimage is the Kaba, the cube-shaped House of God, in which the sacred black stone is embedded. Muslim tradition teaches that the Kaba was originally built by the prophet Ibrahim (Abraham) and his son Ismail. The black stone was given to Abraham by the angel Gabriel and thus is a symbol of God's covenant with Ismail and, by extension, the Muslim community. The Kaba was the object of pilgrimage during pre-Islamic times. Tradition tells us that one of the first things Muhammad did when he marched triumphantly into Mecca was to cleanse the Kaba of the tribal idols that it housed, thus restoring it to the worship of the one true God.

The pilgrimage proper takes place during the twelfth month, Dhu al-Hijja, of the Muslim lunar calendar. As with prayer, the pilgrimage requires ritual purification, symbolized by the wearing of white garments. Men shave their heads, or have a symbolic tuft of hair cut, and don two seamless white sheets. Women may wear simple, national dress; however, many don a long white dress and head covering. Neither jewelry nor perfume is permitted; sexual activity and hunting are prohibited as well. These and other measures underscore the unity and equality of all believers as well as the total attention and devotion required. As the pilgrims near Mecca they shout, "I am here, O Lord, I am here!" As they enter Mecca, they proceed to the Grand Mosque, where the Kaba is located. Moving in a counterclockwise direction, they circle the Kaba seven times. During the following days, a variety of ritual actions or ceremonies take place—praying at the spot where Abraham, the patriarch and father of monotheism, stood; running between Safa and Marwa in commemoration of Hagar's frantic search for water for her son, Ismail; stoning the devil, three stone pillars that symbolize evil. An essential part of the pilgrimage is a visit to the Plain of Arafat, where, from noon to sunset, the pilgrims stand before God in repentance, seeking His forgiveness for themselves and all Muslims throughout the world. It was here, from a hill called the Mount of Mercy, that the Prophet during his Farewell Pilgrimage preached his last sermon or message. Once again, the preacher repeats Muhammad's call for peace and harmony among the believers. Standing together on the Plain of Arafat, Muslims experience the underlying unity and equality of a worldwide Muslim community that transcends national, racial, economic, and sexual differences.

The pilgrimage ends with the Feast of Sacrifice (*Id al-Adha*), known in Muslim piety as the Great Feast. It commemorates God's command to

Abraham to sacrifice his son Ismail (Isaac in Jewish and Christian traditions). The pilgrims ritually reenact Abraham's rejection of Satan's temptations to ignore God's command by again casting stones at the devil, here represented by a pillar. Afterward, they sacrifice animals (sheep, goats, cattle, or camels), as Abraham was finally permitted to substitute a ram for his son. The animal sacrifice also symbolizes that, like Abraham, the pilgrims are willing to sacrifice that which is most important to them. (One needs to recall the importance of these animals as a sign of a family's wealth and as essential for survival.) Some of the meat is consumed, but most is supposed to be distributed to the poor and needy. In modern times, with almost 2 million participants in the pilgrimage, Saudi Arabia has had to explore new methods for freezing, preserving, and distributing the vast amount of meat. The Feast of Sacrifice is a worldwide Muslim celebration that lasts for three days, a time for rejoicing, prayer, and visiting with family and friends. At the end of the pilgrimage, many of the faithful visit the mosque and tomb of Muhammad at Medina before returning home. The enormous pride of those who have made the pilgrimage is reflected in a number of popular practices. Many will take the name Hajji, placing it at the beginning of their name. Those who can will return to make the pilgrimage.

In addition to the *hajj*, there is a devotional ritual, the *umra* (the "visitation") or lesser pilgrimage, which Muslims may perform when visiting the holy sites at other times of the year. Those who are on the pilgrimage often perform the *umra* rituals before, during, or after the *hajj*. However, performance of the *umra* does not replace the *hajj* obligation.

The Struggle for Islam (Jihad)

Jihad, "to strive or struggle" in the way of God, is sometimes referred to as the sixth pillar of Islam. The importance of jihad is rooted in the Quran's command to struggle (the literal meaning of the word *jihad*) in the path of God and in the example of the Prophet Muhammad and his early Companions. In its most general meaning, jihad refers to the obligation incumbent on all Muslims, individuals and the community, to follow and realize God's will: to lead a virtuous life and to spread Islam through preaching, education, example, and writing. Jihad also includes the right, indeed the obligation, to defend Islam and the Muslim community from aggression. Throughout history, the call to jihad has rallied Muslims to the defense of Islam.

These two broad meanings of jihad, nonviolent and violent, are contrasted in an often-cited Prophetic tradition. It is reported that when Muhammad returned from battle he told his followers, "We return from the lesser jihad [warfare] to the greater jihad." Historically, jihad has been subject to many interpretations and usages, spiritual and political, peaceful and violent. The meaning of Quranic passages and their use are questions that are not new—Muslims throughout the ages have debated them.

Like all sacred scriptures, Islamic sacred texts must be read within the social and political contexts in which they were revealed. The Quran, like the Hebrew scriptures, or Old Testament, has verses that address fighting and the conduct of war. Tribal raids and cycles of vengeance and vendetta were common in Arabia. The broader Near East, in which Arabia was located, was itself divided between two warring superpowers, the Byzantine (Eastern Roman) and the Sasanian (Persian) empires. The earliest Quranic verses dealing with armed struggle, or "defensive" jihad, were revealed shortly after the *hijra* (emigration) of Muhammad and his followers to Medina in flight from their persecution in Mecca. At a time when Muslims were forced to fight for their lives, Muhammad is told, "Leave is given to those who fight because they were wronged—surely God is able to help them—who were expelled from their homes wrongfully for saying, 'Our Lord is God'" (22:39–40).

The defensive nature of jihad is clearly emphasized in 2:190: "And fight in the way of God with those who fight you, but aggress not: God loves not the aggressors." At critical points throughout the years, Muhammad received revelations from God that provided guidance for the jihad. The Quran provides detailed guidelines and regulations regarding the conduct of war: who is to fight and who is exempted (48:17, 9:91), when hostilities must cease (2:192), and how prisoners should be treated (47:4).

Most important, verses such as 2:294 emphasized that warfare and the response to violence and aggression must be proportional: "Whoever transgresses against you, respond in kind." Permission to fight the enemy is balanced by a strong mandate for making peace: "If your enemy inclines toward peace, then you too should seek peace and put your trust in God" (8:61) and "Had Allah wished, He would have made them dominate you, and so if they leave you alone and do not fight you and offer you peace, then Allah allows you no way against them" (4:90). From the earliest times, it was forbidden to kill noncombatants as well as women and children and monks and rabbis, who were given the promise of immunity unless they took part in the fighting.

The Quran also has a set of verses, referred to as the "sword verses," often cited by critics to demonstrate the inherently violent nature of Islam and its scripture: "When the sacred months have passed, slay the idolaters [the Meccans] wherever you find them, and take them, and confine them, and lie in wait for them at every place of ambush" (9:5). These verses have also been selectively used (or abused) by Muslim rulers to justify their wars of conquest and political expansion and by religious extremists to develop a "theology of hate" and intolerance and to legitimate uncondi-tional warfare against unbelievers.

During the period of Islamic expansion and conquest, many of the *ulama* (religious scholars), who enjoyed royal patronage, provided a rationale for caliphs to pursue their imperial dreams. They maintained that the "sword verses" abrogated, or overrode, the earlier Quranic verses that limited jihad to defensive war. A further complication has been the tendency to cite verses incompletely and thus distort the full intent of the verse. For example, the full intent of the verse "When the sacred months have passed, slay the idolaters wherever you find them" is missed or distorted when quoted in isolation, for it is followed and quali-fied by "But if they repent and fulfill their devotional obligations and pay the zakat [the charitable tax on Muslims], then let them go their way, for God is forgiving and kind" (9:5). The same is true of another verse:

> Fight those who believe neither in God nor the Last Day, nor hold that forbidden which hath been forbidden by God and His Apostle, nor hold the religion of truth [even if they are] of the People of the Book.

It, too, is often cited without the line that follows, "Until they pay the tax with willing submission, and feel themselves subdued" (9:29).

Jihad has been interpreted and misinterpreted throughout Islamic history to justify resistance and liberation struggles, extremism and ter-rorism, and holy and unholy wars. In addition to historic battles and wars to protect Muslim peoples and lands, rulers, from early caliphs to heads of modern states such as Saddam Hussein, have often used jihad to legiti-mate campaigns to spread the boundaries of their states or empires and fight their enemies.[9] Extremists, past and present, from the Kharijites, who assassinated the caliph Ali, and the assassins of Egypt's president Anwar Sadat to Osama bin Laden and al-Qaeda and a host of modern extremist movements from Egypt to Indonesia, have justified their acts of violence and terror as a jihad. Their failure to abide by the detailed legal and the ethical regulations of Islamic law led to their rejection by the majority of Muslims as religious extremists and terrorists.

Muslim Family Law

As the Five Pillars are the core of a Muslim's duty to worship God, family law is central to Islam's social laws. Because of the centrality of the com-munity in Islam and the role of the family as the basic unit of Muslim society, family law enjoyed pride of place in the development of Islamic law as well as in its implementation throughout history. Although caliphs and modern Muslim rulers might limit, circumvent, and replace penal or commercial laws, Muslim family law has generally remained in force. Today, as in the past, the subject of women and the family remains an important and extremely sensitive topic in Muslim societies.[10]

The special status of family law reflects the Quranic concern for the rights of women and the family (the greater part of its legislation concerns these issues) as well as that of the patriarchal society in which the law was elaborated. The traditional family social structure, the roles and responsibilities of its members, and family values may be identified in the law. The Quran introduced substantial reforms affecting the position of women by creating new regulations and modifying customary practice. These reforms and customary practice constitute the substance of classical family law. To understand the significance of Quranic reforms as well as the forces that influenced the development of family law, some appreciation of the social context in pre-Islamic Arabia is necessary.

The extended family had one head or leader, the father or senior male, who controlled and guided the family unit. The family consisted of the father, his wife or wives, unmarried sons and daughters, and married sons with their wives and children, all of whom had specific roles within the family structure. It served as the basic social and economic unit of the tribe within a male-dominated (patriarchal) society. The paramount position of males was reflected in family matters: their unlimited right to marry or divorce at will and an inheritance system that excluded women. A woman was regarded as little more than a possession, first of her father and her family, and subsequently, of her husband and his family.

The status of women and the family in Muslim family law was the product of Arab culture, Quranic reforms, and foreign ideas and values assimilated from conquered peoples. These regulations and practices—organized in Islamic law under the categories of marriage, divorce, and inheritance—have guided Muslim societies and determined attitudes and values throughout the history of Islam.

The centrality of marriage in Islam is captured by the tradition of the Prophet, which says, "There shall be no monkery in Islam." Marriage is incumbent on every Muslim man and woman unless they are financially or physically unable. It is regarded as the norm for all, a safeguard on chastity, and essential to the growth and stability of the family, the basic unit of society. Marriage is regarded as a sacred contract or covenant, but not a sacrament, legalizing intercourse and the procreation of children. It is not simply a legal contract between two individuals but between two families. Thus, in the traditional practice of arranged marriages, the families or guardians, not the prospective bride and groom, are the primary actors. They identify suitable partners and finalize the marriage contract. The official marriage ceremony is quite simple. It consists of an offer and acceptance

As in other world religions, in Islam marriage is solemnized in a religious ceremony. This Baghdad wedding is an occasion for great joy and celebration among the couple's family and friends.

by the parties (the representatives of the bride and groom) at a meeting before two witnesses. This is followed later by a family celebration. The preferred marriage is between two Muslims and within the extended family. Whereas a Muslim man can marry a non-Muslim woman (i.e., a Christian or a Jew, "People of the Book") (5:6), Muslim women are prohibited from marrying non-Muslims (2:221). As in other religions, in Islam marriage is solemnized in a religious ceremony. This Baghdad wedding is an occasion for great joy and celebration among the couple's family and friends.

Islamic law embodies a number of Quranic reforms that significantly enhanced the status of women. Contrary to pre-Islamic Arab customs, the Quran recognized a woman's right to contract her own marriage. In addition, she, not her father or other male relatives as had been the custom, was to receive the dower from her husband (4:4). She became a party to the contract rather than simply an object for sale. The right to keep and maintain her own dowry was a source of self-esteem and wealth in an otherwise male-dominated society. Women's right to own and manage their own property was further enhanced and acknowledged by the Quranic verses of inheritance (4:7, 11–12, 176), which granted inheritance rights to wives, daughters, sisters, and grandmothers of the deceased in a patriarchal society where all rights were traditionally vested solely in male heirs. Similar legal rights would not occur in the West until the nineteenth century.

Although it is found in many religious and cultural traditions, polygamy (or more precisely, polygyny) is most often identified with Islam in the minds of Westerners. In fact, the Quran and Islamic law sought to control and regulate the number of wives rather than give free license. In a society where no limitations existed, Muslims were not told to marry four wives but instead to marry no more than four. The Quran permits a man to marry up to four wives, provided he can support and treat them all equally. Muslims regard this Quranic command (4:3) as strengthening the status of women and the family, for it sought to ensure the welfare of single women and widows in a society whose male population was diminished by warfare and to curb unrestricted polygamy: "If you are afraid you shall not be able to deal justly with the orphans, marry women of your choice, two or three or four; but if you shall not be able to deal justly [with them] only one."

Islamic law prescribes that co-wives are to be treated equally in terms of support and affection. This includes separate housing (depending on finances, a room, an apartment, or a house) and maintenance. As we shall see, a subsequent verse of the Quran ("You are never able to be fair and just between women even if that is your ardent desire" [4:129]) has been used in modern times by some Muslims to reject the possibility of equal justice among wives and to therefore argue that the Quran preached a monogamous ideal.

The relationship of a husband and wife is viewed as complementary, reflecting their differing characteristics, capacities, and dispositions and the roles of men and women in the traditional patriarchal family. The primary arena for men is the public sphere; they are to support and protect the family and to deal with the "outside" world, the world beyond the family. Women's primary role is that of wife and mother, managing the household, raising children, supervising their religious and moral training. Although both are equally responsible before God to lead virtuous lives, in family matters and in society women are subordinate to men by virtue of their more sheltered lives, protected status, and the broader responsibilities of men in family affairs. Because men were responsible for the economic well-being of all of the women in the extended family, their portion of inheritance was twice that of women. Similarly, because men had more extensive experience in society, in legal affairs the testimony of two women was regarded as equal to that of one man.

Divorce
Alongside the popular images of polygamy, veiling, and seclusion is that of a man's unilateral right to dismiss his wife simply by declaring, "I divorce you." However, ideally divorce is a last resort, discouraged rather than encouraged in Islam. This attitude is preserved in an often-cited tradition of the Prophet that states that "of all the permitted things, divorce is the most abominable with God."[11] The Quran counsels arbitration between

spouses: "If you fear a split between a man and his wife, send for an arbiter from his family and an arbiter from her family. If both want to be reconciled, God will arrange things between them" (4:35). One of the clearest indications of the negative attitude toward divorce, yet reluctant acceptance of it by jurists as a last resort, occurs in the Hedaya, a legal manual, which describes divorce as

> a dangerous and disapproved procedure as it dissolves marriage, an institution which involves many circumstances as well of a temporal as a spiritual nature; nor is its propriety at all admitted, but on the ground of urgency of relief from an unsuitable wife.[12]

However, the Islamic ideal was often compromised by social realities.

Faced with a situation in which Arab custom enabled a man to divorce at will and on whim while women had no grounds for divorce, the Quran and Islamic law established guidelines for men and rights for women based on considerations of equity and responsibility, values that exemplified the Quranic admonition to husbands who were separated and contemplating divorce to "either retain them [their wives] honorably or release them honorably" (65:2).

Several methods of divorce were introduced to constrain a man's unbridled right to repudiate his wife and to establish a woman's right to a judicial (court) divorce. The most common form of divorce is a man's repudiation (*talaq*) of his wife. The approved forms were: (1) a husband's single pronouncement of divorce ("I divorce you"), to take effect after a three-month mandatory waiting period had elapsed to make sure the wife was not pregnant (to determine paternity and maintenance) and to allow time for reconsideration and reconciliation; and (2) the pronouncement of the words of divorce three times, once each in three successive months. At any time during the three months, the couple can nullify the divorce by word or action, such as resuming living together. However, at the end of the three months, the second form of divorce becomes final and irrevocable. The couple may not remarry unless there is an intervening marriage—that is, the wife must have remarried, consummated the marriage, and then divorced. The third form of divorce, more common and problematic, is the husband's pronouncement of the words of divorce three times at once. In this case, the divorce takes effect immediately rather than at the end of a three-month waiting period, bypassing the Quranically mandated waiting period for determining paternity and maintenance obligations and the opportunity for reconciliation. Although this form of divorce is regarded as an unapproved innovation or deviation (*talaq al-bida*, a deviant repudiation), and therefore sinful, it is legally valid. The allowance of this disapproved, although legal, form of divorce is a good example of the extent to which custom was able at times to contradict and circumvent revelation in the development of law:

> When you divorce women, divorce them when they have reached their period. Count their periods   and fear God your Lord. Do not expel them from their houses .... Those are limits set by God. (65:1)

The strong influence of custom is also evident in the more limited divorce rights of women. In pre-Islamic times, Arab women had no divorce rights. In contrast, the Quran states, "Women have rights similar to those [men] over them; while men stand a step above them" (2:228). In the elaboration of Islamic law, the *ulama* extended rights to women while retaining the dominant status of men. In contrast to men, women who wished a divorce had to go before a court and had to have grounds for their action. A wife can sue for divorce if her husband has previously delegated a right to divorce in their marriage contract. She may also request a judicial divorce on such grounds as impotence, insanity, desertion, or nonmaintenance. These grounds varied within the law schools; some were more liberal than others in their interpretation.

Historically, divorce rather than polygamy has been the more serious social problem. This situation has been compounded by the fact that many women have been unable to exercise their legal rights because they were unaware of them or because of pressures in a male-dominated society.

Inheritance

Prior to Islam, the rules of inheritance were concerned solely with the strength and solidarity of the male-dominated tribe. Therefore, inheritance was kept within the male line (patrilineal). Women in Arabia, as in many cultures, were excluded from inheritance, which passed in its entirety to the nearest male relative of the deceased, on whom they were totally dependent. However, Quranic reforms in inheritance strengthened the rights of individual family members, especially women. New rules of inheritance were superimposed on existing practices. The Quran gave rights of inheritance to wives, daughters, sisters, and grandmothers of the deceased, all of whom had previously had no rights. These new "Quranic heirs" received a fixed share from the estate before the inheritance passed to the nearest male relative of the deceased. Only after these Quranic claims were satisfied was the residue of the estate awarded to the senior male.

Veiling and Seclusion of Women

Nothing illustrates more the interaction of Quranic prescription and customary practice than the development of the veiling (**hijab**, *burqa*, or *chador*) and seclusion (*purdah*, harem) of women in early Islam. Both are customs assimilated from the conquered Persian and Byzantine societies and viewed as appropriate expressions of Quranic norms and values. The Quran does not mandate veiling or seclusion. On the contrary, it tends to emphasize the participation and religious responsibility of both men and women in society. However, the Quran does say that the wives of the Prophet should speak to men from behind a partition (*hijab*) and admonishes women to dress modestly:

> And say to the believing women that they should lower their gaze and guard their modesty; that they should not display their beauty and charms except what [normally] appears of them; that they should draw their veils over their bosoms and display their beauty only to their husbands, their fathers. (24:31)

Those who argue for veiling cite Prophetic traditions (*hadith*) from which many of the legal stipulations and practices are derived that stress veiling. It should also be noted that the previous verse also enjoins modesty for men as well as women: "Tell the believing men to lower their gaze and be modest" (24:30).

The Quran and Islamic tradition enjoin modesty, and thus everyone is required to wear modest dress. The diversity of attire found across the Muslim world is reflected in this group of young Muslim women in the United States. Although all are dressed modestly, some wear a headscarf (hijab) and others do not.

In 2014, the White House held a conference featuring leading American Muslims and aspiring young Muslim women. In this group picture, the women display the wide variety of modes of dress across generations, with and without head covering.

The extent to which foreign practices were adopted and legitimated by Quranic interpretation may be seen in the exegesis of al-Baydawi, a thirteenth-century Persian Muslim and one of the most renowned Quranic scholars, who wrote regarding this verse of the Quran:

> Indeed the whole of the body is to be regarded as pudental and no part of her may lawfully be seen by anyone but her husband or close kin, except in case of need, as when she is undergoing medical treatment or giving evidence.[13]

Veiling and seclusion had as their original intent the protection, honor, and distinction of women. They were adopted by upper-class urban women, who lived in great palaces and had mobility and opportunity to participate in activities within their environment. Village and rural women were slower to adopt these practices, as they interfered with their ability to work in the fields. Over the centuries, as the segregation of women in the home spread to every stratum of society, it had unforeseen and deleterious effects. Poorer women were confined to small houses with limited social contacts. They were effectively barred from community life. Because the mosque served as the center of community life, to the extent that women ceased to worship publicly in the mosque they were cut off from social and educational activities. The prominent Egyptian religious scholar Muhammad al-Ghazzali (d. 1996) once claimed: "Ninety percent of our women do not pray at all; nor do they know of the other duties of Islam any more than their names."[14]

To the extent that tribal customs prevailed in the development of Islamic law and in Muslim practice, both the letter and the spirit of Quranic reforms were weakened or subverted by practices such as the *talaq al-bida*. Similarly, despite Quranic passages that talk about the rights of women and counsel that they be treated justly and equitably, regulations were enacted such as the "house of obedience," which requires that a woman obtain her husband's permission to leave the house. If she fails to do so, he may ask the police to forcibly return her and may confine her until she becomes more obedient.

The force of custom can also be seen in the ways in which social customs often contradicted the precepts of Islamic law. Despite a woman's Quranic and legal right to contract her marriage and receive the dower, marriage was often simply arranged by the bride's father and the dower functioned as a bride price given to her family. Thus, she remained the object of sale rather than the subject of a contractual agreement. Women's inheritance rights were also often ignored. Given the social structure of the family, awarding married daughters their rightful share in their

This miniature painting from a sixteenth-century Persian manuscript illustrates the visit of a famous teacher to a mosque. Men and boys sat separately from women and children in different parts of the mosque. The painter showed the children playing among the women and the women relaxing with each other. Such scenes are common in mosques today.

father's estate was often regarded as giving wealth to another, her husband's family. Finally, the pressures of a strong patriarchal society often militated against women exercising their legal right to divorce. As a result, in practice, men could still legally divorce at will and for any reason (a wife's sickness, failure to produce a son), free from legal, although not moral, sanction.

Historically, although the Sharia technically was the sole law and a ruler's source of legitimacy, in fact Islamic empires and states had two complementary legal systems—Sharia courts, which were increasingly restricted to family law and the handling of religious endowments, and Grievance courts, which dealt with public law (criminal, land, and commercial regulations). Although the Sharia remained an essential and integral part of Islamic government, it was only part of a legal system in which the ruler was able to exercise his authority and influence through his power to restrict the scope and jurisdiction of Sharia courts, appoint and fire its judges, issue his own ordinances, and guide his courts. The Sharia set out the law to be followed, but it did not provide constitutional or (independent) judicial restraints. Its ideal nature was reflected in a law that presumed a good Muslim ruler. When faced with the question of what to do about a tyrant, the majority (Sunni) position accepted obedience to the ruler rather than the disorder of civil strife, provided the ruler recognized the supremacy of the Sharia. Acknowledgment by the ruler that the Sharia was the state's official law preserved both the unity and the Islamic character or framework of the community. The supremacy of Islamic law as the eternally valid expression of the straight path of Islam for state and society prevailed both as an ideal and in the practice of official government recognition.

Sufism: The Mystic Path of Love and Knowledge of God

Alongside the exterior path of law (*sharia*) is the interior path or way (*tariqa*) of Sufi mysticism, a major popular religious movement within Sunni and Shii Islam. Whereas the Sharia provided the exoteric way of duties and rights to order the life of the individual and community, **Sufism** offered an esoteric path or spiritual discipline, a method by which the Sufi sought not only to follow but also to know God. Like other mystical movements in Christianity, Judaism, Hinduism, and Buddhism, the Sufi path is a way of purification (*tasawwuf*), a discipline of mind and body with the goal of directly experiencing the ultimate reality. In later generations, Sufism swept across the Islamic world as Sufis became the great missionaries and popular preachers of Islam in Asia and Africa.

While the traditional Islamic way of life was expressed officially and formally in Islamic law, there developed within the Islamic community individuals for whom mere following or obedience to the will of God was

THE SUFI PATH

At the heart of Sufism's worldview and spirituality is the belief that one must die to self (ego-centered self) to become aware of and live in the presence of God. For guidance in the way, Sufis relied on a teacher or master (shaykh or *pir*), one whose authority was based on direct personal religious experience. The master leads his or her disciples through the successive stages of renunciation of the transient phenomenal world, purification, prayer, and insight. Along the way, God is believed to reward and encourage the disciple through special blessings and religious experiences or states of consciousness.

not totally satisfying. Reacting with disdain and dismay to the worldly seductions of imperial Islam, they were motivated by a desire to return to what they regarded as the purity and simplicity of the Prophet's time and driven by a deep devotional love of God that culminated in a quest for a direct, personal experience of the presence of God in this life. These men and women pursued an ascetic lifestyle that emphasized detachment from the material world, which, they believed, distracted Muslims from God, repentance for sins, fear of God, and the Last Judgment. Many took to wearing simple, coarse woolen garments; their detachment from material concerns earned them the name *faqir* or, in Persian, *darwish* (poor or mendicant). Dedicated to a life of prayer and fasting, they meditated on the words of the Quran, seeking deeper or hidden guidance, and scrupulously gathered and imitated the example of the Prophet, strongly motivated by fear of God and His judgment on the Last Day.

Many of the early Sufis were critics and opponents of the Umayyads. They included early *ulama* (*hadith* scholars, jurists, and theologians), who sought to check Umayyad extravagances and refocus the vision and goals of the community. Hasan al-Basri (643–728), an eminent scholar, typifies the ascetic reaction to what they regarded as the decadence of imperial Islam:

> The lower (material) world is a house whose inmates labor for loss, and only abstention from it makes one happy in it. He who befriends it in desire and love for it will be rendered wretched by it, and his portion with God will be laid waste.... For this world has neither worth nor weight with God, so slight it is.[15]

The early emphasis on ascetic practices and detachment from worldly pleasures and meditation was complemented by the contribution of Rabia al-Adawiyya (d. 801), who fused asceticism with an undying devotional love of God. Her joining of the ascetic with the ecstatic permanently influenced the nature and future development of Sufism. An attractive and desirable woman, Rabia declined offers of marriage, not willing to permit anyone or anything to distract her from dedication and total commitment to God. She attracted a circle of followers for whom she served as an example and a guide. Perhaps nothing captures better the selfless devotion she espoused than the following words attributed to her:

> O my Lord, if I worship Thee from fear of Hell, burn me in hell, and if I worship Thee in hope of Paradise, exclude me thence, but if I worship Thee for Thine own sake, then withhold not from me Thine Eternal Beauty.[16]

The joining of devotionalism with asceticism transformed Sufism from its relatively limited elite base into a movement that attracted and embraced all strata of society. Throughout the ninth and tenth centuries, Sufism grew in Arabia, Egypt, Syria, and Iraq. Although its origins and sources (Sufi interpretation of the Quran and life of the Prophet) were clearly Islamic, some outside influences were absorbed from Buddhist monasticism, Hindu devotionalism, Neoplatonism, and the Christian hermits of Egypt (a popular tradition suggests that the word Sufi is a reference to the woolen habits worn by Christian monks).[17]

Mystics like al-Muhasibi of Baghdad (d. 857), Dhu al-Nun of Egypt (d. 859), Junayd of Baghdad (d. 910), and the Persians Abu Yazid al-Bistami (d. 874) and Mansur al-Hallaj (d. 922) made major contributions to the formation of the Sufi way. Their lives and teachings provided the core of beliefs and practices on which later generations would build. They represented a range of mystical doctrines from the "sober" to the "intoxicated," from the doctrinally safe followers of the law and a path of selfless love and service to God to ecstatic rebels like Abu Yazid and al-Hallaj, whose experience of unity with God or of being in union with God drew the ire of many *ulama*. Abu Yazid's consciousness of the transience of the material world and the inner presence of God led him to declare, "Glory to me. How great is my majesty!" Equally blasphemous to orthodox ears was al-Hallaj's claim, "I am the Truth" (*al-Haqq*, one of the traditional ninety-nine names of God) for which he was crucified. However, in his defense, many would argue that his exclamation, "I am the Truth," was not al-Hallaj attributing divinity to himself but that his ecstatic statement reflected or revealed the annihilation of his ego in God and experience that God alone remained.

As Sufism spread in Muslim societies, becoming a mass movement, the gap widened between the Sufi movement and many of the *ulama*, who were often seen by Sufis as co-opted by power, tolerating and supporting the sociopolitical abuses and excesses of the government. As a religious establishment, the *ulama* felt Sufism challenged their authority and prerogatives. Sufis claimed their own authority and guides. They often rejected as religious formalism the official, legal-moral Islam of the *ulama,* seeking to go beyond the letter of the law to its spirit. Sufism claimed to go back beyond religious forms, institutions, and laws to the divine source itself. Although some members of the *ulama* were Sufis, many dismissed Sufi doctrine and practice as heretical, as an unwarranted deviation or innovation from the orthodox consensus of the community. Deep-seated suspicions and hostility led to persecution and even executions, as in the martyrdom of al-Hallaj.

Abu Hamid al-Ghazali: Reconciler and Revivalist
The eleventh and twelfth centuries were a particularly turbulent time in Muslim history. The universal caliphate had disintegrated into a system of decentralized and competing states whose only unity was the symbolic, although powerless, Abbasid caliph in Baghdad. The Ismaili missionary propagandists were actively undermining the Sunni consensus. Muslim philosophers, deeply indebted to Hellenism and Neoplatonism, were offering alternative, and sometimes competing, answers to philosophical and theological questions that often strained or tested the relationship between reason and faith. Sufism had become a mass movement with a strong emotional component and an eclectic propensity to accept superstitious practices. Much of what was taking place seemed out of the reach and control of the *ulama,* many of whom felt that these movements threatened their status and authority in the community. It was the genius and accomplishment of Abu Hamid al-Ghazali (1058–1111) to address all these issues. Amid the turmoil, al-Ghazali emerged, as had al-Shafii centuries earlier, to save the day by providing the needed religious synthesis. His reputed success can be measured by his popular designation as a great reviver (*mujaddid*) of Islam.

Born and raised in Iran, al-Ghazali received the best Islamic education available in his time. After studying at the mosque school in his village of Tus, near modern-day Mashhad, he was trained at Nishapur by the most prominent theologian of the time, al-Juwayni. He mastered law, theology, and philosophy. At a relatively young age, he was appointed in 1091 to the faculty of the Nizamiyya, a theological institute in Baghdad. There, in a series of books, he responded to the challenges posed by the Ismailis and the philosophers. He wrote *The Incoherence of the Philosophers,* in which he refuted those aspects of the philosophy of Avicenna (d. 1037) that he found unacceptable. In particular, he maintained that whereas reason was most effective in mathematics and logic, its application to theological and metaphysical truths merely led to confusion and threatened the fabric of faith.

Al-Ghazali's teaching and writings brought him fame and recognition. Yet, at the peak of his success, he had a spiritual crisis that was to change his life. The brilliant lecturer suddenly found himself unable to speak. Inexplicably, he deteriorated physically and psychologically. Despite his theological knowledge and extraordinary achievements, he felt lost:

> When I considered the circumstances, I saw I was deeply involved in affairs, and that the best of my activities, my teaching, was concerned with branches of knowledge which were unimportant and worthless. I also examined my motive in teaching and saw that it was not sincere desire to serve God but that I wanted an influential position and widespread recognition. I was in no doubt that I stood on an eroding sandbank, and in imminent danger of hell-fire if I did not busy myself with mending my ways.... Worldly desires were trying to keep me chained where I was, while the herald of faith was summoning, "To the road! To the road! Little of life is left, and before you is a long journey. Your intellectual and practical involvements are hypocrisy and delusion. If you do not prepare for the future life now, when will you prepare; if you do not sever your attachments now, when will you sever them?"[18]

Desperate, al-Ghazali resigned his position, left his home and family, and withdrew to Syria, where he studied and practiced Sufism:

> I turned to the way of the mystics.... [I] obtained a thorough intellectual understanding of their principles. Then I realized that what is most distinctive of them can be obtained only by personal experience ["taste," *dhawq*], ecstasy and a change of character.... I saw clearly that the mystics were men of personal experience not of words, and that I had gone as far as possible by way of study and intellectual application, so that only personal experience and walking in the mystic way were left.[19]

For many years, al-Ghazali studied and practiced Sufism, traveling, after his initial stay in Syria, to Sufi centers in Palestine and Arabia. During this period, he wrote what many regard as his greatest work, *The Revivification of the Religious Sciences*, his great synthesis of law, theology, and mysticism. Law and theology were presented in terms that the *ulama* could accept, but these disciplines were grounded in direct religious experience and interior devotion. Rationalism was tempered by Sufism's emphasis on religious experience and love of God. It proved to be a brilliant tour de force, reassuring the *ulama* about the orthodoxy of Sufism and countering the rationalism of the philosophers.

In both his life and his work, al-Ghazali represented the intellectual and spiritual currents of his times. At the end, he had achieved an integration and religious synthesis that earned him a place as one of Islam's great scholars and the title, "Renewer of Islam," a designation based on the popular belief that in each century an individual (*mujaddid*) will come to restore and revitalize the Muslim community, to renew (*taidid*) Islam by returning Muslims to the straight path.[20] Despite continued differences of opinion between the Sufis and many of the *ulama*, al-Ghazali had secured a place for Sufism within the life of the community.

Sufi Orders

The twelfth century proved to be an important turning point both for al-Ghazali's legitimation of Sufism and because of the formation of the first great Sufi orders. In the last years of his life, al-Ghazali had established one of the first Sufi centers or compounds (*zawiyya*), where followers gathered to live and be trained by their spiritual guide. As Sufism became a mass movement, attracting people of all social classes and educational backgrounds, similar centers sprang up and multiplied. Sufism began to be transformed from loose, voluntary associations into organized brotherhoods or religious orders (*tariga*) of mendicants with their own distinctive institutions. Prior to this time, Sufism had tended to be concentrated in urban areas among religious elites who met at mosques or in private homes. Now the spiritual family was organized more formally as a community. By the thirteenth century, Sufi orders had created international networks of centers that transformed Sufism into a popular mass movement whose preachers were the great missionaries of Islam. Among the early founders was Abd al-Qadir al-Jilani, among the most universally celebrated saints of popular Islam from Morocco to the Philippines.

Organizationally, Sufi orders built on the already established relationship of master (**shaykh**, or Persian, **pir**) and student or disciple. Sufi masters drew their authority from their illustrious predecessors. As the authority of traditions was based on a system of links dating back to the Prophet, so too a similar system of linkages of pious predecessors was established going all the way back to Muhammad. Spiritual pedigree or lineage was the source of a master's religious authority, teachings, and practices. Because of his piety, reputation for sanctity, and often miraculous powers, the master was viewed as especially near to God, a friend of God. He served as a spiritual guide and a model to be emulated: his followers wished to be near him to benefit from his teaching, advice, and example as well as to receive his blessing, the product of his spiritual power. Over time the teachings of masters were passed on through their disciples to future generations.

Sufi centers served as the spiritual, social, and cultural center of the community. They consisted of a collection or compound of buildings, which might include the residence of the shaykh and his family, a separate room for recollection, living quarters for his disciples, a mosque, a kitchen, a hospice for visitors, and a school. The focal point was the master's residence. The shaykh would lead prayers, instruct and train, guide and advise individuals, and oversee communal life. Membership was of two kinds: full-time professed members and associate or affiliated members. Professed disciples were those who, after a period of training, were initiated into the order. This ceremony included investiture with the distinctive garb and cap of the order, which symbolized obedience to the rule of the order. The initiate swore an oath of allegiance to his shaykh and clasped his hand, receiving his blessing. Disciples lived nearby in the center, devoting themselves to study, spiritual exercises, and the upkeep and activities of the center. These included a soup kitchen to feed the poor and hungry, care for the sick, a hospice for visitors (travelers, pilgrims, other Sufis), and religious education. Centers were often established and subsidized by pious endowments that permitted the master and his disciples to pursue their spiritual path, free from secular employment and concerns. A large number, often the majority, of members had an associate status, somewhat like "third-order" members of Christian religious orders. These lay associates "lived in the world," engaged in the everyday activities of working and raising families. However, they were also subject to the authority of the shaykh, sought his guidance and advice, participated in community services, and performed the important task of financially supporting the center and its activities. Often associate members formed neighborhoods or even villages around Sufi centers.

Sufi orders developed their own forms of monastic rule that detailed the regulations by which the dervishes or *faqirs* were to live. These varied from order to order and from one geographic area to another. In one of the earliest sets of rules, we find regulations common to many orders, such as:

> 1) The disciple should keep his garments clean and be always in a state of ritual purity.... 2) One should not sit in a holy place gossiping....
> 5) At dawn a disciple should pray for forgiveness.... 6) Then, in the early morning, he should read the Koran, abstaining from talk until sunrise.... 7) Between the two evening prayers, he should be occupied with his recollection [*dhikr*] and the special litany [*wird*] which is given

to him by his master.... 8) The Sufi should welcome the poor and needy, and look after them.[21]

Under the tutelage of a shaykh, disciples progressed along the Sufi path of virtue and spiritual knowledge. The master assigned them prayers to recite and meditate on, monitored and evaluated their progress, and, finally, authenticated their spiritual experiences and insights. He designated the more advanced as *khalifa*, successors. A *khalifa* might be designated to succeed the shaykh after his death, or he might be sent to head one of the centers of the order. The spiritual power of the shaykh was passed on or inherited by his successor. Although some orders retained the practice of selection or election of the shaykh's successor, many opted for hereditary succession. Leadership of the order often passed to a son or relative of the shaykh, keeping control of the order in family hands.

The focal point of a Sufi order was often the domed tomb of its founder, who was venerated as a saint (*wali*, friend) of God. The tomb became a center for pilgrimage as visitors came to appeal to the saint for assistance. His spiritual power and intercession before God could be invoked for a safe pregnancy, success in exams, or a prosperous business, and offerings were made in thanksgiving for answered prayers. Once each year, a great celebration was held to commemorate the anniversary of his birth or death. Pilgrims would come from near and far for several days of rituals, songs or spiritual concerts, and celebration.

The Way: Doctrine and Practice

At the heart of **Sufism** is the belief that one's self must die, that is, one must undergo annihilation (*fana*) of the lower, ego-centered self to abide or rest (*baqa*) in God. Renunciation of that which is impermanent and transient, the phenomenal world, is a prerequisite to realization of the divine that resides in all human beings. The goal of the Sufi is direct knowledge or personal religious experience of God's presence. This mystical knowledge or understanding is reached by means of a series of stages and states. The shaykh leads the disciple through successive stages—renunciation, purification, and insight. Along the way, God rewards and encourages the disciple by granting certain religious experiences or psychological states.

To obtain their goal, the Sufis adapted many practices, some of which were foreign, in the eyes of the *ulama*, to early Islamic values. One of the fundamental tensions between the *ulama* and the Sufis was the extent to which the religious brotherhood offered an alternative sense of community, and the shaykh constituted a threat to the religious authority of the *ulama*. Among the predominant Sufi practices employed to break attachment to the material world and rediscover or become aware of God's presence were:

1. Poverty, fasting, silence, celibacy, and other disciplines of mind and body whose object was the letting go of all attachment to and awareness of the self and the phenomenal world. Only then could the Sufi become aware of the divine, which was always present but ordinarily hidden from view by a preoccupation with the material world. Some orders practiced celibacy, but the majority did not. The interpretation and practice of poverty varied as well. Each order and master had a distinctive approach.

2. Remembrance or recollection of God through a rhythmic, repetitive invocation of God's name(s), accompanied by breathing exercises, to focus consciousness on God and place the devotee in His presence. By themselves or sitting with their shaykh in community worship, Sufis repeated or recalled God's name hundreds and thousands of times for hours during the day or throughout the night. Another form of recollection is the recitation of a litany of God's names or attributes, often counted on a string of prayer beads, similar to a rosary. To become absorbed in recitation is to forget about worldly attachments and rest in God.

3. The use of music and song, spiritual concerts of devotional poems, as well as dance or bodily movements to induce or trigger ecstatic states in which the devotee could experience the presence of God or union with God. Although orthodoxy remained critical, music and dance proved especially popular among the people as a quick way to become intoxicated on God, to experience deep feelings of love for God and to feel His nearness. Groups of Sufis would gather to sing God's praises and loving hymns to Muhammad, or other great leaders like Ali, begging their intercession and assistance. The most famous example of the use of dance is that of the whirling dervishes, followers of the order founded by Jalal al-Din Rumi. Their whirling dance imitated the order of the universe. As dervishes spun in a circle around their shaykh, so, some claimed, did the planets revolve around the sun, the axis or center of the universe.

4. Veneration of Muhammad and Sufi saints as intermediaries between God and people. Muhammad had emphasized that he was only a human being and not a miracle worker. Despite this emphasis in official Islamic belief, the role of the Prophet as a model for Muslim life had early led to extravagant stories about Muhammad's life and extraordinary powers. This tendency became pronounced in Sufi

This circle of Chechen women recite zikr, or remembrance of God in rhythmic song. Such circles of men and women, sometimes mixed, are one expression of Sufism.

piety. Muhammad was viewed as the link between God and man. The most extraordinary powers were attributed to him, given his closeness to God. These wonders were extended to Sufi saints, the friends or protégés of God. Miraculous powers (curing the sick, bilocation, reading minds, multiplication of food) and stories of saintly perfection abounded. Sufi theory organized the saints into a hierarchy, at the apex of which stood Muhammad, the pole of the universe, supervising the world. Shaykhs were venerated during their lifetime; they were honored, loved, and feared because of their miraculous powers. After their death, their burial sites or mausoleums became religious sanctuaries, objects of pilgrimage and of petitions for success in this life as well as the next, for worldly gains as well as eternal life.

The very characteristics that accounted for the strength of Sufism and its effectiveness and success as a popular religious force contributed to its degeneration. That same flexibility, tolerance, and eclecticism that had enabled Islam to spread and incorporate local customs and practices from Africa to Southeast Asia and attract many converts permitted bizarre and antinomian practices. Sufism's healthy concern about legalism and ritual formalism gave way to the rejection by many of official religious observances and laws. Sacred song and dance resulted not only in spiritual intoxication but also in drunkenness and sensuality. Awareness of the divine presence in all of creation became a justification for saint worship, fetishism, and superstitious practices. Mystic/mendicants (*faqir*) of a movement that emphasized poverty and asceticism now came to be regarded as fakers; spiritual heads of some mendicant orders became wealthy feudal landlords.

Sufi excesses came to be regarded as a primary cause of Muslim decline from the seventeenth century onward, and Sufism was subject to suppression and reform by some premodern and modern Islamic revivalist and reformist movements. However, despite these setbacks, Sufism also continued to flourish among many of the *ulama* and the populace, for example, in the Ottoman empire and late Mughal and early British India. Genuine Sufis continued to write, teach, and guide followers. Moreover, a majority of nineteenth- and twentieth-century revivalist movements were linked to Sufism, and even many of the jihad movements against imperial rule were led by Sufis.[22]

Shii Religious Practices

In contrast to official Sunni Islamic ambivalence and/or rejection of popular religious practices, such as visiting the shrines or tombs of saints and belief in their intercession, Shii Islam's worldview incorporated a number of such beliefs and ritual practices. This difference was rooted in their different orientations. For Sunnis, God and human beings have a direct relationship; the *ulama* are not intermediaries but scholar-interpreters of religion. Thus, belief in saintly intermediaries was often viewed as heretical or, more precisely, dangerous deviation (*bida*). For Shii, intercession is an integral part of the divine plan for salvation. Ali and the other Imams were divinely inspired models, guides, and intermediaries between God and the believers. In their absence, the *ulama* or *mujtahids* and local religious leaders (*mullas*) served as community guides, although they had no intermediary or intercessory powers. This belief developed later in contemporary Iran under Ayatollah Khomeini and his idea of *wilayat al-faqih,* the belief that, in the absence of the Imam, a distinguished cleric (or clerics) might serve as the supreme religious guide (*faqih*) and authority. It was not a universal belief in pre-Khomeini Shiism among most Shii religious authorities or in contemporary Shiism among many, including Iraq's Ayatollah Ali al-Sistani, arguably the most influential Shii Ayatollah in the world today.

The special place and veneration of the Imams generated a rich set of religious symbols and rituals that were accepted as integral to Shiism, rather than, as would have been the case in Sunni Islam, peripheral. The central figures are the Fourteen Pure or Perfect Ones.

They consist of (1) the Prophet, Ali and Fatima, and their sons Hasan and Husayn and (2) the remaining nine Imams. Ali and the Imams are the means to an intellectual, esoteric, and legal understanding and interpretation of revelation. They serve as charismatic, infallible, divinely inspired leaders of the community as well as models of suffering and sacrifice in the face of tyranny and oppression. Veneration for the Holy Family is reflected in the special place and honorific title that their descendants have claimed throughout Islamic history, an attitude found in Sunni Islam as well.

Like Sufism, Shiism places great value on the intercession of saints, the "friends" of God who mediate God's grace and blessings to the believers. As in Christianity, suffering and compassion, martyrdom and sacrifice, and atonement and redemption are central motifs in salvation history. In contrast to the Sunni, Shii believe that the intercession of the Imams is a necessary part of history, from the redemptive death of Husayn to the return of the Hidden Imam at the end of time:

> The Imams are also the intermediaries between man and God. To ask for their succour is to appeal to the channel God placed before man so as to enable man to return to him.[23]

Along with those holy days that they share with their Sunni coreligionists, Shii also mourn and celebrate the birthdays and death anniversaries of the Imams. Moreover, a major form of devotion is the visitation of the tomb-shrines of the Holy Family and Imams at Karbala, Kazimiyya, Najaf, Kufa, Qum, and Mashhad. These holy sites draw hundreds of thousands of pilgrims throughout the year. Historically, for financial reasons and ease of access, these pilgrimages have been more popular and common than the *hajj*.

Husayn's Martyrdom and the Rituals of Ashura

Husayn and Fatima serve as major male and female religious symbols, on whom believers are to meditate and pattern their lives. Husayn's martyrdom at Karbala on the tenth day (**Ashura**) of the Islamic month of Muharram in 680 is the paradigmatic event of Shii history. Remembrance and ritual reenactment of the tragedy of Karbala is a cornerstone of faith, personal and communal identity, and piety. It accounts for the special vision and character of Twelver Shii Islam as a disinherited, oppressed community, loyal to God and His Prophet, struggling throughout history to restore God's rule and a just society. The martyrdom motif was extended to all the Imams, who, with the exception of the twelfth, were believed to have been martyred. As a result, the "passion" of Husayn symbolized the historic struggle between the forces of good and evil, God and Satan, and the eschatological hope and belief in the ultimate triumph of justice over tyranny when the Imam will return at the end of time.

The pathos and meaning of Husayn's martyrdom—with its themes of oppression, tyranny, martyrdom, social justice, and atonement—are revealed in liturgical manuals that recount the fateful battle. Husayn was drawn into battle by a request from the citizens of Kufa to liberate them from a land

> where an oppressor now rules, who takes wedded wives and virgin daughters for his own pleasure, and extracts money with threats and violence. It is better to execute a tyrant than to allow the government of sinners. If you, Prince Husayn, do not rescue us from corruption and injustice, we shall accuse you on the Day of Judgment of neglecting your duty, we swear this by the Almighty.[24]

Husayn then set out from Mecca to Kufa with but seventy-seven followers. Along the way he was tested by God but overcame all temptation. Husayn and his army encountered the Syrian forces of the Sunni Umayyad caliph Yazid:

> The Syrians avoided man-to-man battle because Husayn and his men had a reputation as warriors and the Syrians were cowards who limited themselves to shooting arrows at the Alids from behind safe positions. For the sake of the women and children who were with them, Husayn's men tried to fight their way through to the river in the hope of fetching water for those parched creatures.[25]

However, after hours of battle, the the vast Syrian army overcame the small band of Husayn's followers. The casualties included Husayn's eldest and youngest sons as well as the son of Husayn's brother Hasan who, Shii tradition reports, had gallantly killed more than three thousand of the enemy before he, too, fell in battle. Finally, Husayn set out for his final confrontation. The meaning of this event and the intensity of religious belief and feeling it inspires is captured in a scene movingly recalled in Shii religious literature:

> In spite of his admonition, all the women wept bitter tears, and so did the children. Even the angels in heaven cried sadly, and the animals in the wilderness and the birds in the sky lamented in mournful songs; even the fish in the ocean wept.... He mowed down his enemies like a fire raging through the tall grass of the savannah. The earth grew bloodied

and the sky grew dark as if the Day of Judgment had begun. Dark clouds veiled the sun even in Mecca so that its people wondered what caused this gloom which covered Arabia, Syria, and Egypt, reaching as far as Iran and Khurasan .... A voice was heard: Husayn! The enemy has overrun your tent! / The women have been taken and the children killed! / He turned his horse and hurried back to the camp. There in the shrubs the enemy were waiting. They shot at him without their faces showing / Hundreds of arrows flew into his face / Seventy arrows hit his tender body / and pierced the skin and spilled his precious blood. / He knew that he did not have long to live / Just enough time to say: There is no god / but God and Muhammed is His prophet. / His soul flew up into the cloudless sky where it was met by those who loved him most: / His parents and his brother and his sons .... Here ends the sad account of Prince Husayn / Who lived and died a witness for the faith / A ransom for his people, for Mankind.[26]

Fatima, "the Mother of the Imams," has a special claim and role in Shii piety due to her special place in the family of the Prophet. She was the Prophet's only surviving child, the wife of Imam Ali, and the mother of the imams Husayn and Hasan. Her unique status is captured by a widely cited tradition of the Prophet: "Fatima is a part of my body. Whoever hurts her, has hurt me, and whoever hurts me has hurt God."[27] Fatima is the primal mother figure, immaculate and sinless, the pattern for virtuous women, the object of prayer and petition. Like her son Husayn, she embodies a life of dedication, suffering, and compassion. Tradition portrays her as, despite often leading a life of poverty and destitution, sharing whatever she had with others. Like the Virgin Mary in Christian tradition, Fatima is portrayed as a woman of sorrow, symbolizing the rejection, disinheritance, and martyrdom of her husband and sons.

In addition to the *salat* (daily prayer), Shiism developed a number of ritual practices that became major forms of piety and were regarded as earning spiritual merit. All are centered on the tragedy of Karbala, commemorated each year during the month of Muharram through dramatic recitations, passion plays (*taziya*), and street processions. The purpose of these ceremonies is remembrance and mourning. Participants experience profound grief, pain, and sorrow in emotional ceremonies marked by lamentation, breast-beating, weeping, and flagellation as the tragedy and heroism of Husayn are relived. Some of its aspects are reminiscent of practices found at times in a number of Christian contexts: "The Muharram processions are, perhaps, more similar to the Passion Week celebrations which can still be seen in such Christian countries as Guatemala."[28]

Through ritual reenactment and identification with the suffering and patient endurance of Husayn and his family, Shii seek to atone for their sins, merit salvation, and hasten the final triumph:

> Thus lamentations for Husayn enable the mourners not only to gain assurance of divine forgiveness, but also to contribute to the triumph of the Shii cause. Accordingly, Husayn's martyrdom makes sense on two levels: first, in terms of a soteriology not dissimilar from the one invoked in the case of Christ's crucifixion: just as Christ sacrificed himself on the altar of the cross to redeem humanity, so did Husayn allow himself to be killed on the plains of Karbala to purify the Muslim community of sins; and second, as an active factor, vindicating the Shii cause, contributing to its ultimate triumph.[29]

Remembrance of the passion and death of Husayn, like that of Christ in Christianity, occurs not only annually, during the month of Muharram, but also daily. The recitation of sacred stories in homes and specially constructed halls and the performance of passion plays in special theaters, which focus on Husayn and other great Shii martyrs, take place throughout the year in villages, towns, and cities. They constitute popular forms of piety and entertainment and a distinctive way of preserving and reappropriating a sacred history and heritage.

CONCLUSION

As we have seen, despite the unity of Islam, rooted in belief in one God, from the early centuries of Islam, devout Muslims produced a diversity of interpretations. Human understanding and interpretation of sacred texts, influenced by local custom and traditions as well as by reliance on reason, produced multiple and at times contending paradigms. These were reflected in the development of legal, theological, and mystical paths and schools of thought. Common possession of a single revealed sacred scripture yielded many exegetical works (*tafsirs*), whose authors, while striving to remain faithful to the Quran, produced interpretations influenced by their historical and social contexts. The desire to follow the teachings and example (Sunna) of Muhammad led to the collection and preservation of thousands, if not hundreds of thousands of traditions, covering a broad spectrum of diverse topics. Some traditions were authentic, others spurious, but all were capable of sustaining multiple interpretations and norms for Muslim life. Similarly, legal scholars, however much revealed texts served as their reference point, also relied on their intellects and insights and borrowed from the wisdom of their past and the present, customary law as well as Byzantine and Jewish laws.

Hadith scholars, reacting to what they regarded as the dangerous use of personal interpretation or opinion by jurists, sought to limit and circumscribe reason, insisting that Prophetic traditions alone should be employed to corroborate or elaborate Quranic teachings. Muslims, they believed, were to follow God's teaching as revealed in the Quran and the example of Muhammad, not to interpret or create supplementary doctrines and practices.

Early Islamic theological schools struggled over the relationship of reason to revelation both among themselves and in response to the emergence of Muslim philosophers, many of whom were strongly influenced by Greek philosophy. And finally, the Sufis, reacting to the legalism of the Sharia-minded and the intellectual debates of theologians and philosophers, sought to experience and live in the immediacy of God's presence and love. The tensions between reason and revelation, legalism and spirituality, unity and diversity have continued to be played out down to the present.

While the Five Pillars and the Sharia remain the common basis of faith and practice for all Muslims, Islam incorporated a variety of beliefs and activities that grew out of religious and historical experience and the needs of specific Muslim communities. The inherent unity of faith, implicit in statements like "one God, one Book, one [final] Prophet," should not deter one from appreciating the rich diversity that has characterized the religious (legal, theological, and devotional) life of the Islamic community.

KEY TERMS

Ashura	*kalam*
assassins	mufti
dawa	*mujaddid*
faqih	*purdah*
fatwa	*qadi*
fiqh	Sharia
hadith	shaykh or *pir*
hijab	Sufism
ijtihad	*taqlid*
iman	*tariqa*
kafir	*ulama*

QUESTIONS

1. Are "belief" and "practice" opposed to each other? Is Islam better understood through one of these categories?

2. Does Islamic theology go beyond the affirmations of the shahada (profession of faith) and the takbir (declaration of God's oneness)? If so, are there normative Islamic "innovations?"

3. What was the core argument between the Mutazila and the Asharites?

4. What role has Greek philosophy played in shaping Islamic theology? Consider especially al-Ghazali's synthesis.

5. Define "Islamic law." What are its connections to Sharia and *fiqh*? What are the various schools of "orthodox" Islamic law, and what are their most important sources?

NOTES

1. Fazlur Rahman, "The Mesage and the Messenger," in *Islam: The Religious and Political Life of a World Community*, Marjorie Kelly, ed. (New York: Praeger, 1984), p. 43.

2. Morris S. Seale, *Muslim Theology*, 2nd ed. (London: Luzac and Company, 1980), pp. 67–68.

3. Fazlur Rahman, *Islam*, 2nd ed. (Chicago: University of Chicago Press, 1979), p. 91.

4. N. J. Coulson, A *History of Islamic Law* (Edinburgh: Edinburgh University Press, 1964), p. 12.

5. I. Goldziher, *Muslim Studies* (London: Allen & Unwin, 1967), vol. II, pp. 17–254; D. S. Margoliouth, *The Early Development of Mohammedanism* (London: William Norgate, 1914), pp. 65–98; C. Snouck Hurgronje, *Selected Works of C. Snouck Hurgronje*, C. H. Bousquet and Joseph Schacht, eds. (Leiden, Netherlands: E. J. Brill, 1957); Joseph Schacht, *Origins of Muhammadan Jurisprudence* (Oxford: Oxford University Press, 1950), especially pp. 138–76.

6. See, for example, M. Mustafa al-Azami, *Origins of Muhammadan Jurisprudence* (Cambridge, UK: Islamic Texts Society, 1996), and Fazlur Rahman, "Sunna and Hadith," *Islamic Studies* 1 (June 1962), and *Islam*, chap. 3.

7. Rahman, "Sunna and Hadith," p. 4.

8. H. A. R. Gibb, *Mohammedanism* (New York: Oxford University Press, 1962), p. 86.

9. Sherman Jackson, "Jihad and the Modern World," *Journal of Islamic Law and Culture* (Spring/Summer 2002).

10. For a more thorough analysis of Muslim family law, see John L. Esposito, *Women in Muslim Family Law* (Syracuse, NY: Syracuse University Press, 1982).

11. Abu Dawud, *Sunan* (Kanpur, India: Matba Majidi, 1346 A.H.) I: 296.

12. *The Hedaya*, Charles Hamilton, trans., 2nd ed. (Lahore, Pakistan: Premier Book House, 1957), p. 73.

13. R. Levy, *The Social Structure of Islam* (Cambridge: Cambridge University Press, 1955), p. 126.

14. Muhammad al-Ghazali, Our *Beginning in Wisdom*, Ismail R. al-Faruqi, trans. (Washington, DC: American Council of Learned Societies, 1953), p. 111.

15. *Islam*, John Alden Williams, ed. (New York: George Braziller, 1962), pp. 138–39.

16. Margaret Smith, *Rabia the Mystic and Her Fellow-Saints in Islam* (Cambridge: Cambridge University Press, 1928), p. 30.

17. Some scholars had emphasized the influence of outside sources, but more recent scholarship has minimized this influence. See, for example, Carl Ernst, *Shambhala Guide to Sufism* (Boston: Shambhala, 1997), and William Chittick, *Sufism* (New York: Oxford University Press, 2000).

18. W. Montgomery Watt, *Muslim Intellectual: A Study of al-Ghazali* (Edinburgh: Edinburgh University Press, 1963), p. 136. See also W. Montgomery Watt, *The Faith and Practice of al-Ghazali* (London: George Allen & Unwin, 1953).

19. Watt, *Muslim Intellectual,* p. 135.

20. John O. Voll, "Renewal and Reform in Islamic History: *Taidid* and *Isiah*," in *Voices of Resurgent Islam*, John L. Esposito, ed. (New York: Oxford University Press, 1983), p. 33.

21. Reynold A. Nicholson, *Studies in Islamic Mysticism* (Cambridge: Cambridge University Press, 1967), p. 46.

22. See John Voll's *Islam, Continuity and Change in the Modern World* (Syracuse, NY: Syracuse University Press, 1994); Fuad Naeem, "Sufism and Revivalism in South Asia: Mawlana Ashraf Ali Thanvi of Deoband and Ahmad Raza Khan of Bareilly and Their Paradigms of Islamic Revivalism," *Muslim World* 99, no. 3 (July 2009).

23. Seyyed Hossein Nasr, *Ideals and Realities of Islam* (London: George Allen & Unwin, 1966), p. 162.

24. Hamadi ibn Abdullah al-Buhri, *Utenzi wa Sayedina Huseni,* as quoted in *Textual Sources for the Study of Islam*, Andrew Rippon and Jan Knappert, eds. and trans. (New York: Barnes & Noble, 1987), p. 140.

25. Ibid.

26. Ibid., p. 142.

27. Ali Shariati, *Fatima Is Fatima*, Layleh Bakhtiar, trans. (New York: Muslim Students Council, n.d.), p. 136.

28. Peter Chelkowski, *Taziyeh: Ritual and Drama in Iran* (New York: New York University Press, 1979), p. 3.

29. Hamid Enayat, *Modern Islamic Political Thought* (Austin: University of Texas Press, 1982), pp. 182–83.

Chapter 4

Modern Islamic Reform Movements

Although the sultanate period had marked a new and somewhat different beginning after the fall of Baghdad, it began to fall apart by the seventeenth and eighteenth centuries. Political disintegration and social and moral decline once more gripped much of the Muslim world. The internal breakdown of Muslim society was exacerbated by the growing threat from European presence and imperialist designs. Many concerned Muslims and Western observers at that time would have agreed that Islam was a spent force, helpless before the military and political cadres of Europe and rendered religiously impotent by the superstitious and fatalistic tendencies that had infected much of popular Islamic belief and practice. Yet these internal and external threats to the life of the community proved once again to be stimuli for religious revival and reform. Premodern revivalist movements rose up in the eighteenth century to address the social and moral decline, and the nineteenth and twentieth centuries produced the Islamic modernist movement and Islamic societies like the Muslim Brotherhood, which offered Islamic responses to the challenges of European colonialism and modernization. These movements not only contributed to the revitalization of Islam in their own times, they also left a legacy that has informed much of the temper and mood of contemporary Islam. Understanding the background and context of revival and reform, its leadership, and their interpretations of Islam is essential for an appreciation of Islam's dynamism and diversity.

FROM IMPERIAL ISLAM
TO ISLAMIC REVIVALISM

The power, prosperity, and dynamic expansionism of imperial Islam had seriously declined by the eighteenth century. Military revolts and reversals, the decline of a strong central authority, and economic setbacks affected by European competition in trade and manufacturing proved costly. For many of the religiously minded, the causes for this political, military, and economic breakdown were to be found in the spiritual and moral decay that afflicted the community of believers. They believed that the fundamental failure of the community resulted from its departure from true Islam; its revitalization could only come from a return to the straight path of Islam. This call for a moral reconstruction of society did not occur in a vacuum. During the sultanate period, many of the nonofficial *ulama* had concluded that a religious renewal was desirable. This sentiment had an international dimension due to the contacts and exchanges that took place among those scholars who had traveled extensively in their search for knowledge and studied at major Islamic centers of piety and learning in Mecca, Medina, and Cairo (al-Azhar University). At the same time, a new wave of Sufism arose that sought to restrain and purify the excesses of pantheism and eclecticism that had infected Sufism. Influenced by the thought of men like al-Ghazali, Ibn Taymiyya, and Shaykh Ahmad Sirhindi, it reemphasized the importance of divine transcendence and the primacy of the Sharia.[1] These reformist tendencies grew and multiplied with astounding vitality during the eighteenth century, both because the socio-historical conditions were ripe for reform and because the calls for religious renewal occurred within a religious tradition that had strong revivalist precedents and tendencies.

REVIVALISM IN ISLAM

From its earliest days, Islam possessed a tradition of revival and reform. Muslims had been quick to respond to what they regarded as the compromising of faith and practice: Kharijite secession, Shii revolts, the development of Islamic law, and Sufism. In succeeding centuries, a rich revivalist tradition expressed itself in a variety of concepts and beliefs, in the lives and teachings of individual reformers, and in the activities of a host of movements.

The concepts of renewal (*tajdid*) and reform (*islah*) are fundamental components of Islam's worldview, rooted in the Quran and the Sunna of the Prophet.[2] Both concepts involve a call for a return to the fundamentals of Islam (the Quran and Sunna). *Islah* is a Quranic term (7:170, 11:117, 28:19) used to describe the reform preached and undertaken by the prophets when they warned their sinful communities and called on them to return to God's path by realigning their lives, as individuals and as a community, within the norms of the Sharia. This Quranic mandate, epitomized in the lives and preaching of the prophets, especially that of Muhammad, coupled with God's command to enjoin good and prohibit

evil (3:104, 110), provides the time-honored rationale for Islamic reformism, however diverse its manifestations in history.

> In so far as it is on the one hand an individual or collective effort to
> define Islam solely in relation to its authentic sources (i.e. the Kuran and
> the Sunna of the Prophet) and on the other an attempt to work towards
> a situation in which the lives of Muslims, in personal and social terms,
> really would conform to the norms and values of that religion, *islah* is a
> permanent feature in the religious and cultural history of Islam.[3]

Tajdid is based on a tradition of the Prophet: "God will send to this
umma [the Muslim community] at the head of each century those who
will renew its faith for it."[4] The renewer (*mujaddid*) of Islam is believed to
be sent at the beginning of each century to restore true Islamic practice
and thus regenerate a community that tends, over time, to wander from
the straight path. The two major aspects of this process are first, a return
to the ideal pattern revealed in the Quran and Sunna; and second, the
right to practice *ijtihad,* to interpret the sources of Islam. Implicit in
renewal is: (1) the belief that the righteous community established and
guided by the Prophet at Medina already possesses the norm; (2) the
removal of foreign (un-Islamic) historical accretions or unwarranted
innovations (*bida*) that have infiltrated and corrupted community life;
and (3) a critique of established institutions, in particular the religious
establishment's interpretation of Islam. Despite the general tendency
in Sunni Islam after the tenth century to follow (*taqlid*) the consensus of the community, great renewers or revivalists like al-Ghazali,
Ibn Taymiyya, **Muhammad ibn Abd al-Wahhab**, and Shah Wali Allah
claimed the right to function as *muitahids*, practitioners of *ijtihad*, and
thus to reinterpret Islam to purify and revitalize their societies. Both Sufi
excesses and prevailing *ulama* interpretations of Islamic law and belief
were to be corrected by subordination to pristine Islam. In contrast to
the Islamic modernist movement of the nineteenth and twentieth centuries, the purpose of reinterpretation (*ijtihad*) was not to accommodate
new ideas but to get back to or reappropriate the unique and essentially
complete vision of Islam as preserved in its revealed sources. However,
Islamic revivalism is not so much an attempt to reestablish the early
Islamic community in a literal sense as to reapply the Quran and Sunna
rigorously to existing conditions. Thus, we see its militant, even revolutionary, potential as both a moral and a political force, as witnessed
in the eighteenth and nineteenth centuries by the wave of premodern
religiopolitical revivalist movements that swept across the Islamic world
from the Sudan to Sumatra. The orientation and diversity of revivalism

are demonstrated by the cases of several movements in Arabia, Africa, and India.

Arabia: The Wahhabi Movement

The Wahhabi movement is perhaps the best known of the eighteenth-century revivalist movements. Its significance is due not only to its formative influence on Saudi Arabia but also, and more important, to its role as an example for modern revivalism. Its founder, Muhammad ibn Abd al-Wahhab (1703–92), was trained in law and theology at Mecca and Medina, where he was drawn to the Hanbali school, the strictest of the Sunni law schools, including the writings of the rigorous revivalist Ibn Taymiyya (d. 1328). Ibn Abd al-Wahhab regarded the condition of his society as little better than that of pre-Islamic Arabia, the *jahiliyya* or period of ignorance, with which he compared it. He was appalled by many of its popular religious practices, such as the veneration of saints, their tombs, and sacred rocks and trees, which he condemned as pagan superstitions and idolatry (*shirk*), the worst of sins in Islam. Ibn Abd al-Wahhab denounced these beliefs and practices as unwarranted innovations. They compromised the unity of God (**tawhid**, or Islam's radical or absolute monotheism) and the Islamic community, as evidenced by the tribalism and tribal warfare that had returned to Arabia. Living in the Islamic heartland, the homeland of the Prophet and the site of the holy cities of Mecca and Medina, made these conditions all the more reprehensible. The diagnosis of ibn Abd al-Wahhab was similar to that of other revivalists: The political weakness of the community and its moral decline were due to a deviation from the straight path of Islam. Its cure was equally obvious: Muslims must return to true Islamic practice. This could be achieved only by a repetition of Islam's first great reformation, the social and moral revolution led by Muhammad, by living the community life based strictly on the Quran and Muhammad's example.

Ibn Abd al-Wahhab focused on the lifetime of Muhammad and the early Medinan community as Islam's normative period. All subsequent, post-Prophetic developments and the time-honored interpretations of the *ulama* and the law schools were subject to review and reevaluation (*ijtihad*) in the light of Islam's fundamental sources. This rejection of blind imitation (*taqlid*) and embrace of *ijtihad* was designed to purify Islam by weeding out those un-Islamic beliefs and practices that had infiltrated the law and life of Muslims. Because he was in Arabia, ibn Abd al-Wahhab's mode of revivalism was a more literalist re-creation of the life and customs of the early Medinan community, that of the pious forefathers, rather than an attempt to address new circumstances.

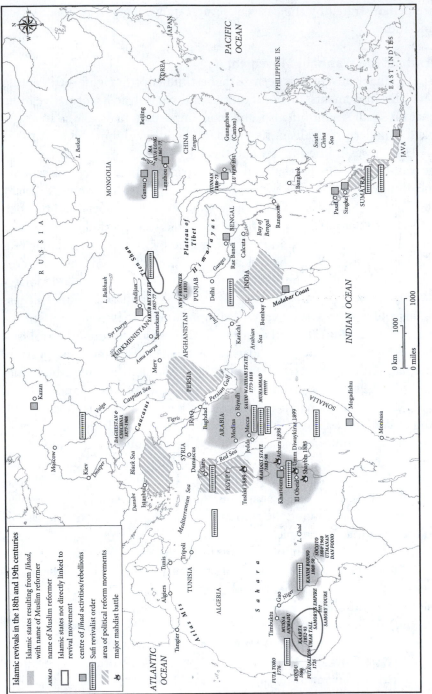

Islamic modernism and revival.

He equated "Arab" and "Islam." This differed somewhat from revival-ist movements outside Arabia, where a return to the Quran and Sunna meant reform through the subordination of Muslim life to God's revela-tion, not simply the appropriation of Arab Islam in toto. It also differed from the process of reinterpretation espoused by the Islamic modernist movement in the next century, which sought to formulate Islamically acceptable solutions for new situations. For ibn Abd al-Wahhab, the Islamic way of life was to be found in its pure, unadulterated form in the seventh-century community.

Islamic Modernism and Revival

Muhammad ibn Abd al-Wahhab entered into a religious-political alli-ance with a local tribal chief, Muhammad ibn Saud (d. 1765), setting into motion a reformist movement that would subdue large areas of Arabia. Although commonly referred to as Wahhabi, its self-designation was the Muwahiddun ("unitarians"), or those who uphold and practice mono-theism (*tawhid*). Initially, the movement focused on the purification of Islamic thought and practice through education. However, over time and according to political need, the movement selectively embraced the teachings of Ibn Taymiyya and increasingly focused on warfare. By the late eighteenth century, after ibn Abd al-Wahhab's death, religious zeal and military power were united in a religiopolitical movement that waged holy war with an uncompromising, Kharijite-like commitment that viewed all Muslims who resisted as unbelievers, enemies of God who must be fought. The tribes of Arabia were subdued and united in the name of Islamic egalitarianism. As Muhammad had cleansed the Kaba of its idols, Wahhabi forces destroyed Sufi shrines and tombs and sacred rocks and trees. By the turn of the nineteenth century, their iconoclastic zeal against idolatrous shrines led to the destruction of sacred tombs in Mecca and Medina, including those of the Prophet and his Companions. In addition, they destroyed the tomb of Husayn at Karbala, a major Shii holy place and pilgrimage center, and massacred portions of the Shii population there, an act that has never been forgot-ten by Shii Muslims and has affected their attitude toward modern-day Saudi Arabia. Finally, in contrast to other revivalists, like the **Mahdi** of the Sudan and the Grand Sanusi of Libya, who reformed Sufism, the Muwahiddun totally rejected it.

The Wahhabi movement influenced other revivalists in Africa and India. In addition, its legacy can be found in the state and society of Saudi Arabia and the ideological worldviews of many contemporary Muslims.

The Sanusi and Mahdi Movements

Born in Algeria, Muhammad Ali ibn al-Sanusi (1787–1859), or, as he came to be known, the Grand Sanusi, studied in Cairo and Mecca, where he earned a reputation as a scholar of law and *hadith*. He rejected the political fragmentation of Muslims resulting from tribalism and regionalism and reasserted the need for Islamic unity and solidarity. A student in Mecca of Ahmad ibn Idris, the renowned scholar of Prophetic traditions and revivalist Sufi, al-Sanusi followed in the footsteps of this great Moroccan reformer in calling for the purification of Sufism and much of Islamic law, which, he believed, had been distorted by *ulama* interpretation. This and his claim to be a *mujtahid* (an independent interpreter of Islam) alienated him from many of the *ulama* and Sufi leaders. Al-Sanusi moved from Arabia to what is modern-day Libya after the death of his teacher and established the Sanusiyyah brotherhood, a reformist and missionary movement that created a network of settlements across central and western Africa.

The Sanusi program pursued a path of militant activism, consciously emulating the example of Muhammad. It involved the unification of tribal factions in the name of their common Islamic brotherhood and the establishment of Sufi centers, or lodges, which served as places of prayer and instruction as well as of military training and social welfare. They were committed to both the creation of an Islamic state and the spread of Islam. Although not hostile to the outside world, descendants of the Grand Sanusi resisted European colonialism. His grandson led the Sanusi resistance to Italian colonial rule and at independence became King Idris I of Libya.

In contrast to the Grand Sanusi, Muhammad Ahmad (1848–85), the founder of the Mandiyyah in the Sudan, proclaimed himself Mahdi in 1881. Although Sunni Islam, unlike the Shii, does not have a formal doctrine of the Mahdi, popular lore did accept the notion of a *mahdi* ("divinely guided one"), a messianic figure who will be sent by God to rescue the community from oppression and to restore true Islam and a just society. This eschatological belief should be distinguished from the more specific Shii expectation that the twelfth imam, Muhammad al-Mahdi, will return at the end of time. Unlike the renewer of Islam who claimed the status of *mujtahid* (one who is qualified to interpret Islam), the Sudanese Mahdi claimed to be the divinely appointed and inspired representative of God. He shared with other revivalist leaders the belief that he was reenacting the paradigmatic drama of early Islam—establishing, as the Prophet had done in the seventh century, God's rule on earth. As with Muhammad's victories, the gains of the Mahdi's forces were attributed to divine guidance and interpreted as divine validation of his mission. He established an Islamic community-state and, in common with other reformers, called for the purification of Islam and the unity of Muslims. Accomplishing this mission meant not only reforming Sufism but also uniting his followers, who, like the Prophet's companions, were called the Ansar, in a struggle against fellow Muslims. Like the early Kharijites, the Mahdi justified waging holy war against other Muslims, in this case the Sudan's Ottoman Egyptian rulers, by declaring them infidels who

> disobeyed the command of His messenger and His Prophet   ruled in a manner not in accord with what God had sent   altered the Sharia of our master, Muhammad, the messenger of God, and blasphemed against the faith of God.[5]

Alcohol, gambling, music, and prostitution were all denounced as foreign (Ottoman Egyptian) and indigenous, un-Islamic practices that had corrupted Sudanese Islamic society.

When the Mahdist forces finally triumphed over Egyptian forces in 1885, an Islamic state was established in Khartoum, governed by Mahdist religious ideology. The Mahdi had supreme power as God's delegate, and the Sharia was its only law. The Mahdist state, which many regard as the forerunner of the modern Sudan, lasted until 1899.

The Indian Subcontinent

Two men in particular stand out in the premodern era of Muslim India: Shaykh Ahmad Sirhindi (1564–1624) and Shah Wali Allah of Delhi (1702–62). Both provided the foundation for Indian revivalism and were formative influences on modern Indian Muslim thought.

Shah Wali Allah lived during a critical period for Indian Muslims. The power of the Mughal empire was in decline. A Muslim minority community faced not only the disintegration of its political rule, challenged by Hindu and Sikh uprisings, but also the internal disunity of conflicting factions: Sunni and Shii, *hadith* and legal scholars, *ulama* and Sufis. Educated in Mecca and a contemporary of Muhammad ibn Abd al-Wahhab, Wali Allah was also a member of the revivalist-oriented Naqshbandi order. He followed in the footsteps of the great revivalist of seventeenth-century India, Shaykh Ahmad Sirhindi. Like Shaykh Ahmad, he asserted the need for Muslims to purge their lives of un-Islamic practices and to reform popular Sufi practices, which he believed were responsible for much of the religious syncretism that threatened the identity, moral fiber, and survival of Indian Islam in its multiconfessional setting. As with other revivalists, for Wali Allah the purification and renewal of Islam were contingent on a return to the pristine Sharia, grounded in its two infallible sources, the Quran and Sunna, which encompassed all areas of life. For Wali Allah, the revivification of Muslim society was a prerequisite for the restoration of Mughal power.

The genius of Wali Allah was his method of reconciliation. He eschewed the rigid, confrontative style of Muhammad ibn Abd al-Wahhab and Sirhindi. His surgery was less radical than that of the Wahhabi. Instead of rejecting the current to restore the past, he sought to modify and refashion present belief and practice in light of early Islamic practice. Like Sirhindi, he sought to reform rather than, as the Wahhabi had done, suppress or eradicate Sufism. Sirhindi's condemnation of error as unbelief was offset by Wali Allah's penchant for a synthesis of contending ideas. In reforming Sufism, Sirhindi had critiqued and condemned Ibn al-Arabi's teaching of the "oneness or unity of being"; Wali Allah softened the condemnation. He resolved the contradictions between the ontological monism of Ibn al-Arabi's unity of being, which denied all existence except God's and declared the ultimate unity of God and the universe, and Sirhindi's "unity of experience," which maintained that Ibn al-Arabi's pantheistic union with God was experiential (based on a subjective experience of illumination or ecstasy) rather than an ontological reality (a union with the divine reality). Wali Allah taught that the seemingly contradictory teachings of Ibn al-Arabi and Sirhindi were two different ways of speaking about the same underlying reality. He denied that there was any substantial difference between the two; instead, the problem was one of semantics.[6] As a result, Shah Wali Allah was able to reconcile contending camps within Indian Sufism and couple this reconciliation with an appeal to Sufi leaders to cleanse their practices of un-Islamic, idolatrous, and antinomian tendencies.

The great legacy of Wali Allah and his major contribution to Islamic modernist thought was his condemnation of blind imitation and his emphasis on reopening the gates of *ijtihad*, the right to reinterpret Islam. As he had used his principle of reconciliation to resolve differences among Sufis and between Sunni and Shii, his teaching regarding *ijtihad* was pivotal to the resolution of a long-standing conflict between jurists and traditionists.

From the tenth century, two opposing trends had developed among the scholars of India. One emphasized strict and exclusive adherence to a particular school of law, and the other opposed this method and instead stressed rigorous following of the clear meaning of the Sunna of the Prophet as found in the accepted compendia of Prophetic traditions (*hadith*). Competition and bitter clashes had become the norm rather than the exception. Wali Allah criticized the partisanship of jurists, which had hardened into a belief that their leaders' interpretations or rulings were infallible and resulted in a rigid doctrine of blind imitation (*taqlid*). He distinguished between blind imitation, which was prohibited, and a more flexible imitation, for those incapable of *ijtihad*, which was subject to change in light of a new understanding of the Quran and Sunna. Wali Allah followed Ibn Taymiyya in calling for the opening of the gates of *ijtihad*, as the rulings of the old jurists were open to correction in light of the Quran and the Sunna. He maintained that the nature of interpretation itself was susceptible to error because of human limitations or because new evidence might arise. In practice, wherever possible, he resolved questions of law by seeking a synthesis of points of agreement among the law schools. However, ultimately he sided with the traditionists, for in doubtful cases he subordinated the fallible opinion of the jurist to Prophetic tradition, because the Sunna of the Prophet, unlike legal opinion, was an infallible source of law.

Shah Wali Allah has often been regarded as the father of modern Indian Islamic thought because of his condemnation of blind imitation of the past and his advocacy of personal interpretation. In this, he opened the door for many reformers who followed, from modernists like **Sayyid Ahmad Khan** and **Muhammad Iqbal** to neorevivalists like **Mawlana Abul Ala Mawdudi**. He established the acceptance in principle of the need for reinterpretation and reform, but it is important to distinguish his meaning from that of others who later broadened and extended its use. For Wali Allah, as for other premodern revivalists, the purpose of reinterpretation was not to formulate new answers but to rediscover forgotten guidelines from the past. Thus, when Wali Allah spoke of the use of *ijtihad* to avoid the rigid particularistic following of one school of law, he did so with the objective of obtaining an answer solely from the "purified past," from a Sharia that was complete and final in its Arabian form, although in need of periodic purification from historical accretions by Islamic reformers or revivalists (*mujaddids*).

Wali Allah believed that the restoration of Mughal power, and thus assurance of Muslim rule, was dependent on the social and moral reform of Muslim society. It was Sayyid Ahmad Barelewi (1786–1831), a disciple of Wali Allah's son, who transformed a reformist school of thought into a jihad movement. For Sayyid Ahmad, effective response to the breakup of the Mughal empire required a jihad against the military threat of Sikh armies and, later, the colonial ambitions of the British. Loss of Muslim power meant that India was no longer an Islamic land but an abode of war. Thus, jihad was obligatory.

Sayyid Ahmad combined a program of religious purification with military power to establish an Islamic state based on social justice and equality for its Muslim citizens. He emphasized pristine monotheism and denounced all those practices (Sufi, Shii, and social customs borrowed from Hinduism) that compromised it. Patterning his revivalist movement on the example of Muhammad, he led a group of his followers on pilgrimage to Mecca. At Hudabiyya, the place where Muhammad's followers had sealed a pact to fight the Meccans, Sayyid Ahmad administered an oath of jihad to these new holy warriors for Islam. Revered as a renewer of Islam, he returned to India where, in 1826, he led his holy warriors three thousand miles to the Northwest Frontier Province (Pakistan) to wage war against Sikh armies that had taken control of the area. Sayyid Ahmad regarded both a holy war against a non-Muslim regime that ruled a predominantly Muslim population and the restoration of Muslim rule as Islamically required and legitimate. After the Muslim warriors defeated the Sikhs at Balakot, they established a religiopolitical state based on Sharia law. Like the early caliphs, Sayyid Ahmad was proclaimed commander of the believers. Although he was killed in battle in 1831, Sayyid Ahmad's movement continued for some years, his followers waging jihad against the British.

Islamic revivalist movements sought to revitalize their societies through a process of moral reconstruction that transformed not only the religious but also the sociopolitical life of their communities. Despite some considerable differences, their strength and legacy included an ideological framework and example that strongly influenced subsequent developments in the history of Islam. This ideological worldview included belief that: (1) the process of renewal requires a reenactment of the first and paradigmatic Islamic revolution or reformation of the Prophet Muhammad; (2) religion is integral to state and society; (3) departure from this norm leads to the fragmentation of the community and a decline in its fortunes; (4) only a purging of un-Islamic behavior and a return to the straight path of Islam, a life governed by Islamic law, can restore the community to its rightful place of ascendancy and power; (5) major causes of Muslim decline are the unchecked cultural syncretism of popular Sufism and the uncritical acceptance of tradition; (6) the reform of Sufism must be accompanied by the practice of *ijtihad*; (7) renewal is the task of both individuals and the community; (8) true believers, like the early Muslims, may need to separate themselves to preserve their faith and form a righteous society or brotherhood; (9) the struggle (*jihad*) to reassert the rightful place of Islam in society requires moral self-discipline and, where necessary, armed struggle; and (10) those Muslims who resist are no longer to be regarded as Muslim but numbered among the enemies of God.

MODERN ISLAMIC MOVEMENTS

Whereas premodern revivalist movements were primarily internally motivated, Islamic modernism was a response to both continued internal weaknesses and the external political and religiocultural threat of colonialism. Much of the Muslim world faced a powerful new threat—European colonialism. The responses of modern Islamic reformers in the late nineteenth and early twentieth centuries to the impact of the West on Muslim societies resulted in substantial attempts to reinterpret Islam to meet the changing circumstances of Muslim life. Legal, educational, and social reforms were aimed at rescuing Muslim societies from their downward spiral and demonstrating the compatibility of Islam with modern Western thought and values. Because of the centrality of law in Islam and the importance of the Muslim family, Islamic modernists often focused their energies on these areas. In many modern Muslim states, governments used Islamic modernist thought to justify reform measures and legislation. For some Muslims, neither the conservative, the secular, nor Islamic modernist positions were acceptable. Their reaction to the "Westernizing" of Islam and Muslim society led to the formation of modern Islamic societies or organizations, such as the **Muslim Brotherhood** and the **Jamaat-i-Islami** (the Islamic Society), that combined religious ideology and activism. These organizations served as catalysts for Islamic revivalism in the middle decades of the twentieth century and have had a major impact on the interpretation and implementation of Islam in recent years.

Islamic Modernism

European trade missions of the sixteenth and seventeenth centuries progressively expanded so that by the eighteenth century many areas of the Muslim world had felt the impact of the economic and military challenge of Western technology and modernization. A major shift in power occurred as declining Muslim fortunes reversed the relationship of the Muslim world to the West, from that of ascendant expansionism to one of defensiveness and subordination. By the nineteenth and early twentieth centuries, Europe (in particular, Great Britain, France, and Holland) had penetrated and increasingly dominated much of the Muslim world from North Africa to Southeast Asia (the French in North Africa, the British and French in the Middle East and South Asia, and the Dutch and British in Southeast Asia).

Western imperialism precipitated a religious as well as a political crisis. For the first time, much of the Muslim world had lost its political and cultural sovereignty to Christian Europe. Although the Muslim world had endured the Mongol conquests, in time the conquerors had embraced Islam. Colonial rule eclipsed the institutions of an Islamic state and society—the sultan, Islamic law, and *ulama* administration of education, law, and social welfare. Muslim subjugation by Christian Europe confirmed not only the decline of Muslim power but also the apparent loss of divine favor and guidance. For the believer, it raised a number of religious questions: What had gone wrong in Islam? Was the success of the West due to the superiority of Christendom, the backwardness of Islam, or the faithlessness of the community? How could Muslims realize God's will in a state governed by non-Muslims and non-Muslim law? In what ways should Muslims respond to this challenge to Muslim identity and faith?

A variety of responses emerged from Muslim self-criticism and reflection on the causes of decline. Their actions spanned the spectrum, from adaptation and cultural synthesis to withdrawal and rejection. Secularists blamed an outmoded tradition. They advocated the separation of religion and politics and the establishment of modern nation-states modeled on the West. Islam should be restricted to personal life, and public life should be modeled on modern (that is, European) ideas and technology in government, the military, education, and law. Conservative religious leaders, including most of the *ulama*, attributed Muslim impotence to divergence from Islam and deviation from tradition. Many advocated withdrawal, noncooperation, or rejection of the West. Western (Christian) ideas and values were as dangerous as their governments and armies, for they threatened faith and culture. Some concluded that where Muslims no longer lived under Islamic rule in an Islamic territory, they were now in a land of warfare that, following the example of the Prophet, necessitated either armed struggle (*jihad*) or emigration (*hijra*) to an Islamically governed land. In India, the son of Shah Wali Allah, Shah Abdul Aziz, issued a *fatwa* declaring India a non-Islamic territory, a land of warfare in which either to fight or to flee was an Islamically appropriate response. While some attempted to emigrate, more joined jihad movements. However, the majority of religious leaders advocated a policy of cultural isolation and noncooperation. They equated any form of political accommodation of Western culture with betrayal and surrender.

A third major Muslim response, Islamic modernism, emerged during the late nineteenth century. It sought to delineate an alternative to Western, secular adaptationism on the one hand and religiously motivated rejectionism on the other. A group of reform-minded Muslims sought to respond to, rather than react against, the challenge of Western imperialism. They proclaimed the need for Islamic reform. They blamed the internal decline of Muslim societies, their loss of power and backwardness, and their inability to respond effectively to European colonialism on a blind and unquestioned clinging to the past (*taqlid*). Islamic reformers stressed the dynamism, flexibility, and adaptability that had characterized the early development of Islam, notable for its achievements in law, education, and the sciences. They pressed for internal reform through a process of reinterpretation (*ijtihad*) and selective adaptation (Islamization) of Western ideas and technology. Islamic modernism was a process of internal self-criticism, a struggle to redefine Islam to demonstrate its relevance to the new situations that Muslims found themselves in as their societies modernized. The Middle East and South Asia produced major modernist movements. Their themes and activities are illustrated in several key figures—in the Middle East, **Jamal al-Din al-Afghani** and his disciples, **Muhammad Abduh** and **Rashid Rida**; and in South Asia, Sayyid Ahmad Khan and Muhammad Iqbal.

The Middle East

Jamal al-Din al-Afghani (1838–97) was an outstanding figure of nineteenth-century Islam and a major catalyst for Islamic reform. A tireless activist, he roamed the Muslim world, calling for internal reform to defend Islam, strengthen the Muslim community, and, eventually, drive out the West. An orator, teacher, journalist, and political activist, he lived and preached his reformist message in Afghanistan, Egypt, Turkey, Persia, India, Russia, France, and England. Afghani attempted to bridge the gap between secular modernists and religious traditionalists. He believed that Muslims could repel the West not by ignoring or rejecting the sources of Western strength (reason, science and technology) but instead by reclaiming and re-appropriating reason, science, and technology, which, he maintained, had been integral to Islam and the grand accomplishments of Islamic civilization. He was an ardent advocate of constitutionalism and parliamentary government to limit the power of rulers. Such statements appealed to many of the young who had had a traditional upbringing but were now also attracted by modern reforms. Afghani also appealed to the *ulama* with his assertion that Muslims needed to remember that Islam was the source of strength and that Muslims must return to a more faithful observance of its guidance.

Afghani rejected the passivity, fatalism, and otherworldliness of popular Sufism as well as the Western secular tendency to restrict religion to personal life or worship. He countered by preaching an activist, this-worldly Islam: (1) Islam is a comprehensive way of life, encompassing worship, law, government, and society; (2) the true Muslim struggles to carry out God's will in history and thus seeks success in this life as well as the next.

[T]he principles of Islamic religion are not restricted to calling man to the truth or to considering the soul only in a spiritual context which is concerned with the relationship between this world and the world to come.... There is more besides: Islamic principles are concerned with relationships among the believers, they explain the law in general and in detail, they define the executive power which administers the law.... Thus, in truth, the ruler of the Muslims will be their religious, holy, and divine law.... Let me repeat   that unlike other religions, Islam is concerned not only with the life to come. Islam is more: it is concerned with the believers' interests in the world here below and with allowing them to realize success in this life as well as peace in the next life. It seeks "good fortune in two worlds."[7]

Like the revivalists of the previous century, Afghani maintained that the strength and survival of the *umma* were dependent on the reassertion of Islamic identity and solidarity. He exhorted Muslims to realize that Islam was the religion of reason and science—a dynamic, progressive, creative force capable of responding to the demands of modernity:

The Europeans have now everywhere put their hands on every part of the world. The English have reached Afghanistan; the French have seized Tunisia. In reality this usurpation, aggression, and conquest have not come from the French or the English. Rather it is science that everywhere manifests its greatness and power.... [S]cience is continually changing capitals. Sometimes it has moved from the East to the West, and other times from West to East   all wealth and riches are the result of science. In sum, the whole world of humanity is an industrial world, meaning that the world is a world of science.... The first Muslims had no science, but, thanks to the Islamic religion, a philosophic spirit arose among them.... This was why they acquired in a short time all the sciences   those who forbid science and knowledge in the belief that they are safeguarding the Islamic religion are really the enemies of that religion. The Islamic religion is the closest of religions to science and knowledge, and there is no incompatibility between science and knowledge and the foundation of the Islamic faith.[8]

Therefore, science and learning from the West did not pose a threat to Islam; they could, and should, be studied and utilized.

Central to Afghani's program for Islamic reform was his call for a reopening of the door of *ijtihad*. He denounced the stagnation in Islam, which he attributed both to the influence of Sufism and to the backwardness of the *ulama*, who lacked the expertise required to respond to modern concerns and discouraged others from obtaining scientific knowledge, erroneously labeling it "European science." The process of reinterpretation and reform that he advocated went beyond that of eighteenth-century revivalism. Although he talked about a need to return to Islam, the thrust and purpose of reform were not simply to reappropriate answers from the past but, in light of Islamic principles, to formulate new Islamic responses to the changing conditions of Muslim societies. Reinterpretation of Islam would once again make it a relevant force in intellectual and political life. In this way, Islam would serve as the source of a renewal or renaissance that would restore Muslim political independence and the past glory of Islam.

In Afghani's holistic interpretation of Islam, the reform of Islam was inseparably connected with liberation from colonial rule. The reassertion of Muslim identity and solidarity was a prerequisite for the restoration of political and cultural independence. Although he preached a pan-Islamic message, he also accepted the reality of Muslim nationalism. National independence was the goal of reformism and a necessary step in revitalizing the Islamic community both regionally and transnationally.

Jamal al-Din al-Afghani articulated a cluster of ideas and attitudes that influenced Islamic reformist thought and Muslim anticolonial sentiment for much of the first half of the twentieth century. His disciples included many of the great political and intellectual leaders of the Muslim world. He is remembered both as the Father of Muslim Nationalism and as a formative influence on Egypt's *salafiyya* (early pious ancestors of the Muslim community) reformist movement and, later, the Muslim Brotherhood.

If Afghani was the catalyst, his disciples Muhammad Abduh (1849–1905) and Rashid Rida (1865–1935) were the great synthesizers of modern Islam. Their Salafiyya movement was to influence reform movements from North Africa to Southeast Asia. Muhammad Abduh was one of the earliest and most remarkable disciples of al-Afghani, destined to become one of Egypt's leading *ulama,* a reformer of al-Azhar University, and the Mufti (chief judge of the Sharia court system) of Egypt, and to be remembered as the Father of Islamic Modernism in the Arab world. During the 1870s and early 1880s, Abduh enthusiastically collaborated with Afghani in writing reformist articles, publishing a journal, and participating in the nationalist movement. He was exiled with Afghani to Paris after they participated in an unsuccessful nationalist revolt against British influence in Egypt. When Abduh returned, he turned his attention away from politics and focused instead on religious, educational, and social reform.

Abduh's theology and approach began with the unity of God, the cornerstone of Islamic belief and the source of the Muslim community's strength and vitality. One of his major reformist works was *The Theology of Unity*.[9] The basis for Abduh's reformist thought was his belief that religion and reason were complementary, and that there was no inherent contradiction between religion and science, which he regarded as the twin sources of Islam. The bases of Muslim decline were the prevalence of un-Islamic popular religious beliefs and practices, such as saint worship, intercession, and miracles, and the stifling of creativity and dynamism due to Sufi passivity and fatalism as well as to the rigid scholasticism of the traditionalist *ulama* who had forbidden fresh religious interpretation. He attributed the stagnation of Muslim society to blind imitation (*taqlid*), the dead weight of scholasticism:

> We must, however, believe that the Islamic religion is a religion of unity throughout. It is not a religion of conflicting principles but is built squarely on reason, while divine revelation is its surest pillar   the Quran directs us, enjoining rational procedure and intellectual inquiry into the manifestations of the universe.... It forbids us to be slavishly credulous.... Well is it said that traditionalism can have evil consequences as well as good.... It is a deceptive thing, and though it may be pardoned in an animal [it] is scarcely seemly in man.[10]

Abduh was convinced that the transformation of Muslim society depended on a reinterpretation of Islam and its implementation through national educational and social reforms. His writings and *fatwas* reflected his underlying message that Islam and science, revelation and reason, were compatible, and thus Muslims could selectively appropriate aspects of Western civilization that were not contrary to Islam.

Abduh sought to provide an Islamic rationale for the selective integration of Islam with modern ideas and institutions. He distinguished between Islam's inner core or fundamentals, those truths and principles that were unchanging, and its outer layers, society's application of immutable principles and values to the needs of a particular age. Therefore, he maintained that whereas those regulations of Islamic law that governed worship (*ibadat*, such as prayer, fasting, and pilgrimage) were immutable, the vast majority of regulations concerned with social affairs (*muamalat*, such as penal, commercial, and family laws) were open to change. As historical and social conditions warranted, the core of Islamic principles and values should be reapplied to new realities and, where necessary, the old layers of tradition discarded. Abduh believed that the crisis of modern Islam was precipitated by Muslim failure to uphold the distinction between the immutable and the mutable, the necessary and the contingent. Abduh followed this approach by championing reforms in law, theology, and education. His reformist ideas were incorporated in his legal rulings and set forth in a journal, *al-Manar* ("The Beacon" or "Lighthouse"), which he published with his protégé, the Syrian Rashid Rida. In education, he worked for national reforms and modernized the curriculum at al-Azhar University during his tenure as its rector. Employing the Maliki law school's principle of public welfare, he gave *fatwas* that touched on everything from bank interest to women's status.

Abduh was particularly critical of the lack of educational opportunities for women and the deleterious effects of polygamy on Muslim society. His handling of the issue reflects his methodology, which combined a modernist interpretation of Scripture and its employment in the name of the public interest. Abduh argued that polygamy had been permitted, not commanded, in the Prophet's time as a concession to prevailing social conditions:

> If you are afraid that you will not treat orphans justly, then marry such women as may seem good to you, two, three or four. If you feel that you will not act justly, then one. (Quran 4:3)

He maintained that the true intent of the Quran was monogamy because marriage to more than one wife was contingent on equal justice and impartial treatment of each wife, which the Quran notes, subsequent to verse 4:3, is not possible: "You will never manage to deal equitably with women no matter how hard you try" (4:129). Abduh maintained that because this was a practical impossibility, the Quranic ideal was monogamy. Abduh's Quranic interpretation and his use of public interest as an Islamic justification for legal reform were adopted by reformers in Egypt and in other Muslim countries to introduce changes in family law.

Rashid Rida has been called the "mouthpiece of Abduh."[11] He traveled from his home in Syria to Cairo in 1897 to become Abduh's close protégé. In 1898, they published the first edition of *al-Manar*, a periodical that became the principal vehicle for Abduh and Rida's Salafi reformism. Rida continued to publish *al-Manar* after Abduh's death (1905) until his own death in 1935. Although regarded as a journal devoted to Abduh's reformist thought, in fact it was greatly affected by Rida's interpretation of his master and Rida's own growing conservatism in later years. It covered the range of reformist concerns—Quranic exegesis, articles on theological, legal, and educational reform, and *fatwas* on contemporary issues.

In general, Rida adopted and carried on the Afghani–Abduh legacy of calling for a reinterpretation of Islam. The development of a modern Islamic legal system was a fundamental priority, given the challenges and requirements of the modern world. Rida, too, rejected the unquestioned authority of medieval formulations of law and regarded much of the social sphere as subject to change. Reform in Islam required more than the eclectic selection of appropriate regulations from one of the established schools of law. New regulations were necessary. He utilized a number of sources to justify this claim. Following Abduh, Rida relied on the Maliki principle of the public interest or general welfare. In classical jurisprudence public interest was a subsidiary legal principle used in deducing new laws by analogy from the Quran and Sunna. Reformers now employed it as an independent source of law to formulate regulations where no clear scriptural text prevailed. Rida also relied on Hanbali law and Ibn Taymiyya. Although Hanbalism is normally regarded as the most rigid of the law schools, its strict formalism pertains to acts of worship, the unchanging essence of Islam based on the Quran and Sunna, as distinct from social laws that are subject to change. Thus, Ibn Taymiyya had been able to maintain the right to exercise *ijtihad* in social affairs. Rida adopted this distinction:

> Creed and ritual were completed in detail so as to permit neither additions nor subtractions, and whoever adds to them or subtracts from them is changing Islam and brings forth a new religion. As for the *muamalat* (social laws), beyond decreeing the elements of virtue and establishing penalties for certain crimes, and beyond imposing the principle of consultation, the Law Giver delegated the affair in its detailed applications to the leading ulama and rulers.[12]

Rashid Rida believed that the implementation of Islamic law required an Islamic government, as law was the product of consultation between the ruler (caliph) and the *ulama,* the guardian-interpreters of law. Like Afghani, Rashid Rida concerned himself with the restoration of the caliphate and pan-Islamic unity. He also shared the modernist belief that the *ulama* were backward and ill equipped to understand the modern world and to reinterpret Islam. Therefore, he advocated the development of a group of progressive Islamic thinkers to bridge the gap between the conservative *ulama* and Westernized elites.

Rida shifted the Salafi movement's orientation toward a more conservative position during the thirty years after the death of Abduh in 1905. Although strongly drawn to Afghani and Abduh, Rida had a much more limited exposure to the West. He neither traveled much in the West nor spoke a Western language. He remained convinced that the British continued to be a political and religious threat: "The British government is committed to the destruction of Islam in the East after destroying its temporal power."[13] He became more critical of the West with the growing influence of Western liberal secular nationalism and culture in Egypt, ironically at the hands of former students of Afghani and Abduh, who wished to restrict religion to private life. An admirer of the Wahhabi movement in Arabia, he was more inclined to emphasize the self-sufficiency and comprehensiveness of Islam. Muslim reformers must not look to the West, but single-mindedly return to the sources of Islam—the Quran, the Sunna of the Prophet, and the consensus of the Companions of the Prophet. Rida's conservatism was reflected in his more restricted understanding of the term *salaf*, ancestors or pious forefathers. For Abduh, it was a general reference to the early Islamic centuries; Rida followed eighteenth-century revivalism's restriction of the term to the first generation of Muslims, the Companions of the Prophet, whose example was to be emulated.

During the post–World War I period, Rida became more wary of modernism and more drawn to the *ulama*. The example of Egyptian nationalism reinforced his fear that modernist rationalism in the hands of intellectuals and political elites would degenerate into the secularization and Westernization of Muslim societies. As a result, he cast his reformism more and more in the idiom of a defense of Islam against the dangers of the West. His rejection of Western secular liberalism and emphasis on the comprehensiveness and self-sufficiency of Islam aligned him more closely with eighteenth-century revivalism and influenced the thinking and ideological worldviews of **Hasan al-Banna** (1906–49), founder of Egypt's Muslim Brotherhood, and other contemporary Islamic activists.

The Indian Subcontinent

Two men dominate the Islamic modernist movement in India—Sir Sayyid Ahmad Khan (1817–98), a contemporary of al-Afghani and Abduh, and Muhammad Iqbal (1875–1938). As the eighteenth century had produced Islamic revivalists like Shah Wali Allah and Sayyid Ahmad Barelewi, the aftermath of the "Mutiny" of 1857, what some Indian historians have called the first war of independence, proved a turning point in Indian Muslim history. The threat to Muslim power, the decline of its society, and the question of whether India was any longer a Muslim empire were all moot points now. The war resulted in British rule and the end of Muslim dominance of India. The Muslim community stood defeated, powerless, and demoralized. Although both Hindus and Muslims had participated in the uprising, the British held the Muslims primarily responsible. In the aftermath, they questioned the loyalty of Muslims in a non-Muslim state. At the same time, the majority of the *ulama* would have nothing to do with these "enemies of Islam." Both British doubts about the loyalty of Muslims and Muslim withdrawal undermined the future of Indian Muslims vis-à-vis their British masters and the Hindu majority. Into the void stepped Sayyid Ahmad Khan. Like al-Afghani and Abduh, he was convinced that the survival of the Muslim community necessitated a bold reinterpretation of Islam and the acceptance, not rejection, of the best in Western thought. However, unlike al-Afghani and Rida, Ahmad Khan preached acceptance of the political reality of British rule and restricted his Islamic concerns to the Muslims of India. He was convinced that both political resistance and appeals to pan-Islam were impractical, given the political reality.

Like his Salafi coreligionists in the Middle East, Sayyid Ahmad Khan believed that the survival of Islam depended on the rejection of unquestioned acceptance (taqiid) of medieval interpretations of Islam and the exercise of ijtihad to produce fresh interpretations of Islam to demonstrate its relevance and validity for modern life. On the one hand, he placed himself within the revivalist tradition of Shah Wali Allah by maintaining that a return to pristine Islam necessitated purifying Islam of many of the teachings and interpretations of the ulama. His goal was to:

> justify without any wavering, what I acknowledge to be the original religion of Islam which God and the messenger have disclosed, not that religion which the ulama and the preachers have fashioned.[14]

On the other hand, Ahmad Khan differed with Shah Wali Allah and other eighteenth-century revivalists in his method. His exercise of ijtihad was not simply to use reason to get back to original interpretations of Islam covered over by ulama scholasticism but to boldly reinterpret Islam in light of its revealed sources.

The extent of his use of reason, the degree to which he reinterpreted Islam, and his borrowing from the West marked him off from revivalists of the previous century. However, Ahmad Khan did see a continuity between his own work and that of previous scholars. Just as in the past Muslim theology had developed out of the need to respond to a social context, so the Muslims of modern India required a new interpretation of Islam to demonstrate the compatibility of Islam and modern science: "Today we need, as in former days, a modern theology by which we either render futile the tenets of modern sciences or [show them to be] doubtful, or bring them into harmony with the doctrines of Islam."[15]

Ahmad Khan's use of reason was far more rationalist than that of Muhammad Abduh. Muhammad Abduh believed that there was no necessary contradiction between true religion and science, but he believed that religion and reason functioned on two different levels or in two different

spheres. Ahmad Khan, influenced by nineteenth-century European rationalism and natural philosophy, much of which he regarded as consonant
with the rationalist principles of the Mutazila and Ibn Rushd (Averroes),
believed that Islam was the religion of reason and nature. There could be no
contradiction between the word of God and the work of God (nature): "If
that religion is in conformity with human nature   then it is true."[16] Islam
was in total harmony with the laws of nature and therefore compatible
with modern scientific thought. These premises, reason and the laws of
nature, governed Ahmad Khan's interpretation of the Quran and Sunna
and his treatment of such questions as evolution, miracles, and the existence of angels. Although he maintained that the Quran was the final
authority, in practice his rationalist approach meant that where a seeming
conflict existed between text and reason, reason prevailed. Quranic texts
that contained miraculous or supernatural language were interpreted
metaphorically or allegorically, because miracles were contrary to the laws
of nature. Yet even here he used his interpretation of the Quran to support
his rationalist position: "I do not deny the possibility of miracles because
they are against reason, but because the Quran does not support the hap-
pening of events or occurrences that are against the laws of nature or violate the usual course of things."[17]

Ahmad Khan also took a hard, critical look at the traditions of the
Prophet. He questioned the historicity and authenticity of many, if not
most, traditions, much as the noted scholars Ignaz Goldziher and Joseph
Schacht would later do. He advocated a critical reexamination of the
hadith, including those in the two major collections of Muslim and
Bukhari, and the acceptance of only those that could be traced directly to
the Prophet himself.

Sayyid Ahmad Khan's approach to Islamic reform was both theoretical and practical. In addition to his prolific writings, which included
a multivolume commentary on the Quran, he recognized the need for
practical implementation through educational reforms. He established
a translation society to make Western scientific thought more accessible and founded the Anglo-Muhammadan Oriental College at Aligarh
(renamed in 1920 Aligarh Muslim University), modeled on Cambridge
University. Through these and other educational societies and journals,
he promoted Western education in Muslim India. Like al-Afghani and
Abduh, he realized that the future of the Muslim community depended
on the ability to produce a new generation of leaders equipped to face
the challenges and demands of modernity and the West. However, his
strong affinity for the West, symbolized by his adoption of a European
lifestyle and his acceptance of knighthood from Queen Victoria of

England, undermined his influence. Many of the *ulama* and antico-lonialists dismissed "Sir" Sayyid's loyalism and reformism as political and cultural capitulation to the British.

Although Ahmad Khan did not produce the integrated curriculum to educate his version of the new Muslim leader or the new science of theology he had deemed so necessary for the future survival of the Muslim community, he did contribute to the spirit of reform in the subcontinent. An heir to the heritage of Wali Allah, he expanded and, in the end, took Islamic reform in new directions, extending its scope to include a rationalist reinterpretation of the Quran and a reevaluation of Prophetic traditions and the law. The issues that his work raised regarding the relationship of Islam to modern Western thought, the place and role of reason in interpreting religion, and the relationship of the Muslim community to the Hindu community were real questions with which future generations would continue to grapple. His modernist orientation remained a major alternative influence to that of the more traditional *ulama*, influencing the education and outlook of many Muslim elite leaders in the subcontinent.[18] Ahmad Khan's place and importance in the chain of Indian reformist thought was acknowledged by the man whose name would come to be synonymous with Islamic reform in the twentieth century, Muhammad Iqbal:

> [Ahmad Khan was the] first modern Muslim to catch a glimpse of the positive character of the age that was coming.... But the real greatness of the man consists in the fact that he was the first Indian Muslim who felt the need for a fresh orientation of Islam and worked for it.[19]

Muhammad Iqbal (1875–1938) represented the next phase in modern Islam. He combined an early Islamic education with advanced degrees from Cambridge and Munich in philosophy and law. In a sense, he represented the best of what Sayyid Ahmad Khan might have wished. Although by the twentieth century the situation in the Indian subcontinent had changed from that of Sir Sayyid Ahmad Khan's age, Muslims, who were now obtaining modern educations, still lived in a society whose *ulama* generally preached an Islam that did not adequately address modern realities.

> No wonder then that the younger generation   demand a fresh orientation of their faith. With the reawakening of Islam, therefore, it is necessary to examine, in an independent spirit, what Europe has taught and how far the conclusions reached by her can help us in the revision, and if necessary, reconstruction of theological thought in Islam.[20]

Muslim corporate identity also continued to be an important issue. However, it was not one of loyalty to the British raj but, instead, independence and national identity. The Muslim community was divided over the question of Muslim participation in the Indian independence movement. Many had joined with Hindus in the Congress party and pressed for the creation of a single, secular nation-state. Others increasingly argued that, given strong communal sentiments and politics, India's Muslim minority would face a serious threat to its identity and survival in a predominantly Hindu secular state. As with much of Islamic history, and certainly the history of Islamic revival and reform movements, religious reflection and interpretation were conditioned by and intertwined with the political life of the community.

Muhammad Iqbal's profession was the law; his passion, writing poetry and prose; his lifelong concern, Muslim religious and political survival and reform. From the time he returned from his doctoral studies in Europe, he devoted himself to the revival of Indian Islam. He did this both as a poet-philosopher and, more reluctantly, as a politician. He placed himself within the revivalist tradition of Ahmad Sirhindi, Shah Wali Allah, and Muhammad ibn Abd al-Wahhab while addressing the questions of Islamic modernism. Islam and the Muslim community were in danger; they remained in decay and decline, were politically powerless, morally corrupted, and culturally backward. All of this, for Iqbal, stood in sharp contrast with the inner nature of Islam, which was dynamic and creative. Drawing on his Islamic heritage and influenced by his study of Western philosophy (Hegel, Bergson, Fichte, Nietzsche), he developed his own synthesis and interpretation of Islam in response to the sociohistorical conditions and events of his time. Nowhere is this synthesis of East and West more evident than in Iqbal's dynamic concept of the self. Rejecting Plato's static universe and those aspects of Sufism that denied the affirmation of the self in the world, Iqbal, utilizing the Quran, developed a dynamic *Weltanschauung* in his theory of selfhood that embraced all reality: individual self, society, and God. For Iqbal, the relationship of God to Islamic society and the Muslim to society incorporates both permanence and change. God, the ultimate or absolute self, has a creative, dynamic life that is both permanent and changing, as creation is the unfolding of the inner possibilities of God in a single and yet continuing act. The individual, the basic unit of Muslim society, is Quranically (2:30) charged as God's vicegerent with the mission of carrying out God's will on earth. Muslims share in this ongoing process of creation, bringing order out of chaos, by endeavoring to produce the model society to be emulated by others. An interdependence exists; the individual is elevated through the community, and the community is organized by the individual.

At the heart of Iqbal's vision of Islam is the unity of God (*tawhid*). The oneness of God applies not only to the nature of God but also to His relationship to the world. As God is the one creator, sustainer, and judge of the universe, so too His will or law governs every aspect of His creation and is to be realized in every area of life. This belief is the basis for Iqbal's view of the community as a religiopolitical state and of the supremacy of Islamic law in Muslim society. Based on the Prophetic tradition that "the whole of this earth is a mosque" and on Muhammad's role as Prophet as well as head of the Medinan state, Iqbal concluded, "All that is secular is therefore sacred in the roots of its being."[21] There is no bifurcation of the spiritual and the temporal.

Church and state are not two sides of the same thing, for Islam is a single, unanalyzable reality.[22] Nowhere is this more evident than in Islamic law. Iqbal reasserted the Sharia's role as the comprehensive guideline for a society of believers and the need for it to be reintroduced into Muslim societies. During the nineteenth century, Islamic law, with the exception of family law, had been displaced in many Muslim countries by European codes. In the Indian subcontinent, the interaction of Islamic law and British law had produced Anglo-Muhammadan law, much of which was based on British common law. For Iqbal, Islamic law was central to the unity and life of the Muslim community: "When a community forsakes its Law, its parts are severed, like scattered dust. The being of the Muslim rests alone on Law, which is in truth the inner core of the Apostle's faith."[23]

Convinced that the survival of Islam and the Muslim community's role as a political and moral force in South Asia were dependent on the centrality of Islamic law, Iqbal emphasized to his friend and coworker Muhammad Ali Jinnah, the leader of the Muslim League party and the founder of Pakistan, the need for a Muslim state or states in India. However, Iqbal did not have in mind the simple restoration of law as it was delineated in the doctrines of the law schools. For Iqbal, just as God has a creative, dynamic life that is both permanent and changing, Islam's way of life as interpreted in Islamic law is itself dynamic and open to change: "[T]he early doctors of law taking their cue from this groundwork evolved a number of legal systems. But with all their comprehensiveness, these systems are after all individual interpretations and as such can not claim any finality."[24]

Iqbal distinguished between eternal, immutable principles of the Sharia and those regulations that were the product of human interpretation and thus subject to change. He regarded the condition of Islam as a "dogmatic slumber" that had resulted in five hundred years of immobility due to the blind following of tradition and believed that the restoration of Islamic vitality required the "reconstruction" of the sources of Islamic law. While acknowledging the role of the *ulama* in the past, Iqbal blamed them for the conservatism that had characterized Islam since the fall of Baghdad. With their perpetuation of what he called the fiction of the closing of the door of *ijtihad*, these scholar-guardians of Islam, who were the followers of those who had developed Islamic law, stopped the dynamic process of reinterpretation and reapplication of Islamic principles to new situations. Instead, they were content to simply perpetuate established traditions. Iqbal rejected the centuries-long tendency to regard Islamic law as fixed and sacrosanct. Like other Islamic revivalists and modernists, he believed that Muslims must once again reassert their right to *ijtihad*, to reinterpret and reapply Islam to changing social conditions. This right belonged to all qualified Muslims and not just the *ulama*. He believed that the traditional criteria used to designate one as an interpreter was both self-serving and shortsighted. The failure of the *ulama* to broaden their training left them ill prepared for resolving many new, modern issues. For these reasons, Iqbal extended and redefined *ijtihad* and *ijma*. He suggested that the right to interpret and apply Islam for the community be transferred from the *ulama* to a national assembly or legislature. This collective or corporate *ijtihad* would then constitute the authoritative consensus (*ijma*) of the community. In this way, he also transformed the meaning of consensus of the community from its traditional one, the agreement of the religious leaders and scholars, to the consensus of modern legislative assemblies, the majority of whose members would have a better knowledge of contemporary affairs. In addition, he recommended that, because of the complex nature of many modem problems, the legislature should seek the advice of experts from traditional and modern disciplines. Shortly after its establishment, Pakistan would establish such a council of experts, the Islamic Ideology Council. Iqbal's approach proved attractive to modernists as a way to enhance the legitimacy of parliamentary government and reforms in family law. However, threatened by an outlook that diminished their status and power in society, the *ulama* were resistant.

Although Iqbal admired the accomplishments of the West—its dynamic spirit, intellectual tradition, and technology—he was critical of its excesses, such as European imperialism and colonialism, the economic exploitation of capitalism, the atheism of Marxism, and the moral bankruptcy of secularism. Therefore, he turned to the past to "rediscover" principles and values that could be employed to reconstruct an alternative Islamic model for modern Muslim society. This resulted in the discovery

of Islamic versions of democracy and parliamentary government, precedents in Islamic belief that, through reinterpretation, could be used to
develop Islamic equivalents to Western concepts and institutions. Thus,
for example, Iqbal concluded that because of the centrality of such beliefs
as the equality and brotherhood of believers, democracy was the most
important political ideal in Islam. Though history, after the period of the
Rightly Guided Caliphs, had prevented the community from realizing this
Islamic ideal, it remains a duty for the Muslim community. That Iqbal did
not believe that he was creating an Islamic rationale for simply copying
Western values and institutions is strikingly evident in his conclusion that
England embodied this "Muslim" quality:

> Democracy has been the great mission of England in modern times
> it is one aspect of our own political ideal that is being worked out in
> it. It is . . . the spirit of the British Empire that makes it the greatest
> Muhammadan Empire in the world![25]

But, for Iqbal, the very bases for Islamic democracy—the equality and
brotherhood of all Muslims—militated against Iqbal's acceptance of
the concept of nationalism. Although as a young man he had been an
Indian nationalist, he returned from his studies in Europe committed to
pan-Islamism. In addition to considering territorial nationalism as anti-
thetical to the universal brotherhood established by Muhammad and
embodied in the caliphate, he regarded nationalism as the tool used by
colonialism to dismember the Muslim world. The political ideal of Islam
was a transnational community that transcended ethnic, racial, and
national ties; it was based on an inner cohesion that stemmed from the
unity of the community's religiopolitical ideal.

As with al-Afghani and others, Iqbal's pan-Islamic commitment was
tempered by political realism. He accepted the need for Muslims to gain
national independence, but believed that as a family of nations based on
a common spiritual heritage, common ideals, and a common law—the
Sharia—they should form their own League of Nations. He applied this
rationale to the situation of Indian Muslims and in 1930 reluctantly concluded that internal Hindu–Muslim communal harmony was impossible.
Iqbal became convinced that the threat of Hindu dominance in an independent India necessitated the establishment of a separate region or state
for the Muslims of India to preserve their identity and distinctive way
of life:

> The nature of the Prophet's religious experience, as disclosed in the
> Quran, is wholly different [from that of Christianity]. It is individual

experience creative of a social order. Its immediate outcome is the fundamentals of a polity with implicit legal concepts whose civic significance can not be belittled merely because their origin is revelational. The religious ideal of Islam is organically related to the social order which it has created. The rejection of the one will eventually involve the rejection of the other. Therefore the construction of a polity on [Indian] national lines, if it means a displacement of the Islamic principles of solidarity, is simply unthinkable to a Muslim.[26]

If Sayyid Ahmad Khan had been the traditionally educated Muslim who sought to make modern Western liberal thought Islamically acceptable, Muhammad Iqbal was the modern, Western-educated Muslim who reinterpreted Islam in conjunction with Western thought to demonstrate its relevance as a viable alternative to Christian European and Marxist ideologies.

Legacy to Islamic Modernism

The legacy of Islamic modernism has been mixed. Islamic modernists were trailblazers who did not simply seek to purify their religion by a return to an Islam that merely reappropriated past solutions. Instead, they wished to chart its future direction through a reinterpretation of Islam in light of modern realities. They were pioneers who planted the seeds for the acceptance of change, a struggle that has continued. Whereas their secular counterparts looked to the West rather uncritically and traditionalists shunned the West rather obstinately, Islamic modernists attempted to establish a continuity between their Islamic heritage and modern change. On the one hand, they identified with premodern revivalist movements and called for the purification of internal deficiencies and deviations. On the other, they borrowed and assimilated new ideas and values from the West. For some, like Sayyid Ahmad Khan, this was accomplished by maintaining that Islam was the religion of reason and nature *par excellence*. For others, like Afghani and Iqbal, the rubric was the reclaiming of a progressive, creative past with a political and cultural florescence that demonstrated that the very qualities associated with the power of the West were already present in Islam and accounted for its past triumphs and accomplishments. Thus, the belief that Muslims already possessed an Islamic rationale and the means for the assimilation of modern science and technology was strengthened. For all, the key was to convince their coreligionists that stagnation and decline were caused by blind imitation of the past and that continued survival and revitalization of the Islamic community required a bold reinterpretation of Islam's religious tradition.

Islamic modernists, like secular modernists, represented a minority position within the community but with less direct influence to implement change at a national level. In general, it would not be unfair to characterize modernism as primarily an intellectual movement, although activist reforms were initiated. Modernists sought to inspire and motivate a vanguard within the leadership or future leadership of their communities and had to contend with the resistance of a more conservative religious majority. The religious establishment was often alienated by the reformers' rejection of their traditional authority as the sole interpreters of Islam. They bridled at modernists' claim to independent interpretation and their attempts to chart the course for modern reforms. Abduh's educational reforms, welcomed by younger *ulama* and students, were resisted by many of the more established religious leaders. Sayyid Ahmad Khan's favorable evaluation of evolution caused *ulama* to condemn him as an infidel. Although he gave the *ulama* control of Islamic studies at Aligarh University, they proved resistant to his reformism.

As noted earlier, Islamic modernism engaged in a process of interpretation or individual investigation (*ijtihad*) that was qualitatively different in its methodology from that claimed by premodern revivalists, who had wished simply to reclaim and implement authentic teachings of the Quran and Sunna. However, modernists, while agreeing with revivalists about the need to reform Sufism and purge Islam of un-Islamic practices in law, also felt free to suggest that many practices acceptable in the past were no longer relevant. Moreover, they claimed the right and necessity to formulate new regulations. Instead of simply engaging in a restoration of the practice of Muhammad and the early community, they advocated an adaptation of Islam to the changing conditions of modern society. In effect, this meant new laws and attitudes toward religious and social reforms. Traditionalists criticized such changes as unwarranted innovations, an accommodationism that permitted alien, un-Islamic, Western Christian practices to infiltrate Islam. Reforms were condemned as deviation from Islam (*bida*). Reformers criticized many of the *ulama* for being out of touch with the modern world, incapable of adequately leading the community, and for being in need of reform; this deepened the resistance of many, although not all, of the religious establishment to Islamic modernism.

What were the effects and accomplishments of Islamic modernism? First, modernists implanted an outlook or attitude toward the past as well as the future. Pride in an Islamic heritage and the achievements of Islamic history and civilization provided Muslims with a renewed sense of identity and purpose. This countered the sense of religiocultural backwardness and impotence engendered by years of subjugation to the West and by the preaching of Christian missionaries. At the same time, emphasis on the dynamic, progressive, rational character of Islam enabled new generations of Muslims to embrace modern civilization more confidently, to regard change as an opportunity rather than a threat.

Second, the example and writings of modernists inspired many like-minded Muslims in other geographic areas. Belief in the absolute relevance, compatibility, and adaptability of Islam to the twin challenges of colonialism and modern culture influenced modernist movements in many other parts of the Muslim world. In North Africa, the influence of al-Afghani and Abduh on the thought and outlook of reformers like Morocco's Bonchaib al-Doukkali (Abu Shuayb al-Dukkali) and Allal al-Fasi, Tunisia's Abd al-Aziz al-Thalabi, and Algeria's Abd al-Hamid ibn Badis (Ben Badis) was such that Islamic reformism in North Africa is often simply referred to as Salafiyya or neo-Salafiyya movements. Salafiyya reformism extended across the Islamic world to Indonesia, where it influenced the Muhammadiyya and Sarekat Islam movements. Although these organizations had significant differences, they were similar in their desire to respond to internal decline and external encroachment. All rejected blind adherence to tradition and un-Islamic popular religious practices and advocated Sufi reform, modernist reinterpretation (*ijtihad*) of the sources of Islam, and educational and social reforms. Most, like the Muhammadiyya, established schools that combined Islamic studies with a modern curriculum and ran social-welfare programs. They published reform-oriented newspapers and journals, such as *al-Islah* ("The Reform") and *al-Muntagid* ("The Critic") in Algeria. Many modernists were anticolonialist and thus participants, often leaders, in nationalist movements that were rooted in religion and harnessed Islam for mass mobilization. Allal al-Fasi organized the Istiqlal (Independence) party in Morocco, combining Islamic reformism with the organization of Sufi orders. Islamic reformers in Algeria joined with some *ulama* and established the Algerian Association of Ulama, whose motto was "Islam is my religion; Arabic is my language; Algeria is my Fatherland."

Third, reformers' espousal of a process of reinterpretation that adapted traditional concepts and institutions to modern realities resulted in a transformation of their meaning to accommodate and legitimate change. As a result, subsequent generations, whether modernist or traditionalist, have come to speak of Islamic "democracy" and to view traditional concepts of consultation and community consensus as conducive to parliamentary forms of government. Similarly, it became quite common for many, including the religious establishment, to accept the use of *ijtihad*.

Fourth, the holistic approach of al-Afghani, Rida, and Iqbal, which viewed Islam as a comprehensive guide for private as well as public life, became part of the modern understanding or interpretation of Islam. Their emphasis on Islam as an alternative ideology for state and society, coupled with the example of eighteenth-century revivalist movements, has been a major influence on modern Islamic activists and movements throughout the twentieth century.

However, the record of Islamic modernism is mixed. Although it was able to prescribe, it proved less successful in implementation. Al-Afghani, Abduh, Rida, Ahmad Khan, and Iqbal failed to provide a systematic, comprehensive theology or program for legal reform. Conservative Muslims continued to see reformism as less an indigenous Islamic movement than an attempt to accommodate Islam to Western thought and culture. Although they attracted a circle of followers, the reformers were not succeeded by comparable charismatic figures, nor did they create effective organizations to continue and implement their ideas. After their deaths, their followers went in many directions. While Rida continued the work of al-Afghani and Abduh, Abduh's associates Saad Zaghlul and Taha Hussein became secular nationalists. Although Muhammad Ali Jinnah and his Muslim League party rallied mass support for the creation of an independent Pakistan through the appeal to Islam, he did not follow Iqbal and implement Islamic law. Islamic reformism tended to become a legacy that was not developed and applied systematically but instead employed or manipulated on occasion, in a diffuse and ad hoc fashion, when convenient by individuals, nationalist movements, governments, and Islamic organizations. The influence and limitations of Islamic modernism are evident in the interpretations of Islam employed in Muslim family law reform, which became the primary arena for Islamic modernist reform, and in the creation of major organizations like the Muslim Brotherhood and the Jamaat-i-Islami.

Muslim Family Law Reform

Muslim family law provides the primary example of the implementation of Islamic reform in the first part of the twentieth century. Reflecting the centrality of the family in Islam and in traditional Muslim society, family law had been the heart of the Sharia and the major area of Islamic law that had remained in force to govern the lives of Muslims throughout the Islamic world.

Modern legal change occurred in many parts of the Muslim world during the nineteenth century, when most areas of Islamic law were replaced by modern codes based on European law. Secular courts were created to handle civil and criminal law, and as a result, the jurisdiction of religious (Sharia) courts was severely restricted. As with educational reform, the modernization of law further eroded the role and authority of the *ulama*, as their tasks were now taken over by Western-educated officials and civil servants. However, the one area that remained essentially untouched and in force was family law, the law governing marriage, divorce, and inheritance. The situation changed in the twentieth century when this important and sensitive area of Islamic tradition was subjected to change. Thus, family law reform constitutes a major example of modem religious reform in Islam.

Early modernists, such as Muhammad Abduh and Ahmad Khan, established rationales for Islamic reform. Their disciples, Qasim Amin in Egypt and Mumtaz Ali in India, developed the social dimension of their programs, in particular as it related to women. Both focused on the plight of Muslim women as a primary cause of the deterioration of the family and society. In his *The Emancipation of Women* and *The New Woman*, Qasim Amin criticized lack of education, child marriages, arranged marriages, polygamy, and easy male-initiated divorce as causes of the bondage of Muslim women. Mumtaz Ali took a similar position. Ali refuted the antifeminist Quranic exegesis of some classical legal scholars, maintaining that their interpretations did not reflect the meaning of Quranic texts but the customs and mores of the exegetes' own times. Fundamental reforms were required. These ideas informed the positions of feminist movements and political elites a generation later in the 1920s and 1930s.

Whereas the modernization of law in the nineteenth century had been accomplished by simply replacing traditional Islamic law with Western-derived legal codes, change in family law was rendered through a process of reinterpretation that sought to provide an Islamic rationale for reforming tradition. Selective changes were introduced through legislation that modified traditional law to improve the status of women and strengthen the rights of the nuclear family. Laws were passed to restrict polygamy (polygyny) and to limit a male's unfettered right to divorce. Women were granted additional grounds for divorce. Child marriages were discouraged by raising the minimum ages of spouses.

To justify their departure from tradition, governments relied on Islamic modernist thought and strategies, employing legal doctrines and methods to establish the Islamic character of their reforms, thus forming a link between legal modernization and traditional jurisprudence. Reforms were proclaimed as resulting from the right to reinterpret (*ijtihad*) Islam. The principle of public interest or social welfare, originally regarded as a subsidiary legal source of law by the Maliki school, was pressed into service to legitimate reforms. Abduh's modernist exegesis of the Quran was used to limit polygamy. Other subsidiary sources of law were used to select a legal doctrine from one school and apply it to another or to patch together laws from different law schools or jurists and create a new regulation. For example, the grounds for divorce were substantially broadened in countries that followed Hanafi law (Egypt, Syria, Jordan, India, Pakistan) by borrowing additional provisions from Maliki law, such as desertion, cruelty, and failure to maintain. Thus, traditional authorities were marshaled or reinterpreted to justify reforms.

Despite the relative success of family law reform, many issues were skirted and remained unresolved. Whereas classical law was the product of the *ulama*, modern reforms were undertaken by governments through the action of parliaments or national assemblies whose members were laymen who lacked the training to qualify as traditional interpreters of law. In most instances, the *ulama* felt disenfranchised and viewed the process of modern legal reform as un-Islamic. They charged that a Western secular elite had used its political power to tamper with Islam and force unwarranted innovations on Muslim society. In some instances, the *ulama* mounted a counterattack. In Pakistan, the *ulama* rejected the findings of the Family Law Commission of 1956, charging that the majority of its members (six out of seven) were not *ulama* and thus were unqualified to exercise *ijtihad,* to reinterpret Islam.

The modernist majority had argued that as the Quran and Sunna could not:

> comprehend the infinite variety of human relations for all occasions and for all epochs, the Prophet of Islam left a very large sphere free for legislative enactments and judicial decisions.... This is the principle of *ijtihad* or interpretive intelligence working within the broad framework of Quran and Sunna.[27]

The modernist majority also denied that the *ulama* had any special role and authority and maintained that all informed Muslims had the right to interpret Islam:

> Islam never developed a church with ordained priests as a class separate from the laity   some may be more learned in the Muslim law than others, but that does not constitute them as a separate class; they are not vested with any special authority and enjoy no special privileges.[28]

The *ulama* countered, reaffirming their traditional role as the qualified expert interpreters of the Sharia and accusing the modernists of wishing to ape the West because they had an inferiority complex and were ashamed of their religious tradition. Although they were not able to prevent the passage of reform legislation, they did limit the extent of the reforms. Similarly, many of the *ulama* in Iran had objected to the Shah's passage of the Family Protection Act and had criticized regulations to prohibit women from wearing the veil. Although some *ulama* accepted the reforms, the majority were willing to bide their time until a more favorable period when traditional Islamic law might once more be implemented. Differences regarding the authority of traditional law, the need for social change, and the authority of the *ulama* as the sole official interpreters of Islam remained critical issues for the majority of the *ulama* and their traditionalist followers. Their voices would be heard in the 1970s.

Muslim family law reform underscores the basic issue underlying Islamic reform in general, the authority of tradition vis-à-vis the need for reinterpretation and reform in Islam. For more conservative traditionalist Muslims, the classical interpretations of Islam, preserved in the legal manuals developed by the law schools, constitute the blueprint for society. They provide the revealed pattern or norm to be followed. The extent to which there was a dichotomy between law and society did not indicate a need for legal reform but society's departure from the straight path of Islam. The remedy was not adaptation and change but a return to established, sacrosanct norms.

However, reformers maintained that a good portion of past legal practice, the regulations in legal manuals, represented the understanding and interpretation of early jurists who had applied the principles and values of Islam to their societies. They argued that changing conditions required that Muslims once again respond to the needs of society. While acknowledging the immutability of Sharia principles and laws found in the Quran and Sunna, modernists distinguished between Sharia, God's revealed law, and its extrapolation and delineation in the corpus of classical law (*fiqh*, understanding), emphasizing the contingency and relativity of the latter. Their position rested on the distinction employed by early Islamic modernists between the eternal validity of religious duties and the flexibility of much of social law. Thus, they asserted that Islamic reform was both necessary and possible.

A major factor undermining the credibility of reformers in the eyes of traditionalists is that the prime movers of reform have been Western-educated or -oriented rulers and political elites, a minority in society legislating for the more traditional majority. Similarly, feminist movements were regarded as organizations of upper-class women who wished to discard the veil to adopt Western dress and lifestyles. Although modernizing elites skillfully appealed to Islam for their methodology, and hence justification, in fact their approach was often superficial and piece-meal. They did not pursue a systematic review and assessment of Islamic law, fearful of its consequences. Because of the considerable resistance to reforms, compromises were often necessary. Indeed, in most Muslim countries, if a man takes a second wife or divorces his wife contrary to reform laws, the action is illegal but not invalid. This tentative approach toward legal reform was denounced as a manipulation and exploitation of Islam. The significance of these unresolved issues and the hold of tradition will be seen in those Muslim countries where the contemporary resurgence of Islam has led to calls for the implementation of Islamic law and the repeal of family law reforms.

Contemporary Islamic Movements

Parallel to modernist reforms initiated in the first half of the twentieth century was the emergence of new religiously based social movements, in particular Hasan al-Banna's Muslim Brotherhood in Egypt and Mawlana Mawdudi's Jamaat-i-Islami (the Islamic Society) in the Indian subcontinent. These movements saw the Islamic community of the twentieth century at a critical crossroads. Like secular and Islamic modernists, they acknowledged the internal weakness of the community, the external threat of Western imperialism, and the value of science and technology. However, the Brotherhood and the Jamaat were more sweeping in their condemnation of the West and assertion of the total self-sufficiency of Islam. Although secularists rejected Western political hegemony, they still looked to the West in charting their present and future. They adopted Western dress, manners, music, and movies and appropriated Europe's political, economic, educational, and legal institutions. Islamic modernists had struggled to provide an Islamic rationale for selective borrowing from the West. However, the Brotherhood and the Jamaat saw their options more clearly and simply. Both capitalism and Marxism represented man-made secular paths that were alien to the God-ordained, straight path of Islam. If Muslims were to remain faithful to God and His divine will, they had to reject Western secularism and materialism and return solely to Islam, whose perfection assured guidance in all aspects of life:

> Until recently, writers, intellectuals, scholars and governments glorified the principles of European civilization   adopted a Western style and manner .... Today, on the contrary, the wind has changed .... Voices are raised   for a return to the principles of Islam   for initiating the reconciliation of modern life with these principles, as a prelude to a final Islamization.[29]

FORMATIVE INFLUENCES FOR CONTEMPORARY ISLAMIC MOVEMENTS

It is difficult to overstate the impact of Egypt's Hasan al-Banna's Muslim Brotherhood and Pakistan's Mawlana Mawdudi's Jamaat-i-Islami and their influence on the formation of other Islamic movements. Combining piety and religious interpretations or ideologies, contemporary Islamic movements represent a spectrum of positions from moderation and gradualism to radicalism and revolutionary violence, from selective criticism of the West to rejection and attacks on all that the West stands for.

John L. Esposito et al., *World Religions Today* (New York: Oxford University Press, 2015), p. 269.

For the Muslim Brotherhood and the Jamaat-i-Islami, Islam was not restricted to personal piety or simply a component in social or political life—it was a comprehensive ideology for personal and public life, the foundation for Muslim state and society.

Hasan al-Banna (1906–49) of Egypt and Mawlana Abul Ala Mawdudi (1903–79) of India were both raised in the shadow of British colonialism in societies where anticolonial national independence movements were active. They were pious, committed Muslims whose upbringing and education exposed them to Islamic education, modernist thought, and Western learning. Hasan al-Banna had studied in Cairo, where he came into contact with Rashid Rida and the Salafiyya movement. He was influenced by the reformist thought of al-Afghani and Abduh, but as channeled through the more conservative, revivalist phase of Rida's life and *al-Manar* in the 1920s, with its emphasis on the dangers of Westernization and the complete self-sufficiency of Islam. He established the Muslim Brotherhood in 1928. Mawlana Mawdudi, on the other hand, had been given a traditional Islamic education in which modern education was assiduously avoided. It was only later that he learned English and taught himself modern subjects. In 1938, at the invitation of Muhammad Iqbal, he moved to Lahore and in 1941 founded the Jamaat-i-Islami. Despite distinctive differences in their movements due to local conditions, both Hasan al-Banna and Mawlana Mawdudi combined religion with social activism. They shared a revivalist ideology and established activist organizations that remain vibrant today and have served as an example for others throughout much of the Muslim world.

Hasan al-Banna (1906–49), the founder of the Muslim Brotherhood.

Both the organization and the ideological outlook of the Brotherhood and the Jamaat were modeled on the example of the Prophet Muhammad and his first Islamic religiosocial reformation or revolution. The Islamic paradigm was reinterpreted and reapplied by these modern religious societies as it had been by revivalists and reformers in the past. Like Muhammad, they established communities of true believers who were distinguished from the rest of society and were totally committed to the struggle (*jihad*) to transform society. They did not leave (*hijra*) their societies but instead organized their followers into an Islamically oriented community or party within the broader (un-Islamic) society, forming a group of committed, like-minded Muslims who were to serve as the dynamic nucleus to transform society from within. In a sense, they were the vanguard of a religiously motivated elite. They were not a political party but an ideological fraternity, as their names, the Society of Muslim Brothers (Jamaat al-Ikhwan al-Muslimin) and the Jamaat-i-Islami (Islamic Society), signified. Each developed a well-knit socio-religious organization with a network of branches and cells. Members were trained and reinforced in their faith and commitment to create a more Islamically oriented state and society; this was their reformist struggle or jihad. They were carefully selected and underwent a period of training and ideological indoctrination that emphasized religious knowledge and moral fitness and concentrated on moral and social programs. Religious instruction, youth work, schools, hospitals, religious publications, and social-welfare projects were among the activities utilized to create a new generation of leaders in a morally strong society.

The Muslim Brotherhood grew rapidly as a mass movement, soon expanding beyond its rural lower- and lower-middle-class background to include many members of the new middle class in urban areas. It attracted a broad following: clerks, policemen, merchants, teachers, lawyers, physicians, civil servants, soldiers, and university students. At its height, its membership was estimated to be between 500,000 and 1 million. In contrast, the Jamaat had a more restricted membership, focusing on developing a new elite leadership. For Mawdudi, change resulted from a vanguard working within society, and therefore, in contrast to the Brotherhood, the Jamaat was primarily an elite rather than a populist organization, concerned with training a core of well-educated and Islamically committed leaders. Although an activist, Mawdudi focused on a systematic presentation of Islam. A gifted and prolific writer, he attempted to provide a theoretical blueprint for the revival of Islam, or what he termed the process of Islamic revolution. His books and articles discuss such themes as the Islamic way of life, Islam and its relationship to the state, law, marriage and the family, veiling and the seclusion of women, and economics.

Under the leadership of the Supreme Guide, Hasan al-Banna (and later, its prolific and influential ideologue **Sayyid Qutb**), and Mawlana Mawdudi, the Muslim Brotherhood and the Jamaat-i-Islami reinterpreted Islamic history and tradition to respond to the sociohistorical conditions of the twentieth century. Both regarded Islam as the all-embracing ideology. The union of religion and society, the relationship of Islam to all aspects of life, followed from the doctrine of God's unity (*tawhid*) and sovereignty over all creation as embodied in the comprehensive nature of the Sharia: "The sharia is a complete scheme of life and an all embracing social order."[30] As they looked at their societies, and the Muslim world in general, both Hasan al-Banna and Mawlana Mawdudi attributed the impotence of their communities to political disunity, social dislocation, moral laxity, and a growing indifference to religion. Western secularism, with its separation of church and state, and the unbridled materialism of capitalism and Marxism were regarded as the major culprits. In contrast, they argued, Islam's organic relationship among religion, politics, and society distinguished it from the West. The separation of religion from the state represented for the Brotherhood and the Jamaat the inherent fallacy of Western secularism. Withdrawal of divine guidance would be the basis for its moral decline and ultimate downfall. Western culture, and all who do not follow Islam, exist, as did pre-Islamic society, in a state of ignorance and darkness.

Both the Brotherhood and the Jamaat incorporated the ideology, symbols, and language of revivalism within their reformist interpretation of Islam. There were two historic options—ignorance and Islam. Modern Muslim society was compared with that of pre-Islamic Arabia, a period of ignorance (*jahiliyya*), disunity, exploitation, and superstition. They felt that much of the Muslim world was gripped by factionalism, Sufi excesses, and acculturated, alien European institutions, practices contrary to Islam. The unity of the brotherhood of believers must replace the religious, political, and socioeconomic factions that divided and weakened the *umma*. Following revivalist logic, they called for a return to the Quran, the Sunna of the Prophet, and the practice of the early community to establish an Islamic system of government. Like Islamic revivalists and modernists, they rejected *taqlid* and upheld the right of *ijtihad*. They followed modernists in their acceptance of change through legal reform, although not accepting its application in modern family law reforms, which they regarded as Western in inspiration and intent. Unlike Islamic modernists who looked to the West and provided an Islamic rationale for the appropriation of Western learning, these contemporary revivalists emphasized the perfection and comprehensiveness of Islam and, hence, its self-sufficiency. All that Muslims needed could be found in or derived from the Islamic tradition. Although open to science and technology, they denounced Muslim intellectuals and governments for their dependence on the West. They believed that the renewal of Muslim society and its social transformation or modernization must be rooted in Islamic principles and values.

Instead of speaking of democracy as such, the Brotherhood and Jamaat accepted the modernist reinterpretation of traditional concepts of consultation and community consensus, but noted that in an Islamic democracy the will of the people remained subordinate to the divine will. Mawlana Mawdudi called this a theo-democracy to distinguish it from a theocracy, or a clergy-run state, which he rejected. In an Islamic state, democracy could never mean that the majority had the power to legislate laws that contradicted religious belief regarding alcohol, gambling, prostitution, and so forth. Emphasizing the universality of the *umma* and its mission, they rejected nationalism and European-inspired legal codes, which they regarded as un-Islamic and a threat to Islamic identity, and called instead for an Islamic state to be governed by the Sharia. However, both Hasan al-Banna and Mawlana Mawdudi tempered their idealism with a realistic pragmatism. Mawdudi had rejected both Hindu and Muslim nationalism in India and initially refused to support the establishment of Pakistan as a separate homeland for Muslims. Like al-Afghani, Rida, and Iqbal, pan-Islamic aspirations gave way to a reluctant acceptance of political reality, and thus al-Banna and Mawdudi focused on Egypt and Pakistan, respectively, while remaining committed to the eventual restoration of worldwide unity and involved in the broader concerns of the *umma*.

Mawlana Abul Ala Mawdudi (1903–79), the founder of the Jamaat-i-Islami, had a far-reaching impact on Muslim thinkers and activists throughout the Islamic world. Although the Jamaat and Muslim Brotherhood were founded as a political party, their holistic vision, their belief that the Islamic community was to exist in a state and society governed by Islamic law, drew the Brotherhood and the Jamaat into the political arena. Both had understood their social revolution or reformation as occurring within society; their paths differed as a result of differences in political conditions. The Muslim Brotherhood's dissatisfaction with the failure of Egypt's government to establish an Islamic state escalated into violence, armed conflict, and the assassination of its founder in 1949. Government repression drove the Brotherhood deeper underground and subsequently led to a series of confrontations, imprisonments, executions,

Mawlana Abul Ala Mawdudi (1903–79), the founder of the Jamaat-i-Islami, had a far-reaching impact on Muslim thinkers and activists throughout the Islamic world.

and, finally, its suppression and proscription in Egypt in the mid-1960s. In Pakistan, the Jamaat often found itself in opposition to governments and resorted to political action and participation in elections. Although Mawdudi and his followers were sometimes imprisoned for their activities, by and large they were able to work within the system.

The Muslim Brotherhood and the Jamaat-i-Islami demonstrate the strength and attractiveness of neorevivalist movements. After the Brotherhood was banned in Egypt and apparently crushed as its leaders were executed, imprisoned, or driven into exile, Muslim Brotherhood organizations continued to grow in many other parts of the Muslim world—the Sudan, Syria, Jordan, Palestine, and Kuwait. Similarly, the Jamaat-i-Islami established organizations in India, Afghanistan, and Kashmir as well as Pakistan. What was the basis of the appeal of neorevivalists? First, they presented themselves as an indigenous movement. Although similar to modernists in their critique of Sufi excesses, saint worship, and the backwardness of the *ulama* and in their appeal to the process of premodern revivalism, neorevivalists did not seek to address modern life by demonstrating the compatibility of Islam with the West. Instead, they claimed that Muslims could adapt to the demands of modernity by reference to Islam alone. There was no need to go outside Islam's way of life, no need to be dependent on the West and run the danger of Westernizing Islam. Second, the organization and activism of neorevivalists contrasted sharply with the tendency of modernism to consist of a loose circle of intellectuals. Their emphasis on discipline, loyalty, and training as well as social-activist programs resulted in more cohesive and effective organizations. Third, although criticizing blind adherence to medieval Islam and claiming the right to *ijtihad*, neorevivalist condemnation of Western values (Westernization) and insistence on the self-sufficiency of Islam proved more attractive to many of the *ulama* and the more traditional sectors of society. This was more akin to the traditional interpretation of Islam that they had learned and the lifestyle and values they cherished. Quite simply, the degree of change advocated by neorevivalists seemed less radical than that of the modernists, less of a departure from tradition.

Whereas neorevivalists and modernists advocated legal change, in practice, in sensitive areas like family law reform, the Brotherhood and the Jamaat made common cause with the majority of the traditionalist-oriented *ulama*. They also tended to agree in their condemnation of the free mingling of the sexes, Western dress and manners, movies, and banking interest. The Islamic credentials of modernists, on the other hand, were eroded by the tendency of many of the colleagues or students of early modernists to follow a liberal, Western secular path.

Neorevivalism blended the worldview that informed the activism of premodern revivalist groups, like the Wahhabi and Mahdi movements, with the holistic vision of Islam articulated in theory by modernists like al-Afghani, Abduh, and Iqbal. The result was an ideology grounded solely on Islam, an Islamic alternative that presented Islam as a timeless, rational, comprehensive faith with a transcendent message that was relevant to this life as well as the next. Islam was identified with the everyday lives and concerns of Muslims. Poverty, illiteracy, economic exploitation, education, and health care were all issues to which the Islamic message was relevant. The transcendent was made immanent not by Sufi withdrawal or indifference to the material world but by involvement in it. For the Brotherhood and the Jamaat, Muslim submission to God implied the molding of the individual and society. The Quranic teaching that human beings were God's representatives or vicegerents on earth, charged with realizing and spreading His will for humankind, became the theological basis for the social and moral reformism that characterized the work of the Brotherhood and Jamaat. The preaching of Islam was not just a propagation of the faith among non-Muslims but a revivalist call or mission to those born Muslim to awaken and become better Muslims. The message or interpretation of Islam that they preached and practiced addressed the totality of the human experience.

Their strengths also implied distinct weaknesses. Defending and establishing the appropriateness, indeed superiority, of Islam often degenerated into a one-sided attack on the ills of Western culture. The worst characteristics or social problems (prostitution, alcoholism, high crime rates, sexual promiscuity) of the West were exploited in a polemic that selectively compared Western realities with Islamic ideals, Western Christendom at its worst with Islam at its best. Secularism was equated with godlessness, an absence or denial of religious belief and values, rather than a separation of church and state to guarantee religious freedom in pluralistic societies. Women's emancipation movements were dismissed as Western-inspired, anti-Islamic attacks on the sanctity of the family without a serious consideration of changing social realities.

The perception and experience of modernity as a threat of Western political and cultural domination and assimilation resulted from the state of siege posed by both European powers and Muslim secular elites, who were regarded as indigenous domestic colonizers responsible for the Westernization of Muslim society: "The faction which works for the separation of Egypt from Islam is really a shameless, pernicious, and perverse group of puppets and slaves of Europe."[31] The need to respond to this internal and external threat motivated revivalists to assume a defensive posture, to defend Islam and its way of life "against" Westernization, instead of adequately reexamining and reinterpreting Islam. Yet this did not mean that the Brotherhood and the Jamaat were not open to change. Nothing could be more mistaken than to stereotype their goals as a simple, literalist return to the seventh century. However, the interpretation of Islam implicit in their ideological worldview was limited by its failure to reexamine Islamic history more thoroughly.

Lacking an awareness of the actual historical (as distinguished from the idealized) development of their faith, revivalists could not fully appreciate the nature of the dynamic, creative process of Islamization that characterized the development of Islamic law and theology. They were unable to realize the extent to which human reasoning and socio-historical conditions affected the formulation of belief and practice: the role of local customary practice in law, social practice as a source of *hadith*, and the influence of political considerations on theological doctrine. The breadth of the process of Islamization by which Muslims had adopted and adapted foreign social and cultural practices, integrating them within a framework of Islamic principles and values, remained forgotten. (In contrast, the failure of Islamic modernists like Muhammmad Abduh and Ahmad Khan to produce a systematic reconstruction of Islam meant that their isolated, ad hoc reforms were not seen as part of an integrated whole but instead as the result of an eclectic borrowing from the West. Therefore, modernists came to be regarded as Westernizers.) For revivalists, Islamic history provided *the* authoritative interpretation of revelation rather than *an* authoritative interpretation open to subsequent substantive reinterpretation and reform as circumstances change. Although revivalists advocated change through *ijtihad*, they tended to accept past practice and undertake change only in those areas not already covered by Islamic law.

CONCLUSION

Revival and reform have been dominant themes in Islam since the eighteenth century, as Muslims responded to internal and external forces that challenged their faith and social order. Islam was used effectively in the formation of Islamic sociopolitical reform organizations and Islamic modernist movements. Revivalist movements in the eighteenth and nineteenth centuries demonstrated the power of an appeal to Islam in providing a rationale for community decline and initiating religio-political movements bent on social and moral reform. Despite their differences, premodernist movements left a legacy to modern Islam in their ideological interpretation of Islam and their activist methods and organization. Islam proved a potent force in both the response to internal decline and the reaction to European imperialism. Islamic modernists reinterpreted Islamic sources to obtain new answers and to assimilate some Western ideas and institutions. Islamic modernism influenced attitudes toward Islam regarding both its past significance and its modern relevance. Its emphasis on Islam as a progressive, dynamic, rational religion generated a sense of pride, identity, and conviction that Islam was relevant to modern life. Although Islamic modernism did not produce a systematic reinterpretation of Islam and splintered in many directions, its outlook and modernist vocabulary penetrated Muslim society and enabled a new generation of Muslims to confidently embrace modern civilization with the belief that Islam was compatible and adaptable to the demands and challenges of modernity. However, some of these Muslims—neorevivalists—who grew up during the independence struggles of the post–World War I period rejected the accommodationist spirit of Islamic modernism. They combined a holistic interpretation of Islam and an organizational activism, calling for a social order based not on modernist acculturation but on a self-sufficient Islamic alternative. The struggle to produce viable Islamic responses to the new demands of modernity preoccupied many in the latter half of the twentieth century, as evident in the reassertion of religion in Muslim politics and society.

KEY TERMS

Hasan al-Banna (1906–49)	Muhammad Iqbal (1875–1938)
Jamaat-i-Islami (Islamic Society)	Muslim Brotherhood
Jamal al-Din al-Afghani (1838–97)	Rashid Rida
Mahdi	*salafiyya*
Mawlana Abul Ala Mawdudi	Sayyid Ahmad Khan (1817–98)
Muhammad Abduh	Sayyid Qutb
Muhammad ibn Abd al-Wahhab	*tawhid*

QUESTIONS

1. Compare the neorevivalist movements of the Muslim Brotherhood and Jamaat-i-Islam. In spite of their geographic separations, what do they share in common?

2. Compare Rashid Rida/Salafism with ibn Abd al-Wahhab.

3. What have been the dominant points of intersection between Islam and the West in Modernity?

4. Trace the history of Islamic renewal/reform on the Indian subcontinent between the sixteenth and twentieth centuries.

5. How have various Muslim reformers understood the terms jihad and *ijtihad*?

NOTES

1. For an excellent discussion of revivalism in the eighteenth century, see John O. Voll, *Islam: Continuity and Change in the Modern World* (Boulder, CO: Westview Press, 1982), chap. 2.
2. John O. Voll, "Renewal and Reform in Islamic History: *Tajdid* and *Islah*," in *Voices of Resurgent Islam*, John L. Esposito, ed. (New York: Oxford University Press, 1983), chap. 2.
3. A. Merad, *"Isiah,"* in *The Encyclopedia of Islam*, new ed., vol. 4, H. A. R. Gibb et al., eds. (Leiden, Netherlands: E. J. Brill, 1960), p. 141.
4. Voll, "Renewal and Reform," p. 33.
5. John O. Voll, "The Sudanese Mandi: Frontier Fundamentalist," *International Journal of Middle East Studies* 10 (1979), p. 159.
6. Yohann Friedmann, *Shaykh Ahmad Sirhindi: An Outline of His Thought and a Study of His Image in the Light of Posterity* (London, 1971), p. 67, and J. M. S. Baljon's *Religion and Thought of Shah Wali Allah ad-Dihlawi* (Leiden, 1983), pp. 60–62.

7. Jamal al-Din al-Afghani, "Islamic Solidarity," in *Islam in Transition: Muslim Perspectives*, John J. Donohue and John L. Esposito, eds. (New York: Oxford University Press, 1982), pp. 21, 23.

8. Jamal al-Din al-Afghani, "An Islamic Response to Imperialism," in *Islam in Transition*, pp. 17–19.

9. Muhammad Abduh, *The Theology of Unity*, Ishaq Musaad and Kenneth Cragg, trans. (London: George Allen & Unwin, 1966).

10. Ibid., pp. 39–40.

11. Albert Hourani, *Arabic Thought in the Liberal Age: 1798–1939* (Oxford: Oxford University Press, 1970), p. 227.

12. Malcolm H. Kerr, *Islamic Reform: The Political and Legal Theories of Muhammad Abduh and Rashid Rida* (Berkeley: University of California Press, 1966), p. 190.

13. Rashid Rida, *al-Wahabiyyun wal Hijaz* (Cairo: Manar Press, 1926), p. 47.

14. Ahmad Khan, "Lecture on Islam," in *Islam in Transition*, p. 42.

15. Ibid.

16. *Majmua*, I, 213–14, as quoted in J. M. S. Baljon, *The Reforms and Religious Ideas of Sir Sayyid Ahmad Khan* (Lahore, Pakistan: Sh. Muhammad Ashraf, 1964), p. 78.

17. *Tafsir al-Quran*, Vol. III, p. 32, as quoted in B. A. Dar, *Religious Thought of Sayyid Ahmad Khan* (Lahore, Pakistan: Sh. Muhammad Ashraf, 1957), p. 182.

18. See, for example, Kemal A. Faruki, "Pakistan: Islamic Government and Society," in *Islam in Asia: Religion, Politics, and Society*, John L. Esposito, ed. (New York: Oxford University Press, 1987), pp. 54, 75.

19. Muhammad Iqbal, *Thoughts and Reflections of Iqbal*, S. A. Vahid, ed. (Lahore, Pakistan: Sh. Muhammad Ashraf, 1964), p. 277.

20. Muhammad Iqbal, *The Reconstruction of Religious Thought in Islam*, rev. ed. (Lahore, Pakistan: Sh. Muhammad Ashraf, 1968), p. 8.

21. Ibid., p. 155.

22. Ibid., p. 154.

23. Muhammad Iqbal, *The Mysteries of Selflessness* (London: Oxford University Press, 1953), p. 37.

24. Iqbal, *Reconstruction*, p. 168.

25. Muhammad Iqbal, "Islam as a Political and Moral Ideal," in *Thoughts and Reflections of Iqbal*, Vahid, ed., p. 52.

26. Muhammad Iqbal, as quoted in "A Separate Muslim State in the Subcontinent," in *Islam in Transition*, pp. 91–92.

27. *Report of the Commission on Marriage and Family Laws*, as excerpted in *Islam in Transition*, pp. 201–2.

28. Ibid., p. 202.

29. Hasan al-Banna, "The New Renaissance," in *Islam in Transition*, p. 78.

30. Mawlana Abul Ala Mawdudi, *The Islamic Law and Constitution*, 6th ed., Khurshid Ahmad, ed. (Lahore, Pakistan: Islamic Publications, 1977), p. 5.

31. Muhammad al-Ghazzali, *Our Beginning in Wisdom*, Ismail R. al-Faruqi, trans. (Washington, DC: American Council of Learned Societies, 1953), p. 54.

Chapter 5

The Resurgence of Religion in Politics

For several decades, in much of the Muslim world, Islam has been reasserted into personal and public life. This phenomenon has variously been described as the Islamic resurgence, **Islamic revivalism**, Islamic fundamentalism, Islamism, and political Islam. The struggle and debate over issues of identity, faith, culture, and practice occurs today not only in the Muslim world but also among Muslim minorities in the West. In the twenty-first century, the sharp distinction between Islam and the West no longer exists. Islam today is indeed a global religion. Muslims in Muslim-majority countries from North Africa to Southeast Asia struggle with the role of Islam in state and society. Muslim-minority communities in Europe and America grapple with issues of faith and identity, cultural and economic integration, or assimilation.

THE ISLAMIC RESURGENCE

To speak of an **Islamic revival or resurgence** since the late twentieth century is not to imply that Islam was dead or irrelevant in previous Muslim societies. However, the contemporary revival increased the importance of religious identity and practice in individual and corporate life and the role of religion in Muslim politics and society. It has been reflected in an increased emphasis on religious observances (mosque attendance, fasting during Ramadan, abstention from alcohol and gambling, new forms of Islamic dress); a new vitality in Sufism; the proliferation of religious literature, television and radio programs, audio and video cassettes, and DVDs; Islamically oriented websites; the growth of new Islamic associations committed to socio-religious reform; and the reassertion of Islam in Muslim politics.

Understanding the meaning, causes, and significance of the role of religion in Muslim politics and society today requires that certain contrasting presuppositions be recognized. The first is the modern Western secular tendency to separate religion and politics or to presume that secularization is the only modern option possible. The second is the realization that, for many Muslims, Islam is a total way of life and thus speaking of religion and politics as two utterly distinct arenas is not acceptable. Muslims believe that religion and society are interrelated and thus Islam is relevant and integral to politics, law, education, social life, and economics. There is no sharp dichotomy between the sacred and the profane. The question is not if but when and how religion should inform life. Religious orthodoxy (or more accurately, orthopraxy/correct practice) and cultural authenticity require it. For many Muslims, the mixing of religion and politics is not the issue; the issue is whether religion is utilized to produce a more moral and just society or distorted to manipulate and control people.

Throughout many parts of the Muslim world, Islamic symbols, slogans, ideology, and actors have become prominent fixtures. Islam has been used by governments and by reform and opposition movements alike. Rulers in Libya, Saudi Arabia, the Sudan, Egypt, Morocco, Iraq, Iran, Afghanistan, Pakistan, Malaysia, and Indonesia have used Islam to enhance their legitimacy and policies, while resistance, reform, and opposition movements have also appealed to Islam in Afghanistan, Lebanon, Palestine, Egypt, Turkey, Syria, Iraq, the Persian Gulf, Pakistan, and the southern Philippines. Why and how has Islam reemerged so significantly in Muslim life?

In the post–World War II period, modernity was no longer a new external European colonial force infiltrating or invading Muslim lands. Instead it became the established internal order of newly independent Muslim nation-states, their political, legal, and educational institutions, and the outlook of their leaders. Most governments had tackled the arduous task of nation building by establishing states with a more secular orientation, circumscribing the role of religion in public life, and fostering various forms of secular nationalism, both local (Egyptian, Sudanese, Tunisian) and regional (Arab and Baath nationalism/socialism). However, during the 1960s, Arab socialist regimes that had seized power in Egypt, Syria, Iraq, and Algeria buttressed their appeal for popular support by a deliberate, selective use of religion to legitimate their socialist ideologies and governments. Gamal Abd al-Nasser in Egypt provides a classic case. Determined to emerge as a pan-Arab leader and legitimate his Arab socialist revolution and ideology, Nasser created a state-supported periodical, *Minbar al-Islam* ("The Pulpit of Islam"), in which leading scholars and religious leaders linked Arab socialist policies to the Islamic tradition. The shaykh (rector) of al-Azhar gave fatwas reconciling socialism and state policies with Islam. Yet, the general trend in these and in most Muslim countries was to restrict religion to personal matters and personal laws, with the exception of those instances when regimes found it useful to appeal to religion.

The late 1960s signaled a turning point and the dawn of a new phase, a retreat from the secular path and the growth and spread of religious revivalism.

Why did religion again become such a visible force?

For the Arab world and many in the broader Muslim world, the **Six-Day War with Israel in 1967** generated a period of soul-searching and self-criticism as Muslims tried to fathom why and how they had reached this nadir in their history. From its creation in 1948, Israel and its Arab neighbors had been at odds over the issue of a Jewish state in Palestine. However, the 1967 war transformed an Arab and Palestinian problem into an Islamic issue. The decisive rout of the combined forces of Egypt, Syria, and Jordan in just six days and their massive loss of territory (the West Bank, especially East Jerusalem, Gaza, and the Golan Heights) raised serious questions about the force of Arab regimes and their nationalist policies, in particular Nasser's Arab nationalism/socialism. Most important, the loss of Jerusalem—the third holiest city in Islam—and its sacred shrines was a major blow to Muslim pride and faith, precipitating a crisis

---

COMMON CAUSES OF THE RELIGIOUS RESURGENCE IN ISLAM

The original causes of the resurgence are many and need to be appreciated within the specific contexts of individual countries and regions. However, several common phenomena were:

1. an identity crisis precipitated by a sense of failure, loss of identity, and lack of self-esteem;
2. disillusionment with the West—the failure of many Muslim rulers and their Western-inspired governments to respond adequately to the political and socioeconomic needs of their societies;
3. the newfound sense of pride and power that resulted from military (Arab–Israeli war) and economic (oil embargo) success in 1973 and the Iranian revolution of 1978–79; and
4. as a result, a quest for a more authentic personal and public/political and social identity, rooted in Islam and Islamic history.

of confidence and identity. The "liberation of Jerusalem" became not only a regional political problem but also a worldwide (Islamic) religiopolitical slogan and issue.

For many, the 1967 war, remembered in Arab literature as "the disaster," demonstrated the continued state of decline and the utter impotence of Muslims despite their independence from colonial rule. If Islamic belief and history taught that success and power were signs of a faithful community, many again asked, as they had during the colonial period: What has gone wrong in Islam? Why has God seemingly abandoned His community? Whereas some blamed the hold of an outmoded traditional way of life and saw religion as the culprit, religious leaders asserted that Islam had not failed the Muslims. Muslims had failed Islam by relying on the West for their guidance and development. Adopting the discourse of religious revivalism, they called for a return to Islam. Behind this call was the belief that it was Islam that had united Arabia under Muhammad, inspired the early expansion and conquests, informed the glories of Islamic empires and civilizations, and served as a motivating force in revivalist reforms. The lessons of faith and history were clear. Muslim strength and success were dependent on faithfulness to God's Word and Prophet. Massive failure could only be a sign of waywardness and faithlessness. Coping with modernity did not require new, foreign-inspired alternatives when the community (*umma*) had a tried-and-true faith and way of life.

Many Western-oriented intellectuals and elites were also disillusioned. They had relied on a process of modernization that borrowed heavily from the West; and their hopes and expectations had been shattered. They could not claim to have strengthened their societies or to have built secure bridges with their Western mentors and allies.

The ignominious defeat of Arab forces and Israel's movement of its capital from Tel Aviv to Jerusalem symbolized both Muslim military failure and the failure of the West as an ally. Israel was regarded as a Western state or colony in the Arab world, created and sustained by support from Western powers, in particular the United States. The message seemed clear: relying on the West for its models of development or as an ally had not worked. The sense of disenchantment and failure felt by many modern elites coincided with the criticisms of more traditional religious sectors of society. This disenchantment was reflected in Muslim literature in the late 1960s and early 1970s.[1] Whereas previously the content and concerns of secular and religious literature had generally differed, now popular, intellectual, and religious literature had common themes—a growing criticism and rejection of the West; a quest for identity and authenticity, manifested in a nostalgia for a past golden age of Islam; efforts to recover and incorporate an awareness of native (Islamic) cultural and historical identity; and emphasis on traditional moral values. Many believed that Muslims had failed to produce a viable, authentic cultural synthesis and social order that was both modern and true to indigenous history and values. Western models of political, social, and economic development were criticized as imported transplants that had failed, fostering continued political and cultural dependence on the West and resulting in secularism, materialism, and spiritual bankruptcy. Neither Western liberal nationalism nor Egypt's Gamal Abd al-Nasser's Arab nationalism/socialism had succeeded.

Behind their democratic parliamentary facades, problems of authoritarianism, legitimacy, and limited political participation plagued most Muslim countries. Government promises and development programs had created rising expectations that often went unfulfilled. Poverty and illiteracy remained unchecked. Modernization seemed to benefit a disproportionate few, the new urban-based middle and upper classes, fostering conspicuous consumption and corruption. The negative impact of modernization on village and family life and traditional religious and social values seemed to threaten the religious and moral fabric of society. The adoption of a Western lifestyle (its institutions, values, dress, music, cinema), once enthusiastically embraced as a symbol of progress and modernity, was now increasingly criticized as responsible for the Westernization and secularization of Muslim societies, a threat to cultural identity, and the cause of moral decline and spiritual malaise. Many revivalist themes reemerged: the need for greater self-reliance and a desire to reclaim the accomplishments of the past and to root individual and national self-identity more indigenously (to find pride and strength inside, not outside, the community) in an Islamic tradition that had once been a dominant world power and civilization. The prevailing mood was reflected in the language of authenticity, religiocultural revival (*tajdid*), reform (*islah*), and renaissance.

Events in 1973 and 1979 provided a new source of pride and served as catalysts for Islamic revivalism. In the eyes of many Muslims, October 1973 reversed the ignominious Arab defeat of 1967. Although the Israeli army was ultimately victorious, many in the Arab world felt vindicated by Egyptian successes in the war. Most importantly, Anwar Sadat's use of Islamic symbols and rhetoric to mobilize and motivate Egyptian forces gave a decidedly religious character to its battles and led to its being regarded as an Islamic war and moral victory. This was the Ramadan war (named for the sacred month of fasting during which it occurred); its code name was Badr, the first great victory for Islam under the Prophet

Muhammad; its battle cry was Allahu Akbar ("God is most great"), the traditional summons to the defense of Islam as well as to prayer. Those who died in this holy war were not regarded simply as patriots but as religious martyrs.

The Arab oil embargo of 1973 was a second major catalyst for the resurgence. For the first time since the dawn of colonialism, the West seemed dependent on the Muslim world. The Arabs were no longer client-states but a world economic power to be reckoned with. For many, these new signs of wealth and power were a source of enormous pride and a sign of the return of God's blessings. Remembering a once-glorious past, the Muslims believed the return of God's favor and a new renaissance seemed at hand. Major oil powers like Saudi Arabia, Libya, and the United Arab Emirates used their petrodollars to foster revivalism both out of conviction and to extend their political influence. They assisted other Muslim governments (on condition that they foster Islamic measures), supported Islamic organizations and movements, and underwrote the publication and distribution of Islamic literature and the building of mosques, hospitals, and schools.

The **Iranian revolution of 1978–79** seemed a triumphant watershed for Sunni and Shii Muslims alike. The prominence of its Islamic ideology and leadership reinforced its portrayal as an "Islamic revolution." Success in effectively mobilizing Iranians against a seemingly invincible shah seemed to validate Islamic activist claims that a return to Islam would restore religious identity and vitality and enable Muslims, with God's guidance, to implement a more autonomous and self-reliant way of life despite a regime's military power and Western allies. The initial euphoria of postrevolutionary days sparked an enthusiasm and strong sense of pride among many in the Muslim world. The Ayatollah Khomeini's insistence that Iran's revolution was an Islamic, not just a Shii, revolution and his call for others to follow suit inspired not only Shii outbursts in Saudi Arabia and the Gulf but also initial admiration among Sunni Muslims and organizations. The Islamic (Student) Association of Cairo University's "Lessons from Iran" echoed the sentiments of many who saw in the revolution a clear sign of the power of God, a reminder of the Muslim community's vocation as an example and world leader, a vindication of the true nature of Islam as the sole, comprehensive guide for life and the basis of a just society.

Say, O God, possessor of all sovereignty, you give sovereignty to whom you wish and take sovereignty from whom you wish (Quran 3:26)
the importance of this unique and amazing revolution [is] to awaken

Muslims and to restore their confidence in their religion and their adherence to it, so that they may assume the reins of world leadership of mankind once again and place the world under the protection of the esteemed Islamic civilization. *"You are the best* umma *given to mankind; you prescribe the good and prohibit evil and you believe in God. (Quran 3:110)*

The first lesson is the influence of the creed on the Islamic people. What spirit that was which moved in the being of this people who had appeared servile and submissive to injustice and tyranny. They exploded like a volcano, not fearing death and not concerned about life   flesh conquered steel. The spirit is the spirit of faith. This revolution indicates the nature of this religion which refuses to let injustice befall its followers and guarantees strength and dignity for them .... The revolution also indicates the nature of this religion from another perspective, namely it is a comprehensive religion   It is religion and state, governance and politics, economics and social organization, education and morals, worship and holy war.

.... Perhaps the most profound lesson which this revolution embodied was the fruit of working for countries of the East and West. Rulers sold their countries   and were transformed into puppets in the hands of rulers of East and West.[2]

From Cairo to Kuala Lumpur, Iran's revolution became tangible corroboration for those who sought explanations for the apparent failures of their governments and believed that less dependence on outside forces, greater self-reliance, and the reaffirmation of Islam offered an alternative. Important differences of belief and perspective existed between those for whom greater cultural autonomy and authenticity meant reclaiming an Islamic cultural heritage and those for whom the foundation and point of departure was Islam, an all-embracing religious tradition. For the former, Islam was an element in national cultural identity. For the latter, it was the basis for community identity and life. The heart of contemporary revivalism has been this ideologization of Islam, interpretation of Islam as a total ideology for political, social, and cultural life. This belief is reflected in the belief that Islam encompasses religion and state, that it is a system of belief and law that governs both spiritual and temporal affairs.[3]

The use of Islam in politics has taken a number of forms or modes of expression conditioned as much by local sociopolitical realities as by religious belief. The ideology of Islamic political activists is the product of faith and experience, a religious worldview interpreted and applied within the context of a specific country or region. This then accounts for the diversity of Islamic revivalism, its actors, organizations, strategies, and tactics. The increased emphasis on religion in Muslim societies has meant

IDEOLOGICAL WORLDVIEW OF REVIVALISM

There are distinctive differences of interpretation, but the general or common ideological framework of Islamic revivalism includes the following beliefs:

1. Islam is a total and comprehensive way of life. Religion is integral to politics, law, and society.
2. The failure of Muslim societies is due to their departure from the straight path of Islam and their following a Western secular path, with its secular, materialistic ideologies and values.
3. The renewal of society requires a return to Islam, an Islamic religiopolitical and social reformation or revolution that draws its inspiration from the Quran and the Prophet Muhammad.
4. To restore God's rule and inaugurate a true Islamic social order, Western-inspired civil codes must be informed by or replaced by the Shariah.
5. Although the Westernization of society is condemned, modernization as such is not. Science and technology are readily accepted, but they are to be subordinated to Islamic belief and values to guard against the Westernization and secularization of Muslim society.
6. The process of Islamization, or, more accurately, re-Islamization, requires Muslim organizations, who by their example and activities call upon others to be more observant and who are willing to struggle (jihad) against corruption and social injustice.

more widespread attention to such common aspects of worship as prayer and fasting, and it has also included a rich and. at times confusing agenda as governments and Islamic associations have formulated or implemented policies and programs in the name of Islam. The impetus for the implementation of Islam has come from above, imposed by the state or government, or from below, from society, through the pressure of religious organizations or political parties.

State Islam is government imposed, implemented by ruling regimes often with the cooperation of the religious establishment, state-supported clerical leaders. Rulers as diverse as Libya's **Colonel Muammar Qaddafi** (1969–2011), Egypt's **Anwar Sadat** (1970–81), Iran's **Ayatollah Khomeini** (1979–89) and his successors, Sudan's **Colonel Jafar al-Numayri** (1969–85) and **General Omar ul-Bashir** (b. 1989), Pakistan's **General Zia ul-Haq** (1977–88), and the **Taliban** rule in Afghanistan (1996–2001) have used Islam to enhance their legitimacy and policies. State Islam has reflected a broad spectrum, ranging from the conservative Saudi monarchy to Qaddafi's radical populist "state of the masses," from General Zia ul-Haq's martial law regime to Ayatollah Khomeini's model of a clerically guided governance by the (Islamic) jurist and Taliban rule in Afghanistan. It has included the contrasting styles of monarchs, the military, and the clergy.

Islamic organizations and movements reflect an equally pluriform rather than monolithic Islam, ranging from moderates who work within

Ayatollah Khomeini (1902–89), leader of the 1979 Iranian Revolution.

existing political systems to violent revolutionaries who seek to topple governments; from open membership to secret cells; from the relatively democratic to the totalitarian. Contrary to popular stereotypes, most activists are neither uneducated peasants from rural areas minimally exposed to modern education nor seminary students. They are not anti-modern reactionaries trying to take refuge in the seventh century. Many combine a traditional upbringing with modern education. The majority have been university graduates in engineering, law, medicine, science, or education from major national universities in Muslim countries as well as from centers of learning in Europe and America such as MIT, Cornell, Indiana, Oxford, London, and the Sorbonne.

Whereas the *ulama* and theological faculties played a more important role among the Shii, Sunni organizations have been predominantly lay rather than clerical, their membership drawn heavily from students and young professionals (teachers, lawyers, engineers, doctors) recruited from schools and mosques. They have included both city dwellers and villagers, members of the lower middle and middle classes. Many have been serious, pious, highly motivated people disaffected with the socioeconomic realities of their societies. These were not Muslims reacting to the introduction of modernization, reflexively rejecting a new and unknown reality. They were, instead, from the modern sector of society. Unlike some of their peers, their experience of modernization did not lead them to embrace it but to criticize and reject its excesses and espouse an alternative to the dominant, Western form of modernization prevalent in much of the world.

The moderate (nonviolent) majority pursued reform through the gradual transformation of Muslim society; a radical minority advocate violent revolution. Moderate organizations and parties have participated in electoral politics: the **Muslim Brotherhood of Egypt and Jordan** (the Jordanian Islamic Action Front), the **Renaissance Party (Ennahda) in Tunisia**, the **Justice and Development Party in Morocco**, the **Reform Party in Algeria**, the *Ummah* **Party in Kuwait, Turkey's Welfare Party**, the **Yemeni Reformist Union**, the Jamaat-i-Islami **in Pakistan**, ABIM **(Malaysian Islamic Youth Movement** and PAS **(Party of Islam) in Malaysia**, and the **Muhammadiya** and **Nahdatul Ulama in Indonesia**. Many ran educational and social programs, youth camps and centers, and legal aid societies and hospitals; they participated in government and student campus elections and even served in the cabinets of Pakistan, Lebanon, Jordan, Turkey, Yemen, and Malaysia. Extremist groups like Egypt's **Takfir wal Hijra** (Excommunication and Emigration), **al-Jihad** (Holy War), **Gamaa Islamiyya** (Islamic Group), **Jund Allah** (God's Army), **and Algeria's Armed Islamic Group** pursued a policy of violent

---

IDEOLOGICAL WORLDVIEW
OF RADICAL ACTIVISTS

Militant extremists operate on the following assumptions, believing that
theological doctrine and political realism necessitate violent revolution:

1. A Crusader mentality, European and more recently American neo-
    colonialism, and the power of Zionism pit the West against the
    Islamic world.
2. Establishment of an Islamic system of government is not simply an
    alternative but an Islamic "imperative," God's command and mandate
    that all Muslims must obey and implement.
3. Because the legitimacy of Muslim governments is based on the Sharia,
    governments that do not follow it are illegitimate. Those who fail to
    follow Islamic law, governments and individuals, are guilty of unbelief,
    are no longer Muslim, and must be fought and if necessary killed.
4. The official religious establishment of *ulama* and state-supported
    and controlled mosques and preachers have been co-opted by the
    government.
5. Jihad as armed struggle in the defense of Islam or Muslims against
    their enemies (Muslim as well as Western governments, groups or
    individuals), who threaten their existence, is a religious duty. Like
    the Kharijites in early Islam, radicals demand total commitment and
    obedience. The army of God is locked in battle or holy war with the
    followers of Satan. One is either a true believer or an infidel, saved or
    damned, a friend or an enemy of God.
6. Christians and Jews are unbelievers rather than "People of the Book"
    because of their connections with Western (Christian) neocolonialism
    and Zionism. They are seen as partners in a Judeo-Christian conspir-
    acy against Islam and the Muslim world.

---

confrontation, based on their conviction that the political realities of
Muslim life require armed struggle or jihad.

Militants viewed most Muslim governments as anti-Islamic
regimes that either co-opt and control religion or repress the attempts
of authentic Islamic movements to implement Islam. Many criticized
or condemned such government policies, but extremists saw them as a
general pattern that made most established governments the object of
jihad. Radicals believe that the refusal of Muslim governments to implement Islamic law and their repression of Islamic activism necessitate

violence and armed struggle against the enemies of God, despotic rulers and their foreign allies. Indeed, they saw it as a religious obligation to resist and fight. In contrast to conservative and modernist leaders, who tended to emphasize nonviolent interpretations of jihad, militants believed that Islam is in danger, locked in a defensive war against repressive anti-Islamic or un-Islamic rulers and states. They regarded themselves as the "true" defenders of Islam, in whose name they assassinated opponents like Egypt's Anwar Sadat and attacked government installations and foreign embassies. Although many spoke of an Islamic alternative, shared aspirations, when translated into ideology and strategy, often yielded differing interpretations and agendas.

Religion in Modern Muslim Nation Building

A more detailed review of several Muslim countries reveals the multiple uses of Islam by governments and activist organizations in Turkey, Egypt, Libya, Iran, Lebanon, Saudi Arabia, and Pakistan.[4] Modern nation building in the Muslim world demonstrated three patterns: secular, Muslim, and Islamic.

Turkey

At one end of the spectrum, Turkey, under the leadership and direction of Mustafa Kemal (Ataturk, Father of the Turks, d. 1938), was the only Muslim country to choose a completely secular path, restricting religion to private life. At the other end of the spectrum, Saudi Arabia became a self-proclaimed Islamic state. The vast majority of countries in the Muslim world fall in between. After independence, most pursued a path of political development that was heavily indebted to the West for political, legal, economic, and educational institutions. Most are Muslim states in that the majority of the population and their heritage are Muslim. Moreover, most of these states have "Islamic" provisions, such as a requirement that the head of state must be Muslim, a declaration that Islam is the state religion, or state control of religion through a ministry of religious affairs. Yet the prevailing tendency in the postindependence period was to foster secular forms of national identity and solidarity and to limit religion to private rather than public life. Thus, local (Egyptian, Syrian, Libyan) or regional/linguistic (Arab or Baath) forms of nationalism or socialism prevailed. The secular trend changed almost imperceptibly in the 1960s and 1970s, for reasons we will now discuss.

Egypt

When Gamal Abd al-Nasser and the Free Officers overthrew the Egyptian monarchy in July 1952, they came to power in a nation that had for more than a century pursued a Western-oriented path of development. Despite the initial support Nasser had received from the Muslim Brotherhood, he continued to steer Egypt on a secular nationalist course. However, by the late 1950s, faced with opposition from the Brotherhood and wishing to establish his leadership in the Arab world as well as Egypt, Nasser broadened Egyptian nationalism into an Arab nationalism/socialism, rooted in the region's common Arab-Islamic heritage. He preached a common Arab unity and identity—based on a shared language, history, and religion—whose concerns and interests transcended national borders.

Increasingly, Nasser used religious symbols, language, leaders, and rhetoric to legitimate and win support for his Arab socialist ideology and policies. State control of al-Azhar University and a state-sponsored Supreme Council of Islamic Affairs were used to legitimate and promote the Islamic character of Arab socialism. Official pronouncements or legal decrees (fatwas) were obtained from Islamic scholars at al-Azhar University, which had been nationalized in 1961, to establish the compatibility of Arab socialism and Islam. The state-sponsored Supreme Council of Islamic Affairs published a journal, *The Pulpit of Islam*, in which articles interpreted traditional Islamic beliefs regarding the equality of believers and social justice to legitimate Nasser's socialist policies and programs of land reform, nationalization, and birth control.

Nasser's use of Islam was challenged internationally and domestically. Saudi Arabia resented this popular and charismatic leader's scathing denunciation of conservative Arab monarchies and his regional influence. The Saudis obtained decrees from their *ulama* condemning socialism and preaching a pan-Islamic, which included a pan-Arab, message. The Egyptian Muslim Brotherhood, which had been disaffected by Nasser's failure to create an Islamic state, stepped up its opposition. In 1965, the Brotherhood was accused of attempting to assassinate Nasser. Their leaders were imprisoned and a number were executed, among them **Sayyid Qutb**, who is remembered as the martyr of Islamic revivalism. The Brotherhood was ruthlessly suppressed. Although it seemed to be effectively eliminated, the Brotherhood continued to exist in prison, in exile, and underground and reemerged under Nasser's successor, Anwar Sadat.

The shock and grief that Nasser's unexpected death caused in the Arab world was reflected in the millions who took to the streets of Cairo for his funeral. However, the pride that Nasser had fostered and the hopes of his Arab socialism had been shattered by the catastrophe of the Arab defeat in 1967. Yet, Nasser's charismatic personality created a void that few men could have filled. Sadat had been completely eclipsed by Nasser's shadow. Upon Sadat's accession to power, he was careful to see that his picture was displayed alongside that of Nasser. As Sadat sought to emerge as a leader in his own right, enhance his political legitimacy, and counter the opposition of Nasserites and leftists who opposed his pro-Western policies, he relied heavily on Islam. Sadat appropriated the title "The Believer President," had the mass media cover him praying at the mosque, increased Islamic programming in the media and Islamic courses in schools, built mosques, and employed Islamic symbols and rhetoric in his public statements. Sufi brotherhoods and the Muslim Brotherhood, suppressed by Nasser, were permitted to function publicly. The Sadat government encouraged and supported Islamic student organizations on campuses to offset the influence of Nasserite and Marxist student groups. He marshaled the support of al-Azhar's religious establishment to legitimate key government policies such as the Camp David Accords and family law reforms and to denounce as extremists the Islamic activists who increasingly challenged the regime during the latter part of the 1970s.

As Islamic organizations like the Muslim Brotherhood and student groups gained momentum, they became more independent and critical of Sadat policies: his support for the Shah of Iran and early condemnation of the Ayatollah Khomeini, the Camp David Accords, and Sadat's pro-Western economic and political ties. They were also more vocal in their demands for the implementation of Islamic law. A new crop of secret revolutionary groups, some funded by disaffected and radicalized former Muslim Brothers who had been imprisoned under Nasser, began to challenge both what they regarded as Sadat's hypocritical manipulation of Islam and the moderate posture of the Muslim Brotherhood. Militant groups like Muhammad's Youth (also known as the Islamic Liberation Organization), the Army of God, and Excommunication and Emigration (*Takfir wal Hijra*) resorted to acts of violence in an attempt to overthrow the government.

Springing up in both cities and provincial towns, these groups recruited heavily from schools, universities, and local mosques. Many members were educated and highly motivated. Despite their differences, all condemned Sadat and Egyptian society as un-Islamic, politically corrupt, controlled by infidels (that is, people who were not "true believers"), and dominated by alien and decadent Western laws and lifestyles that fostered secularism, materialism (conspicuous consumption), and a spiritually lax and permissive society. They believed that the liberation of Egyptian society required that all true Muslims undertake an armed struggle or holy war against a regime they regarded as oppressive, anti-Islamic, and a puppet of the West. Their concern was not only over Egypt's political and military dependence but also its cultural penetration and acculturation, the more insidious threat. Their grievances erupted into attacks against bars, nightclubs, cinemas, Western tourist hotels, as well as government institutions and personnel.

Sadat's growing authoritarianism and suppression of any dissent came to a head in 1981, when more than 1,500 people from a cross-section of Egyptian society (Islamic activists, lawyers, doctors, journalists, university professors, political opponents, ex-government ministers) were imprisoned. On October 6, 1981, Tanzim al-Jihad assassinated Anwar Sadat as he reviewed a parade commemorating the 1973 war. Lieutenant Khalid Islambuli, the leader of the assassins, had cried out: "I am Khalid Islambuli, I have killed Pharaoh and I do not fear death." Sadat's popularity in the West and his international image as a flexible, enlightened leader stood in sharp contrast to his growing unpopularity at home, where his secular and religious opposition referred to him as pharaoh.

If Islamic revivalism or fundamentalism in Egypt during the 1970s seemed to be a movement of confrontation and violence, the 1980s witnessed the fruits of the broader based, quiet revolution that had been overshadowed or eclipsed by the conflict between Sadat's growing authoritarianism and his militant opposition. The most important characteristic of Islamic revivalism in Egypt since the 1980s, as in many parts of the Muslim world when Islam is not controlled or suppressed by governments, is the extent to which Islamic activism has become part of moderate, mainstream life and society rather than merely a marginal phenomenon. Islamic identity is expressed not only in formal religious practices but also in the social services offered by psychiatric and drug rehabilitation centers, dental clinics, day-care centers, legal aid societies, and organizations that provide subsidized housing and food distribution or run banks and investment houses.

The *ulama* and the mosques have also taken on a more prominent role. The popularity of preachers has made some of them religious media stars. Their presence is known not only through television but also from their regular newspaper columns, cassettes, DVDs, websites, and books, which enjoy widespread distribution in bookstores, in airports and hotels, and through street vendors. Their popularity extends beyond Egypt to much of the Arab world. Mosques and their imams (leaders) are also part of the mainstreaming of revivalist activities.

During the late 1980s and early 1990s, the two faces of political Islam (violent and nonviolent) were evident in Egyptian politics and society. Extremist organizations like the Gamaa Islamiyya (Islamic Group) and Islamic Jihad attacked and killed government officials, intellectuals, and foreign tourists as well as Egyptian Christians in clashes in southern

Egypt. At the same time, Egypt's "quiet revolution" became more evident as Islamic activism became increasingly more visible as an effective social and political presence, institutionalized within mainstream society. Islamically motivated associations and societies ran schools, hospitals, clinics, and other social services as well as banks and publishing houses. At the same time, the Muslim Brotherhood, banned as a political party, formed coalitions with legal political parties and emerged as the leading opposition in parliamentary elections. Islamic activists also proved successful in professional associations (medicine, law, engineering, education) and university faculty elections.

The prominence of Islamic activism in mainstream society proved a tacit critique of the ineffectiveness of the Mubarak government in delivering adequate social services and mobilizing popular support. In its early years, the Mubarak government had distinguished between violent extremists, whom it silenced, and nonviolent opposition, which it tolerated. However, in the 1990s, the government increasingly moved to silence any and all opposition, blurring the line between violent revolutionaries and those who participated within the system. It charged that there was little difference (other than tactics) between the Muslim Brotherhood and the Gamaa Islamiyya or Islamic Jihad. Muslim Brothers were arrested and convicted in special, extrajudicial, military courts ostensibly created to counter terrorism. The government moved to pass new laws to prevent or disqualify Islamists from office as heads of professional associations and moved to take control of (nationalize) all private or independent mosques (many of which were sources of opposition).

Egypt has long been regarded as a leader in the Arab world—politically, militarily, and religiously. Among the most modern of Muslim countries, it has experienced the full array of Islamic revivalist activities. Once a barometer for a modernization that was predominantly Western and somewhat secular in orientation, Egypt provides a full-blown example of the more complex, and at times volatile, experience of many Muslim societies attempting in a variety of ways to integrate their Islamic heritage and values with their sociopolitical development. The Muslim Brotherhood enjoyed considerable success in parliamentary elections despite government harassment and repression, and Egyptian society continued to reflect the growing strength of Islam in society. As we shall see, in 2011 Mubarak would be forced to resign and the Brotherhood would briefly come to power.

Libya
During the late 1960s revolutionary regimes came to power in military coups d'état in Libya and the Sudan. Both colonels Muammar Qaddafi of

Libya and Jafar al-Numayri of the Sudan were admirers of Egypt's Gamal Abd al-Nasser, patterned their revolutions on Nasser's model, and justified their coups in the name of Arab socialism. However, by the 1970s, both had found it necessary to buttress their secular nationalist ideology with an appeal to religion.

Libya was the site of one of the earliest and most controversial state implementations of Islam. Although Qaddafi had emulated the policies of his hero, Nasser, regarding religion, by the 1970s Qaddafi was reinforcing nationalist slogans and ideology with an espousal of Islam. Qaddafi embarked on a series of reforms aimed at eradicating the vestiges of European colonialism and reaffirming Libya's Arab-Islamic heritage. He declared that Libya's Arab socialist path was the socialism of Islam, "a socialism emanating from the true religion of Islam and its Noble Book."[5] Churches were closed and missionary activities curtailed. Arabic replaced European languages in official transactions, names of localities, and street signs. In the early 1970s, Qaddafi announced the introduction of Islamic law. In fact, however, Islamic law was never fully implemented. Instead, Qaddafi introduced Islamic penal laws and punishments for gambling, alcohol, theft, and adultery. Full implementation of Islamic law was replaced by his grand design, the Third Way or Third Universal Theory, in which he provided an Islamic alternative to capitalism and Marxism for Libya and the world. The blueprint was delineated in *The Green Book*. The symbolism and significance of this title was not lost on a Muslim audience. The Quran is the Noble Book; Jews and Christians are "people of the book," possessors of revelation; green is the color of the Prophet Muhammad. The Chinese in mainland China at that time were followers of Mao Tse Tung's *Red Book*. *The Green Book* (published in three installments—in 1975, 1977, 1979) was billed as an alternative to prevailing ideologies and blueprints for society, whether Western European (Judeo-Christian) capitalism or Soviet or Chinese Marxism.

Publication of *The Green Book* signaled Qaddafi's own modern and idiosyncratic interpretation of Islam. He claimed *The Green Book* replaced the traditional position of Islamic law as the blueprint for society. He radically redefined Islam and Arab nationalism, stamping them with his own interpretation. Islam in Qaddafi's hands was transformed into a form of Islamic revolutionary socialism. Muhammad was portrayed as a revolutionary leader whose battle with the power and wealth of the Arab political establishment is likened to the modern-day struggle against kings and princes. For Qaddafi, the principal cause of Muslim backwardness was not Islam but the legacy of European colonialism and the forces of modern political and economic imperialism. He maintained that Islam was a progressive, socialist movement that stands for a worldwide political and social revolution against these forces of oppression. Qaddafi's linkage of Islam with a "progressive, populist revolutionary universalism" could be seen in his assertion that to achieve their God-ordained goal, Muslim nations must support liberation movements wherever they occur, whether or not they are Islamically inspired.[6]

The ire of many of the *ulama*, and indeed many Muslims, across the Islamic world was particularly aroused by Qaddafi's methodology and interpretations of Islam. He challenged the status and role of the *ulama* by emphasizing that all Muslims had a right to interpret Islam and by interpreting Islam himself in a rather sweeping style with innovations that broke with traditional belief and practice. Raising his *Green Book* to the status of the Sharia, interpreting Islam for state and society, and encouraging others to do so—all these actions flew in the face of the traditional role of the *ulama*. Qaddafi also encouraged Muslims to break with the centuries-long Islamic practice of dating the Muslim calendar from the emigration (*hijra*) of Muhammad and his followers from Mecca to Medina. Instead he introduced a new Muslim calendar, which began with the death of the Prophet.

For many, the proof of Qaddafi's hubris and unorthodoxy was his position regarding the authenticity and binding nature of the corpus of Prophetic traditions, the *hadith*. Like some Muslim scholars and much of Western scholarship, Qaddafi questioned the authenticity of the traditions of the Prophet, given alterations, interpolations, and fabrication. He concluded that due to this lack of certitude regarding the Sunna of the Prophet, only the Quran should be regarded as binding and as an infallible guide. Many of his critics charged that Qaddafi was merely clearing the way for the authority of his own statements and teachings. Indeed, Qaddafi rejected the binding nature of the Sunna, the schools of Islamic law (which he regarded as sectarian movements), and the traditional religious establishment. Moreover, in a direct assault on the authority of the *ulama*, he had encouraged his youthful followers to take over the mosques.

In the final analysis, Qaddafi advocated an ideology and system of government based less on revelation than on his own personal guidance and dictates. Muammar Qaddafi's idiosyncratic, and for some heretical, populist reinterpretation of Islam and Arab socialism, which he imposed on Libyan religious leaders, earned the opposition of the religious establishment in the Arab world and Libyan Islamic movements, including the Muslim Brotherhood, who were targeted as "public enemies" and repressed, driven into exile, and silenced. Qaddafi remained in power until he was overthrown and killed in October 2011 during the Arab Uprisings.

Iran

For many in the West, the Iranian revolution was the occasion for their encounter with Islam and its role in Muslim politics. For more than a decade thereafter, events in the Muslim world would be viewed primarily through the prism of the Islamic revolution and Ayatollah Khomeini's Iran: the fall of the Shah, long regarded by the Western media as an enlightened, modernizing monarch and a staunch ally of the United States; the wrenching spectacle of the seizure of the American embassy in Tehran and of "America Held Hostage" by Islamic militants, shown nightly on television and in the press shouting "Death to America"; and the kidnapping of Americans and bombings of American embassies and Marines in Lebanon, attributed to Iranian-inspired and supported Islamic radicals. The Iranian experience exemplifies a publicly proclaimed "Islamic" revolution and government as well as the clash of interpretations of Islam that accompany the politicization of Shii Islam.

During the 1960s and 1970s, the Shah of Iran's White Revolution had attempted to implement a wide-ranging modernization program. Despite noteworthy gains, the real impact and advantages of modernization had primarily benefited urban areas and a new modern middle class of technocrats and professionals. Most important, modernization had not included significant political reform. Many sectors of Iranian society had become increasingly critical of the Shah's growing autocratic rule and the rapid, uncritical pace of modernization, which posed a threat to Iranian national autonomy, identity, and culture.

In the face of the regime's refusal to grant broader political participation and its suppression of dissent, an alliance evolved between the traditional, religiously oriented classes (religious leaders, merchants, and artisans), who felt many of the Shah's modern reforms to be an assault on both their religion and livelihood, and many modern, Western-educated intellectuals and professionals. Both shared common concerns about political freedom, the dangers of military and economic dependence on the United States, and the threat of cultural alienation due to the Westernization of Iranian education and society—what one secular intellectual termed "Westoxification" or "Weststruckness," that is, indiscriminate borrowing from and dependence on the West. Although all shared the goals of overthrowing the Shah and creating a more indigenously rooted government and society, their religious and political outlooks and agendas were in reality quite diverse. For many, the Islamic alternative meant a return to Islam, the establishment of an Islamic state and society. Others wished to restore national pride and identity through a conscious preservation and incorporation of Iran's Persian–Shii identity and cultural heritage. Their differences would emerge once the Shah was overthrown and Iran's new leaders moved from opposition to a common foe to the implementation of an Islamic republic.

As opposition to the Shah mounted, the reinterpretation and politicization of Shii Islam emerged as the most viable and effective vehicle for articulating national concerns, for legitimating demands for reforms, and for gaining popular support. Islam provided an indigenous, non-Western alternative—a sense of identity, a common set of religiocultural symbols and values and thus an ideological framework within which a variety of factions could coexist. The ideological worldview of Shii Islam, in particular its religious history, gave meaning and legitimacy to a mushrooming opposition movement. Indeed, early Shii religious history and belief lent itself to the interpretation of Shiism as a religion of protest and revolution: the disinheritance of Ali, Husayn, and the early Imams by Sunni caliphs; Shii revolts against Umayyad and Abbasid Sunni rulers; and especially the martyrdom of Husayn at Karbala. All these events offered inspirational examples and symbols for the ensuing battle against oppression and injustice and the legitimacy of protest, martyrdom, and, if necessary, revolution.

Modern Iranian history had also provided selective examples or precedents for the use of Islam in protest movements to preserve Iranian independence and national interests. In the Tobacco Protest (1891–92) to prevent the selling of tobacco concessions to Europeans and the Constitutional Revolt (1905–11), which set some limits on the Shah's power by instituting liberal reforms, a modern constitution, and parliamentary form of government, local religious leaders (mullahs) were pressed into service, joining with other sectors of society in the protests. In both cases, religious leaders and institutions were part of broad-based movements to safeguard Iranian identity and autonomy and check an autocratic Shah. Similarly, during the 1970s the mullah-mosque network offered a ready-made system of organization and mobilization.

The imprisonment of many key secular leaders and the imposition of martial law accentuated the more independent status and role of religious leaders, who represented a vast reservoir of grassroots leadership. Their mosques, situated throughout Iran's cities, towns, and villages, became centers for political organization and agitation. Government regulations could not restrict the functioning of mosques, the economic support that religious leaders received from wealthy merchants and others who paid their Islamic tithes or taxes (the annual tithe on wealth for the poor, *zakat*, and the Shii religious tax on income, *khums*, which is paid directly to religious authorities), or the sermons at Friday community prayer that drew on Shii religious history to excoriate the evils of imperial oppression. The battlefield at Karbala in the seventh century became the streets of Tehran and other Iranian cities in the twentieth century; the confrontation between the armies of Caliph Yazid and the martyred Husayn was transformed into the contemporary confrontation between the Shah (the new Yazid) and the modern-day forces of Husayn, the Iranian people. Thus, the classic Shii myth of good and evil, the army of God versus that of Satan, with its lessons of sacrifice and martyrdom, had its modern-day meanings and application. Similarly, traditional Twelver Shii belief in the return of the hidden Twelfth Imam, its promise of ultimate victory and a reign of perfect social justice, could be drawn on to inspire and motivate.

The Islamic component in Iran's revolution had many sources, drawing on a variety of Islamically oriented leaders and their ideological interpretations of Islam. Among the more prominent and influential were Mehdi Bazargan, Dr. Ali Shariati, and the Ayatollah Khomeini. Bazargan (1907–96), who would become the provisional prime minister of the Islamic Republic of Iran in 1979, was a French-trained engineer and Islamically inspired political activist who had been a longtime critic of the Shah and had been imprisoned for his beliefs. Bazargan was particularly effective because he combined a traditional religious outlook and vocabulary with modern concerns and was thus able to speak to the *ulama* as well as modern, educated students and professionals.

Ali Shariati (1933–77), the son of a preacher-scholar, was a Sorbonne-educated intellectual and teacher. He had been active in Bazargan's Liberation Movement of Iran in the 1960s and influenced by the example of the Algerian and Cuban revolutions. Shariati synthesized Shii Islam and Western social scientific language to develop a thoroughgoing reinterpretation of traditional Islam, a kind of liberation theology. He denounced "world imperialism, including multinational corporations and cultural imperialism, racism, class exploitation, class oppression, class inequality, and *gharbzadegi* [Weststruckness]."[7]

Shariati's teachings disturbed both the political and the religious establishments. The Shah regarded Shariati as an Islamic Marxist and revolutionary, and many of the *ulama* condemned his innovative reinterpretation of traditional Shii beliefs, which was critical of the *ulama's* role in Iranian history. Shariati distinguished between original Islam (the Islam of Ali and his early followers)—which he claimed was dynamic, progressive, scientific, and revolutionary—and the scholastic, institutionalized, bureaucratic Islam (Safavid Islam) of the *ulama*, who had been co-opted by the Safavid rulers. The *ulama* produced a rigid, passive and retrogressive religion of the establishment. For Shariati, both Western imperialism and a retrogressive religious leadership were responsible for the decline of Muslim society. The *ulama* had too often become government advisers or fallen into quietism rather than asserting their true role as protectors of Islam against oppressive governments. Thus Shariati believed that reform must come primarily from lay intelligentsia rather than from the traditional religious leaders. His dynamic revolutionary Islam, which preached a more indigenous ideology—Iranian-Islamic rather than Western-imperialist—proved very effective among many of Iran's modern, educated professionals and students. More than 100,000 copies of his lectures were published and distributed, and thousands flocked regularly to hear him speak. For them, Shariati demonstrated the relevance of Shii Islam to modern life and to serve as the basis for a much-needed social revolution.

In sharp contrast to Shariati stands the champion of clerical rule, the Ayatollah Ruhollah Khomeini (1902–89). If Shariati was the ideologue of the Iranian revolution, Khomeini was its living symbol and guide. An early, outspoken critic of the Shah, he had been forced to live in exile from the 1960s until his triumphant return from France in 1979. The freedom and independence he enjoyed in exile enabled him to remain vociferous in his call for reform and to cultivate his image and role as the symbol of opposition to the Shah, the outspoken voice and conscience of Islam and the Iranian people. From exile, he continued to guide his followers in Iran; his speeches and writings were smuggled into Iran on audiocassettes and pamphlets and widely distributed through the mullah-mosque network. Khomeini, like many others in Iran and throughout the Islamic world, condemned Western imperialism, the Westernization of Muslim societies with its threat to Islamic identity and culture, and Israel, which he regarded as an outpost of American neocolonialism.

In contrast to Bazargan and Shariati, Khomeini remained religiously conservative in his education, vocation, worldview, and lifestyle. Although all three shared common national and religious concerns—the experience of government repression, opposition to the Shah, rejection of political quietism, and the struggle for Islamically oriented sociopolitical reforms—Khomeini's outlook was shaped by his clerical background and interests. For Khomeini, the comprehensiveness of Islam and its integral relationship to society were inseparably linked to clerical dominance.

However, religious traditionalism did not preclude change and development in his interpretation of Islam. His doctrine of jurist rule asserted that because an Islamic government is one based on Islamic law, the most qualified to rule would be an expert (*faqih*) or group of experts in Islamic law. However, Khomeini's opinions would have remained academic if the political situation had not deteriorated so badly in the mid-1970s.

The increasingly repressive measures of the Shah transformed an opposition movement demanding reform into a resistance movement, organized under the umbrella of Islam, calling for a new political and social order. This movement comprised diverse groups in the Iranian political and ideological spectrum: from secularists to Islamic activists, from liberal democrats to Marxists. In 1970, the Ayatollah had spoken of an Islamic revolution that might take centuries; he could not foresee that events in 1979 would lead to his triumphant return to Iran and the establishment of the Islamic Republic of Iran.

Khomeini and his clerical followers consolidated their power and dominated Iran's government, parliament, judiciary, military, Revolutionary Guards, the press, and media. Censorship of news and publishing, ideological control of university curricula and professors, and prohibitions on alcohol, gambling, drug use, and sexual offenses were all enforced in the name of Islam. Islamic courts and judges sentenced and punished those convicted of offenses ranging from drug smuggling and homosexuality to political dissent. Dissent, both Islamic and secular, was silenced. Competing interpretations of Islam were often no longer tolerated but eclipsed or displaced by a doctrinaire ideology that left little place for the followers of Islamically oriented laity like Shariati and Bazargan or for dissenting clerics. Many were driven out of office, fled the country, imprisoned, or executed.

Khomeini's espousal of a nonsectarian, universalist Islam, transcending Sunni–Shii differences, informed Iran's advocacy of a universal Islamic revolution to liberate all the oppressed and justified Khomeini's outspoken leadership on Islamic issues internationally. This doctrine was used to justify the incitement, of revolts in Saudi Arabia, Bahrain, and Iraq; to support the Moro in the southern Philippines; to legitimate Iranian intervention in Lebanon; and to justify Khomeini's condemnation of Salman Rushdie. Debate over the interpretation and application of Islam has continued throughout the existence of the Islamic Republic of Iran.

Critical to understanding the Islamic Republic have been and continue to be its factions and shifts of power, a history of factionalism, and the loss of equilibrium and increasing polarization among the governing elites. The contending forces within Iran were reflected in 1997, when many were stunned when the "favorite son" of the ruling elites lost in a landslide to the "Cinderella candidate," Seyyed Mohammad Khatami, who received 69 percent of the vote. Khatami had run on a liberal platform in a country where "liberal" was synonymous with "Western decadence."

During Khatami's presidency open public discussion and debate on topics like democratization, civil society, and the rule of law were accompanied by factional disputes over the concept and future of the institution of the *faqih* (jurist). The debate included a questioning of the historical and theological legitimacy of the concept of *vilayat-i faqih* (guardianship of the jurist) or the Supreme Leader of the government as well as the limits of popular sovereignty, civil society, and rule of law.

The hardliners bounced back with the election of the sixth president of the Islamic Republic, who enjoyed the support of a coalition of conservative political groups. Mahmoud Ahmadinejad espoused a hardline religious and political position, winning 62 percent of the votes in a runoff election to become president in August 2005.

Ahmadinejad proved to be a very controversial figure within Iran and internationally. Criticism crested with his election to a second term in June 2009, the results of which were rejected by the major opposition opposition candidates, Mir-Hossein Mousavi, a former prime minister under Ayatollah Khomeini, and Mehdi Karroubi, former Speaker of Iran's parliament, charging the elections were rigged and also widely criticized internationally. On June 23 and 25, 2009, two years before the Arab Uprisings in Tunisia, Egypt, Libya, Yemen, and Syria, in protest against Ahmadinejad's declared victory, up to 3 millions demonstrators in Tehran poured into the streets in a pro-democracy movement that came to be called the Green Movement, whose supporters included former president Khatami and other reform-minded politicians and clergy, many chanting the slogan "Where is my vote?" Mass demonstrations and civil disobedience continued in major cities until February 2010 when police and other security forces suppressed the demonstrations. More than seventy-two were killed and thousands arrested and tortured. The government in Tehran shut down and attempted to block social media and banned public rallies. Mousavi and Karrubi and more than one hundred other leaders of the movement were arrested, subjected to show trials, and imprisoned.

In June 2010 Mousavi issued a Covenant for the Green Movement, calling for democratic reforms. In contrast to the Arab uprising that led to the overthrow of Arab dictators, the Green Movement continued to call for pro-democracy reforms and civil rights. While recognizing the role of Islam in society, the covenant called for the separation of religious institutions from institutions of the state," although it acknowledged that "religion will certainly have a presence" in Iran's democratic future.

Lebanon

The dominant reality of Lebanon during the late 1970s and the 1980s was its civil war. Lebanon also offers the second major example of militant Shii politics. Ironically, the two Middle Eastern countries most torn by violence and civil strife, Iran and Lebanon, were once regarded as the most stable, modern, and Western-oriented. It was not uncommon for Lebanon to be referred to as the Switzerland of the Middle East or for Beirut to be described as the Paris of the Middle East (reflecting the influence of French culture and fashions). Moreover, Beirut's banks, shops, boutiques, cinemas, and leading universities (the French Jesuit Universite St. Joseph and the American University of Beirut) reflected Western influence and offered the best that was available in the United States and Europe.

Shii organizations such as **AMAL, Hizbollah**, and **al-Jihad**, which mobilized Shii Muslims in protest and revolutionary activities, were major actors in the Lebanese civil war. Since the late 1970s, a Shii community, long a distant third in political and economic power in a state dominated by Maronite Christians and Sunni Muslims, has become a formidable force. The Shii of Lebanon existed in a confessional or sectarian state whose government was based on the balancing of several major religiopolitical communities or confessional groups' interests.

Historically, with the division of the Ottoman empire after World War I, Lebanon and Syria had been placed under French rule, known as the French Mandate. The French subsequently oversaw the creation of modern Lebanon, with a government that was based on an informal agreement, the National Pact of 1943, designed to assure the dominance of France's Christian Lebanese allies. A sectarian system of government, based on the census of 1932, which identified the Maronite Christians as the largest community, institutionalized the relative population strengths of Lebanon's major religious communities: Maronites, Sunni Muslims, Shii Muslims, and Druze. Thus, the president was to be a Maronite, the prime minister a Sunni Muslim, and the speaker of the chamber of deputies a Shii. Key positions in the government, cabinet, parliament, ministries, and military were apportioned along confessional, or sectarian, lines. Within this system, the Shii minority were a distant third to the more numerous and prosperous Christian and Sunni Muslim communities. However, Shii prominence in political affairs increased in the 1970s, and a major catalyst for this turn of events was an Iranian-born and educated Shii cleric, Imam Musa Sadr. As the Ayatollah Khomeini had come to symbolize the hopes and aspirations of Iran's dispossessed, so too the charismatic Musa Sadr came to represent the reinvigorated and mobilized Lebanese Shii community.

Musa Sadr had come from Iran to Lebanon in 1959. The Lebanese Shii were primarily rural, poor, and disorganized. By the early 1970s, he had become the leading Shii cleric in Lebanon, a major force in organizing a weak, disparate community. Musa Sadr appealed to Shii identity and community solidarity to sustain a populist movement for social and political reform, and in 1974 he organized the Movement of the Disinherited. Musa Sadr reinterpreted Shii religious history and belief. Early Shii suffering at the hands of Sunni rulers was likened to the tyranny, discrimination, and exploitation suffered under the Christian-dominated Lebanese political system. He identified AMAL ("Hope": the militia that had evolved from this movement) with the liberation of Lebanon's oppressed and disinherited. In a land of militias and escalating sectarian warfare, AMAL, originally organized to provide the Shii community with protection, to defend the rights of a community who had now grown in numbers to become Lebanon's largest confessional group, became radicalized.

Four events precipitated a radicalization of Shii politics: the Lebanese Civil War of 1975, the disappearance of Musa Sadr in 1978, the Iranian revolution of 1978–79, and the Israeli invasions of Lebanon in 1978 and 1982. The failure of Lebanon's Christian-dominated government to acknowledge the changed demographics (no census was taken after 1932!) and redistribute power more equitably to reflect a Muslim (Sunni and Shii combined) majority and of the Christian and Sunni Muslim leadership to respond to the needs of a Shii community that had grown from 18 percent in 1968 to 30 percent, or approximately 1 million, of the population, plus the presence of significant numbers of Palestinians in the south had exacerbated an already fragile and volatile political situation.

The mysterious disappearance of Musa Sadr while visiting Muammar Qaddafi in Libya in 1978 transformed Musa Sadr from a symbol of Shii protest to a cult hero and breathed new life into AMAL. Musa Sadr's disappearance fit nicely into the Shii paradigm of martyrdom and the occultation of the Hidden Twelfth Imam. He was transformed into a religious hero, a worthy descendant of Husayn. Many maintained that Imam Musa Sadr had not died; he had merely disappeared and would return.

The Iranian revolution and the Israeli invasions of 1978 and 1982 significantly contributed to the further deterioration of Lebanon's war-torn politics and the radicalization of the Shii. The impact of the Iranian revolution, with its heightened sense of Shii pride and identity, testified to the power of Shii faith and ideology and verified the politicized Shii model of resistance and its promise of ultimate triumph. However, by 1982, AMAL, under Musa Sadr's lay successor, Nabih Berri, had increasingly pursued a moderate, pragmatic policy, maintaining relations with Lebanon's Christian-dominated government and Western powers. The Israeli invasion of Lebanon and the massacres at Shatilla and Sabra in 1982, attributed to a Christian militia, discredited Berri in the eyes of more alienated and radicalized Shii youth and Iranian-influenced militants. They rejected

AMAL and Berri as collaborators with the Christian government, Israel, and the United States, regarded as an ally and sponsor of both the Lebanese and Israeli governments.

With the assistance of Iran, radical Islamic organizations like Islamic AMAL, Hizbollah, and Islamic Jihad emerged in Baalbek, a Shii center in the Beqaa Valley. Calling for an "Islamic revolution," Iran offered a more militant, confrontational, and explicitly Islamic alternative to the Shii of Lebanon. Like Islamic AMAL, which broke with Berri and opted for a more explicit Islamic identification, all rejected AMAL's secular nationalism and, influenced by the example of Iran, called for an Islamic republic for Lebanon and the implementation of a more Islamic way of life. The groundwork had been well prepared. Ideologically, like the Ayatollah Khomeini, Lebanese Shii religious leaders such as Musa Sadr and Shaykh Muhammad Husayn Fadlallah (Hizbollah's ideologue and adviser) had been engaged in a powerful reinterpretation of Shii Islam that supported a populist, militant, political activist movement of resistance and protest.

Hizbollah, the Party of God, had sprung up in the wake of the Iranian revolution with the support of Iranian Revolutionary Guards ostensibly sent to Lebanon to fight Israel. Its motto ("the Party of God will surely be the victors") was taken from Quran (58:22), for they perceived their battle as that of the Party of God against the Party of Satan (58:19–20)—whether Christian militias, Israeli forces, Western imperialism, or even AMAL. Quoting Khomeini, Hizbollah ideologues maintained that "the original objective of the imperialist countries is to destroy the Holy Koran and to obliterate it, and to destroy Islam and the Muslim ulama (leadership) and their plan is to keep [Islamic countries] backward, and in the name of encouraging education   they have suppressed religious schools."[8]

Pro-Iranian Shii clerics provided leadership and guidance for Hizbollah. Their mosques became centers for recruitment, training, and mobilization. The clerics attracted students and young professionals, who regarded their situation as so desperate as to justify armed struggle (jihad) in their defense against political oppression, imperialism, and social injustice. Iran provided training, arms, and substantial financial aid to Hizbollah and supported its military operations as the building of mosques and the reconstruction of war-torn homes, hospitals, clinics, schools, and farms.

Throughout the 1980s Hizbollah grew to be an umbrella group with which a variety of smaller groups, such as Islamic Jihad, allied themselves. Within the shifting alliances of Lebanon's civil war, it fought Christian militias, Israeli and Syrian troops, and AMAL and engaged bombings such as those of the American and French embassies as well as the barracks of multinational forces in Beirut in 1983.

With the end of civil war in 1990 and return to parliamentary government, both AMAL and Hizbollah remained significant, although differing, Shii voices in Lebanese society. In the 1990s, both participated in parliamentary elections. AMAL's leader Nabih Berri became Speaker of the Parliament. Both AMAL and Hizbollah joined with Sunni Muslim, Christian, and Druze in rebuilding Lebanon and participated in institutes, conferences, and projects to improve interreligious understanding and cooperation. Hizbollah kept up its substantial military resistance to Israeli occupation in southern Lebanon, claiming a victory when the last Israeli troops withdrew from southern Lebanon in May 2000.

Six years after the last Israeli troops withdrew from southern Lebanon, Israel launched a full-scale war on Lebanon in the summer of 2006 in retaliation for Hizbollah's raid on Israeli Defense Forces (IDF) that killed seven IDF soldiers and captured two others. Hizbollah responded with rocket attacks targeting northern Israeli cities. The air strikes on Lebanon's airport, runways, gas stations, lighthouses, bridges, buses, residences, and power plants left an estimated 1,200 Lebanese dead, most of them civilians, and a million people homeless. Israel lost 117 soldiers and forty-one civilians in the war.

On August 11, 2006, the United Nations Security Council voted for a ceasefire that went into effect three days later. After intense fighting between Hizbollah and Israel, Hizbollah's leader, Hassan Nasrallah, declared a strategic victory over Israel and emerged as the most popular figure in the Middle East. According to *The Washington Post*, "Nasrallah managed what the tens of thousands in the armies of Egypt, Syria and Jordan were unable to do for half a century—force Israel to retreat. Today, his is the last private army left in Lebanon."[9] Israeli Prime Minister Ehud Olmert countered, claiming that Israel dealt a major blow to Hizbollah.[10] Subsequent history would see Hizbollah's continued influence both in Lebanese politics and in the Syrian civil war, where it provided significant military support to Syria's President, Bashar Al Assad.

Saudi Arabia

A visitor to Saudi Arabia is initially struck by a host of images that seem to confirm the Islamic character of the state—a seemingly endless number of mosques; a society that seems to stop at prayer time as shops close and the faithful, wherever they are, face Mecca to pray; prohibition of alcohol; and women veiled and segregated in public life. Saudi Arabia provides a striking and at times paradoxical example of a traditional yet modern self-styled Islamic state. The Saudis proudly proclaim their Islamic heritage and traditions.

Hassan Nasrallah (1960–92), Secretary General of Hizbollah.

Religion is the basis of Saudi Arabia's national identity, society, law, and politics. The House of Saud has relied on Islam to unite and rule its tribal society, to legitimate its authority and institutions, and to assert its leadership in the Islamic world. Saudi Arabia encompasses an area that is the original birthplace of Muhammad and the homeland of Islam. It is the guardian of the holy cities of Mecca and Medina and of the annual pilgrimage (hajj) to Mecca.

Although the modern Kingdom of Saudi Arabia was officially established as a nation-state in 1932, its roots date back to the eighteenth-century Islamic revivalist Wahhabi movement, with the alliance of religion and political power under **Muhammad ibn Abd al-Wahhab** (1703–92) and **Muhammad ibn Saud** (d. 1765). The Saudi flag, which combines the Muslim confession of faith ("There is no god but the God....") and the crossed swords of the House of Saud and ibn Abd al-Wahhab, reflects this union of faith and politics. The Wahhabi spirit and strict interpretation of Islam have remained a prominent force in Saudi politics and society.

Islam provides the ideological basis for Saudi rule. The Quran is its constitution and the state is said to be governed by Islamic law, applied by a Sharia court system whose judges and legal advisers are ulama. The House of Saud has been careful to cultivate its relationship with the ulama, the guardians of Islamic law, through intermarriage and state patronage. The monarchy itself has been justified or rationalized by maintaining that the king himself is subject to the Sharia, God's law. For example, a ruling (fatwa) from the ulama cited the Islamic legal principle of "public interest" or general welfare of society was used to legitimate the removal in 1964 of King Saud ibn Abd al-Aziz, an inept ruler, and transfer of power to his brother, King Faisal. Thus, the ruler, government, law, and judiciary are in principle Islamically rooted and accountable.

Wahhabi Islam's ultraconservative interpretation of Islam—literalist, puritanical, exclusivist, and intolerant—is based on the belief that they follow the pristine, pure, unadulterated message of the Prophet. Their brand of Islam is not shared by many other Sunni or Shii Muslims, whom many Wahhabis would condemn as unbelievers or religious hypocrites. Like hardline Christian fundamentalists, Wahhabis aggressively seek to convert the world and can be intolerant of other faiths as well as other Sunni, Shii, and Sufi Muslims.

Wahhabi ultraconservatism is reflected in the activities of Committees for the Enforcement of Virtue and the Prohibition of Vice. An adaptation of a traditional Muslim institution, religious officials or police, who in the early Islamic era supervised public markets and morals, monitor proper "Islamic" public behavior; making sure that shops close during prayer times, the fast of Ramadan is observed, alcohol is not consumed, and men and women dress and act modestly. Their activities have included raiding homes where they suspect alcohol, caning women for not covering properly, arresting unrelated males and females caught socializing and priests or ministers suspected of conducting religious services, banning

Valentine's Day gifts, and beating or flogging violators. The House of Saud Islam has employed Islam both domestically and internationally. Religious interpretations and justifications have been used to outlaw political parties and trade unions as un-Islamic and at the same time to justify the infusion of modern technology and social change. Thus, although tradition has been the source of strict separation of the sexes in public life and the veiling of women, the limits of revelation and the application of the rather rigid and strict Hanbali interpretation of Islamic law have paradoxically proven quite flexible in other ways. Islam has been utilized to demonstrate the compatibility of religion and modernization. The Quran and the traditions of the Prophet have been interpreted to justify using foreign workers and to gain acceptance of everything from television and automobiles to women's education. The Quran and Islamic law are strictly enforced, but reforms have been implemented where revelation is silent. In these areas, the Saudi government has claimed the right to interpret (ijtihad) and apply Islam. In the name of Islamic legal principles, such as public interest, regulations, or royal decrees (as distinguished from human legislation, which is technically proscribed) can introduce modern commercial regulations or laws.

Internationally, Islam has been a factor in Saudi Arabia's diplomacy and foreign policy. When Egypt's Gamal Abd al-Nasser sought to extend his influence in the Arab world as the leader of a pan-Arab nationalist movement in the 1960s and to present Arab socialism as an "Islamic socialism," King Faisal responded to the challenge of pan-Arabism by invoking Islam as a counter-ideology and placing himself at the head of an alternative pan-Islamic movement. Saudi–Egyptian rivalry for leadership in the Arab world became an occasion for the king to reinforce Saudi leadership in the broader Islamic world as well.

King Faisal set Saudi Arabia on a course of Islamic leadership that has lasted to the present day. The king emphasized his role and that of Saudi Arabia as protectors of the holy sites and, by extension, of Islam and the interests of the Islamic world. Ideologically, Saudi Arabia has cultivated its image as the defender of Islam against Arab and Islamic radicalism (whether it be the brand of Nasser, Qaddafi, or Khomeini), Zionism, and atheistic communism.

A host of international Islamic organizations, such as the Muslim World League, the Organization of the Islamic Conference (OIC), and the Islamic Development Bank (IDB), have been established, based in and funded in large part by Saudi Arabia. The Muslim World League, based in Mecca but with branches throughout the world, seeks to promote Saudi Arabia's interpretation of Islam; it funds programs, conferences, and other

Islamic activities and projects. The OIC fosters intergovernment cooperation among Islamic governments, and the IDB supports economic development projects in Muslim countries. Over the years the Saudis have
used their oil wealth to support and spread their Wahhabi brand of Islam,
promote missionary activities worldwide, translate and distribute Islamic
literature, and encourage and provide financial incentives to Muslim governments to further Islamize their societies.

The Saudi appeal to Islam has proven to be a two-edged sword. Islam
has been used as a yardstick by which opponents of the House of Saud have
attacked the government. As a result of the Islamic revival, the Iranian
revolution, and Saudi domestic politics, the Saudi monarchy became even
more attentive to its Islamic image in the 1980s. Religious symbolism and
social values were reemphasized. The influx of foreigners was more strictly
controlled, as was their observance of prohibitions on alcohol and modest
dress and behavior in public. At times the religious police became more
assertive in their enforcement of public morality.

The Gulf War of 1991 and its legacy brought new challenges for the
monarchy. Although the religious establishment rallied to support the
House of Saud and even provided fatwas to legitimate royal decisions,
sharp voices of dissent, including that of Osama bin Laden, condemned
the presence of American (foreign, non-Muslim) forces on Saudi soil.
In addition, the leaders of many Islamic movements, some of whom
long enjoyed Saudi financial support, also joined the opposition. In the
post–Gulf War period, the House of Saud faced growing criticism and
demands from diverse sectors of society.

By the mid-1990s, the government appeared to have effectively silenced
its opposition, co-opting some, imprisoning others, and driving still others underground. That silence was shattered by bombings, which targeted
the American military, in Riyadh at the National Guard Headquarters
in November 1995 and the U.S. military housing compound in Dhahran
in June 1996. The bombings were seen by many as a reaction by militant
Islamists to the government crackdown and a warning to Saudi Arabia
and other Gulf states about their ties to and dependency on America and
the West.

Despite Saudi Arabia's creation as an Islamic state and its deliberate Islamic profile, the House of Saud's security, legitimacy, and leadership domestically and internationally would continue to be threatened
by domestic terrorists as well as the Saudi-born and raised Osama
bin Laden and **al-Qaeda** and its leadership and perceived security in
the Gulf challenged by Iran and its nuclear program. As we shall see,
Saudi Arabia would play a major role in its opposition to prodemocracy

movements of the Arab Spring and indeed be a significant political and financial supporter of the military coup in Egypt and the restoration of authoritarian rule.

Pakistan

Pakistan offers the most sustained example of the evolution of a modern Islamic republic. From the late 1930s when Muhammad Ali Jinnah and the Muslim League seized the banner of Islam and mobilized mass support for Muslim national independence in India with the cry, "Islam in Danger," religion has been a factor in Pakistan's political development: a source of national identity, legitimacy, and mass mobilization, as well as opposition.[11] A review of Islam's role in Pakistan reveals the diverse, shifting, and often contending interpretations and usages of religion as well as its potential to divide rather than unite.

Religion played an important role in Pakistan's independence movement. Muhammad Ali Jinnah (1876–1948) used Islam to mobilize popular support among the Muslims of the Indian subcontinent. Pakistan was established as a Muslim homeland in August 1947. The ethnically and linguistically diverse Muslims in West and East Pakistan, a country separated by more than a thousand miles of Indian territory, were united in the name of a Muslim nationalism, rooted in an appeal to a common Islamic heritage. However, its meaning and implications were as diverse as the country's population, often the subject of compromise and manipulation rather than precise definition.

For Jinnah, Islam was simply the common cultural heritage and identity of the Muslim majority, and in this sense, Pakistan was a Muslim homeland or state. Many others believed that the creation of Pakistan necessitated an Islamic state whose institutions and law should be based on Islam. The renowned Islamic modernist, Muhammad Iqbal, differed from Jinnah in regarding Islam as a religiosocial order, believing that Islamic law (the Shariah) should be the law of Pakistan.

Whereas many of the *ulama* in the Indian subcontinent had initially been divided in their response to the Pakistan movement, after independence those who were in Pakistan accepted the political reality and with the Jamaat-i-Islami (the Islamic Society) clamored for an Islamic state during the often heated constitutional debates in the late 1940s and the early 1950s.

The governments of General Ayub Khan (1958–69), Zulfikar Ali Bhutto (1971–77), General Zia ul-Haq (1977–88), and Benazir Bhutto (1988–90, 1993–96) revealed the formative and contending influences on Pakistan's national identity, the interplay, rather than separation, of religion and politics in Pakistan and the continued tensions between modernists' and traditionalists' interpretations of Islam and its proper role in society.

In 1958, Field Marshal Muhammad Ayub Khan established the first of what would later become three martial law regimes in Pakistan. A Western-oriented modernist Muslim, Ayub Khan was primarily concerned with establishing a strong centralized government and fostering rapid socioeconomic change. His secular pursuits did not preclude the attempt to use religion and religious institutions to legitimate selective reforms, to define and interpret Islamic belief and practice in a "rational and liberal manner" and thus bring out its "dynamic character in the context of the intellectual and scientific progress of the modern world."[12]

Islamic socialism replaced modernist Islam during the rule of Zulfikar Ali Bhutto (1971–77). Although Bhutto was a secular socialist, political realities led him to increasingly appeal to religion in his domestic and foreign policy to buttress and legitimate his populism. Pakistan's 1971 civil war resulted in the transformation of East Pakistan into independent Bangladesh and refocused attention on the issue of Pakistan's identity and raison d'être as a Muslim homeland. Like the post-1967 Arab experience, many Pakistani Muslims concluded that the disastrous loss of East Pakistan and failure to achieve national integration were due to their departure from Islam (both in their failure to sufficiently realize an Islamic identity that was supposed to bind West and East Pakistan and in the effective penetration of Western culture during Ayub Khan's liberal Western regime) and called for a reaffirmation of Pakistan's Islamic roots. At the same time, Bhutto turned to Arab oil countries (Libya and especially Saudi Arabia, the United Arab Emirates, and Kuwait) for foreign aid and as an outlet for Pakistani products and labor. In exchange, Bhutto increased emphasis on Pakistan's Islamic identity in his public discourse and politics, and his government sponsored Islamic conferences and introduced Islamic laws restricting alcohol, gambling, and nightclubs. In many ways Bhutto unwittingly set the stage for General Zia ul-Haq's July 5, 1977, coup d'état in the name of Islam.

If during the Ayub Khan and Zulfikar Bhutto years (1956–77) Pakistan was an avowed Islamic republic with a modernist bent, under Zia ul-Haq a more conservative or "fundamentalist" orientation would prevail. General Zia ul-Haq moved quickly to legitimate his coup and impose martial law rule in the name of Islam, promising an Islamic system (*nizam-i-Islam*) of government. Islam became the core symbol for his regime, informing both domestic and foreign policy. Zia employed Islam as a source of national identity, legitimacy, cultural integration, and public morality to a degree that exceeded that of any previous government. Islam was used as an excuse for continued military rule. As the years passed, many religious leaders who had been swift to support Zia's nizam-i-Islam (Islamic system) and to tolerate some of the harsher aspects of martial law moved from support to criticism of the government's slow pace in implementation and even its actual commitment.

Although touted as a source of national unity and pride, the increased appeal to religion, **Islamization,** exacerbated religious and ethnic divisions. Unity of faith in Islam did not mean a common interpretation or understanding of Islamic belief and practice. Islamization intensified differences between Sunni and Shii as well as among diverse Sunni groups, fanning the fires of sectarianism.

Zia ul-Haq's Islamic system of government had negative repercussions for women and minorities and threatened the status and role of Muslim and Christian minorities in society. In 1974, Zulfikar Ali Bhutto and the National Assembly had amended Pakistan's Constitution to legally declare the Qadiani (Ahmadiyya) a non-Muslim minority. After a worldwide Qadiani conference in 1983 drew 200,000 participants, Sunni and Shii *ulama* met in January 1984 and passed a series of resolutions that resulted in Zia's government's Ordinance, which stipulated punishments for any Qadiani who called himself a Muslim, referred to his faith as Islam, preached or propagated his faith, used Islamic terminology such as *masjid* (mosque) or *adhan* (call to prayer), "or in any manner outraged the religious feelings of Muslims."

For Christians, who constitute about 1 percent of the population, the greater emphasis on Islamization of state and society under Bhutto and Zia ul-Haq meant nationalization of religious schools and anxiety about the impact of greater emphasis on Pakistan's Islamic heritage and the introduction of Islamic laws. A general concern for all minorities was that Pakistan would retreat to classical Islamic law's designation of non-Muslim "People of the Book" as *dhimmi* (protected people), a status that, however advanced in its original context, by modern standards would amount to a second-class citizenship of restricted rights and duties vis-à-vis Muslim citizens.

Pakistan's eleven-year experiment with Islamization under General Zia ul-Haq came to an abrupt end on August 17, 1988, with a plane crash. In democratically held national elections in November 1988, Benazir Bhutto, the daughter of Zulfikar Ali Bhutto, became Pakistan's first freely elected prime minister in eleven years and the Muslim world's first woman prime minister.

Whatever her personal preferences, the Islamic trajectory set in motion reluctantly by her father and with great fanfare by Zia could not easily be halted or reversed. Bhutto herself found it necessary to project a profile in accord with Pakistan's Islamic religiocultural traditions. Shortly after her election, she made a much publicized pilgrimage (*umra*, the lesser pilgrimage) to Mecca, entered an arranged marriage, and began raising a family. Although she had distinguished between a correct interpretation of Islam and Zia ul-Haq's Islamization program, political realities prevented her from substantially changing the Islamic laws introduced during Zia's rule or initiating substantive women's reforms.

The President of Pakistan dismissed Prime Minister Benazir Bhutto's government on August 6, 1990. While her successor Nawaz Sharif pursued a pragmatic policy on international and domestic Islamic issues, the symbolic significance of Islam and its continued linkage to national identity were reflected in a Gallup poll, in which an overwhelming majority supported passage of a Sharia bill in 1991.

When General Pervez Musharraf carried out a bloodless coup in 1999, he promised a reformist government of "enlightened moderation," including a moderate Islam. Yet he was forced to withdraw his attempt to reform the Blasphemy law in the face of protests from Islamist groups, and his government continued to support the Taliban in Afghanistan. Government attempts to gain greater control over the madrasa system through legislation and educational reform were opposed by most religious groups and parties.

Benazir Bhutto returned to Pakistan in October 2007, after reaching an understanding with President Musharraf by which she was granted amnesty. However, on December 27, 2007, two weeks before the scheduled Pakistani general election of 2008, in which she was the leading opposition candidate, she was assassinated after a Pakistan Peoples Party rally in Rawalpindi. On August 18, 2008, Pervez Musharraf resigned as president under impeachment pressures from Pakistan's coalition (the Pakistan Peoples Party and the Pakistan Muslim League) government and was succeeded on September 6, 2008, by Asif Ali Zardari, Benazir Bhutto's husband, as Pakistan's eleventh president. Pakistan's government would continue to be challenged by deep ethnic, regional and religious divisions, sectarian (Sunni–Shia) violence, and terrorism, especially in its northwest tribal region along the border of Afghanistan. Pakistan earned a reputation as a haven for terrorists and terrorist camps. In 2007 some 13 militant Taliban groups were united to form Tehrik-i-Taliban Pakistan, and on May 2, 2011, U.S. Navy SEALs killed Osama bin Laden in his secret compound in Abbottabad.

A QUIET ISLAMIC REVOLUTION

Although the 1980s had been dominated by fears of an Iranian-inspired wave that would destabilize governments and come to power through violence and terror, by the 1990s failing economies and widespread public unrest produced an unexpected result. Viewing Islam and events in the Muslim world primarily through the prism of violence and terrorism had resulted in a failure to see the quiet revolution. Islamic movements were no longer on the periphery of society but had become part of mainstream Muslim life.

Islamically oriented social and political movements pursued reform within mainstream civil society. They included professional associations (journalists, physicians, engineers, and professors), as well as human rights and women's organizations. Many, where permitted, participated in electoral politics. Islamic movements also provided schools, clinics, hospitals, day care, legal aid, youth centers, and other social services. Private (non–government-controlled) mosques and financial institutions such as Islamic banks and insurance companies also proliferated. The emergence of an alternative elite, modern and educated but more Islamically oriented, offered an alternative that challenged the Western, secular presuppositions and lifestyles of many in the establishment.

In response to failed economies and "food riots," public protests and mass demonstrations, countries like Jordan, Tunisia, Sudan, Algeria, and Egypt held elections. Islamic political parties or individual activists (in countries that banned Islamic political parties) were "permitted" to participate. To the shock of many regimes and Western countries, Islamic candidates from North Africa to Southeast Asia proved a credible—often the only—political opposition, winning in local and national elections and assuming leadership in professional associations and trade unions. If much of the 1980s had been dominated by fears of Iran's export of a radical revolutionary Islam, in contrast, by the late 1980s and early 1990s, Islamically oriented candidates were elected as mayors and parliamentarians in countries as diverse as Morocco, Egypt, Turkey, Lebanon, Jordan, Kuwait, Bahrain, Pakistan, Malaysia, and Indonesia. They served in cabinet-level positions and as speakers of national assemblies. In Turkey, the bastion of secularism in the Middle East, Dr. Ecmettin Erbakan became the first leader of an Islamic party (Welfare) to become a prime minister (1996–97); in Malaysia, Anwar Ibrahim, the founder in 1971 of ABIM, the Muslim Youth Movement, served as the Deputy Prime Minister from 1993 to 1998; Abduraahman Wahid in Indonesia, head of the country's largest Islamic movement, Nahdatul Ulama, was elected President by the People's Consultative Assembly in 1999.

At the dawn of the twenty-first century, religiously oriented parties and candidates continued to prove successful at the polls. Islamic candidates and Muslim parties increased their influence in 2001 parliamentary elections in Morocco and in Pakistan; Islamic candidates in Bahrain won nineteen of forty parliamentary seats. In Turkey's secular republic, the **Justice and Development Party** (AKP), whose principal founders were former leaders of the Islamist Welfare Party, came to power in 2002 parliamentary elections and were reelected in July 2007 with a stunning victory in which the AKP took 47 percent of the vote.

In post-Saddam's Iraq's general elections in late 2005, the Shiite alliance won 128 of 275 seats.[13] Islamic activist candidates performed strongly in Saudi Arabia's 2005 polls, winning all the seats on the municipal councils in the cities of Mecca and Medina.[14] Sunni and Shii Islamic parliamentarians were a formidable force in Kuwait's National Assembly.

Among the most surprising performances, the officially "outlawed" (as a political party) Muslim Brotherhood's 2005 electoral performance rocked the government-controlled Egyptian political system. The authorities used many means to bar Brotherhood candidates from elections or to limit dramatically the size of its participation, including harassment by government-supported thugs, widespread arrests (of nearly nine hundred Brotherhood members and supporters), and the imprisonment of many, accompanied by government tampering with the electoral process. Although the Brotherhood ran for only one third of all parliamentary seats in order not to provoke the Mubarak government, its candidates still managed to win a surprising eighty-eight seats, more than any other opposition party, and therefore to control 20 percent of Egypt's parliament. As we shall see in the next chapter, during the Arab Spring, the Muslim Brotherhood would dominate Egypt's first parliamentary and presidential elections.

Without doubt the most stunning political victory belonged to **Hamas**. After winning local elections in late 2005 in the West Bank's largest cities, Hamas overwhelmingly defeated the ruling Fatah party, sweeping to power in early January 2006 in Palestinian parliamentary elections, sending shock waves through the region and beyond. Unprepared to accept the results of what was widely regarded as a free and fair election, the United States and Europe, along with Israel, refused to accept the Hamas electoral victory, to recognize and deal with Hamas's democratically elected leadership, and instead engaged in policies to isolate Hamas and undermine its influence.

The continued performance and success of Islamic movements in many countries reflected the failures of their governments and the extent to which mainstream Islamic movements were prepared to participate in the electoral process and remain a potent force in mainstream Muslim politics. The rise of al-Qaeda and the threat of global terrorism reinforced regimes, their security states and policies, and Western support.

GLOBAL TERRORISM

September 11, 2001, signaled a major crisis and struggle not only in global politics, but also within Islam and among Muslims. The terrorist attacks against the World Trade Center and the Pentagon raised disturbing questions about the nature of Islam itself: Was it a religion of peace or a peculiarly violent religion? Many in the West asked "Why do they hate us?" and expressed strong concerns about the religion of Islam and about Muslims and their relationship to violence and terror. The most persistent questions revolved around Islam's relationship to global terrorism, democracy, and modernity: Is Islam more militant than other religions? What does the Quran have to say about jihad, or holy war? Does the Quran condone this kind of violence and terrorism? Is there a clash of civilizations between the West and the Muslim world? Are Islam and democracy compatible? Can Muslims in Europe and America be loyal citizens? These questions continued as America pursued its war against global terrorism, eventually toppling Saddam Hussein via a multinational military coalition. Terrorists countered with attacks from Spain and Morocco to Saudi Arabia and Indonesia.

Osama bin Laden and al-Qaeda symbolized a global jihad, a network of extremist groups threatening both Muslim countries and the West, whose roots proved deeper and more pervasive internationally than most had anticipated. This new global threat, which had emerged from the jihad against the Soviet Union's occupation of Afghanistan, exploded across the Muslim world, from Central, South, and Southeast Asia to Europe and America. It also highlighted a struggle for the soul of Islam between mainstream Muslims and religious extremists.

THE GLOBALIZATION
AND HIJACKING OF JIHAD

The war in Afghanistan, the subsequent emergence of al-Qaeda and role of global communications and travel, the meaning and use of jihad became more complex and widespread. On the one hand, jihad's primary Quranic

Osama bin Laden (1957–2011), leader of al-Qaeda.

religious and spiritual meanings, the "struggle" or effort to follow God's path, to lead a good life, and build a just society, became more widely applied to contemporary social and political problems. Jihad was used to characterize the spiritual struggle to lead a moral personal life as well as to create a more just society by engaging, for example, in educational, community, and social service projects. On the other hand, in response to authoritarian regimes and political conflicts, jihad became a clarion call used by resistance, liberation, and terrorist movements alike to legitimate their causes, mobilize support, and motivate their followers.

Militant groups like the Afghan mujahidin, the Taliban, and the Northern Alliance each waged a "jihad" in Afghanistan against foreign powers and among themselves; Muslim movements in Kashmir, Chechnya, Dagestan, the southern Philippines, Bosnia, and Kosovo have fashioned their struggles as jihads; Hizbollah, Hamas, and Islamic Jihad in Palestine characterized war with Israel as a jihad; Algeria's Armed Islamic Group engaged in a jihad of terror against the government and their fellow citizens; Osama bin Laden and al-Qaeda waged a global jihad against Muslim governments and the West.

The politicization of Islam in Muslim societies enabled militant extremists to use religion to legitimate the use of violence, warfare, and terrorism. However different, militant groups shared a common worldview, a theology of hatred that sees the world in mutually exclusive, black-and-white categories: the world of belief and unbelief, the land of Islam and of warfare, the forces of good against the forces of evil. Whether Muslim or non-Muslim, those who are not with them are enemies to be fought and destroyed in a war with no limits and no proportionality. Extremists legitimated their acts of violence and terror by appealing to and reinterpreting the Islamic doctrine of jihad, creating a jihadi culture taught in mosques, schools, and seminaries.

Most militants and movements have been directly or indirectly influenced by the most prominent and influential ideologue of modern Muslim extremism, the late Egyptian, Sayyid Qutb. In the late twentieth century, Osama bin Laden and al-Qaeda became the most visible symbol of the new global jihad. Bin Laden's upbringing and exposure to Wahhabi Islam in Saudi Arabia, coupled with the strong influence of Qutb's vision of a new Islamic order and global jihad, transformed this somewhat shy, serious, devout, polite young man into a godfather of worldwide terrorism.

SAYYID QUTB: MARTYR
OF ISLAMIC RADICALISM

Sayyid Qutb's (1906–66) journey took him from educated intellectual to militant ideologue and activist who inspired many militants, from the assassins of Anwar Sadat to the followers of Osama bin Laden and al-Qaeda. Qutb received a modern education and, after graduation from university, worked as an official in Egypt's Ministry of Public Instruction in Cairo. He was also a poet and literary critic and became a great admirer of Western literature.

Qutb's visit to America in the late 1940s proved a turning point in his life. His observations and experiences produced a culture shock that made him both more religious and highly critical of the West's moral decadence, from its materialism and sexual permissiveness to its use and abuse of alcohol to its racism. In addition, Qutb's stay in America coincided with the creation of the modern state of Israel. He felt betrayed by what he considered America's anti-Arab bias in government and the media. Returning to Egypt, Qutb joined the Muslim Brotherhood. He quickly emerged as a major voice in the organization and its most influential ideologue amid a growing confrontation with Nasser's regime.

Imprisoned and tortured for alleged involvement in a failed attempt to assassinate Nasser, Qutb became increasingly radicalized, convinced that the Egyptian government and its security forces was repressive and un-Islamic and had to be overthrown. Qutb's revolutionary vision is set forth in his most influential tract, *Milestones*, in which he sharply divided Muslim societies into two diametrically opposed camps, the forces of good and of evil, those committed to the rule of God and those opposed, the party of God and the party of Satan. Qutb saw no middle ground. He emphasized the need to develop a special group of true Muslims, a righteous vanguard, within a corrupt and faithless society. Given the authoritarian and repressive nature of the Egyptian and many other Muslim governments, Qutb concluded that change from within the system was impossible. Because the creation of an Islamic government was a divine commandment, he believed that it was a divinely mandated imperative that Muslims strive to implement or impose it immediately. Islam was on the brink of disaster; jihad as armed struggle, he urged, was the only way to implement a new Islamic order.

Qutb came to regard the West as the historic enemy of Islam and Muslims, demonstrated by the Crusades, European colonialism, and the Cold War. He saw this Western threat as political, economic, and religio-cultural. Equally insidious, he believed, were the elites of the Muslim world, who ruled and governed according to Western secular principles and values that threatened the faith, identity, and values of their own Islamic societies. Qutb denounced governments and Western secular-oriented elites as atheists against whom all true believers must wage holy war. Sayyid Qutb's radicalized worldview became a source for militant extremists from the founders of Egypt's Islamic Jihad group to Osama bin Laden and other terrorists who call for a global jihad.

As we have seen, the Wahhabi movement takes its name from Muhammad ibn Abd al-Wahhab, an eighteenth-century scholar, and his revivalist movement. Wahhabi Islam over the years has been subject to multiple interpretations, including the ultraconservative exclusivist theology of the religious establishment and militant theologies of hate and violence. Many Wahhabi preachers and followers tend to be literalist, rigid, puritanical, and religiously intolerant, believing that they are right and all others (people of other faiths as well as Muslims who do not follow their version of Islam, which they believe is the pristine, pure, unadulterated message of the Prophet) are wrong. Saudi Arabian Wahhabis have sought to propagate and impose beliefs and interpretations throughout the Muslim world as well as Europe and America.

In the last half of the twentieth century, Islamic activists from other countries, mainstream and extremist, often fleeing their home governments, found refuge in Saudi Arabia. They found jobs teaching in universities and religious schools as well as working in government ministries and organizations. After Sayyid Qutb's execution in 1966 and the suppression of the Brotherhood, Muslim Brothers including Muhammad Qutb, Sayyid Qutb's brother, fled to Saudi Arabia, where he taught at King Abdulaziz University in Jeddah, where Osama bin Laden majored in civil engineering. Among bin Laden's teachers was Dr. Abdullah Azzam, a Jordanian member of the Palestinian Muslim Brotherhood, who would later become prominent in Afghanistan. Azzam was an advocate of a militant global jihad ideology and culture, sometimes popularly called the "Godfather of Global Jihad," seeing it as a duty incumbent on all Muslims: "This duty will not end with victory in Afghanistan; jihad will remain an individual obligation until all other lands that were Muslim are returned to us so that Islam will reign again; before us lie Palestine, Bokhara, Lebanon, Chad, Eritrea, Somalia, the Philippines, Burma, Southern Yemen, Tashkent and Andalusia [southern Spain]."[15]

Bin Laden was also a keen student of Islamic studies. As a result, he was exposed to the more militant theological interpretations of Islam present among Saudi and foreign Muslim professors and fostered by Saudi support for the militant Islamic groups and **madrasas** (seminaries) in Afghanistan and Pakistan.

Internationally, Saudis, both government-sponsored organizations and wealthy individuals, funded the export of Wahhabi Islam, in its mainstream and extremist forms, to other countries and communities in the Muslim world and the West. They offered development aid; built mosques, libraries, and other institutions; funded the publication and distribution of religious tracts; and commissioned imams and religious scholars to preach and teach abroad. Wealthy businessmen as well as private and government organizations (knowingly or unknowingly) in Saudi Arabia and the Gulf region provided financial support to extremist groups who spread a militant brand of Islam with its "jihadi" culture. As with forms of religious fundamentalism in all faiths, there often seemed to be a fine line between those who propagated an ultraconservative, exclusivist theology and militant religious extremists, such as Osama bin Laden and al-Qaeda, who then turned to violence and terror to implement their vision of God's will.

THE MAKING OF A TERRORIST
AND HIS GLOBAL JIHAD

Osama bin Laden had fought against the Soviets in Afghanistan, a struggle that allied him with a cause supported by the United States, Saudi Arabia, Pakistan, and many other nations. However, after the war bin Laden became alienated from the House of Saud and radicalized by the prospect that an American-led coalition coming to oust Saddam Hussein from his occupation of Kuwait in the Gulf War of 1991 would lead to the increased presence and influence of America in Saudi Arabia and the Gulf.[16]

Bin Laden was regarded as an inspiration to and major funder of terrorist groups suspected in the bombing of the World Trade Center in February 1993, the slaughter of eighteen American soldiers in Somalia in October of the same year, bombings in the Saudi cities of Riyadh in November 1995 and in Dhahran in June 1996, the killing of fifty-eight tourists at Luxor, Egypt, in November 1997, and threatened attacks against Americans who remained on Saudi soil and promised retaliation internationally for cruise missile attacks.[17]

In February 1998 bin Laden and other militant leaders announced the creation of a transnational coalition of extremist groups, the Islamic Front for Jihad against Jews and Crusaders. Al-Qaeda was linked to a series of acts of terrorism: the truck bombings of American embassies in Kenya and Tanzania on August 7, 1998, that killed 263 people and injured more than five thousand, followed on October 12, 2000, by a suicide bombing attack against the USS *Cole* that killed seventeen American sailors.

Afghanistan and Pakistan became primary centers for the globalization of jihad and the culture of jihad through networks of madrasas and training camps. The Taliban and al-Qaeda provided refuge and training for militants, many of whom had had to flee their home countries, from Egypt, Algeria, Yemen, Saudi Arabia, Malaysia, Thailand, the Philippines, Uzbekistan, Tajikistan, Kyrgyzstan, Chechnya, and Xinjiang province in China. A hitherto little noted part of the world spawned a Taliban–al-Qaeda alliance that became the base for a network of organizations and cells from across the Muslim world that hijacked Islam, indiscriminately slaughtering non-Muslims and Muslims alike.

The attacks of 9/11 and subsequent acts of terrorism in Muslim countries and in Europe brought into sharp relief the magnitude of global terrorism. Jihad has been waged not only against unjust rulers and governments but also against a broad spectrum of civilian populations in the Muslim world, who have been its primary victims, as well as civilian populations in the West.

Osama bin Laden, like the secular Saddam Hussein and the cleric Ayatollah Khomeini before him, cleverly identified and exploited specific grievances against Muslim regimes and against America that are shared across a broad spectrum of Muslims, most of whom are not extremists. He then interpreted or used religious texts and doctrines to justify his jihad of violence and terrorism. Anti-Americanism is driven not only by terrorists' blind hatred but also by a broader-based anger and frustration with American foreign policy among many in Arab and Muslim societies. Many admired Western principles and values (political participation, accountability, basic freedoms of speech, thought, the press) but believed that these principles are applied selectively or not at all when it comes to the Muslim world.

To understand the love–hate relationship, the attraction and repulsion toward America that exists in many parts of the world and is widespread in the Muslim world, we must not only know who we think we are but try to understand how others might see us. As Paul Kennedy has observed, few of us ask:

> [H]ow do we appear to them, and what would it be like were our places in the world reversed.... Suppose that there existed today a powerful, unified Arab-Muslim state that stretched from Algeria to Turkey and Arabia—as there was 400 years ago, the Ottoman Empire. Suppose this unified Arab-Muslim state had the biggest economy in the world, and the most effective military. Suppose by contrast this United States of ours had split into 12 or 15 countries, with different regimes, some conservative and corrupt. Suppose that the great Arab-Muslim power had its aircraft carriers cruising off our shores, its aircraft flying over our lands, its satellites watching us every day. Suppose that its multi-national corporations had reached into North America to extract oil, and paid the corrupt, conservative governments big royalties for that. Suppose that it dominated all international institutions like the Security Council and the IMF. Suppose that there was a special state set up in North America fifty years ago, of a different religion and language to ours, and the giant Arab-Muslim power always gave it support. Suppose the Colossus state was bombarding us with cultural messages, about the status of women, about sexuality, that we found offensive. Suppose it was always urging us to change, to modernize, to go global, to follow its example. Hmm   in those conditions, would not many Americans steadily grow to loathe that Colossus, wish it harm? And perhaps try to harm it? I think so.[18]

The Gallup World Poll, which surveyed Muslims in some thirty-five countries from North Africa to Southeast Asia, representing the voices of a billion Muslims, found that of the 7 percent who reported they believed the actions of 9/11 were justified, not a single respondent who condoned the attacks cited the Quran for justification. Instead, this group's responses were markedly secular and worldly—speaking in terms of revenge and revolution, not religion.

Political grievances, in particular the threat of political domination and occupation, emerge as the primary catalyst or driver of extremism and of suicide bombing, often seen as inseparable from the threat to Muslim religious and cultural identity.

TERRORISTS AND SUICIDE BOMBING

While the atrocities and acts of terrorism committed by violent extremists are often enshrouded in religious rhetoric, Osama bin Laden and others went beyond classical Islam's criteria for a just war. They recognized no limits but their own, employing any weapons or means. Like those who would justify preemptive strikes and torture, they often argued that today's circumstances are so dangerous and unjust that extraordinary measures are justified. Thus, they rejected Islamic law's regulations regarding the goals and means of a valid jihad (that violence must be proportional and that only the necessary amount of force should be used to repel the enemy), that noncombatants should not be targeted, and that jihad must be declared by a legitimate religious or political authority. Their targets included civilians, women and children, Jews, Christians, people of all faiths, and other Muslims who do not agree with them.

At the same time, prominent Islamic scholars and religious leaders across the Muslim world have denounced this hijacking of Islam by terrorists. The Islamic Research Council at al-Azhar University, one of the oldest universities in the world and a leading center of Islamic learning, issued strong, authoritative declarations against bin Laden's initiatives:

> Islam provides clear rules and ethical norms that forbid the killing of non-combatants, as well as women, children, and the elderly, and also forbids the pursuit of the enemy in defeat, the execution of those who surrender, the infliction of harm on prisoners of war, and the destruction of property that is not being used in the hostilities.[19]

A critical and contentious issue is the distinction between legitimate and illegitimate forms of violence as well as the difference between resistance and liberation versus terrorist movements. Although most people would agree in condemning the illegitimate use of force and acts of terrorism, they do not always agree on who is right and who is wrong. The differing perspectives of America's Founding Fathers and the British monarchy or more recently between Israeli Jews and Palestinian Muslims and Christians underscore the problems when speaking of a defensive versus offensive war and who is a freedom fighter and who is a terrorist.

September 11 and its aftermath were a wake-up call for many Muslims. Although some were in a state of denial, many others recognize the global threat of religious extremism and understand the need to delegitimate and marginalize extremists. However, they differ in their definitions of legitimate versus illegitimate acts of violence and what constitutes terrorism.

Many Muslim leaders denounced the September 11 attacks and other acts of terrorism and drew a sharp line between "true" Islam and extremist Islam. Timothy Winter, a Cambridge University professor and prominent Muslim religious leader, strongly condemned extremists like al-Qaeda as religiously illegitimate and inauthentic. He decries extremists' failure to adhere to the classical canons of Islamic law and theology and denounced their fatwas as "neither formally nor in their habit of mind deducible from medieval exegesis."[20] He unequivocally rejected all acts of terrorism and condemned suicide bombing as an act of suicide and the killing of noncombatants as always forbidden, noting that some Islamic sources regard it as worse than murder. Winter dismissed bin Laden and others like him as unqualified, un-Islamic vigilantes who violate basic Islamic teachings:

> [T]heir proclamations ignore 14 centuries of Muslim scholarship [they use] lists of anti-American grievances and of Koranic quotations referring to early Muslim wars against Arab idolaters .... All this amounts to an odd and extreme violation of the normal methods of Islamic scholarship .... An insurrectionist who kills non-combatants is guilty of baghy, "armed transgression," a capital offence in Islamic law. A jihad can be proclaimed only by a properly constituted state; anything else is pure vigilantism.[21]

Yusuf Qaradawi, a prominent and controversial scholar and religious leader with an international following and one of the first leading Muslim scholars to condemn the 9/11 terrorist attacks, emphasized that Muslims are not allowed to kill anyone except those fighting Muslims directly and that it is immoral to kill innocent civilians for their government's actions. So far so good, but Qaradawi went further, and according to critics, he and others crossed the line when, unlike Winter and like-minded Islamic religious authorities, they supported the Palestinian struggle as a legitimate jihad and equate suicide bombing with martyrdom, relinquishing one's life for the faith.

Suicide Bombing and the War of the Fatwas
The use of suicide bombing in attacks has become a contentious "weapon" in the waging of jihad, used in the September 11 attacks against the World Trade Center and the Pentagon, in Afghanistan, Pakistan, Lebanon, India

and postwar Iraq, and by ISIS subsequently in many extremist attacks globally.

Traditionally, suicide was unconditionally forbidden in Islam, because only God has the right to take the life he has granted. Only one verse in the Quran may be relevant to suicide: "O you who believe! Do not consume your wealth in the wrong way—rather only through trade mutually agreed to, and do not kill yourselves. Surely God is Merciful toward you" (4:29). The subject of suicide is therefore little discussed in exegetical literature. The Prophetic traditions (*hadith*), however, frequently, clearly, and absolutely prohibit suicide.

Historically, both Sunni and Shii Muslims have generally forbidden "religious suicide" and acts of terrorism. The Nizari Ismailis, popularly called the assassins, who in the eleventh and twelfth centuries were notorious for sending suicidal assassins against their enemies, were rejected by mainstream Islam as fanatics.

Attack on the World Trade Center, September 11, 2001.

Suicide Bombing in Israel and Palestine

The use of suicide bombing in Palestine dates back to the mid-1990s. On February 25, 1994, Dr. Baruch Goldstein, a Jewish settler who had immigrated to Israel from the United States, opened fire, killing twenty-nine Muslim worshippers during their Friday congregational prayer in the Mosque of the Patriarch in Hebron. In response, Hamas (Islamic Resistance Movement) promised swift revenge for the Hebron massacre; its militia, the Qassem Brigade, undertook suicide bombing operations within Israel itself, in Galilee, in Jerusalem, and in Tel Aviv. The question of whether suicide bombing is legitimate or illegitimate crystallized during the second Palestinian intifada (uprising) that began in September 2000. Increased Israeli military violence and targeted assassinations and the lack of comparable weapons to fight and defend themselves (in their eyes) reinforced the belief among many Palestinians that suicide bombers were not committing an act of suicide but one of self-sacrifice, their only option for resisting and retaliating against an enemy with overwhelming military power and foreign support. As student posters at universities in the West Bank and Gaza declared: "Israel has nuclear bombs, we have human bombs."

Suicide bombings in Palestine have been the subject of much debate in the Muslim world, the subject of both support and condemnation on religious grounds. Prominent religious leaders have differed greatly in their legal opinions (*fatwas*). The late Sheikh Ahmad Yasin, religious leader and founder of Hamas, and Akram Sabri, the mufti of Jerusalem, as well as many other Arab and Palestinian religious leaders, argued that suicide bombing is necessary and justified.

Yusuf al-Qardawi, among the most influential religious authorities in the world, despite his condemnation of the 9/11 attacks and the targeting of noncombatants, has given fatwas as early as the mid-1990s that recognize suicide bombing in Israel and Palestine as an act of self-defense, the giving of one's life for God with the hope of Paradise. Qardawi legitimated the killing of Israeli civilians, arguing that Israel is a military society in which both men and women serve in the military and reserves and that if an elderly person or a child is killed in such acts, it is an involuntary killing.

However, other senior religious authorities have condemned suicide bombings, in particular those that target civilians, as terrorism. Sheikh Abdulaziz bin Abdallah al-Sheikh, Grand Mufti of Saudi Arabia, like Timothy Winter, condemned all suicide bombings without exception as un-Islamic, as acts of suicide as well as attacks against civilians as forbidden by Islam.

The acts of shedding the blood of innocent people, the bombing of buildings and ships, and the destruction of public and private installations are criminal acts and against Islam. Those who carry out such acts have deviant beliefs and misguided ideologies and are to be held responsible for their crimes…. Islamic Law clearly prohibits leveling such charges against non-Muslims, warns against following those who carry such deviant beliefs, and stresses that it is the duty of all Muslims over the world to consult truthfully, share advice, and cooperate in piety and righteousness.[22]

In contrast, Sheikh Muhammad Sayyid Tantawi, former Grand Mufti of Egypt and Grand Sheikh of al-Azhar University and thus among the highest religious authorities globally, drew a sharp distinction between suicide bombings that constitute self-sacrifice and acts of self-defense versus killing noncombatants:

Attacking innocent people is not courageous; it is stupid and will be punished on the Day of Judgment…. It is not courageous to attack innocent children, women and civilians. It is courageous to protect freedom; it is courageous to defend oneself and not to attack.[23]

A War against Global Terrorism or against Islam?
In the aftermath of the September 11 attacks, President George W. Bush emphasized that America was waging a war against global terrorism, not against Islam, which he said was a religion of peace. However, America's pursuit internationally and domestically of its broad-based war, the rhetoric and policies of the administration that accompanied its actions, and the mass arrests and detention of Muslims and erosion of civil liberties of American Muslims raised many questions and concerns.

The trajectory of American and British foreign policy and military action: the broadening of the American-led military campaign's scope beyond the invasion and occupation of Afghanistan to second frontiers, the identification of an "axis of evil" (comprised of a majority of countries that were Muslim), the invasion and occupation of Iraq, and the Bush administration's failed leadership in the Palestinian-Israeli conflict and the Hezbollah-Lebanon war fed anti-American sentiment among the mainstream population as well as the hatred of America among militant extremists. America was seen not only as a global but also a neo-colonial, imperial country, whose overwhelming military and political power were at times used unilaterally, disproportionately and indiscriminately.

The grievances of mainstream and potential extremists vary from one Muslim country to another, but a prominent concern involves America's longtime support for authoritarian Muslim regimes over the years from Hosni Mubarak's Egypt and Zeine Abedin Ben Ali's Tunisia to Saddam Hussein's Iraq (1980–88) and Pervez Musharraf's Pakistan. Critics charged that America had a double standard in promoting its fundamental principles and values (democracy, political participation, human rights, and basic freedoms of speech, assembly, and the press) selectively or not at all when it comes to the Muslim world. Majorities in virtually every predominantly Muslim nation surveyed in a Gallup World Poll report in 2005–06 doubted that the United States was serious about establishing democratic systems in the region.

Accordingly, majorities of Muslims, like many others in the world, regarded the invasion of Iraq as a war of occupation. Claims of a commitment to democratization were dismissed as a "guided democracy" under American trusteeship. Outside of Iraq, 90 percent of Muslims agreed that the American initiative had done more harm than good.

The war in Iraq, waged without the support of a broad-based coalition, did not remove a major regional or global threat that possessed weapons of mass destruction, nuclear weapons, or a major supporter of Osama bin Laden and al-Qaeda. The occupation reduced substantially Iraqi quality of life (employment, electricity, water) and safety and security; it pushed Iraq to the brink of civil war, inflamed sectarianism, and ironically had the unintended consequence of transforming Iraq into a training ground for terrorists. It created political and economic conditions that fed radicalization and terrorism, threatened the stability of regional powers like Turkey, Jordan, Syria, Saudi Arabia, Kuwait, and other Gulf States, and enhanced Iran's stature as a major political player in the Middle East.

Abuses in Iraq, Abu Ghraib and Haditha, as well as Guantanamo Bay, and the rendition of prisoners and transfer of suspected terrorists overseas to "CIA prisons" in countries that employ harsh interrogation techniques and torture all undermined the U.S. record on human rights and outraged not only Muslims but many others across the world. This war, condemned by the heads of many mainstream religious faiths, including President Bush's own United Methodist denomination, as an unjust war, but supported by the political power of neoconservatives and the militant Christian Right, led to the circumvention of international law and accountability before international tribunals for preemptive strikes, water boarding and other forms of torture, disproportionate use of force, and controversial drone attacks.

ARAB SPRING/ARAB WINTER?

If the 9/11 attacks stunned the world, threatened global security, and generated warnings of a clash of civilizations, a decade later 2011 stunned Arab dictators and American and European policymakers and experts. The Arab Uprisings or Arab Spring, with its toppling of entrenched authoritarian regimes, signaled a major transformation in the Arab world.

The "Arab Spring" or "Arab Awakening," as it has been called, marked a historic transition in the political makeup of countries like Tunisia, Egypt, Libya, Syria, Yemen, and Bahrain. A broad sector of society, eager for change and democratic reforms, made their voices heard, reclaiming their dignity and national pride and insisting that they would decide the direction and the future of their countries.

From Spring to Winter

Three years after pro-democracy revolutions swept Tunisia, Egypt, Libya, Syria, and Yemen, all except Tunisia reversed to an Arab Winter. In Syria, the uprising led to deep rivalries within the country caused by a number of factors: Sunni vs. Shia (Alawi) supporters of Assad and Christians feared their fate if they lost the protection of the Assad government; Syrian nationalists' main militias were unable to forge a united front and were weakened by the failure of the international community to provide weapons and other forms of significant assistance; another factor was the influx of foreign Sunni jihadist militias. The al-Nusra Front, or Jabhat al-Nusra, is a branch of al-Qaeda operating in Syria and Lebanon, whose goal is to overthrow the Assad regime and replace it with a Sunni Islamic state. The second major group, the Islamic State of Iraq and Syria (ISIS), also known by its Arabic acronym Daish and subsequently renamed the Islamic State (IS), is based in Iraq and Syria, where it controls a significant swath of territory. As the civil war dragged on, the death toll in the fight to oust the Bashir Al-Assad rose to more than 250,000 with more than 4.million refugees in Turkey, Jordan, and North Africa.

Libya too, within three years after the overthrow and killing of Muammar Qaddafi, was in a state of civil war with rival militias (tribal, nationalist, and Islamist) battling for control of different parts of the country. In contrast to Egypt and Tunisia, Islamists in Libya suffered a stunning defeat in parliamentary elections. Libyan Dawn, from the Misrata district, allied with other Islamist militias and broke with the newly elected parliament, charging that the supporters of Qaddafi controlled the parliament and engaged in an all-out war with the nationalist tribal militias. The

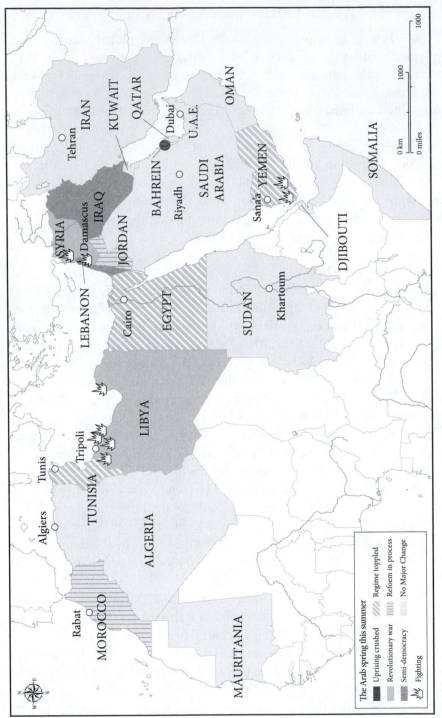

The Arab spring this summer

- Uprising crushed
- Revolutionary war
- Semi-democracy
- Fighting
- Regime toppled
- Reform in process
- No Major Change

Arab Spring.

newly elected parliament fled to Tobruk in the east of the country while militant Islamists (Libyan Dawn) captured the capital, Tripoli, and most of Benghazi, the country's second city, and Derna, the next town up the coast, was declared an Islamic caliphate. Libya now had two governments, one Islamist in Tripoli and one in Tobruk.

Egypt and Tunisia

In contrast to the chaos and civil war in Syria and Libya, Egypt and Tunisia's democratically elected leadership proceeded on the path to democratization but had distinctively different experiences and results. Egypt's democratic experiment hit a dead end with the toppling of the Morsi government in a coup and restoration of military backed authoritarianism. Only Tunisia produced a functioning parliamentary system.

Egypt

Initially the Islamist parties—Egypt's Muslim Brotherhood and Tunisia's Ennahda (Renaissance) Party—were not among the leadership in their countries' uprisings. However, in subsequent presidential and parliamentary elections, in Egypt the Muslim Brotherhood's Freedom and Justice Party and in Tunisia the Ennahda swept into power. While many voted for Islamists, others were dismayed and feared an increased role of religion in politics.

Though the electoral process in Egypt and Tunisia was heated and at times polarizing, elections themselves were the product of a free and fair process. This process was to be a first step on a path toward a future that would hopefully consist of more free and fair elections, a vibrant civil society, and the evolution of democracy in a region where it had long been absent.

The new governments in Egypt and Tunisia faced formidable challenges: the need to satisfy the expectations of diverse sectors of society and in particular to jump-start failed economies and reverse high unemployment. At the same time, they were undermined by entrenched remnants of the Mubarak and Ben Ali regimes often referred to as "the deep state."

While the Muslim Brotherhood did not officially endorse the popular Tahrir uprising that toppled Mubarak in February 2011, many individual members, especially youth, did participate. After a bitter presidential contest, in June 2012, the Brotherhood's political party, the Freedom and Justice Party (FJP), and its candidate, Mohammed Morsi, won in Egypt's first free and fair democratic election after six decades of authoritarian rule. Mohammed Morsi became Egypt's first civilian president in June 2012. However, although he officially resigned from the Muslim

Brotherhood, he and his government would continue to be perceived as a Muslim Brotherhood government.

President Morsi faced formidable circumstances. The military, police, security, judiciary and bureaucracy, all Mubarak government appointees, remained in their positions. The military, which had in particular always been influential in politics and society, also controlled between 33 and 45 percent of the Egyptian economy. The Supreme Council of the Armed Forces (SCAF), a group of senior Egyptian military officers who took over power to govern Egypt after President Hosni Mubarak's departure, had ruled from February 2011 until June 2012, the start of President Mohamed Morsi's term of office. Its close relationship with the courts was evident. The Supreme Constitutional Court consistently issued invasive decisions such as dissolving the Brotherhood's FJP and the Brotherhood and Salafi–dominated parliament as well as the Constitutional Assembly.

The Morsi government also made mistakes and mishandled multiple opportunities: they failed to build a more representative coalition government with liberals, Christians (especially Coptic Christians), secularists, and leftists, and they completely excluded Arab youth leaders and groups who were the backbone of the revolution. In reacting to the SCAF and in particular the Constitutional Court's interventions, Morsi unilaterally implemented policies that alienated sectors of society who charged that his Muslim Brotherhood–dominated government was intent upon imposing an Islamic state. Most polarizing was Morsi's decision to issue constitutional decrees granting himself the power to act without judicial oversight or review, claiming that he would protect the nation from the Mubarak-era power structure. He dismissed the Mubarak appointed prosecutor-general, protected the Islamist-dominated parliament and the constituent assembly from dissolution by the Constitutional Court, and immunized his presidential decisions from judicial review. In response to opponents' charges of an "Islamist coup," he maintained that these actions would protect the work of the Constituent Assembly, allowing them to draft the new constitution without judicial interference, and that these actions would only last until the draft constitution was completed and ratified by a national referendum.

After one year in power, Morsi faced demonstrations by millions across Egypt demanding reforms and early elections. Sectors of the deep state (military, judiciary, security forces), with assistance from the media, used this growing dissent to move from demands for major reforms to a call for Morsi either to resign or to be driven from office. The result was a military-led coup under General Sisi, Morsi's minister of defense. The democratic process was bypassed to topple the first democratically elected government in Egypt's history and usher in a return to authoritarianism in the guise of a restoration of a secular, democratic secure future.

Three weeks after the removal of President Mohamed Morsi and the Muslim Brotherhood from power, the interim government appointed nineteen generals as the governors of Egypt's provinces. It systematically shut down independent television stations, blocked satellite channels, imprisoned Egyptian, Arab, and Western journalists, and initiated a policy to suppress and eradicate the Brotherhood.

Backtracking and reversing his promise of a neutral and inclusive political process for Egyptians, General al-Sisi now moved to outlaw, suppress, and eradicate the Muslim Brotherhood as a terrorist organization. He called upon Egyptians to take to the streets to support the army's use of force in its "war against terrorism" and suppression of the Muslim Brotherhood. The charges and actions flew in the face of the decades-long track record of the Brotherhood.

For more than forty years, despite provocation, arrest, detention, rigged elections, and state-sponsored violence, the Brotherhood had not engaged in political or religious violence. Militant Egyptian Islamist organizations, as well as Ayman Al-Zawahiri, the current Egyptian leader of al-Qaeda, have long opposed the Brotherhood because of its gradualism and willingness to compromise even during the Morsi presidency.

The post-coup military-backed government with support from the courts initiated a massive wave of arrests and imprisonment of Morsi and Muslim Brotherhood leaders and supporters. On August 14, 2013, faced with large nonviolent sit-ins by the Muslim Brotherhood at Rabaa al-Adawiya and al-Nahda Squares in Cairo, Egyptian security forces used lethal force and snipers to clear and expel Muslim Brothers and other Morsi supporters, the vast majority of whom were unarmed civilians, including women and children. Human Rights Watch (HRW) and other experts described the raids as the most serious incident of mass unlawful killings in modern Egyptian history. According to the post-coup interim government's statistics, 638 people were killed—595 civilians and 43 police officers—and some 3,994 injured at Rabaa Square. However, other more independent estimates ranged from 2,600 or more dead and more than 4,500 injured in what came to be called the Massacre at Rabaa Square.

The Rabaa killings sparked serious sectarian violence and attacks on Christian churches and Christians by militant extremists, many reportedly incensed by the Coptic Pope Tawadros II's public backing of the military-led coup and his support for the security forces' crackdown and massacre at Rabaa. While the Brotherhood leadership publically counseled against violence, some outraged followers as well as non-Muslim

Brotherhood Islamic militant groups and thugs destroyed at least thirty-two churches and attacked and robbed Christian-owned shops, businesses, and schools, leading a senior official for HRW to comment, "Security forces did little or nothing to protect churches, despite the high likelihood of such attacks.... Egyptian security officials bear responsibility not only for what they did in breaking up the protests but for their failure to protect churches and Christian communities against predictable reprisal attacks."

Government repression increasingly extended beyond the Brotherhood. In February 2014, HRW reported, Egyptian authorities "demonstrated almost zero tolerance for any form of dissent, arresting and prosecuting journalists, demonstrators, and academics for peacefully expressing their views. Prosecutors on January 29, 2014, referred three Al Jazeera English journalists to trial on politicized charges such as disseminating "false information" and belonging to a "terrorist organization," some of which carry prison sentences ranging from five to 15 years. At least 17 other journalists and opposition figures face similar charges in the same case, with the trial scheduled to begin on February 20. On January 19, prosecutors referred 25 people to trial on charges of "insulting the judiciary," including Amr Hamzawy, an academic and former member of parliament."[24]

Amnesty International in "Roadmap to repression: No end in sight to human rights violations" (January 23, 2014), reported, "On the eve of the third anniversary of the '25 January Revolution.' the human rights outlook in Egypt remains grim.... The Egyptian authorities are using every resource at their disposal to quash dissent and trample on human rights.... Across the board the Egyptian authorities have tightened the noose on freedom of expression and assembly.... Security forces have been given free rein to act above the law and with no prospect of being held to account...."[25]

In March and April Egyptian courts set a new record in judicial history. In March 2014, an Egyptian court condemned 529 alleged supporters of Morsi to death on charges of killing a single police officer. In April 2014, 683 people were sentenced to death in the biggest capital punishment sentence in modern Egyptian history and without hearing the defense arguments.

New presidential elections were held with only one candidate, al-Sisi, in May 2014. After an initial very low voter turnout, government officials extended voting to a third day and threatened nonvoters with a large fine. Cairo's main shopping mall, City Stars, and other stores closed early on Tuesday to encourage shoppers to vote, and well-known pro-Sisi TV hosts begged their viewers to vote. Some 46 percent of Egypt's 53 million eligible voters participated, substantially lower than the 80 percent turnout Sisi had called for in the days before the election. Abdel Fatah al-Sisi won more than 90 percent of the vote in the presidential elections.

On November 29, 2014, Egypt's Criminal Court, despite their convictions and imprisonment for several years, acquitted Mubarak and his minister of interior of all murder and corruption charges. A judge also acquitted Mubarak's sons of all corruption charges. Mubarak was sentenced in June 2012 to life imprisonment over the killing of protesters during Egypt's 2011 uprising. In May 2014 he was sentenced to three years in prison for embezzlement and ordered to pay back $17.6 million.

Tunisia

In contrast to Egypt, Tunisia, on the whole, made significant strides toward democratization. Despite strong disagreements, some violence, and politically and religiously motivated roadblocks, Tunisia's political elites demonstrated a commitment to national unity and the institutional formation of a robust democracy, characterized by an inclusive constitution, a progressive electoral law, and an institutional setting that prioritized dialogue and compromise over exclusion and partisanship. This process was aided by a favorable context. In the wake of the uprisings, Tunisia's brutal security apparatus collapsed and its small yet professionalized military, which historically had no interest in politics, remained silent in the wings. In civilian politics, Islamists and secular factions were evenly matched; the Isamist party, Ennahda (Renaissance), won a plurality in Tunisia's first free democratic elections and had reached out to include secular opposition parties in the government.

The lack of compromise among Egyptian political elites had led to an exclusive system in which the winners exercised unchecked authority over the very foundations of their country's political and economic institutions. In contrast, the Tunisian case, while not entirely unflawed, can illustrate how inclusive transitional processes can lead to the development of balanced and accountable institutions.

Key features account for the difference between the Tunisian and Egyptian cases, both tied to the will of the political elite. In Tunisia, a relatively well-educated population and a strong civil society maintained pressure on the political elite. Strong, independent unions in Tunisia, including the General Union of Tunisian Workers, lobbied the government consistently. Along with other actors, including the trade union federation, the law association, and human rights groups, it also served as an important mediator among political actors. In Egypt, civil society and unions were neither as powerful nor as independent.

Egypt, with its much larger, diverse, failed economy and less educated population, more restricted civil society, and politicized military and court system enabled political actors to treat the postrevolutionary period as a winner-takes-all rivalry rather than a process of negotiation and compromise. Once in power, in contrast to Ennahda's more inclusive political process, the Morsi government installed many Islamists (Muslim Brotherhood and Salafis) in key power positions, often to the exclusion or minimal representation of the April 6 movement, secularists and Copts. In a similar vein, the military, after the 2013 coup, dominated political development and sought to completely eradicate the Brotherhood and leftist opposition and shaped foundational documents and institutions to its favor. The El-Sisi government used overwhelming and lethal force, killing and wounding thousands of civilians, as well as military courts and mass death sentences, arresting and detaining 22,000 (some human rights organizations put this figure at reportedly 40,000).

In contrast, Tunisia's Ennahda party, taking a lesson from Algeria's decades-long civil war, avoided polarizing stances. It demonstrated its emphasis on national unity and inclusion by promising before elections that, if victorious, it would appoint a non-Ennahda citizen as president and reach out to opposition parties to create a coalition government. It backed away from pushing for the integration of Islamic law in the constitution and, after two years in power and engaging with opposition in dialogue, opted to step down in favor of technocratic leadership to preserve national unity. The military stayed out of direct involvement in politics, enabling political actors to negotiate a new system.

The year 2014 proved a turning point for Ennahda's political fortunes. In parliamentary elections on October 26, 2014, Nidaa Tounes won eighty-five seats in the 217-member assembly, ahead of sixty-nine secured by Ennahda. Nidaa Tounes, a self-styled liberal secular democratic coalition party, like its leader, Beji Caid Essebsi, was composed in large part of Tunisia's traditional, political elite who portrayed themselves as a liberal democratic alternative to Ennahda. Ennahda's loss of political power was finalized with the victory of Nidaa Tounes's Essebsi in the presidential elections on December 21, 2014. Ironically, Ghannouchi overriding his party's wishes and not allowing a law to be passed in May 2014 forbidding former members of Ben Ali's government and the RCD (Democratic Constitutional Rally) from running made possible the Nidaa Tounes parliamentary victory and Essebsi candidacy and presidential victory.

ISIS

ISIS, the Islamic State of Iraq and Syria, renamed the "Islamic State," has existed in various forms since the 1990s. Shortly after the U.S. invasion of Iraq in 2003, Abu Musab Al Zarqawi established Jamaat al-Tawhid wal-Jihad (the Party of Monotheism and Jihad), the precursor of the Islamic State. Zarqawi's main targets were Shia (rather than the Americans). The group carried out civilian attacks and beheadings. By 2004, Zarqawi had gained recognition and the endorsement of bin Laden; he joined his group under the umbrella of al-Qaeda by rebranding it as al-Qaeda in Iraq (AQI). Zarqawi was killed by American forces in 2006, and the MSC (Mujahideen Shura Council) declared the Islamic State of Iraq, or AQI/ISI. In 2011, Abu Bakr al-Baghdadi (who assumed the position of emir in 2010) became the leader of AQI/ISI, now largely made up of Iraqis—whose leadership were former Baathist (Saddam's political party) military and intelligence officers (nearly all previously imprisoned by the United States). With thousands of fighters and instability in Syria, al-Baghdadi opened a second front against Bashar al-Assad and Shia/Alawis in Syria. The group was renamed the Islamic State of Iraq and Syria/the Levant (ISIS or ISIL) to reflect the group's expanding ambitions. In 2014 Baghdadi renamed the movement the Islamic State (IS), claiming its goal was the restoration the caliphate, and took the title of caliph.

ISIS expansion was made possible by political conditions in Syria and Iraq, ethnic-religious/sectarian divisions and violence and terror in the region, and the failure of the United States and the international community to respond effectively. Bashar al-Assad's unprincipled and disproportionate military response to the "threat" of the democratization wave, the Arab Spring, with the slaughter of Syrian opposition groups both radicalized the situation and heightened sectarian (Sunni–Alawi) divisions.

The inability or reluctance of the United States and European Union to respond early on with significant assistance to the moderate Syrian opposition and the opposition's failure to unite or work effectively together enhanced the ability of foreign jihadists. In Iraq, Nouri al-Maliki's installing of a Shia-dominated government and the political marginalization of Sunnis increased an already polarized situation and sectarian violence that would result in alienated Sunnis welcoming ISIS.

ISIS "Islamic Pedigree and Vision"
Like al-Qaeda and other extremist groups, ISIS offers a warped militant Salafi rationalization to justify, recruit, legitimate, and motivate many of

its fighters. Their unabashed acts of barbarism and terrorism—slaughter of civilians, savage use of beheadings, killing of innocent Muslims and Christians—all violate Islamic law.

While there are similarities in ideological worldviews and tactics between ISIS and other terrorist groups like al-Qaeda, distinctive differences exist. ISIS seeks to create a state, to occupy and control areas, to govern, and to impose their version of a transnational caliphate, with its harsh version of law and order. They are far more ruthless in driving out, suppressing, and executing Shia and Kurds, Sunni imams-religious leaders, and others who disagree; they demand conversion to their warped and extraordinarily violent brand of Islam from minorities such as Christians and Yazidis, forcing populations to publically pledge their allegiance (*baya*) to the caliphate in exchange for security, in a mafia like version of "protection" and social services.

Is religion (Islam) the primary driver of the so-called Islamic caliphate?

Like al-Qaeda and others, ISIS's appeal to a harsh and barbaric version of religion/Islam captures headlines. Religion, as well as other factors, does play a role to legitimate, recruit, and motivate followers. However, studies of most jihadist movements like ISIS show that the primary drivers and motivations are most often political: a declared outrage at the occupation and oppression of Muslims and Muslim lands. Thus, for example, ISIS execution videos (released October 2006–April 2013 via its Al-Furqan Media Foundation) reveal the primacy of political grievances: foreign military invasion and occupation and killing of tens of thousands of civilians as well the "crimes" committed by individuals and groups (Iraqi soldiers, police, and government workers).

ISIS Recruitment of Western Muslim Youth

U.S. intelligence as well as many nongovernment experts and studies confirm that ISIS preys on Western youth (estimated at several thousand from Europe and the United States) who are disillusioned and have no sense of purpose or belonging. Like the Mafia and gangs, ISIS offers a sense of family and purpose:

> The general picture provided by foreign fighters of their lives in Syria suggests camaraderie, good morale and purposeful activity, all mixed in with a sense of understated heroism, designed to attract their friends as well as to boost their own self-esteem.... What the jihadis are actually pushing is a specific narrative, which is: Your people

(Muslims) are being oppressed in this place called Syria; your government is doing nothing; we're the only ones who are actually going
to help you out.[26]

Although a constellation of narratives influences Western Muslim
recruits to ISIS, many believe that the West is at war with Islam in the
United States and Europe and in Muslim countries. They are alienated
and marginalized politically, economically, and socially by the growth
of xenophobia and Islamophobia as reflected in American and European
politics, society, and media and believe that the invasion and occupation of
Muslim lands and support for un-Islamic authoritarian Muslim regimes
are the product of U.S. and European imperialism.

This issue is not new. Studies of domestic radicalization in Europe
post-9/11 by the European Commission's European Network of Experts
on De-Radicalization in Europe found that identity and political issues,
rather than religion or religious fervor, were the primary sources of
most extremist behavior. An MI5 (British military intelligence, a
national security service) report on radicalization (2008) noted: "far
from being religious zealots, a large number of those involved in terrorism do not practice their faith regularly. Many lack religious literacy
and could   be regarded as religious novices." Analysts concluded that
"a well-established religious identity actually protects against violent
radicalization."

ISIS use of professionally crafted media to lure Western Muslim youth
(some three thousand from Europe and the United States) also played on
identity, alienation, and political issues, attracting recruits, many of whom
had not been particularly religious, as reflected in a July 2014 ISIS-related
terrorism case. Two jihadi wannabes, Yusuf Sarwar and Mohammed
Ahmed, pled guilty to terrorism offenses. The previous May, prior to setting out for Syria, they had ordered two books from Amazon: *Islam for
Dummies* and *The Koran for Dummies*.

That said, ISIS members, like bin Laden and al-Qaeda, do appeal to
Islam, using an extremist ideological interpretation to legitimate their
jihad and its savage and disproportionate slaughter of military and civilians, Muslims, Christians, and Yazidis alike, as well as other actions and
policies that in fact violate the prescriptions of mainstream Islam and
Islamic law that: war should be defensive, to defend against aggression
of an enemy; proportionality is required in using force; noncombatants,
especially women and children, are to be protected; and prisoners are to
receive humane treatment. This belief motivated condemnations and fatwas against ISIS by Muslim leaders worldwide, who ruled that there is no

Islamic rationale for ISIS extremist claims, rhetoric. and actions, and the launching of a Twitter campaign #NotInMyName and other social media campaigns denouncing ISIS atrocities.

CONCLUSION

The Islamic resurgence has had a significant impact on personal and public life in Muslim politics and society as well as militant movements that have wrought havoc in Muslim counties and the West. Rulers, religious leaders, and Islamic movements, mainstream and extremist, from Egypt, Libya, and Iran to Pakistan, Afghanistan, and Southeast Asia have appealed to Islam. The events of 9/11 brought into sharp relief the global dimension and magnitude of the threat from terrorist movements, in particular Osama bin Laden and al-Qaeda and subsequently ISIS. However, the focus on "the global war on terrorism" also buttressed entrenched Muslim authoritarian regimes and their suppression not only of militants but also of genuine popular discontent and a desire among many Muslims for a more democratic future, an end to dictatorship and massive corruption, and the rule of law, greater equality, and human rights.

As we shall see in the next chapter, reform-minded Muslims from North Africa to Southeast Asia have responded to the realities of many Muslim societies in the twenty-first century. As in other faiths and societies, reformers have grappled with the challenges of authoritarian regimes, greater democratization, the relationship between religion and the state, gender relations and equality, religious pluralism, and the dangers of religious extremism. A vanguard of religious reformers and activists have reread their scripture and reinterpreted and reapplied Islam to counter the dead weight of well-meaning but often intransigent interpretations of ultraconservatives. They seek to revitalize their faith and its relevance to the challenges of the twenty-first century, one that promotes pluralism, mutual understanding, and respect both within Islam and in Muslim relations with other believers and nonbelievers.

KEY TERMS

al-Qaeda

al-Jihad (Holy War)

Anwar Sadat

Ayatollah Khomeini

Gamaa Islamiyya

Hamas

islah

Islamic revivalism

Jafar al-Numayri

Jamaat-i-Islami (Pakistan)

Jemaah Islamiya (Indonesia)

Justice and Development Party
  (Turkey)

Justice and Development Party
  (Morocco)

Muammar Qaddafi

Muhammadiya (Indonesia)

Muslim Brotherhood (Egypt)

Muslim Brotherhood (Jordan)

Omar ul-Bashir

Nahdatul Ulama (Indonesia)

Renaissance Party (Tunisia)

Sayyid Qutb

tajdid

Takfir wal Hijra

Taliban rule (Afghanistan)

Yusuf Qaradawi

Zia ul-Haq

QUESTIONS

1. How have reformers and established governments used Islam for their own political ends?

2. Does democracy require a "wall of secularism"? If so, does this preclude "Islamic democracy"? If not, what could/does this concept look like?

3. What effect did the Iranian Revolution have on Shii and Sunni Muslim states? Is its paradigm still relevant today?

4. How does the revivalism described in this chapter compare to that of Chapter 4?

5. What do Muslim "radicalization" and "terrorism" look like? Are they related?

NOTES

1. See, for example, John J. Donohue, "Islam and the Search for Identity in the Arab World," in *Voices of Resurgent Islam*, John L. Esposito, ed. (New York: Oxford University Press, 1983), chap. 3; and Ali Merad, "The Ideologisation of Islam," in *Islam and Power*, Alexander S. Cudsi and Ali E. Hillal Dessouki, eds. (Baltimore: Johns Hopkins University Press, 1981), chap. 3.
2. "Lessons from Iran," in *Islam in Transition: Muslim Perspectives*, John J. Donohue and John L. Esposito, eds. (New York: Oxford University Press, 1982), pp. 246–49.
3. Merad, "Ideologisation of Islam," p. 38.
4. For a more extended analysis of the roles of Islam in politics, see John L. Esposito, *Islam and Politics*, 2nd ed. (Syracuse, NY: Syracuse University Press, 1987), which has been a source for this discussion.
5. "The Libyan Revolution in the Words of Its Leaders," *The Middle East Journal* 24 (1978): 208.
6. As quoted in Mahmoud Mustafa Ayoub, *Islam and the Third Universal Theory: The Religious Thought of Muammar al-Qadhdhafi* (London: KPI, 1987), p. 88.
7. As quoted in Ervand Abrahamian, "Ali Shariati: Ideologue of the Iranian Revolution," *MERIP Reports* 102 (January 1982): 26.

8. Marius Deeb, "Shia Movements in Lebanon: Their Formation, Ideology, Social Basis, and Links with Iran and Syria," *Third World Quarterly* 10, no. 2 (April 1988): 694.

9. Wright, Robin, "Inside the Mind of Hizbollah." *The Washington Post*, July 16, 2006.

10. http://www.cbc.ca/news/background/middleeast-crisis/index.html.

11. For my analysis, I have drawn on my previous work, in particular, John L. Esposito, *Islam and Politics*, 3rd rev. ed. (Syracuse, NY: Syracuse University Press, 1991), pp. 162–78, 275–76; and John L. Esposito, "Islam: Ideology and Politics in Pakistan," in *The State, Religion, and Ethnic Politics*, Ali Banuazizi and Myron Weiner, eds. (Syracuse, NY: Syracuse University Press, 1986), chap. 12.

12. Ayub Khan, as quoted in *Islam and Politics*, p. 116.

13. "Shiite Parties Win Iraq Poll," *Gulf News*, January 20, 2006. http://archive.gulfnews.com/indepth/iraqelection/sub_story/10013187.html.

14. Ghattas, Kim. "Conservatives 'Win Saudi Polls.'" *BBC News*, April 23, 2005. http://news.bbc.co.uk/2/hi/middle_east/4477315.stm.

15. As quoted in Peter L. Bergen, *Holy War: Inside the Secret World of Osama bin Laden* (New York: Free Press, 2002), p. 53.

16. For perceptive discussions of Osama bin Laden, see A. Rashid, *Taliban: Militant Islam: Oil and Fundamentalism in Central Asia* (New Haven, CT: Yale University Press, 2000); Peter L. Bergen, *Holy War: Inside the Secret World of Osama bin Laden* (New York: Free Press, 2002); Jason Burke, *Al Qaeda: Casting a Shadow of Terror* (London: I.B. Taurus, 2003); and J. K. Cooley, *Unholy War: Afghanistan, America and International Terrorism* (London: Pluto Press, 2000).

17. Transcript of Osama bin Laden interview, CNN/Time, *Impact: Holy Terror?* August 25, 1998.

18. Paul Kennedy, "As Others See Us," *The Wall Street Journal*, October 5, 2001.

19. *Al-Hayat* (November 5, 2001).

20. Shaikh Abdal-Hakim Murad, "Bombing without Moonlight: The Origins of Suicide Terrorism," October 2004, http://www.masud.co.uk/ISLAM/ahm/moonlight.htm.

21. Timothy Winter (aka Dr. Abdul Hakim Murad), "Bin Laden's Violence is Heresy Against Islam," http://groups.colgate.edu/aarislam/abdulhak.htm.

22. "Initiatives and Actions Taken by the Kingdom of Saudi Arabia in the War on Terrorism," Royal Embassy of Saudi Arabia, Washington, DC, September 2003.

23. "Muslim Reactions to September 11," http://www.crescentlife.com/ heal%20the%20world/muslim_reactions_to_sept_11.htm.

24. http://www.hrw.org/news/2014/02/19/egypt-high-price-dissent.

25. http://www.amnesty.org/en/news/egypt-three-years-wide-scale-repression-continues-unabated-2014-01-23.

26. Richard Barrett, "Foreign Fighters in Syria," January 2014, pp. 17–18. http://soufan-group.com/wp-content/uploads/2014/06/TSG-Foreign-Fighters-in-Syria.pdf.

The Struggle for Islam
in the Twenty-First Century

CONTEMPORARY ISLAMIC RELIGIOUS REFORM

The struggle (jihad) in Islam today is religious, intellectual, political, social, spiritual, and moral. The threat from religious extremists and terrorists has accelerated the need to face critical issues of Islamic reform.

Islam today exhibits a rich, and at times bewildering, array of interpretations. Indeed, some observers maintain that there is not one but many Islams, many interpretations of Islam, as there are multiple interpretations of Christianity and other faiths. Many devout Muslims take issue with this and instead assert that there is only one Islam and that the distinction must be made between the one Islam and the many Muslims. The many interpretations and uses of Islam by governments, religious leaders, movements, and individuals have produced a diversity of theologies, ideologies, actors, organizations, and programs.

The struggle for the future of Islam is between competing voices and visions: the vast majority of mainstream Muslims and a dangerous and deadly minority of militant extremists. Some wish to restore an idealized and romanticized past, while others press for more substantial and widespread reforms. Extremists grab the headlines and often overshadow the existence of a current generation of diverse reformers active in reinterpreting Islam.

Reformers face formidable obstacles: overcoming the ultraconservatism of many (although not all) *ulama* (religious scholars and clergy); meeting the need for curricula reform in seminaries (**madrasas**) and universities that train the next generation of religious leaders, scholars, students, and citizens; and effectively discrediting militant jihadist ideas and ideologies. The obstacles to reform are compounded by political and economic realities that encourage growth of extremist movements (repressive authoritarian governments, widespread corruption, failed economies, joblessness, and social injustice) as well as the legacy of a bifurcation in education and society.

THE BIFURCATION OF SOCIETY

The bifurcation of society in many parts of the Muslim world is rooted in two parallel systems of education: traditional religious training and modern secular education, a product of European colonialism and a Western-oriented process of modernization. Many religious schools, despite some modern curriculum reform, continue to produce graduates with predominantly traditional religious educations who continue to serve as local religious leaders, teachers, and scholars. Many are ill prepared to appreciate the need for substantive reforms and for a fresh reinterpretation of Islam, and thus they fail to provide the kind of religious leadership and guidance required in modern society. Unsurprisingly, most of the leaders of the mainstream Islamic movements are lay intellectuals who are graduates of modern schooling and not the products of traditional institutions.

Modern secular schools that provide the "new" knowledge and academic credentials for prestige positions in modern society (medicine, law, engineering, government service) often enjoy increased government funding and support. However, although their graduates are well versed in modern disciplines, they often lack knowledge of their religious and cultural traditions necessary to formulate changes with sufficient sensitivity to the history and values of their cultural milieu. The educational situation is further compounded by the fact that many traditional religious schools and universities suffer from a lack of adequate government support and human resources (well-trained faculty), and although their graduates are qualified to be imams or to teach religion, their degrees are regarded as second class or not acceptable for the job market in general.

For many conservative and ultra conservative religious leaders fixated on the past, tradition is not so much a source of inspiration and direction as a literal map to be followed in all its details. This blueprint for Muslim society, contained in the traditional (classical) legal manuals, is not seen as a time-bound response to a specific sociohistorical period but rather as a final, comprehensive guide. Conservatives fail to distinguish adequately between revealed, immutable principles and historically conditioned laws and institutions produced by the early jurists' fallible human reasoning as well as assimilated foreign influences and practices. Moreover, the hold of tradition can be seen in its more subtle and hidden form among those who, in principle, advocate reinterpretation (***ijtihad***) and change but, when pressed on specific changes, often exhibit a "***taqlid*** mentality." This is a tendency to reflexively follow or imitate (*taqlid*) past practice because of either intellectual conviction or a pragmatic need to defer to the dominant traditionalist culture.

THE *ULAMA* AND REFORM

Many of the *ulama* see the erosion of their traditional power and authority as the legacy of European colonialism and Westernization and its continuation in the institutions of the modern state system and in society. Modern educational and legal reforms greatly curtailed the *ulama*'s dominant role in education and law, restricted their sources of revenue, and raised serious questions about their competence and relevance. In most Muslim countries, modern secular educational systems were privileged over traditional religious schools (madrasa) that in many countries attract fewer talented students and whose diplomas have a more limited value. State control and administration of religious endowments has further reduced the *ulama*'s economic independence and social role. Government ministries of religious affairs or endowments control many social welfare programs as well as religious schools and institutions, influencing appointments, teachers' and preachers' salaries, and, in some countries, the content of sermons. Moreover, the greater value placed on modern education contributed to the general tendency to hold the *ulama* responsible for the ills of Muslim societies since they are viewed as "monopolizing" the explanations of religion, claiming to be the only ones who should speak in the name of religion and because they teach that any laws, decisions, and solutions having to do with doctrine or daily life that originated from early religious sources were binding and could not be changed in any way.

Although the majority of *ulama* continue to maintain that they should be the ultimate authority determining what the law is or should be, increasingly one finds Muslim voices who, although not directly challenging the existence of the *ulama* as an institution, redefine their role and areas of competence. To limit the scope of *ulama* authority and justify lay input, they note that Islam knows no ordained clergy and that all Muslims are equal and responsible before God. They argue that the title *alim* (pl. *ulama*) means "learned," one who has knowledge or is an expert. Thus, the title belongs properly not to a specific clerical group or class but to any Muslim who is qualified. However, since many *ulama* resist any attempt to limit the area of their competence, their authority and the nature of Islamic law and the question of legal reform remain pivotal issues and sources of conflict.

A response to the perceived failures resulting from training two distinct mind-sets or outlooks—conservative or traditional versus modern—can be seen in the emergence of an alternative elite, those who are modern educated but more Islamically oriented and committed. These new elites, trained in Muslim countries and in the West, have been strongly visible in politics and society. However diverse, they all call for more Islamically informed political, social, legal, and economic institutions. But how can tradition be effectively integrated with or accommodate modern reforms and institutions?

TRADITION: ANCHOR OR ALBATROSS?

During the formative centuries of the Muslim community, several factors led to the development of a sacralized tradition that blurred the line between divine revelation and human interpretation. Time-honored tribal and regional traditions were Islamized and sacralized. The authority of this tradition was attributed not to a human community but to God's revelation. In particular, the notion of tribal practice (*sunna*) was transformed and became Prophetic Sunna, the practice and precedent of Muhammad. The authoritative basis for the Muslim community's practice was thus grounded in what the Prophet said, did, or permitted or was attributed to him. "Islamic" tradition replaced tribal, ethnic, or regional traditions.

The development of Islamic law and the notion that it was the product of God's revelation (scripture and Prophetic tradition) and an insufficient recognition of the role of human interpretation further reinforced the belief that Islamic tradition was an expression and source of God's divinely revealed law. The tendency of some pious Muslims to seek approbation for their beliefs and practices by attributing them to Prophetic traditions obscured the creative human role in developing many beliefs and practices. For many, Islamic law was no longer viewed as the product of God's revelation and human interpretation. Instead, the majority of *ulama* simply regarded it as the divinely revealed, perfect blueprint for society.

By the tenth century many Sunni jurists had come to believe that because the guidelines for individual and community life were established, personal interpretation (*ijtihad*) was no longer necessary or permitted. Society was simply to emulate or follow (*taqlid*) the guidelines of sacred tradition as delineated and preserved in Islamic law. Thus, tradition was effectively standardized, fixed, and sanctified by grounding it in revelation and sacred law (Shariah). As such, it became a strong source of community identity and cohesion, providing an underlying sense of unity, certitude, and guidance amid the diversity of local cultures and popular religious practices that characterized the lands of Islam.

However, the benefits of community cohesion were obtained at a cost—the tendency to forget the dynamism, diversity, and human creativity that had contributed to the development of Islam. The human input into the formation of Islamic tradition and law (the role of reason, human interpretation, assimilation, and Islamization of local customs) became obscured as later generations preserved and transmitted a more static, romanticized sense of Islamic history. Islamic tradition became relatively fixed and sacrosanct; future generations were simply to follow Islam's way of life, the straight path of Islam, as authoritatively and comprehensively set forth in Islamic law. Substantive change was regarded as unwarranted innovation (*bida*), departure from the revealed law or practice of the community.

The sacrosanct nature of Islamic tradition is of primary importance today in the struggle for reform by both conservatives and many modern reformers, although they differ in their approaches: (1) conservatives and traditionalists tend to emphasize the centrality and restoration of tradition; and (2) modern Islamic reformers see tradition as an important reference point, but one that is historically conditioned and subject to change or reconstruction. As a result, there are major differences about the nature and degree of change. They part ways when they respond to two fundamental questions: Whose Islam? What Islam?

Whose Islam?

Who is to interpret, formulate, and implement Islam? In the past, the traditional Sunni religious leadership (*ulama*) claimed the prerogative to interpret Islam, while the caliph was responsible for its implementation. In traditional Shii Islam, the *ulama* were sources of guidance and emulation in the absence of the imam (the descendant of Muhammad and infallible and sinless religious and political leader of Shia Islam). In recent decades non-*ulama*, lay intellectuals (men and women) and leaders of Islamic movements, have also asserted their right to interpret or reinterpret Islam. Who then today should oversee, approve, and implement Islam: rulers, clerical leaders, a committee of *ulama*, or an elected national assembly?

In contemporary times, there have been many abuses in the name of Islam. Muslim governments and individual rulers have interpreted Islam to enhance their legitimacy and policies and to justify authoritarian rule, suppress political parties, and impose censorship. Islamic activists, mainstream and extremist, have opposed self-proclaimed Muslim rulers. However, critics charge that, like political leaders, they are also manipulating religion for political ends, especially those that have resorted to violence to achieve their goals.

Manipulation of religion can be seen by the selective use of a "negative Islam" in countries such as Afghanistan, Iran, Saudi Arabia, and Sudan. For example, in Afghanistan, the Taliban's forced code of dress (the tent-like burqa for women and beards for men) and severe restrictions on women's education, work, and human rights are enforced by flogging and even stoning. Iran, Saudi Arabia, and Sudan have been criticized by international human rights organizations for their policies and violations of human rights.

What Islam?

What interpretation(s) of Islam are normative and appropriate? The central issue here is the relationship of tradition to modernization. Does a return to Islam mean the reclamation and implementation of the traditional legal blueprint of Muslim society, or does it mean a return to the sources of Islam, to those principles and values on which new laws and institutions can be constructed?

In classical terms, is the implementation of Islam in state and society simply to be a process of imitation (*taqlid*) of the past or of reinterpretation (*ijtihad*) and reform of tradition? Is there one classical Islamic model, or are there many possible models for development? In the struggle and debate over whether a new synthesis is needed and, if so, how it will be accomplished, many approaches exist.

Thus, it is important to remember, first of all, that categories and terminology are always arbitrary because individuals and groups often overlap in their use of one category or another; second, although all models might reflect some reform, the category of Islamic reformism is used for those who are more sweeping in their modernist orientation.

A SPECTRUM OF REFORMERS AND APPROACHES

Today's reformers reflect a broad diversity of orientations, from secular to religious. Secularists advocate the exclusion of religion from public life. Sometimes dismissed as nonbelievers by their critics, most counter that they are religious but believe that religion should be restricted to private life (i.e., to prayer, fasting, pilgrimage, personal morality). They believe that mixing religion with politics is inappropriate in modern nation-states and regard those who do so as manipulating Islam for political rather than religious ends. Three religiously oriented positions advocate a return to Islam: conservatives and traditionalists, Islamic activists, and Islamic modernists or reformers. However, their methods and interpretations vary.

Conservatives and traditionalists emphasize the classical formulation of Islam, developed during the early Islamic centuries and embodied and preserved in manuals and commentaries on Islamic law. However, the conservative position, represented by the majority of the *ulama*, does not believe significant change is necessary. Although they accept *ijtihad* in principle, in practice they emphasize reapplying traditional Islamic laws. In contrast, traditionalists, who also revere the Islamic tradition, pursue fresh or new interpretations of Islamic law as we have seen previously. Although traditionalists are open to significant change, and some are open to a break with Islamic tradition, others mine the breadth and depth of classical/medieval Islamic law and traditions in an attempt to establish a continuity and hence the authenticity of their reforms.

Conservatives see little need to develop new answers because, for them, Islam is an already comprehensive religious and cultural system fully articulated in the past. They rely quite strictly on following and imitating (*taqlid*) past tradition. They see significant change as unacceptable innovation (*bida*) in religion. Because Islamic law is the divinely revealed path, it is not the law that must change or modernize, they say, but society that must conform to God's will. To the extent that there is a dichotomy between law and society, society has departed from the straight path of Islam and must return to long-established norms. Persistent conservative attitudes can be seen in countries like Pakistan and Egypt. The majority of the *ulama* and their followers, faced with modern reform movements, voiced their objections but were willing to compromise, to cooperate, or to remain quiescent. However, with the contemporary resurgence of Islam in politics and society, many then called for repealing modern family law reforms and restoring classical/medieval Islamic laws. Similarly, when the mullahs who dominated the Iranian parliament came to power, they moved to abolish Iran's Family Protection Act to implement traditional Islamic laws. Where change did occur, it was gradual and by way of exception and it occurred in areas not covered by traditional law.

Islamic activists advocate a return to Islam and the Sharia. Because of the popular use of the term *fundamentalism*, the broad ideological diversity and orientations of Islamic activists, who range from rigid to flexible, political to apolitical, and nonviolent to violent is often obscured. Instead, they are often simply stereotyped as literalist, puritanical, antimodern, antidemocratic, and antipluralist. Such descriptors are true for **Wahhabi** and **Salafi Muslims**, but many Islamic movements are far more progressive. Although respecting the classical formulations of Islamic law, many are not wedded to them. Instead, they claim the right to go back to the fundamental sources of Islam, Quran and Prophetic example, to reinterpret (*ijtihad*) and reapply them to contemporary needs and conditions. Thus, over the years, many have participated in democratic elections and supported reforms in human rights and the status of women.

Islamic activists are political and social reformers who often challenge the political and religious establishments. They are more flexible than conservatives in their ability to adapt to change. Their leadership is predominantly lay rather than clerical, as was the case of the Egyptian Muslim Brotherhood's Hasan al-Banna and the Jamaat-i-Islami's Mawlana Mawdudi in the past. Today, diverse movements such as the Muslim Brotherhoods of Egypt, Sudan, and Jordan; the Jamaat-i-Islami in Pakistan and Bangladesh; Ennahda in Tunisia; as well as movements in Morocco, Algeria, the Gulf States, and South and Southeast Asia have a lay leadership cadre. However, the predominance of lay reformers in this group has not precluded the significant role played by prominent religious scholars like Shaykh Fadlallah of Lebanon; Ali Gomaa, the former Grand Mufti of Egypt; Mustafa Ceric, former Grand Mufti of Bosnia-Herzegovina; Yusuf Qardawi of Qatar; Habib Al Jifri of Yemen and Abu Dhabi; and Ayatollah Ali Sistani of Iraq; as well as senior Ayatollahs in Iran and Iraq.

Both Islamic activists and conservatives insist that their reinterpretation of Islam is based solely on Islamic sources and tradition, which can provide the answers for Islamic society today. They see secularizers as agents of Western imperialism, "native Westernizers" who undermine Islam, and see Islamic modernists or reformers as well-intentioned reformers who "Westernized" Islam and thus sacrificed its authentic vision and voice. However, although excessive dependence on the West is rejected, selective modernization is not. Science and technology, they say, needs to be appropriated and "Islamized," or subordinated to Islamic values and purposes. This attitude is exemplified by popular slogans like "Islamic economics equals economics minus Western values plus Islamic values."

Islamic activists or fundamentalists, unlike religious conservatives, tend to ideologize Islam, to interpret Islam as an alternative system or worldview for politics, law, education, and banking. Because of the variety that exists in human interpretation, as well as changes in leadership and circumstances, many differing Islamic positions can be seen on the same issue. Whereas Muslim Brotherhood leaders like Sayyid Qutb and Mustapha al-Sibaii advanced Islamic socialism as a means to promote social justice in the late 1950s and early 1960s, today the Brotherhood tends to emphasize private ownership as the Islamic norm. In addition, the Brotherhood's original tendency to regard Arab nationalism and unity as a necessary stage in the revival of Islam has given way to an emphasis today on Islamic rather than Arab solidarity. Similarly, Mawlana Mawdudi originally rejected democracy as inherently Western and as part of European colonization. He also maintained that a ruler might regard *shura* (consultation) as simply informative and nonbinding, regardless of the number of its supporters. However, in later years Mawdudi taught that *shura* was indeed binding, and members of his organization, the Jamaat, came to accept and participate in Pakistan's democratic process, serving in its Senate, National Assembly, and cabinet and also accepting the results of elections in which they did not fare well.

Finally, the most adaptable group is Islamic modernist reformers. In many ways they build on the legacy of Muhammad Abduh's and Muhammad Iqbal's Islamic modernism in the late nineteenth and early twentieth centuries. Yet today they must respond to a more globalized "postmodern" world in which the meaning of modernity itself has changed. In contrast to the past when modernity or becoming modern was equated solely with a Western secular paradigm, we live today in a more cosmopolitan world of "multiple modernities" that go far beyond the standard, homogeneous Western secular paradigm for modernization.

Like other Muslims, Islamic modernists look to the early Islamic period as embodying a normative ideal. However, they distinguish more sharply than others between substance and form, between the principles and values of Islam's immutable revelation and the historically and socially conditioned institutions, laws, and practices. They maintain that the classical or medieval regulations enshrined in the law books represent the understanding of early jurists who applied the principles and values of Islam to their societies. They distinguish revealed immutable Sharia principles and laws from man-made regulations in Islamic law that are historically relative and that might need to be reformulated in light of modern social needs.

Many reformers have obtained advanced degrees at major universities in their countries or regions or major universities in the United States and Europe. In their view, however, they are not as Western oriented as earlier generations of Islamic modernists. Islamic reformers do not see themselves as responding primarily to the West but instead as seeking in a more independent, authentic manner to meet the changing needs of their societies. They have learned from the West but do not wish to Westernize Muslim society. They remain Islamically oriented and emphasize commitment to "Islamic modernization," a future in which political and social development are more firmly rooted in past Islamic history and traditional values. However, in contrast to many others, their rhetoric is not as critical of the West, and they are more open to a selective adoption and adaptation of Western knowledge and institutions.

Like fundamentalists, they interpret Islam as a way of life and seek to implement Islamic values in public as well as private life. Unlike many fundamentalists, they are not necessarily advocates of an Islamic polity and are more creative and wide-ranging in their reinterpretation, less tied to the traditional interpretations. For this reason, the more conservative members of the *ulama* regard them as a threat to their authority. They attack their "Western deviationism" and challenge their qualifications as reinterpreters of Islam.

Reform-minded Muslims include academics, lawyers, physicians, journalists, and religious scholars from North Africa to Southeast Asia. They respond to the realities of many Muslim societies, the challenges of authoritarian regimes and secular elites, the dangers of religious extremism, and the need for fresh interpretations of Islam to counter the deadweight of well-meaning but often intransigent religious scholars and leaders. They seek to identify and build on a common ground of shared beliefs and values and to foster change through the peaceful cultural and educational transformation of society rather than regime change.

Distinguishing between unchanging principles and values and historically and culturally conditioned practices, these reformers have addressed issues of belief and practice: gender equality, full citizenship rights for non-Muslims, democratization, religious extremism and terrorism, Islamic banking (differentiating the Quran's condemnation of usury and acceptable forms of banking interest), abortion, and in vitro fertilization. They denounce the use of violence by militants as contrary to Islamic teachings; call for government reforms to address political, social, and economic grievances; and are critical of Western political and cultural imperialism.

Abdurrahman Wahid (d. 2009) is a good example of a reformer, a traditional and modern educated religious scholar and political leader. He was the president of the **Nahdatul Ulama** (Renaissance of Religious Scholars), the largest Islamic organization in the world's largest Muslim country with more members (40 million) than the populations of Saudi Arabia and all the Gulf emirates combined. As head of the Nahdatul Ulama, he strongly opposed making Sharia the law of the land. Wahid later became the first democratically elected president in Indonesian history (1999–2001).

Wahid and an increasing number of Muslims, like many non-Muslim scholars, see a world of multiple modernities, multiple paths rather than just a Western secular paradigm. Muslims, they believe, can choose an

Islamic modernity that is appropriate to their social context. Thus, for example, Indonesian Islam will differ from Arab Islam. In contrast to those who advocate the Islamization of Indonesia, Wahid argues for the Indonesianization of society, the contextualization of Islam within local culture. Bridging the worlds of traditional Islam and "modern" thought, Wahid espouses a cosmopolitan Islam, responsive to the demands of modern life and reflecting Indonesian Islam's diverse religious and ethnic history and communities. His reform is an inclusive religious, democratic, pluralistic force.

Wahid believes that contemporary Muslims are at a critical crossroads. Two choices, or paths, confront them: to pursue a traditional, static, legal-formalistic Islam or to reclaim and refashion a more dynamic cosmopolitan, universal, pluralistic worldview.[1] He rejects the notion that Islam should form the basis for the nation-state's political or legal system,[2] which he characterizes as a Middle Eastern tradition alien to Indonesia. Indonesian Muslims should apply a moderate, tolerant brand of Islam to their daily lives in a society where "a Muslim and a non-Muslim are the same," a state in which religion and politics are separate.[3] Rejecting legalistic formalism and fundamentalism as aberrations and a major obstacle to Islamic reform and to Islam's response to global change, Wahid affirms the right of all Muslims, laity as well as religious scholars (*ulama*), to "perpetual reinterpretation" (*ijtihad*) of the Quran and tradition of the Prophet in light of "ever changing human situations."

CYBERSPACE AND HIGH-TECH ISLAM

The globalization of communications has produced a new breed of popular well-known scholars like **Yusuf Qardawi** and **Tariq Ramadan** and a new breed of charismatic and enormously successful preachers like Egypt's Amr Khaled, Pakistan's Farhat Hashmi and Javed Ahmad Ghamidi, and Indonesia's Abdullah Gymnastiar. These tele-preachers, or what some call televangelists because of their preaching style and outreach, captivate millions, sometimes hundreds of millions, filling huge auditoriums and sports stadiums and disseminating their message on the Internet and through DVDs, video- and audiotapes, satellite television, and radio. Some, like Qardawi, have traditional religious educations, whereas others, like Khaled and Ramadan, have modern or secular educations.

Many media preachers and scholars provide a religious alternative to ultraconservative clerics and mosques, muftis and fatwas. If many *ulama* seek to shore up their religious authority, these popular alternative outlets enable Muslim televangelism, like Christian televangelism, to move in the opposite direction, toward a decentralization of religious authority. Most preach a direct, down-to-earth message, dispensing advice on everyday problems, promoting a practical, concrete Islamic spirituality of empowerment and success in this life as well as the next. Their audiences are drawn not as much by their religious or scholarly credentials as by their personalities, preaching styles, and distinctive messages.

Amr Khaled has been called "the Arab world's first Islamic tele-evangelist, a digital age Billy Graham who has fashioned himself into the anti-Bin Laden to turn around a generation of lost Muslim youth."[4] Clean-shaven and well dressed in a fashionable Western suit, Khaled speaks in colloquial Arabic to millions of young Muslims, ages fifteen through thirty-five. He targets upper-middle-class Muslims in the Arab world and Arab immigrants living in the West because he believes they are the ones most capable of changing the Islamic world for the better.

Like evangelical Christian preachers, Khaled blends conservative religious belief with a charismatic personality and speaking style, Western self-help, management training jargon, and an emotive, crowd-pleasing performance full of stories, laughter, and tears. He doesn't talk politics, preferring to emphasize God's love and issues of personal piety, daily prayer, family relationships, community responsibility, veiling, and dating. Muslim youth, in particular, are drawn to his down-to-earth religious and spiritual messages, emphasizing values and a positive, proactive attitude toward life. He replaces the ultraconservatives' and fundamentalists' negative "No, no Islam" with an affirmative "Yes to life Islam."

Aa Gymnastiar

For theater and drama, few can compete with Aa Gym. Abdullah Gymnastiar was Indonesia's most popular preacher. His fame nationally exceeded that of Indonesian film stars and cuts across the social spectrum: rich and poor, educated and uneducated, men and women, Muslims and many Christians have been drawn by his emphasis on religious pluralism and belief that all religions ultimately preach the same message.

A household name, the flamboyant Aa Gym disseminated his message on a weekly television program and to a radio audience of 60 million people in addition to his books, cassettes, videos, management training seminars, and aphorisms displayed on the red cans of Qolbu Cola, the soft drink he markets.[5] His message has been likened to American Protestant evangelism's emphasis on people's ability to take control of their lives and their fortunes. Spiritual success for Aa does not preclude temporal success. His optimistic message is that you can succeed in the "here and now" if you follow religious values and work hard, and his message is embodied in his own lifestyle. Like Khaled's, Gymnastiar's credibility and appeal stem from his emphasis on Islam's relevance to the everyday life of Muslims.

Aa combines religion, popular Western business motivational principles and techniques, entrepreneurship, marketing, and modern media to produce a model that joins modern principles of business organization with the teachings of Islam and Indonesian culture. He calls his teaching method "Management by Conscience"[6] and offers popular management seminars for business executives and middle managers where they train to be better professionals in a program that includes ethics and Quranic studies.

Farhat Hashmi: Veiled Reformer?

Although she has a Ph.D. from the University of Glasgow, in contrast to what might be the popular image of a Muslim woman reformer, Farhat Hashmi fully veils her face and body. Hashmi insists that she is committed to the liberation, empowerment, and education of women; her critics dismiss her as fundamentalist, patriarchal, and even Taliban-like. Modernists and feminists as well as conservative *ulama* have often been her severest critics.

Ironically, Hashmi's greatest popularity is among "Westernized," English-speaking, educated women in Pakistan, who have traditionally been the torchbearers of the women's movement. Some have credited her with spawning an Islamic resurgence among elite Pakistani women. Indeed, her influence and popularity in Pakistan and internationally are reflected in crowds of up to ten thousand who attend her talks.

Hashmi focuses on the day-to-day practical aspects of Islam and attributes the popularity of her lectures to the fact that people are desperate for religion: "There is a search for direction, for guidance," she says. She identifies her goal as reforming Islamic society by reviving authentic Islamic education. Her admirers travel from across Toronto, where she now lives and works, and from as far away as Australia to her Al-Huda Institute, which serves full-time students as well as working women and homemakers and has graduated more than ten thousand women. Al-Huda also reaches out to women in rural areas, staff and inmates in the prison system, and women in hospitals.[7]

Despite Hashmi's seemingly "progressive" views on women's education, career opportunities, and right to be a religious authority, her choice of dress, preference for hijabs, and support of gender segregation have worked against her and drawn sharp criticism. When asked if her teachings might encourage the talibanization of society and result in the loss of women's rights, Hashmi responds:

When I myself have done my Ph.D. and gone to a foreign land to study, how can I tell others not to do the same? My point of view is that a woman's primary responsibility is her home, after she has fulfilled that it is up to her to go into whatever field suits her best .... A woman's role as a home-maker should not be sacrificed at the altar of ambition.[8]

Fethullah Gulen and the Hizmet Movement

Described by major Western publications such as *The Economist* and *Foreign Policy* as well as scholars as one of the world's most important Muslim figures, Fethullah Gulen, religious leader and preacher, was born in Izmir, Turkey, in 1941. He rose from being a popular preacher to become a state-approved preacher. Gulen traveled extensively throughout the provinces and villages preaching and organizing coffeehouse discussion groups, student summer camps, and high school study and boarding halls. Students trained in such summer camps in the 1970s became teachers themselves for a new generation of followers.

By the 1980s, the Gulen or **Hizmet** (service) **Movement** expanded from a regional to a national movement and then a three-dimensional (religious, educational, and social) global movement aimed at transforming society and the world. Today the Gulen Movement promotes religious-social reform with a global presence and impact, from the Middle East, Central and Southeast Asia, and Africa to Europe and the United States.

Fethullah Gulen advocates a "moderate Islam," religious views that are pragmatic and contemporary, without necessarily being "liberal." His reformist thinking and activities, rooted in his interpretation of the Quran, focus on emphasizing service (*hizmet*), especially for culturally, educationally, and economically excluded groups, Muslim and non-Muslim alike, nationally and globally. Gulen advocates local and international interfaith dialogue with "People of the Book" (Jews and Christians) and has personally met with major religious leaders including Pope John Paul II, the Greek Orthodox Patriarch Bartholomeos, and Israeli Sephardic Head Rabbi Eliyahu Bakshi-Doron.

In contrast to the political ideology of Islamists, Gulen emphasizes a civil Islam that accommodates both religion and secular nationalism but does not support implementation of Shariah law. Civil Islam in contrast to political Islam focuses on the spiritual and educational development of individual Muslims and civil society, human rights, religious freedom, social justice, and economic development. His inclusive approach embraces the sciences, West and East, and Islam and other religions as well as Islam's compatibility with democracy and market economy.

The Hizmet Movement's educational projects, include more than 1,100 schools and universities globally, 130 (mostly charter schools) in the United States, in over 140 countries. Their curriculum includes modern science and technology, and they feature dormitories for tens of thousands of students, tutorials, financial aid, and book publication and distribution.

The Gulen Movement's aim is to educate and expand a counterelite (to the entrenched Westernized secular elite), a "golden generation" equipped with education in the modern sciences and in Islamic ethics to work in business, government, education, and media as well as among the working poor. Thus, Gulen moves beyond leading a purely religious movement and instead spearheads a social and educational revolution. A complex web of business networks (large holding companies, banks, investment houses, insurance companies, and chain stores) and a large media empire (a major international newspaper [*Zaman*], published in Turkish and English, as well as scientific and theological journals, an environment-related magazine, an English-language religious publication, and popular radio and television stations support and disseminate the movement's message). In addition, a global network of organizations (Rumi Forum, Niagara, Cosmos and Sky Foundations, Rainbow, and many others) promotes interfaith and intercultural dialogue activities globally.

The Two-Way Superhighway

In contrast to the past, when ideas and influence flowed one way, from Muslim countries to the West, today information, ideas, financial resources, and influence flow on a superhighway whose traffic travels in both directions. Indeed, given the more open religious, political, and intellectual climate in Europe and America, Muslim intellectuals and activists have increasingly had a significant impact on Islamic thought and activism through their training of a new generation of university students and through their writings, which often reflect fresh reinterpretations (*ijtihad*) of critical issues. They represent a movement that encompasses diverse people and orientations.

Two-way communication and exchange occur through Muslim and non-Muslim scholars' and religious leaders' travel, speaking engagements, publications, cassettes, and DVDs, and increasingly in cyberspace (Facebook, Twitter, etc.). Their influence also occurs through their Muslim students who return to their home countries. At the same time, diverse voices in the Muslim world have a similar presence and impact in Europe and America through their writings, workshops, preaching (live and on the Internet, videos, and DVDs), and fatwas.

The result is a process of reform that addresses issues of faith and practice, religious leadership and authority, religious and political pluralism, tolerance, minority rights (Muslim and non-Muslim), and gender. European and American Muslim diaspora communities can have almost instant access to the fatwas *of* muftis throughout the Muslim world and can obtain answers to their own specific questions on Internet sites that feature segments such as "Ask the Mufti." Indeed, one of the clearest examples of the struggle for reform, its diverse voices, and the issues involved is the "war of the fatwas." The opinions of prominent religious scholars, or muftis, mainstream and extremist, are circulated and debated globally in the media and via the Internet. Issues include terrorism and suicide bombings, organ transplants, marriage and divorce, abortion, polygamy, the veil (hijab), women in the home and workplace, Sunni–Shii and Muslim–non-Muslim relations, and citizenship and voting, especially that of Muslim minorities in America, Europe, and elsewhere.

CRITICAL AREAS OF ISLAMIC REFORM

Many critical questions and issues are the subject of hot debate in Islam today. Some of the most important include the compatibility of Islam and democracy, the meaning and role of Sharia, the status of women, the relationship of jihad and terrorism, and the rights of non-Muslims.

Islam and Democracy

For years, the question "Are Islam and democracy compatible?" has been raised, and with seemingly good reason. As in many other parts of the world, including the former Soviet Union, Eastern Europe, Latin America, and Africa until recently, the history of the modern Muslim world reveals a majority of authoritarian regimes. The Muslim experience has been one of kings and military and ex-military rulers possessing tenuous legitimacy and propped up by their military and security forces. Only one in four Muslim-majority nations had democratically elected governments. Many have been authoritarian states with democratic facades: parliamentary institutions and political parties that existed at the sufferance of rulers. Where "elections" occurred, they resulted in fairy-tale outcomes. Tunisia's president, **Zine al-Abidine Ben Ali**, won 99.4 percent of the vote in the 1999 presidential elections and 94.5 percent in 2004. In Egypt, **Hosni Mubarak** in 1999 won with 94 percent and in 2005 with 88.6 percent of the vote. Indeed, a majority of Muslim governments control or severely limit opposition political parties and nongovernmental organizations. At the same time, militant Islamic movements have often projected a religious

ISLAM AND DEMOCRACY

A primary example of Islamic reform and its method today is the debate over the relationship of Islam to democracy. Some Muslims reject any discussion of the question, maintaining that Islam has its own system of government. Others believe that Islam and democracy are incompatible, claiming that democracy is based on un-Islamic Western principles and values. Still others reinterpret traditional Islamic concepts like consultation (*shura*) and consensus (*ijma*) of the community to support the adoption of modern forms of political participation or democratization, such as parliamentary elections. Thus, just as it was appropriate in the past for Muhammad's senior Companions to constitute a consultative assembly (*majlis al-shura*) and to select or elect his successor through a process of consultation, Muslims now reinterpret and extend this notion to the creation of modern forms of political participation and government, parliamentary governments, and the direct or indirect election of heads of state. This process is sometimes called "Islamization." Similarly, in legal reform, some Muslims believe that Islam is totally self-sufficient; they demand the imposition of Islamic law and reject any outside influences. Others argue that Islamic law can be reinterpreted today to incorporate new interpretations or formulations of law as well as laws from elsewhere that do not contradict the Quran and Sunnah.

authoritarianism and political intolerance of divergent viewpoints that parallels that of secular authoritarianism.

The absence of democracy in many Muslim countries led many to ask whether this is due to peculiar characteristics of Arab and Muslim culture. Some maintain that Arab culture and/or Islam are inherently authoritarian and thus incompatible with democracy. Others asserted that the introduction of democracy is premature. Still others believe that democracy is a product of the Western experience that may well be inappropriate or nontransferable to other cultures.

Movements for democratization in the Muslim world, in common with other developing societies, have faced serious obstacles: authoritarian governments who rely heavily for their legitimacy and stability upon security forces, economic underdevelopment (chronic unemployment, lack of adequate housing), ethnic and regional strife (often a legacy of the artificial borders created by colonial powers), and weak institutions and infrastructures. Equally important, the U.S. and European democracies, although publically committed to the right of self-determination, democratization, and human rights, have in fact have been allies of authoritarian regimes, providing financial aid, weapons and training to their militaries and security forces. As Richard Haass, a senior State Department official in the George W. Bush administration, acknowledged in a major policy address, both Democratic and Republican administrations had practiced what he termed "Democratic Exceptionalism" in the Muslim world: subordinating democracy to other national interests such as accessing oil, containing the Soviet Union, and grappling with the Arab–Israeli conflict.

Islam, like the world's other major religions, supported empires and monarchies and feudal societies in premodern times. Just as Jews, Christians, and followers of other religions have in modern times debated the merits of democracy and generally moved to accommodate modern forms thereof, many Muslims have done the same. On the one hand, authoritarian regimes in the Muslim world raised questions about the compatibility of Islamic teachings with democracy. On the other, many Muslims wished for greater political participation, the rule of law, government accountability, freedoms, and human rights.

A diversity of Muslim voices has existed, from those who totally embrace democracy to others who reject it as un-Islamic. Secularists argue for the separation of religion and the state. Rejectionists (both moderate and militant Muslims) maintain that Islam's forms of governance are not compatible with democracy, which they regard as a foreign, Western institution that grew out of and reflects the experiences of the West but not of the Muslim world. The late King Fahd of Saudi Arabia maintained that "the democratic system prevalent in the world is not appropriate in this region.... The election system has no place in the Islamic creed, which calls for a government of advice and consultation and for the shepherd's openness to his flock, and holds the ruler fully responsible before his people."[9] However, in response to pressures at home for greater political participation and reform and the growing threat from terrorists, the government eventually introduced limited elections. Extremists condemn any form of democracy as *haram*, forbidden, an idolatrous threat to God's rule (divine sovereignty). Their jihads to topple governments aim to impose an authoritarian "Islamic" rule. Conservatives often argue that Western notions of popular sovereignty contradict the sovereignty of God; some call for the restoration of the caliphate, while others have often accommodated some form of monarchy.

Modern Islamic reformers have reinterpreted key traditional Islamic concepts and institutions to develop Islamic forms of parliamentary governance, representative elections, and religious reform: mutual consultation (shura) of rulers with those ruled, consensus (***ijma***) of the community, reinterpretation (*ijtihad*), and legal principles such as the public welfare (*maslaha*) of society. Just as it was appropriate in the past for Muhammad's senior Companions to constitute a consultative assembly (*majlis al-shura*) and to select or elect his successor (caliph) through a process of consultation, these Muslims now reinterpret and extend this notion to the creation of modern forms of political participation, parliamentary government, and the direct or indirect election of heads of state.

In recent years the call for greater liberalization and democratization has become more common and widespread. Throughout much of the Muslim world, diverse sectors of society, secular and religious, leftist and rightist, educated and uneducated, increasingly use greater political participation or democratization as the litmus test by which to judge the legitimacy of governments and political movements alike. Many have believed that just as the modern democracies of America and Europe accommodate diverse relationships with religion, so too Muslims can develop their own forms of democracy that reflect and are responsive to indigenous values.

Sharia Reform

Whatever Muslim religious and cultural differences exist, the role of Sharia law is a key issue throughout the Muslim world. The rule of thumb employed by many to judge the Islamic commitment and character of Muslim society (and for others its backwardness) has been the presence or absence of Islamic law. Countries as different in degree of modernization and Westernization as Egypt, Sudan, Libya, Afghanistan, Iran, Pakistan, Nigeria, Malaysia, and Mauritania have had to face this issue. Many, out of conviction or political expediency, have declared the Sharia as *the* source of law, even if such a claim has merely amounted to mention of Sharia in a constitutional provision rather than substantive change. Some, like Iran, Pakistan, Libya, Afghanistan, and Sudan, enacted legislation to enforce traditional Islamic penalties for theft, fornication, and adultery or regulations to curb gambling, nightclubs, and alcohol consumption and to censor television and the cinema.

The introduction of Islamic laws has often consisted of a restoration of traditional laws instead of a reinterpretation and reformulation of fresh laws and regulations. This is due primarily to the predominance of conservative and traditional forms of Islam and the continued failure to distinguish adequately between Sharia, God's law in revelation, and *fiqh*, the understanding and elaboration of law by early jurists that produced the corpus of Islamic law.

The real issue in law, as in sociopolitical change in general, is the question of the degree of change possible. How much change in the Islamic

tradition is necessary? How much departure from tradition is legitimate? Conservatives see little need or justification for substantive change.
Although in principle they accept the need for change, they so revere traditional law that they are often reluctant to support substantive changes
and reflexively opt to imitate or follow tradition ("*taqlid* mentality"). The
majority of Muslims tend to share these attitudes, and thus the resurgence
of Islam has often tended to be a process of restoration instead of reform
through the reinterpretation and reformulation of tradition.

What do Muslims want?

Polls confirm that majorities of Muslims want key democratic components
like self-determination, the rule of law, free speech, and a free press and
see these rights as compatible with their faith. Muslims say they admire
freedom and an open political system, but many do not believe they must
choose between Islam and democracy and instead believe that the two can
coexist. Thus, Muslims surveyed in the Gallup World Poll also indicated
widespread support for Sharia.[10] Although majorities of Muslims report
they want Sharia as "*a*" source—but not "*the*" sole source—of legislation,
they differ as to what that might mean: formal constitutional lip service,
a system where no law is contrary to Sharia values, or a situation where a
country's laws are a blend of those derived from Western legal codes and
selected Islamic laws.

Support for Sharia does not mean that Muslims want a theocracy in
their countries. Only a minority in each country say they want religious
leaders to be directly in charge of drafting their country's constitution,
writing national legislation, drafting new laws, determining foreign policy
and international affairs, and deciding how women dress in public or what
is televised or published in newspapers.[11]

Muslim Women Reclaiming Their Rights

Like all of the world's religions, in Islam and Muslim societies patriarchy has played, and in many cases continues to play, an influential role
affecting the status of women. Despite Quranic concerns for women's
rights, their place in the family and society was heavily influenced by
a male-dominated patriarchal structure and values of the societies in
which Islamic law was developed and elaborated. Patriarchy as much as
religion—indeed patriarchy linked to religion—accounts for many customs that became long-standing traditions affecting gender relations. The
primary interpreters of Islam (of the Quran, traditions of the Prophet, and
law) were men functioning in and reflecting patriarchal societies. Thus,
even where there were no clear Quranic texts, Muslim exegetes interpreted

verses of the Quran to justify the customs of veiling and seclusion. These interpretations became so embedded in tradition that they came to be regarded as integral to Islam, although such practices have varied over time and from one region to another. For example, veiling was less common among village women who had to work in the fields and was less visible in Africa and Southeast Asia compared with the Arab world and South Asia. However, any attempt to change these customs has often been dismissed as an attack on an Islamic ideal from those influenced by the West. As Mawdudi argues:

> People have tried their very best to prove that the present form of Purdah was a custom in pre-Islamic communities, and that the Muslims adopted this custom of ignorance long after the time of the Holy Prophet. The question is: Where was the necessity of carrying out this historical research in the presence of a clear verse of the Quran, the established practice of the time of the Holy Prophet, and the explanations given by the Companions and their pupils? Obviously this trouble was taken in order to justify the objective of life prevalent in the West. For without this, it was not possible to advocate the Western concepts of "progress" and "civilization" that have got deeply fixed in the minds.[12]

The record of self-styled Islamic governments in Saudi Arabia, Pakistan, Iran, the Sudan, and Afghanistan and the policies of some Islamic movements that have reinforced women's restricted subordinate status and led to their abuse and exploitation continue to raise serious questions about the status of women in Islam. At the same time, significant changes have occurred in the lives of many Muslim women.

Increasingly, educational and employment opportunities as well as legal reforms and voting rights have improved and broadened women's roles in many societies. In addition to being wives and mothers, Muslim women in many countries play a more prominent role in public life as teachers, lawyers, physicians, heads of state, parliamentarians, and cabinet ministers. Admittedly, these changes vary from one country or region to another and have affected a small proportion of the population in some countries. However, there is strong momentum in women's social and educational development in many Muslim societies.

Majorities of Muslim women reflect a growing desire and call for change and reform in virtually every country in the Gallup World Poll's survey of some thirty-five countries. Majorities of women (as well as men) said that women deserve the same legal rights as men, to vote without influence from family members, to work at any job for which they are qualified, and even to serve in the highest levels of government. In Saudi

WOMEN AND EMPOWERMENT

Muslim women in the twentieth century had two clear choices or models before them: the modern Westernized lifestyle common among an elite minority of women and the more restrictive traditional "Islamic" lifestyle of the majority of women who lived much as their grandmothers and great-grandmothers had lived. The social impact of the Islamic revival produced a third alternative that is both modern and firmly rooted in Islamic faith, identity, and values. Muslim women, modernists, and Islamists have argued on Islamic grounds for an expanded role for women in Muslim societies. Rejecting the idea that Islam itself is patriarchal and distinguishing between revelation and its interpretation by all-male *ulama* in patriarchal settings, Muslim women have reasserted the right to be primary participants in redefining their identity and role in society. In many instances this change has been symbolized by a return to the wearing of Islamic dress or the donning of a headscarf, or hijab. Initially prominent primarily among urban middle-class women, this new mode of dress has become more common among a broader sector of society. For many it is an attempt to combine religious belief and Islamic values of modesty with contemporary freedoms in education and employment, to pair a much-desired process of social change with indigenous Islamic values and ideals. The goal is a more authentic, rather than simply Westernized, modernization.

Arabia, for example, where women are not allowed to vote or drive, majorities of women say that women should be able to drive a car by themselves (61 percent), vote without influence (69 percent), and work at any job they are qualified to fill (76 percent). Egyptian women, who have faced far fewer restrictions than their Saudi counterparts, speak even more strongly in favor of women's rights, with 88 percent of Egyptian women saying that they should be allowed to work at any job for which they qualify. In Egypt, as in other parts of the Muslim world, this attitude is not just a theory, as a full third of professional and technical workers in Egypt are women, on a par with Turkey and South Korea. In the United Arab Emirates and Iran, women make up the majority of university students.[13]

Today, Muslim women have become active participants who are reclaiming their rights in Islam, employing religious principles and mosque participation as a source of empowerment. Reformers emphasize that just as women during the time of the Prophet prayed in the mosque, so too today they must actively exercise that right. In the centuries after the death of Muhammad, women played a significant role as transmitters

A female scholar speaks to a gathering in a Damascus mosque. Islamic history and law includes a long tradition of women as scholars, teachers, and transmitters of *hadith*, which is experiencing a revival in the present day.

Eid Al-Fitr prayers mark the end of the Ramadan month of fasting for Muslims.

of *hadith* (prophetic traditions) and in the development of Sufism (Islamic mysticism). Gradually, however, women's religious role and practice, particularly their access to education and public worship, was severely restricted. Male religious scholars cited a variety of reasons—from the need to protect women from moral degeneration in society to the temptations and social discord women might cause—to restrict their presence in public life, schools, and the mosque.

Increasingly, women globally, from the United States to Malaysia, write, organize, and speak out as individuals and through women's organizations. In contrast to the past, they can now draw on a growing number of female scholars who utilize an Islamic discourse to address women's role in education, employment, political participation, and religion.

In many Muslim countries and communities, women lead and participate in Quran study and recitation groups as well as mosque-based educational and social services. Women serve as prayer leaders (imams) for congregational prayers; although they are currently restricted to leading groups of women, this long-held tradition is being challenged. Some have recently argued that because Islam has no ordained clergy to lead prayer or officiate at weddings, nothing in revelation prohibits women from performing such roles.

On March 18, 2005, Amina Wadud, an American scholar of the Quran and Islamic studies and a Muslim feminist who has taught in Malaysia and the United States, broke a centuries-old Islamic tradition requiring a male to lead the Friday communal prayer. Wadud took this role for herself at a mosque in New York City, with a congregation of more than one hundred men and women. Although it is still uncommon, women have led mixed-gender prayers in the United States, Canada, and elsewhere in the face of objections from other Muslims around the world and even some death threats; a small but growing minority has begun to support Wadud and others in their bold actions.

Wadud's efforts for reform are empowered by a career focused on rereading the Quran to challenge literalist, misogynist laws and policies and achieve legal, political, and social reform. Her central thesis is that prejudice against women is attributable to the Quran's interpreters, not to the Quran itself. Those who believe that men are superior to women have interpreted the Quran based on those assumptions. The problem in modern times, Wadud argues, is not simply patriarchy and the fact that men formulated and developed Islamic law or customs, but the continued influence of patriarchal structures today and their hegemonic presumption of dominance and superiority. Male religious scholars, she says, continue to abuse their power. In *Gender Jihad* she urges, "the proactive inclusion of women's experiences and interpretations is crucial to transforming gender status toward its higher egalitarian potential."[14]

The distinctiveness and radical reformist approach of Amina Wadud contrasts strongly with the traditionalist methodology of Cambridge University's Timothy Winter, an Oxford- and al-Azhar–trained scholar and religious leader. Winter relies on classical or medieval Islam as his primary authoritative reference point. Islamic societies, he maintains, are simultaneously both matriarchal and patriarchal. Men dominate public space; private space is dominated by women, who, he claims, consider their sphere to be of greater importance. Islam's emphasis on a woman's obedience to her husband is complemented or balanced, in Winter's view, by the traditional veneration of mothers.

At the heart of Winter's interpretation of Islam is not just respect for but the "sacralization" of tradition that many modernist reformers warn against. It is epitomized by Winter's belief in the "normative" status of gender relations in traditional Islam. Despite his admission that no Quranic or *hadith* text explicitly prohibits women from leading men in prayer, nevertheless Winter, like many prominent traditionalist religious authorities, still uses the consensus of classical Sunni Islamic law to argue that the imam (leader of the prayer) must be male if men and women are praying together. Winter opposes going back directly to the Quran and Prophetic traditions to derive a ruling that differs from the consensus of early Muslim scholars.[15]

Today, an increasing number of women scholars of the Quran and Islamic sciences represent leading voices of reform. In some countries (Syria, Iran, Turkey, India, Indonesia) they serve as *qadis,* muftis who give fatwas, or as deputies to muftis. Even in the more conservative Saudi Arabia, when women called for appointing female muftis, Sheikh Abdullah Al-Manea, a member of the Council of Senior Islamic Scholars, agreed that the council should consider having women members, commenting, "I don't see anything in Shariah law which prevents women from becoming a scholar, mufti or working in any consultative body."[16]

The continued complexity of women's status is illustrated by many country-specific contradictions. In most Muslim countries (including Iran, Pakistan, Turkey, Indonesia, and Bangladesh), women vote and a woman can run for political office and serve in the parliament or as head of state or vice president.

Although women cannot vote or be elected in Saudi Arabia, Saudi women own 70 percent of the savings in Saudi banks and 61 percent of private firms in the kingdom. They also own much of the real estate in Riyadh and Jeddah and can own and manage their own businesses. However, they are sexually segregated, restricted to "appropriate" professions, and cannot drive cars. In nearby Kuwait, women freely function in society and hold responsible positions in many areas, but, despite getting the right to vote in 2005, by 2009 women had won only four seats in parliamentary elections.

Across the globe, depending on the country, women's basic literacy and education reflect both serious inequality and significant change. On the one hand, in Yemen, women's literacy is anywhere from 26 percent[17] to 47 percent (vs. 81 for men);[18] in Pakistan, the rate is anywhere from 12 percent[19] to 40 percent[20] (vs. 69 percent for men). On the other hand, the women's literacy rate in Iran is 70 percent,[21] the rate in Saudi Arabia is 81 percent,[22] and rates are as high as 89 percent[23] in Jordan and 85 percent[24] in Malaysia. In the United Arab Emirates, as in Iran, the majority of university students are women.

Terrorism

Osama bin Laden and other terrorists transformed Islam's norms about the defense of Islam and Muslims under siege to legitimate the use of violence, warfare, and terrorism. Their theology of hate espouses a bipolar view of a cosmic struggle between the armies of God and of Satan, the forces of good and evil, right and wrong, belief and unbelief. Those who are not with them, Muslim or non-Muslim, are judged to be against them. These extremists have "hijacked" the Islamic concept and institution of jihad in an attempt to lend legitimacy to their acts of violence and terror and their violation of clear regulations in the Quran and Islamic law.

Bin Laden and other terrorists ignore Islamic criteria for a just jihad and recognize no limits but their own. They reject the tenets of Islamic law regarding the goals and means of a valid jihad: that the use of violence must be proportional; that innocent civilians, noncombatants, should not be targeted; and that jihad can be declared only by a ruler or head of state. Today, extremists from Madrid to Mindanao legitimate unholy wars in the name of Islam itself, bypassing the Quranic requirement that authorization for jihad be given by a nation's ruler.

Although bin Laden and al-Qaeda have enjoyed support from a significant minority of Muslims and religious leaders, the majority of Muslims and major Islamic scholars and religious leaders across the Muslim world have roundly condemned the organization's attacks. For example, the Gallup Organization's World Poll found that 91 percent of those interviewed in some thirty-five Muslim countries, representing the voices of

1 billion Muslims, said the 9/11 attacks were morally unjustified; 7 percent said the attacks were completely justified.[25] Reflecting the majority view, other prominent religious leaders have issued authoritative declarations (fatwas) against bin Laden's and other terrorists' initiatives.

As we saw in Chapter 5, denunciations by Muslim scholars and religious leaders like Cambridge University's Timothy Winter and the members of the Islamic Research Council at Egypt's al-Azhar University, regarded by many as the highest moral authority in Islam, reflect the positions of a majority of Muslims, individuals, religious leaders, and organizations globally, who have publically denounced terrorist attacks, both because they believe these acts are contrary to Islam and, not to be forgotten, they have often been the primary victims. Despite this fact, a common and recurring charge for many years has been: Why haven't Muslim leaders condemned 9/11 and Islamic terrorism? The failure of media to cover such statements is offset by the collection and availability of Muslim statements and fatwas condemning terrorist attacks on the Internet.[26]

The struggle for the future of Islam is between competing voices and visions: a dangerous and deadly minority of religious extremists and terrorists, represented by Osama bin Laden and al-Qaeda, and the vast majority of mainstream Muslims, those who wish to restore an idealized and romanticized past and others who press for more substantive and widespread reforms. Although the extremists grab the headlines and threaten Muslim as well as Western societies, the moderate mainstream, like most religious believers, continue to pursue normal everyday lives and goals. The focus on extremists often overshadows the extent to which the current generation of reformers are active in reinterpreting Islam and advocating an Islam that is progressive, pluralistic, and tolerant.

Non-Muslim Minorities

Religious minorities in the Muslim world, in countries where they are constitutionally entitled to equality of citizenship and religious freedom, increasingly fear the erosion of those rights—and with good reason.

Interreligious and intercommunal tensions and conflicts from Nigeria and Egypt and Sudan to Iraq, Afghanistan, Pakistan, Bangladesh, Malaysia, and Indonesia have raised major concerns about deteriorating rights and security for religious minorities in Muslim countries. Conflicts have varied, from acts of discrimination to forms of violence escalating to murder and the destruction of villages, churches, and mosques.

Pakistan's blasphemy laws exemplify the issue. These laws cover a range of "violations/crimes," chief among them defiling the Quran, for which the punishment is imprisonment for life, and defaming Prophet

Mohammed, which is punishable by death. Although no government execution of a person charged with blasphemy has occurred in Pakistan, charges of blasphemy against the Prophet and the desecration of the Quran have often been used against Christians.

On Saturday, August 1, 2009, after several days of rioting and violence over allegations that Christians had desecrated the Quran, an estimated crowd of one thousand stormed a Christian neighborhood in Gojra, Pakistan. The mob killed nine, including six women, and burned and looted dozens of houses. The Human Rights Commission of Pakistan reported that the riots were preplanned, including announcements in some mosques the day before at the Friday congregational prayer. The government and National Assembly were quick to condemn these actions as contrary to Pakistan's constitutional tradition and reiterated Pakistan's commitment to ensure protection of the minorities as equal citizens. Christians and many Muslims called for repealing Pakistan's blasphemy laws.

Another case proved equally explosive. In November 2009 Asia Bibi, a Christian and forty-five-year-old mother of four, was sentenced to death on charges of insulting Islam, a charge she strongly denied. The case sparked international outrage that was heightened in 2011 by the brutal assassination of Salman Taseer, the governor of Punjab and an outspoken critic of the blasphemy law, and the assassination of Pakistani Chief Minister Shahbaz Bhatti, a Christian and outspoken opponent of Pakistan's blasphemy law.

Interreligious and intercommunal tensions and conflicts varying from discrimination, violence, and the destruction of villages, churches, and mosques to murder and slaughter have flared up not only in Pakistan but also in Egypt, Sudan, Nigeria, Iran, Iraq, Malaysia, and Indonesia. In Iran, the Bahai community, whom many of the *ulama* regard as apostates from Islam, have at times been imprisoned and executed and their property seized. Moreover, in Pakistan and Sudan, Muslim groups whose teachings have been regarded as unorthodox have been suppressed. In Pakistan and Indonesia, the Ahmadiyya have been denounced and persecuted as heretics and non-Muslims. Pakistan declared them a non-Muslim minority, and in Indonesia conservative religious groups have used violence and large demonstrations to call for an outright ban on Ahmadiyya. Christians in Iraq and Syria have been under siege—churches burned and Christians killed by militant Iraqi and Syrian militias and ISIS, driving many to flee their countries. Militants often link Christian minorities with the Crusades and European colonialism to recruit followers and justify their barbaric actions.

Muslims today are strongly challenged to move beyond older notions of "tolerance" or "co-existence" to a higher level of religious pluralism based on mutual understanding and respect. Regrettably, a significant minority, like many ultraconservative and fundamentalist Christians, Jews, and Hindus, are not pluralistic but rather strongly exclusivist in their attitudes toward other faiths and even co-believers with whom they disagree.

THE CHALLENGE OF RELIGIOUS PLURALISM

A robust religious pluralism is a prerequisite in our modern globalized world. Most of the great world religions have struggled historically with issues of religious pluralism and tolerance, but the three Abrahamic monotheistic faiths, in particular Christianity and Islam, have had checkered histories. Belief in a special covenant with God, possession of the final revelation, and, for Christians and Muslims, a mandate to spread their faith globally have fostered an attitude of religious triumphalism.

Muslims are challenged to move beyond older notions of tolerance or coexistence to a religious pluralism based on mutual understanding and respect. Regrettably, a significant minority of Muslims, like very conservative and fundamentalist Christians and Jews who strongly affirm their faith, are less pluralistic in their attitudes toward other faiths and Muslim groups with differing interpretatons of Islam. In the twenty-first century, they will need to incorporate an internal pluralism, a generous space in their religious discourse and behavior for alternative opinions and dissenting voices within Islam.

Too often, some who call for greater Islamization in practice engage in a policy of "kafirization," condemning not just followers of other faiths but also Muslims with whom they disagree as unbelievers or infidels. Some practice theological exclusivism and intolerance and remain nonviolent, but others are militant extremists who threaten and commit acts of violence and terror.

A key Islamic issue and debate today regarding pluralism and tolerance is the relationship of past doctrine to current realities. As discussed earlier, Jews and Christians are regarded as "People of the Book" (*dhimmi*), people who have also received a revelation and a scripture from God (the Torah for Jews and the Gospels for Christians), a status that in later centuries was extended to other faiths. To reinforce tolerance, some call for a reinstatement of this "protected" (*dhimmi*) status for non-Muslims. However, although progressive in the past when compared to Christendom, where other forms of Christianity as well as Muslims and Jews were not tolerated,

The Muslim community in America is a rich racial, ethnic, and cultural mosaic of indigenous believers, the majority of whom are African American and immigrant Muslims. Thousands of Muslims from New York's varied ethnic communities pray next to Coney Island's landmark Parachute Jump to celebrate the Feast of Sacrifice (*Id al Adha*). This major religious holiday commemorates God's command to Abraham to sacrifice his son Ismail.

the reassertion of traditional Islamic law's status for non-Muslims today amounts to second-class citizenship for non-Muslims who would not enjoy equality of citizenship or access to senior government and military positions, which are reserved for Muslims.

As with women's status and rights, the tendency to legislate change from above, without adequately addressing traditional norms and values that remain a part of faith and religious history, creates a dichotomy between modern practices and traditional ideals that must be addressed. The unresolved contradictions between the two are like a smoldering fire, barely visible until a strong change in the direction of the wind causes it to ignite and erupt.

Recognizing the power of the Islamic tradition, other reformers maintain that pluralism is the essence of Islam as revealed in the Quran and practiced by Muhammad and the early caliphs, rather than a purely Western invention or ideology. Reformers turn to Quranic texts for this pluralistic vision, pointing out that God deliberately created a world of diversity in which all peoples were to know and understand each other: "O humankind, We have created you male and female and made you nations and tribes, so that you might come to know one another" (49:13).

Emphasis on religious diversity in the human community and support for religious pluralism rather than exclusivism is also found in Quranic texts like: "To everyone we have appointed a way and a course to follow" (5:48) and "For each there is a direction toward which he turns; vie therefore with one another in the performance of good works. Wherever you may be, God shall bring you all together [on the Day of Judgment]. Surely God has power over all things" (2:148).

Thus, Muslims are to recognize and respect the faith of others. Asked the question "Can a person who is Muslim choose a religion other than Islam?" Shaykh Ali Gomaa, the former Grand Mufti of Egypt, responded, "The answer is yes, they can because the Quran says, 'Unto you your religion, and unto me my religion' [Quran, 109:6], and, 'Whosoever will, let him believe, and whosoever will, let him disbelieve' [Quran, 18:29], and, 'There is no compulsion in religion. The right direction is distinct from error' [Quran, 2:256]."[27]

Sarah Joseph, executive editor of *Emel: The Muslim Lifestyle Magazine*, an influential United Kingdom–based magazine circulated in more than thirty countries, offered another perspective on the Quran and religious pluralism in an editorial, "Who Is a muslim vs. a Muslim?" In conducting her Ph.D. research, Joseph discovered and was struck by how "people went from being 'muslim' to being 'Muslim.'" She explains the Quranic distinction between a "muslim," that is, anyone and everyone who surrenders to God, and Muslim, as an institutionalized religious identity, in this way:

> The word Islam comes from the Arabic root s-l-m, meaning to surrender, to give something or someone up. In a religious context, it means to surrender one's life to God. The word Muslim is derived from that. In Arabic, the prefix "mu-" at the beginning of a word often signifies the doer of an action, so "mu-" added to the form "Islam" yields "one who surrenders him/herself to God.
>
> However, we are in a situation [today] where Islam and Muslim are only understood in the institutionalized form. Textbooks describe the proscriptive elements of Islam as an institutionalized religion, the five pillars of Islam, the dress and practice of a Muslim, the do's and don'ts. We are told about Islam the proper noun, but we get no sense of islam the dynamic verb.
>
> Muhammad himself spoke of how he was bringing nothing new; the Qur'an repeatedly asserts that it is a reminder of what was previously revealed. The Qur'an even describes Abraham as a muslim, that is someone who surrendered himself to God as opposed to a member of an institutionalised religion post the 7th century.
>
> God says in the Qur'an, "Behold, the only true religion in the sight of God is man's self-surrender unto Him" (3:19). This was the message of all the prophets from Adam onwards."[28]

Despite the writings and activities of reformers, the backgrounds of the majority of religious leaders and Muslim masses and the Islamic ideology of self-styled Islamic governments and some religious organizations remain very conservative in orientation. Thus, when religious forces gain power (Iran, Sudan, and Afghanistan) or influence (Pakistan) or become more vocal in calling for a more Islamically oriented society, the Islam many advocate is predominantly an Islam of the past, not simply in its revealed principles but often in its derivative prescriptions and forms.

The force of religious conservatism among many *ulama* was evident in Indonesia in 2005, when three hundred members of the Indonesian Ulama Council (MUI) at the end of a four-day international conference issued fatwas that included a ruling declaring liberal thought, secularism, and religious pluralism to be unlawful (a position not unlike that of early twentieth-century popes). Other controversial rulings included a ban on interfaith marriage and one on participating in prayers with people of other faiths. The fatwas were criticized by a number of moderate Muslim leaders, including Azyumardi Azra, rector of the State Islamic University, and M. Syafii Anwar, head of the International Center for Islam and Pluralism, who described the fatwa as a symptom of the MUI's "creeping 'shariazation' of the state."

Acceptance of modern notions of religious pluralism, like opposition to them, will be influenced as much by semantics as by theology. Many very conservative and fundamentalist Muslims as well as their counterparts in Christianity see their faith as the only path to heaven or salvation. Thus, they oppose modern pluralism because they see it as emphasizing that all religions are of equal validity and therefore legitimating conversion to other faiths as well as intermarriage.

As Muslim countries today grapple with issues of religious pluralism, from status and rights of non-Muslims in Muslim countries to Sunni–Shii relations, the swelling numbers of Muslim refugees and the migration of Muslims to Europe, America, Canada, and Australia challenge established notions of pluralism in Western secular societies.

GLOBAL MUSLIM MULTIFAITH AND INTERCIVILIZATIONAL INITIATIVES

The aftermath of 9/11 witnessed an exponential increase in multifaith and intercivilizational initiatives, sponsored by governments, religious leaders, and international organizations, including the World Economic Forum's Council of 100 leaders (C-100), the UN Alliance of Civilizations, the Archbishop of Canterbury's Building Bridges project, the Vatican–al-Azhar dialogue, the Parliament of the World's Religions, and the Organization of the Islamic Conference (OIC). Two especially important initiatives are the Jordanian-sponsored **Amman Message (2004–2005)** and **"A Common Word Between Us and You" (2007)**. Both are examples of unique, broad-based Muslim efforts to mobilize religious leaders globally to counter and delegitimate religious extremism and global terrorism in the name of Islam and to partner with major Christian churches and leaders addressing common threats to global peace and survival.

The Amman Message

Faced with the ongoing threat of al-Qaeda and other terrorist groups, the inflammatory preaching of religious extremists, sectarian warfare, and the lack of a central religious authority in Islam, many ask, "Who speaks for Islam?" For the first time in history, more than five hundred diverse religious leaders and leading Muslim scholars, together representing global Islam, joined together to endorse unanimously an important authoritative statement, the Amman Message.[29] The process began in 2004 when King Abdullah of Jordan sought to address religious extremism and militancy by bringing religious leaders together to develop a statement on the nature of "true Islam," "to declare what Islam is and what it is not, and what actions represent it and what actions do not," emphasizing Islam's core values of compassion, mutual respect, acceptance, and freedom of religion.[30]

The Amman Message rejected extremism as a deviation from Islamic beliefs and affirmed Islam's message of tolerance and humanity as a common ground among different faiths and peoples. Twenty-four senior religious scholars in the Muslim world were asked to answer three key questions: (1) Who is a Muslim?; (2) Is it permissible to declare someone an apostate (*takfir*)?; and (3) Who has the right to issue fatwas? The opinions of these scholars then became the basis in July 2005 of a major international Islamic conference of two hundred Muslim scholars from more than fifty countries. Based on fatwas provided by three of the most senior Sunni and Shii religious authorities, among them Sheikh Muhammad Sayyid Tantawi of al-Azhar University, Iraq's Grand Ayatollah Ali al-Sistani, and Yusuf Qaradawi, scholars addressed intra-Muslim conflict and violence and worked to delegitimate extremists who issue fatwas to justify their agendas. Participants issued a final declaration that did the following:

- Emphasized the underlying unity and validity of the three major branches of Sunni, Shia, and Ibadi Islam and agreed on a precise definition of a Muslim: anyone who recognizes and follows one of the eight law schools of Sunni, Shia, and Ibadi Islam (the latter being the dominant form of Islam in Oman).
- Forbade any declarations of excommunication or apostasy (*takfir*) between Muslims.
- Delineated the conditions for a valid fatwa: No one may issue a fatwa without the requisite personal qualifications that each school of Islamic jurisprudence determines for its adherents and without adhering to the prescribed methodology of the schools of Islamic jurisprudence.

These guidelines were unanimously adopted in December 2005 by the Organization of the Islamic Conference, which represents the political leadership of fifty-seven Muslim-majority countries, and in July 2006 by six other international Islamic scholarly assemblies, including the International Islamic Fiqh (Jurisprudence) Academy of Jeddah.

"A Common Word"

"A Common Word Between Us and You," an open letter initially signed by some 138 prominent Muslim religious leaders, academics, intellectuals, government ministers, and authors from across the world, was sent in 2007 to the heads of the world's major Christian churches. The purpose and heart of their message was this:

> Muslims and Christians together make up well over half of the world's population. Without peace and justice between these two religious communities, there can be no meaningful peace in the world. The future of the world depends on peace between Muslims and Christians.
>
> The basis for this peace and understanding already exists. It is part of the very foundational principles of both faiths: love of the One God, and love of the neighbour. These principles are found over and over again in the sacred texts of Islam and Christianity. The Unity of God, the necessity of love for Him, and the necessity of love of the neighbour is thus the common ground between Islam and Christianity.

Thus, the writers maintain, the relationship between these two religious communities cannot be overemphasized:

> With the terrible weaponry of the modern world; with Muslims and Christians intertwined everywhere as never before, no side can unilaterally win a conflict between more than half of the world's inhabitants. Thus our common future is at stake. The very survival of the world itself is perhaps at stake ....[31]

The response to "A Common Word" from Christian leaders and scholars was immediate and global. Pope Benedict XVI, the Archbishop of Canterbury, Orthodox Patriarch Alexei II of Russia, the presiding bishop of the Lutheran World Federation, and many others acknowledged its importance, as did a multitude of individuals and groups that posted comments and criticisms on the official website of "A Common Word."[32] More than three hundred leading American mainline and evangelical leaders and scholars responded in an open letter endorsing the statement, "Loving God and Neighbor Together," published in the *New York Times* and elsewhere. The number of Muslim leaders and scholars who signed the initiative increased from the original 138 to more than 300, with more than 460 Islamic organizations and associations also endorsing it.

As a follow-up to the letter, international conferences of religious leaders, scholars, and nongovernmental organizations took place at Yale, Cambridge, and Georgetown Universities, as well as at the Vatican, to explore the theological, biblical, and social implications of this initiative. The conferences at Yale and Cambridge and the Vatican brought together global religious leaders and academic experts who explored the theological and scriptural bases and implications of the foundation of "A Common Word," the two great commandments. The Georgetown conference, "A Common Word: A Global Agenda for Change," addressed these questions: How do we respond to and put "Love of Neighbor" into action to address the many shared challenges and threats we face in our world? How do we transform a common word into common works? The networks established among these diverse leaders have strengthened the continuation of their work and collaboration.

THE CHALLENGE OF PLURALISM FOR WESTERN SECULAR DEMOCRACIES

If some have questioned whether Islam and Muslims can accommodate other faiths, the challenge to American liberalism and pluralism, long accustomed to think of itself as Judeo-Christian or secular, is to broaden the borders of its pluralism to include large numbers of Muslims, Hindus, Buddhists, and Sikhs. The realities of globalization and immigration and the influx of new national, ethnic, and religious groups all challenge accepted notions of modern religious and cultural pluralism in the West. Although immigrants need to accept primary responsibility for making their own way, new homelands are equally responsible for providing the institutional structures and the educational and employment opportunities that immigrants need to advance and become part of the dominant culture.

Like other immigrants before them, Muslims in the West are looking for a level playing field; to have the same rights, duties, and opportunities; and to be judged by the same standards as their fellow citizens. Despite the fact that Islam is the third largest religion in America, that Muslims have lived in America for decades, and that they are making significant progress in their economic and educational status today, they continue to face serious problems.

Although prejudice toward and discrimination against Muslims on the basis of their religion or religious identity (**Islamophobia**) is ascribed to fallout from 9/11, in fact the decades before 9/11, the 1980s and 1990s, actually set the stage for an exponential increase in anti-Muslim discourse and behavior.

Political events in the Muslim world and the West, as well as statements by government leaders, policymakers, and commentators in the media perpetuated notions of a global Islamic threat and a clash of civilizations. Magazine and newspaper articles and editorials spoke of Islam's war with the West and its incompatibility with democracy. Islam was painted as a triple threat: political, civilizational, and demographic.

Belief in an impending "clash of civilizations" between the Muslim world and the West was reflected in American and European media headlines and television programs such as "A Holy War Heads Our Way," "Jihad in America," "Focus: Islamic Terror: Global Suicide Squad," "I Believe in Islamophobia," and "Don't Look for Moderates in the Islamist Revolution."[33]

9/11 and Media Impact on Popular Culture

The 9/11 attacks on the World Trade Center and the Pentagon by al-Qaeda in the United States and terrorist attacks in Europe (London, Madrid, Glasgow) and Bali, Indonesia, precipitated what the came to be called the "Global War on Terrorism" leveled against Osama bin Laden and al-Qaeda and other terrorist groups. A significant side effect was an exponential growth in Islamophobia. Mainstream Islam and Muslims were brush-stroked by the atrocities committed by a dangerous and deadly minority of terrorists and often demonized as the radical "other" in media: in political commentary and cartoons, movie and TV villains, and anti-Muslim social media websites and diatribes.

Far right political and religious commentators asserted with impunity what would never appear in mainstream broadcasts or print media regarding American Jews, Christians and established ethnic groups.

Conservative columnists like Ann Coulter declared: "We should invade their countries, kill their leaders and convert them to Christianity."[34] Michael Savage ranted: "I think these people [Arabs and Muslims] need to be forcibly converted to Christianity.... It's the only thing that can probably turn them into human beings." [35]

Daniel Pipes charged: "The Muslim population in this country is not like any other group, for it includes within it a substantial body of people—many times more numerous than the agents of Osama bin Ladin—who share with the suicide hijackers a hatred of the United States and the desire, ultimately, to transform it into a nation living under the strictures of militant Islam."[36] Rush Limbaugh, reacting to criticism of the abuse of Iraqi prisoners at Abu Ghraib, commented, "They're the ones who are sick.... They're the ones who are perverted. They are the ones who are dangerous. They are the ones who are subhuman. They are the ones who are human debris, not the United States of America and not our soldiers and not our prison guards."[37]

Religious Leaders

President Bush, in his September 20, 2001, Presidential Address to the Nation, drew a sharp distinction between Islam and Muslim extremists: "The terrorists practice a fringe form of Islamic extremism that has been rejected by Muslim scholars and the vast majority of Muslim clerics; a fringe movement that perverts the peaceful teachings of Islam." However, his distinction has often been overshadowed by statements by prominent members of the American administration, Congress, the U.S. military, and especially by leaders of the hardline Christian Right. For example, Franklin Graham maintains: "Islam has attacked us.... The God of Islam is not the same God.... Islam is a very evil religion." Pat Robertson says: "This man [Muhammad] was an absolute wild-eyed fanatic. He was a robber and a brigand. And to say that these terrorists distort Islam, they're carrying out Islam...." And Jerry Falwell referred to the Prophet Muhammad as a "terrorist" on the CBS news program *60 Minutes*.

In the immediate months following the 9/11 attacks, nearly 60 percent of the American population expressed that they had a generally favorable opinion of Muslims and Islam. However, by 2004 the climate had deteriorated to such an extent that Kofi Annan, then Secretary General of the United Nations, called a 2004 UN conference, "Confronting Islamophobia: Education for Tolerance and Understanding," Annan signaled the international scope of the problem:

> "[when] the world is compelled to coin a new term to take account of increasingly widespread bigotry — that it is a sad and troubling development. Such is the case with 'Islamophobia'.... Since the September 11 attacks on the United States, many Muslims, particularly in the West, have found themselves the objects of suspicion, harassment and discrimination.... Too many people see Islam as a monolith and as intrinsically opposed to the West . [38]

The conference and Annan's warning received little attention in the media.

By 2006, a *Washington Post*/ABC News poll found that nearly 46 percent of Americans expressed a negative view of Islam. A 2006 *USA*

Today–Gallup Poll found that substantial minorities of Americans admitted to having negative feelings about or prejudices against Muslims. Fewer than half of the respondents believed U.S. Muslims were loyal to the United States. Nearly one quarter of Americans, 22 percent, said they would not like to have a Muslim as a neighbor; 31 percent said they would feel nervous if they noticed a Muslim man on their flight, and 18 percent said they would feel nervous if they noticed a Muslim woman on the flight. About four in ten Americans favored more rigorous security measures for Muslims than those used for other U.S. citizens—requiring Muslims who are U.S. citizens to carry a special ID and undergo more intensive security checks before boarding airplanes in the United States. The impact and influence of anti-Muslim bias could also be seen in American elections, media commentary, the rhetoric of hardline Christian Zionist preachers, the Park 51 ("so-called building of a mosque at Ground Zero), and country-wide anti-mosque and anti-shariah actions as well as the fact that by 2011, one decade after the 9/11 attacks, 59 percent expressed a negative view of Islam.

Presidential elections in 2008 and 2012 as well as the 2010 congressional elections reflect the politicization of Islamophobia and its impact in American politics. In the 2008 presidential campaign "The Muslim Problem" surfaced as an issue for both Barack Obama and John McCain, the Republican candidate. "I am not a Muslim." "I am not a Muslim." "I am not a Muslim." During the U.S. presidential election of 2008, it was difficult to count the number of times Barack Obama or his campaigners believed it necessary to reassure the American electorate that the Democratic candidate for president was not a Muslim. Although an avowed and practicing Christian, Obama's Muslim name (Barack Hussein), his Kenyan nonpracticing Muslim father, and his two-year attendance at a Muslim school while his mother lived in Indonesia fed intense rumors among those who wished to derail his candidacy that Obama was a Muslim.

When President Obama visited Dearborn, Michigan, in the 2008 presidential campaign, his people avoided his being photographed with young women wearing a hijab by asking them to move out of the picture. Throughout his presidency, Mr. Obama has avoided visits to a mosque in America or being photographed near a mosque. This situation was exacerbated by persistent rumors and growing beliefs that the president was a Muslim. In March 2008, a survey conducted by Pew Research Center found that 10 percent of respondents believed the rumors. By August 2010 the number climbed to 18 percent of Americans and 30 percent of Republicans; by 2012, the Pew Research Center still reported that more than one in seven Americans (including one third of conservative Republicans) believed Obama was a Muslim.

In contrast to his 2004 bid for the presidency, in 2008 Republican candidate John McCain, who had avoided the Christian Right, now aggressively sought their votes. McCain received endorsements from Ron Parsley and John Hagee, prominent televangelists and hardline Christian Zionists who believed that the establishment of the State of Israel in 1948 and the return or "restoration" of the Jews to the Holy Land are a prerequisite for the Second Coming of Jesus Christ, rooted in Biblical prophecies. Parsley and Hagee, like Falwell and Robertson, take a hardline Zionist position, welcomed by Israeli leaders from Menachem Begin to Ariel Sharon and Benjamin Netanyahu.

Rev. Ron Parsley, leader of a twelve-thousand-member megachurch and hailed as John McCain's spiritual adviser and strong supporter in the Ohio primary, devoted an entire chapter in his 2005 book *Silent No More* to warning of a "war between Islam and Christian civilization." Parsley identified Islam as an "anti-Christ religion" predicated on "deception" and said Muhammad "received revelations from demons and not from the true God." Parsley makes no distinction between violent Muslim extremists and mainstream Muslims, believes that Islam "inspired" the 9/11 attacks, and urges us to see Islam as a "faith that fully intends to conquer the world."[39]

Rev. John Hagee, also a strong supporter of McCain, broadcasts on television and radio in over 190 nations around the globe. In February 2006, he and four hundred Christian and Jewish leaders formed Christians United for Israel (CUFI), an organization that addresses Congress, regarding the biblical justification for the defense of Israel. Hagee warned his followers: "Jihad has come to America. If we lose the war to Islamic fascism, it will change the world as we know it…. [A]bout 200 million Islamics believe they have a command from God to kill Christians and Jews. This is a religious war."[40] When informed of Hagee's extreme statements about Islam, McCain initially refused to disassociate himself from this pastor. It was only after Hagee's past anti-Catholic comments—that Adolf Hitler built on the work of the "Roman Church," which he called "the Great Whore of Babylon"—were revealed that McCain finally severed his ties.[41]

Many in the Republican Party seemed undisturbed by the offensive campaigns of rumors that Obama was in fact a Muslim to discredit him. As Colin Powell observed: "I have heard senior members of my own party drop the suggestion, 'He's a Muslim and he might be associated with terrorists.' … This is not the way we should be doing it in America." Perhaps

Powell's most compelling remarks came from his story about American Muslims not often seen in the media:

> I feel strongly about this particular point because of a picture I saw in a magazine. It was a photo essay about troops who are serving in Iraq and Afghanistan. And one picture at the tail end of this photo essay was of a mother in Arlington Cemetery, and she had her head on the headstone of her son's grave. And as the picture focused in, you could see the writing on the headstone. And it gave his awards—Purple Heart, Bronze Star—showed that he died in Iraq, gave his date of birth, date of death. He was 20 years old. And then, at the very top of the headstone, it didn't have a Christian cross, it didn't have the Star of David, it had crescent and a star of the Islamic faith. And his name was Kareem Rashad Sultan Khan, and he was an American. He was born in New Jersey. He was 14 years old at the time of 9/11, and he waited until he can go serve his country, and he gave his life. Now, we have got to stop polarizing ourselves in this way. And John McCain is as nondiscriminatory as anyone I know. But I'm troubled about the fact that, within the party, we have these kinds of expressions.[42]

Four years later, not surprisingly, Islam remained an issue in the 2012 presidential campaign. More than one in seven Americans (including one third of conservative Republicans) believed Obama was a Muslim. Major Republican candidates (Newt Gingrich, Michele Bachman, Rick Santorum, and Herman Cain) espoused positions such as questioning the loyalty of Muslims to America, asking whether a Muslim could serve in the cabinet, or urging the banning of Sharia law.

Park 51: The Mosque at Ground Zero

In contrast to Europe, where the term "Islamophobia" had been used in countries like Britain to identify anti-Islam and anti-Muslim bias, this prejudice was never labeled in the United States until the 2010 "Park 51" controversy. In August 2010, *Time* magazine was the first publication to release a cover story asking: "Is America Islamophobic?" A poll that accompanied the issue found that 28 percent of voters did not believe that Muslims should be eligible to sit on the U.S. Supreme Court, and nearly one-third believed that Muslims should be barred from running for president.

What was this controversy all about? Plans to build a Muslim community center, Park 51, which would be much like the Jewish Community Center in Manhattan whose facility and programs serve the broader community, had been approved by New York officials and not been a major issue. However, in the summer of 2010 Robert Spencer and Pam Geller mobilized media and led large public protests, which drew participants from other states, opposing what they called the "Mosque at Ground Zero," despite the fact that the planned center was not a mosque and was not located at Ground Zero but rather in the broader vicinity. The protests drew national media attention. Spencer and Geller were the creators of the "Freedom Defense Initiative" and "Stop Islamization of America," organizations that have been labeled "hate groups" by U.K. government officials, and had also run websites including "Jihad Watch" and "Islamization of America." Spencer, who has no academic credentials in Islamic studies, has written books such as *The Truth about Muhammad: Founder of the World's Most Intolerant Religion, Did Muhammad Exist?, Obama and Islam*, and *Not Peace but the Sword: The Chasm between Christianity and Islam*. He and American anti-Muslim blogger Geller co-authored *The Post-American Presidency: The Obama Administration's War on America* in 2010. On November 22, 2010, Geller posted the following on her Atlas Shrugs website: "Jihadist Developers of Ground Zero Mosque Hit Up 9/11 Fund to Rebuild Lower Manhattan for $5 Million Jizya to Erect Islamic Supremacist Mega-Mosque." In 2013 both Spencer and Geller were barred from entering the United Kingdom by a Home Office identifying them as leaders of "anti-Muslim hate groups."

Charges that Park 51 was a "monument to terrorism" and a "command center for terrorists" unleashed a tsunami-like wave of anti-mosque activities extending from New York to California. Efforts to erect mosques across America were met with a fierce backlash; standing mosques were defaced, desecrated, and vandalized in Connecticut, New York, Wisconsin, Texas, California, and many other cities throughout the United States. According to a report from the Pew Center on Public Life and Religion, municipalities and city councils have consistently blocked the building of new mosques.[43] In addition, anti-Sharia, sometimes referred to as anti-foreign legislation, has been introduced in some twenty-nine states despite the fact that there has been no significant attempt to introduce Sharia in America and in fact it is impossible to do so under the American Constitution.

The Role of Media

Media focus on "headline events," which often emphasize the negative, sensational, and violent coverage of Islam and Muslims, is compounded by a robust network of far right and Islamophobic websites. A major study by Media Tenor, "A New Era for Arab-Western Relations,"[44] found that out of nearly 975,000 news stories from U.S. and European media outlets, networks have tended to reduce coverage on events in the

Middle East and North Africa region (MENA) to actions of Muslim militants. Audiences of BBC, ABC, and CBS were not presented with nuanced pictures of Muslims as nonmilitants or nonextremists. A comparison of media coverage in 2001 versus 2011 demonstrates the problem. In 2001, 2 percent of all news stories in Western media presented images of Muslim militants, while just over 0.1 percent presented stories of ordinary Muslims. In 2011, 25 percent of the stories presented militant image, while again 0.1 percent presented images of ordinary Muslims. The net result is an astonishing imbalance of coverage: a significant increase in news of militants but no increase at all over ten years in news about ordinary Muslims.

Social Media and Popular Culture

In recent years, the Internet has emerged as a major source for information and opinion, and therefore a primary instrument in shaping popular culture. Unfortunately, the Internet has also become a primary platform for the spread of sites and bloggers promoting coordinated campaigns of misinformation that into popular media and from there into popular culture. Two major studies demonstrate the magnitude of financial resources supporting these websites and narratives. In 2011, using information based on IRS returns, the Center for American Progress conducted a study called Fear Inc., which documented that during a ten-year period $42.6 million flowed from seven major foundations to Islamophobic authors and websites. A second study by the Council on American-Islamic Relations (CAIR), also based on IRS returns, showed that between 2008 and 2011, $119,662,000 in total revenue was given to U.S.-based Islamophobic networks. Islamophobia has many dire implications. The Norwegian terrorist Anders Breivik, responsible for murdering 77 people, mostly teenagers at a youth camp, cited many of these Islamophobic writers and websites 112 times to justify the hatred described in his Manifesto, which describes his worldview encompassing Islamophobia and support for "far-right" **Zionism**.

CONCLUSION

Today, as throughout its history, the study of Islam encompasses the interaction of religion, history, and politics as Muslims struggle to define their faith and identity in the modern world. Like followers of other faiths, Muslims are engaged in an ongoing debate over religious reform influenced by diverse readings of sacred texts, history, and traditions. Integral to debates over reform is the degree to which differing groups recognize that normative Islamic laws and theologies, espoused in a particular time and place, are often time-bound, not timeless, and are the product of human interpreters and their contexts.[45] The diversity found in the schools and manuals of Islamic law reflects the influence of reason, differing cultural contexts, and changes in the history of the community. So today, traditional beliefs, practices, and institutions take on new meanings in the teachings of even those who regard themselves as the most orthodox of believers.

Many Muslims have been disillusioned by the abuses or manipulation of religion by some governments and radical organizations. At the same time, majorities of Muslims believe that religion is a very important part of their lives, essential for the future progress of their societies. The influence of religion continues to inform broad-based socio-religious movements, functioning today within virtually every Muslim country and internationally. These movements are rooted in the Quranic command to summon (*dawa*, call) Muslims to follow God's Will and to invite non-Muslims, through preaching and mission, to Islam.

When comparing the struggle for reform in the Muslim world with that of the West, it is important to remember that Western processes of modernization developed over a period of several centuries. The establishment of modern states, the creation of a sense of national identity and political legitimacy, and the development of appropriate economic and social institutions took time and experimentation. This process was accompanied by heated debates, riots, and revolutions (American, French, and Russian). Similarly, the accommodation of religion and modernity (religion and science, revelation and reason) and the resolution of issues of modernization (democracy and pluralism, women in religion and society, changing family, sexual, corporate, and medical ethics) continue to challenge the faith and unity of modern Judeo-Christian communities. Questions of identity and the relationship of religion to politics, society, and culture remain important hot-button issues in the West today.

In contrast to the West's more gradual and often bottom-up process of modernization, in the Muslim world this process has not been organic and long-term. It was originally imposed by colonial regimes and then by Westernized elites who were often out of touch with their own societies in the postindependence period. The legacy of European colonialism and the political and economic realities of the post–World War II independence period hampered and often undermined the process of self-determination in many parts of the Muslim world. Muslims have had only decades, rather than the several centuries enjoyed by the West, to cope with the religious and social challenges of modernity. The pace of reform has been slow in many countries and societies dominated by authoritarian regimes, entrenched elites, and a global politics in which Western governments, despite their democratic principles and values, are often willing to support autocrats to protect their own national interests.

An Islamic revolution is occurring in many parts of the Muslim world. Its most significant and pervasive aspect is not global terrorism but Islamic reform, led by religious leaders, preachers, scholars, and other professionals (teachers, doctors, lawyers, dentists) rather than warriors. The battle is one of the pen, tongue, and heart rather than the sword, a broad-based religiosocial revolution that is affecting many societies and communities. The violent actions, explosive headline events, of a dangerous minority should not obscure the lives and activities of most Muslims today.

In divergent ways, the majority of Muslims continue to grapple with the task of defining (or redefining) more clearly a framework of meaning within which they can understand, interpret, and respond to today's world. For many, being a Muslim means greater awareness and observance of their faith in diverse ways: study of the Quran, prayer, fasting, dress, and Sufism. For others, a greater affirmation of Islam in personal and community life implies that Islam knows no clear separation of the sacred and profane, the spiritual and the mundane. They believe that the

In 1934, immigrants in Cedar Rapids, Iowa, built the first permanent structure in the United States to serve as a mosque. In 1990, the mosque was restored as shown here.

restoration of Islam to its rightful place in Muslim life requires bridging the secular gap between religion and society, through political action and social action to persuade, pressure, or coerce the political and religious establishments to comply.

Muslims face a period of reexamination, reformation, and renewal similar to the Protestant Reformation or Vatican II in Roman Catholicism, although the path of Islamic reform must be indigenously rooted. Religious, like political, reform is revolutionary. The Protestant Reformation was not simply a theological movement influenced by or a product of the Enlightenment but also led to an extended period of bloody religious wars (1516–1750). The line between orthodoxy and heresy, belief and unbelief depended on the religious community or church to which one belonged. Thus, for Roman Catholics, celebrated Protestant reformers like Luther, Calvin, and Wesley were heretics. Similarly, Islamic reform not surprisingly is and will be a process not only of intellectual or theological reinterpretation but also of religious differences and debate as well as political unrest and violence.

As the history of Islam has shown, belief in one God, one final revelation, and one final Prophet has been the basis for a strong, vibrant monotheistic faith. The unity of Islam, from its early formation to contemporary developments, has encompassed a diversity of interpretations and expressions of faith. However, as in Judaism and Christianity, monotheistic has not meant monolithic, and unity has not precluded diversity. Today, the lives of one-fourth of the world's population testify to the dynamism but also the struggle of Islam and the continued commitment of Muslims to follow "the straight path, the way of God, to whom belongs all that is in the heavens and all that is on earth" (Quran 42:52–53).

KEY TERMS

"A Common Word Between Us
　and You"
Amman Message
Fethullah Gulen
Hizmet Movement
Hosni Mubarak
ijma
ijtihad
Islamophobia

madrasas
Nahdatul Ulama
Salafi Muslims
taqlid
Tariq Ramadan
Wahhabi Muslims
Abdurrahman Wahid (d. 2009)
Zine al-Abidine Ben Ali

QUESTIONS

1. In today's Islam, who has the authority to interpret or narrate the tradition?

2. Describe and differentiate between the three religiously oriented positions that advocate a return to Islam in the twenty-first century.

3. Western critiques of Islamic values often boil down to the rights of women and religious minorities living in Muslim-majority societies. How is this issue being contested in the twenty-first century?

4. Describe the Amman Message and the broader push toward Islamic ecumenism. Is interfaith or intra-faith concord more important to the future of Islam?

5. Is Islam compatible with democratic pluralism? If so, how does this look in a specifically Islamic context? If not, does the tradition contain the resources for another form of multiculturalism?

6. What have the Arab Spring and Arab Winter done to influence the future trajectory of Islamism?

NOTES

1. Mujiburrahman, "Islam and Politics in Indonesia: The Political Thought of Abdurrahman Wahid," *Islam and Christian-Muslim Relations* 10, no. 3 (1999): 342.
2. "Islam in Indonesia: Where to?" *Inside Indonesia* (October 8, 1986): 3.
3. "Yes, I have enemies. But it is important that I do the right things." *Business Times (Singapore)*, March 24, 1999.
4. David Hardacker, "Amr Khaled: Islam's Billy Graham," *Independent* (January 4, 2006): http://news.independent.co.uk/world/middle_east/article336386.ece.
5. Alan Sipress, "Indonesian Cleric's Media Empire" *Washington Post* ,June 2, 2004.
6. Shahed Amanullah, "Post–Feng Shui: Muslim Scholar Now a Management Guru," (April 7, 2002): http://www.altmuslim.com/perm.php? id¼262_0_26_30_C28.
7. Sharmeen Obaid-Chinoy, "Islamic School for Women: Faithful or Fundamental?" *Globe and Mail* (October 29, 2005); "Al-Huda at a Glance," Al-Huda International, 2005: http://www.alhudapk.com//home/about-us.
8. "[Tariqas] Samina Ibrahim's Interview of Dr. Farhat Hashmi," *Newsline* (February 2001): http://stderr.org/pipermail/tariqas/2001-May/000581.html.
9. *Mideast Mirror*, March 30, 1992, p. 12.
10. John L. Esposito and Dalia Mogahed, *Who Speaks for Islam?* (Washington, DC: Gallup Press, 2008), chap. 4.
11. Ibid., p. 93.
12. Abul Ala Mawdudi, *Purdah and the Status of Women in Islam*, al-Ashari, trans. and ed. (Lahore, Pakistan: Islamic Publications, 1972), pp. 200–1.
13. *Who Speaks for Islam?*, p. 103.
14. Amina Wadud, *Gender Jihad* (Oxford, UK: Oneworld Publications, 2006), p. 17.

15. Timothy Winter, "Islam, Irigaray, and the Retrieval of Gender," April 1999. http://www.masud.co.uk/ISLAM/ahm/gender.htm
16. "Saudi Arabia: Calls to Enroll Women in Council of Scholars," *Arab News* (February 8, 2008): http://www.7cgen.com/lofiversion/index.php?t26307.html.
17. "Adult and Youth Literacy, 1990-2015," *UNESCO Institute for Statistics*, 2012: http://www.uis.unesco.org/literacy/Documents/UIS-literacy-statistics-1990-2015-en.pdf, p 6.
18. "Literacy" *The World Factbook*, Central Intelligence Agency: https://www.cia.gov/library/publications/the-world-factbook/fields/2103.html 2010 est.
19. Aamir Latif, "Alarming situation of education in Pakistan," UNESCO: http://www.unesco.org/education/efa/know_sharing/grassroots_stories/pakistan_2.shtml.
20. "Literacy," *The World Factbook*, Central Intelligence Agency: https://www.cia.gov/library/publications/the-world-factbook/fields/2103.html2009 est.
21. "Literacy," *The World Factbook*, Central Intelligence Agency: https://www.cia.gov/library/publications/the-world-factbook/fields/2103.html 2002 est.
22. "Literacy," *The World Factbook*, Central Intelligence Agency: https://www.cia.gov/library/publications/the-world-factbook/fields/2103.html2010 est.
23. "Literacy," *The World Factbook*, Central Intelligence Agency: https://www.cia.gov/library/publications/the-world-factbook/fields/2103.html2010 est.
24. "Literacy," *The World Factbook*, Central Intelligence Agency: https://www.cia.gov/library/publications/the-world-factbook/fields/2103.html 2000 est.
25. *Who Speaks for Islam?*, p. 69
26. http://www.unc.edu/~kurzman/terror.htm; http://www.beliefnet.com/story/111/story_11121_1.html; http://theamericanmuslim.org/tam.php/features/articles/muslim_voices_against_extremism_terrorism_part_ii_statements_by_organizatio/0012210.
27. Ali Gomaa, Written response to series of questions author posed to him (January 14, 2008).
28. Sarah Joseph, ed., "Text Book Islam," *EMEL Magazine* 46 (July 2008): 7.
29. The Amman Message, 2007: http://ammanmessage.com/index.php?option=com_content&task=view&id=16&Itemid=30.
30. Gallup poll, 2007. See also, Lydia Saad, "Anti-Muslim Sentiments Fairly Commonplace," *Gallup*, August 10, 2006: http://www.gallup.com/poll/24073/AntiMuslim-Sentiments-Fairly-Commonplace.aspx.
31. "A CommonWord between Us and You," October 10, 2007: "A CommonWord"official Web site, http://www.acommonword.com/index.php?lang¼en&page¼option1.
32. Gallup poll, 2007. See also, Lydia Saad, "Anti-Muslim Sentiments Fairly Commonplace," *Gallup*, August 10, 2006: http://www.gallup.com/poll/24073/AntiMuslim-Sentiments-Fairly-Commonplace.aspx.
33. Peter Rodman, "Don't Look for Moderates in the Islamic Revolution," *International Herald Tribune*, January 4, 1995.
34. Ann Coulter, "This Is War," National Review Online, September 13, 2001: http://national.review.com/coulter/coulter/091301.shtml.
35. On his radio show, "The Savage Nation," 5/12/03.
36. "The Islamic States of America?" by Daniel Pipes, FrontPageMagazine.com, September 23, 2004.
37. http://www.rushlimbaugh.com/daily/2004/05/12/what_i_saw_was_unspeakable
38. Kofi Annan, Conference on Islamophobia, December 4, 2007: http://www.un.org/press/en/2004/sgsm9637.doc.htm

39. David Corn, "McCain's Spiritual Adviser: Destroy Islam," *Mother Jones*, March 12, 2008: http://www.motherjones.com/washington_dispatch/2008/03/john-mccain-rod-parsley-spiritual-guide.html. See also Rod Parsley, *Silent No More* (Lake Mary, FL: Charisma House, 2005), p. 96.

40. Ron Brown, "John Hagee Warns against Radical Islam," *The News and Advance*, September 3, 2006: http://www.religionnewsblog.com/15816/john-hagee-warns-against-radical-islam.

41. Jeff Greenfield, "McCain Faces Fire over Minister's Views: Presumptive GOP Nominee Faces Questions over Rev. John Hagee's Provocative Preachings," February 29, 2008: http://www.cbsnews.com/news/mccain-faces-fire-over-ministers-views/.

42. http://www.pewforum.org/files/2012/09/2012Mosque-Map.pdf.

43. *Meet the Press* transcript for October 19, 2009: http://www.msnbc.msn.com/id/27266223/page/2/.

44. Media Analysis by Media Tenor International, Presented at Arab League Conference, April 6, 2011, Cairo, Egypt.

45. Dale F. Eickelman, "The Study of Islam in Local Contexts," *Asian Studies* 17 (1982): 12.

Timeline

c. 570–632 Prophet Muhammad

c. 595 Muhammad marries Khadija, his first and only wife until her death and mother of his four daughters, Zaynab, Ruqayya, Umm Kulthum, and Fatima, and two sons who died in infancy, al-Qasim and Abd Allah

610 Muhammad receives call to prophethood through first revelation of the Quran, continues to receive prophecies for twenty-two years; Khadija is first to believe in Muhammad's prophethood, becoming first convert to Islam

613 Muhammad begins public preaching in Mecca; first emigration of Muslims to Abyssinia, although Muhammad remains in Mecca to continue preaching against polytheists

619 Deaths of Muhammad's wife, Khadija, and uncle, Abu Talib, leaving Muhammad without a protector; Muhammad tries to leave Mecca

622 Migration (*hijra*) of early Muslims to Medina; Islam takes form of political state; first year of Islamic calendar

623 Muhammad marries Aisha, his favorite wife, daughter of first caliph, Abu Bakr, and exemplary female figure for Muslims

622–3 Series of compacts among Muslims, Jews, and Christians in the Arabian Peninsula, examples of treaty relations establishing interfaith cooperation and peaceful coexistence

624 Battle of Badr: Muslims outnumbered, but victorious; serves as symbol for Muslims of divine intervention and guidance

625 Battle of Uhud: Muhammad and Muslims attacked and defeated by Meccans

626–80 Husayn ibn Ali, son of Ali and Fatima, grandson of Muhammad and third Shii imam

627 Battle of the Trench/Ditch: Muhammad and Muslims victorious over Meccans and Bedouin mercenaries; Muhammad consolidates leadership in Medina; Aisha accused of adultery in "Affair of the Necklace," but exonerated by Quranic revelation

628 Treaty of Hudaybiyah permits Muslims to make pilgrimage to Mecca by establishing temporary truce; Muslims defeat and expel Jews of Khaybar after repeated violations of treaties by Jews

629 Qibla (direction of prayer) changed from Jerusalem to Mecca

632 Death of Muhammad; Abu Bakr becomes first caliph

632–61 Reign of the Four Rightly Guided Caliphs: normative period for Sunni Islam

633 Death of Fatima, daughter of Muhammad, wife of Ali, and mother of Hasan and Husayn

634 Death of first caliph Abu Bakr; Umar ibn al-Khattab becomes second caliph

637 Battle of Qadisiyah, Muslim Arabs defeat the Persians

638 Muslims occupy Jerusalem; construction of al-Aqsa mosque complex begins

639 Expansion of Islam into Central Asia and Caucasus begins

644 Caliph Umar ibn al-Khattab assassinated; Uthman ibn Affan becomes third caliph; Quran is collected and put in final format during reign of Uthman, within twenty years of Muhammad's death

656 Caliph Uthman ibn Affan assassinated; Ali ibn Abi Talib becomes fourth caliph

656–61 First Muslim civil war over succession, leading to Sunni–Shii split; Battle of the Camel with Aisha leading Muslim forces against caliph Ali ibn Abi Talib

657 Battle of Siffin: Kharijites secede from Ali's camp

661 Caliph Ali ibn Abi Talib assassinated; Muawiya ibn Abi Sufyan founds Umayyad Dynasty

661–750 Umayyad caliphate: Arab military aristocracy

670 Muslim conquest of northwest Africa; death of Muhammad's grandson, Hasan; Great Mosque of Qayrawan, Morocco, built

680–92 Second Muslim civil war

680 Husayn, son of Ali and grandson of Muhammad, leads rebellion against Umayyad Caliph Yazid and is martyred at Karbala, Iraq, creating paradigm of protest and suffering for Shiis; martyrdom on tenth day of Muharram is commemorated annually as Ashura by Shiis

691 Dome of the Rock completed in Jerusalem by Caliph Abd al-Malik; earliest extant coins from Umayyad caliphate date to this time

692–1099 Muslims rule Jerusalem, permitting Muslims, Jews, and Christians to live and worship there freely

699–767 Abu Hanifa, founder of Hanafi school of Islamic law, dominant in Ottoman and Moghul empires

705–15 Great Umayyad Mosque of Damascus built

711 Berber converts to Islam cross Straits of Gibraltar and enter southern Iberia, expanding Islam into Europe

713–95 Malik ibn Anas, founder of Maliki school of law, dominant in Africa

714 Death of fourth Shii imam, Ali Zayn al-Abidin, results in creation of Zaydi (fiver) branch of Shii Islam

c. 717–801 Rabia al-Adawiyya, Sufi saint and teacher credited with introducing selfless love of God into mystical tradition

728 Death of Hasan al-Basri, pivotal early Sufi

732 Charles Martel defeats Muslims at Battle of Tours, France, halting expansion of Islam into Europe

733 Death of fifth Shii imam, Muhammad al-Baqir

744–50 Third Muslim civil war and defeat of Umayyads by Abbasids

750–1258 Abbasid caliphate: height of Islamic civilization, development of Islamic law, patronage of art and culture, booming trade, commerce, agriculture, and industry

754–75 Rule of Caliph al-Mansur, who establishes translation bureau in Baghdad that develops into Bayt al-Hikmah (the House of Wisdom)

756 Emirate of Cordoba founded by Umayyad prince Abd al-Rahman

762 Baghdad founded as Abbasid capital

765 Death of sixth Shii Imam and founder of Jafari school of Islamic law, Jafar al-Sadiq; succession disputed, creating split between Sevener and Twelver Shiis

767–820 Muhammad al-Shafii, founder of Shafii school of Islamic law, dominant in Arabic-speaking areas of eastern Mediterranean

780–850 Abu Jafar Muhammad ibn Musa al-Khwarizmi, father of modern algebra and major scientist

780–855 Ahmad ibn Hanbal, founder of Hanbali school of Islamic law, dominant in Saudi Arabia and prominent among conservative groups

785 Great Mosque at Cordoba built

786–809 Harun al-Rashid caliph (legendary exploits recounted in *The Thousand and One Nights*), height of Abbasid caliphate

799 Death of Musa al-Kazim, recognized by Twelver Shiis as the seventh imam

9th century Universally accepted orthography and system of vocalization for Quranic text compiled under Uthman fixed

813–33 al-Mamun caliph: period of intellectual activity including translation of ancient Greek materials into Arabic, thus preserving them for Western culture.

830 Caliph al-Mamun establishes "House of Wisdom" (Bayt al-Hikmah) in Baghdad, responsible for translating manuscripts from other languages and cultures into Arabic

833–945 Emergence of regional states within Abbasid territories (present-day Iraq, western Iran, Khurasan, Egypt, and Syria)

864–1126 Zaydi imamate in northern Iran

865–925 al-Razi, Muslim physician

870 Death of al-Bukhari, major Sunni compiler of hadith

874 Twelfth imam, Muhammad al-Mahdi, goes into occultation/hiding; end of direct rule of Shii imams; death of Yazid al-Bistami, founder of Bistamiyah Sufi order

878–950 Abu Nasr al-Farabi, philosopher and author of *The Virtuous City*

893–1962 Zaydi Dynasty rules Yemen as imamate

899 Ubayd Allah al-Mahdi declares himself Imam of Sevener Shiis, leading to split between Ismailis and followers of Ubayd Allah who founded a state in North Africa and the Fatimid Dynasty in Egypt

10th century Peak of cultural and artistic flowering of Cordoba caliphate

920–1171 Fatimid dynasty rules North Africa, Egypt, and Syria

929 Andalusian caliphate founded by Abd al-Rahman III

936–1013 Abu al-Qasim al-Zahrawi, Andalusian physician and father of modern surgery

941–present "Complete" or "Greater" Occultation for Twelver Shiis during which "general deputies" guide believers until the return of the Hidden Imam

965–1039/1040 Abu Ali al-Hasan Ibn al-Haytham, mathematical scientist and founder of modern optics

969 Fatimids conquer Egypt; oldest continuous university in the world, Al-Azhar, founded in Cairo, Egypt

973–1048 Abu Rayham al-Biruni, major Muslim scientist and philosopher

980–1037 Abu Ali al-Husayn ibn Abd Allah Ibn Sina (Avicenna), philosopher and author of *The Just City* and *The Book of Healing*

11th century Foundation of Bohra movement in Ismaili Shiism

1017 Fatimid Caliph al-Hakim proclaims himself manifestation of the divine, resulting in foundation of Druze faith seeking to establish millennial world order

1055 Seljuk Turks overtake Baghdad, seat of Abbasid caliphate

1058–1111 Abu Hamid al-Ghazali, theologian, legal scholar, and mystic who integrated Sufism into mainstream Sunni thought

1065–7 Nizamiyah founded as institution for higher learning by Seljuks

1095 Pope Urban II calls Crusade against Islam at Council of Clermont

1099 Crusaders capture Jerusalem, slaughtering the inhabitants, and establishing Latin Kingdom

Early 11th century–1147 Almoravid Dynasty in North Africa and Spain

1126–98 Ibn Rushd (Averroes), philosopher, physician, and chief religious judge of Cordoba

1130–1269 Almohad Dynasty in North Africa and Spain

1138–93 Saladin (Salah al-Din), legendary Muslim general during the Crusades and founder of Ayyubid Dynasty in Egypt

1165–1240 Muhyi al-Din ibn al-Arabi, great medieval Muslim Sufi mystic and writer

1171 Saladin conquers Egypt, ending Fatimid Dynasty and restoring Sunni rule

1192 Treaty between Saladin and Richard I permitting Christian pilgrimage to the Holy Land during the Crusades

1201–74 Abu Jafar Muhammad ibn Muhammad ibn al-Hasan Nasir al-Din al-Tusi, father of non-Euclidean geometry and intellectual

1206–1370 Mongols rule Central Asia

1206–1555 Delhi sultans

1207–73 Jalal al-Din Rumi, Sufi mystic, musician, poet, and patron saint of Mevlevi (Whirling Dervish) Sufi order

1207–1574 Zaytunah emerges as one of the most important Islamic institutions of higher learning

1220–60 Mongol invasions of Muslim territories

1225 Almohad rulers abandon Spain

1256 Assassin stronghold in Alamut falls to Mongols; last grand master of the Assassins is executed

1258 Mongols sack Baghdad and execute Abbasid caliph al-Musta'sim; end of Abbasid caliphate

1260 Mamluks defeat Mongols at Ayn Jalut

1261–1517 Abbasid caliphate in Cairo

1263–1328 Ibn Taymiyya, Syrian Hanbali religious and legal scholar and source of inspiration to many contemporary extremists due to legal rulings justifying rebellion against ruler of ummah on the basis of the ruler's impiety

Mid- to late 13th century Founding of Mevlevi (Whirling Dervish) Sufi order

1281–1922 Ottoman empire

12th century Sufi orders begin to provide organizational framework for social movements

1332–1406 Ibn Khaldun, philosopher of history and author of *Muqaddimah*

1389 Ottomans defeat Serbians at Battle of Kosovo and take control over western Balkans

1453 Ottomans capture Constantinople

1478 Islamic conquest of Majapahit kingdom in Java

1491 Granada, last Muslim stronghold in Spain, falls to Christian rulers Ferdinand and Isabella

1492 Spain expels Jewish population, which largely flees to Muslim lands; death of Persian poet Abd al-Rahman Jami

1500 Ottomans control Greece, Bosnia, Herzegovina, and Albania

1501–1722 Safavid Dynasty in Persia

1517 Ottoman conquest of Egypt, Syria, Mecca, and Medina

1520–66 Suleyman the Magnificent ruler, high point of Ottoman empire

1520–1857 Mughal empire in India

1529 Failed first siege of Vienna by Ottomans

1564–1624 Shaykh Ahmad Sirhindi, advocate of Islamic state and society in India

1571 Battle of Lepanto: Europeans block Ottoman advance into Mediterranean

c. 1645 Taj Mahal completed

1660–present Alawi Dynasty rules Morocco

1683 Ottoman-Hapsburg War; second unsuccessful Ottoman siege of Vienna marking end to Ottoman expansion into Europe; reported to have led to creation of pastry known as croissant

1702–62 Shah Wali Allah of Delhi, India, leader of Islamic revival in India

1702–92 Muhammad Ibn Abd al-Wahhab, founder of Muwahhidun (Wahhabi) revival and reform movement in Arabia

1744–present Al Bu Said dynasty rules Oman, claiming title of imam until the late eighteenth century

1745 Beginning of Wahhabi movement in Arabia

1754–1817 Uthman Dan Fodio, leader of northern Nigerian reformist opposition to Hausa states

1786–1831 Sayyid Ahmad Barelwi, leader of jihad movement in north India against Sikhs and British

1787–1859 Muhammad Ali ibn al-Sanusi of Libya, founder of Sanusiyyah tariqah and Islamic state

1794–1864 Jihad state in area of present-day Mali and Senegal

1798 French occupation of Egypt under Napoleon; Muhammad Ali comes to power, initiating period of reform of political and economic structures along Western lines

19th century European imperial expansion in the Muslim world; study of Islam becomes separate field of university study known as Orientalism

1801–2 Major Shii shrines destroyed in Karbala and Najaf by Wahhabiyah

1803–37 Padri Movement in Sumatra; Sokoto caliphate in Nigeria

1804–5 Jihad in northern Nigeria against Gobir state led by Uthman Dan Fodio

1808–83 Abd al-Qadir, leader of Algerian independence movement and Sufi mystic and poet

1809–1903 Sokoto caliphate in western Africa

1817–92 Mirza Husayn Ali Nuri (Baha' Allah), prophet and founder of the Baha'i faith

1817–98 Sir Sayyid Ahmad Khan, leader of Islamic modernist movement in India

1818–45 Faraidi of Bengal opposes Hindus and British

1819–50 Sayyid Ali Muhammad Shirazi, popularly known as the Bab in Iran, a non-clerical messianic religious leader who declared himself the "gate" (Bab) to the Twelfth Shii Imam, an interpreter of the Quran, and ultimately the Hidden Imam

1821–38 Padri War in Indonesia

1830 French invade and colonize Algeria; Abd al-Qadir, leader of Qadiriyah tariqah, leads resistance until 1847 and tries to establish Islamic state

1835–1908 Mirza Ghulam Ahmad, self-proclaimed Mahdi and founder of Ahmadiya movement in Pakistan

1838–97 Jamal al-Din al-Afghani, father of Islamic modernism

Late 1830s–1908 Mirza Ghulam Ahmad, founder of Ahmadiya movement in India

1840–88 Mehmet Namik Kemal, Turkish Islamic reformer, poet, and Young Ottomanist

1841–1920 Ayatollah Sayyid Muhammad Tabataba'i, leading religious leader in Constitutional Revolution in Iran

1844–95 Chiragh Ali, Indian modernist author and supporter of Aligarh movement

1848–85 Muhammad Ahmad, Mahdi of Sudan and founder of Islamic state

1849–1905 Muhammad Abduh, Egyptian scholar and reformer regarded as the architect of Islamic modernism

1849–1928 Syed Ameer Ali, Indian jurist and Islamic modernist

1851–1914 Ismail Gasprinski, Crimean Tatar reformer and sponsor of schools combining Russian and Muslim education to achieve modernization

1856–1921 Ahmad Riza Khan Barelwi, leader and ideologue of Barelwi school of Islamic thought

1857 Failed Indian Mutiny, revolt against British occupation, resulting in formal British colonization of India and dissolution of Mughal empire

1862–67 Jihad in Senegal led by Ma Ba against French

1865–1908 Qasim Amin, Egyptian proponent of expanded women's rights

1865–1935 Muhammad Rashid Rida, co-founder of Salafiyah movement in Egypt and Islamic modernist movement

1867 Foundation of Dar al-Ulum in Deoband, to combine hadith studies and Sufism; center of Deobandi Indo-Pakistani reform movement

1868–1923 Hadji Ahmad Dahlan, founder of Indonesian Muhammadiyah movement

1873–1908 Ulama lead resistance to Dutch occupation of Aceh

1873–1960 Bediuzzaman Said Nursi, Turkish Islamist

1875 Muhammadan Anglo-Oriental College (Aligarh University) founded in India by Sayyid Ahmad Khan

1875–1938 Muhammad Iqbal, Islamic modernist and ideologue for foundation of Pakistan

1875–1962 Mohammad Hosayn Borujerdi, Iranian theologian and religious leader who was recognized as marja al-taqlid for Iranian Shiis

1878 Emergence of Pan-Islam as ideology

1878–1944 Reza Shah Pahlavi, founder of the Iranian Pahlavi Dynasty

1879–1947 Huda Sha'rawi, Egyptian activist and founder of Egyptian Feminist Union

1881 Mahdist mission declared in Sudan under leadership of Muhammad Ahmad ibn Abdallah as imamate led by Ansar religiopolitical movement; France establishes protectorate in Tunisia

1881–1938 Mustafa Kemal Ataturk, father of the Turkish Republic

1885–98 Mahdist state in Sudan

1885–1944 Maulana Muhammad Ilyas, Indian activist and founder of Tablighi Jama'at

1888–1958 Abu al-Kalam Azad, Indian Urdu journalist and stylist, Islamic thinker, and religious universalist opposed to partition of India

1888–1966 Ali Abd al-Raziq, Egyptian intellectual, religious scholar, and judge

1889 Ahmadiya founded by Mirza Ghulam Ahmad in India as Islamic messianic movement; first mosque established in England

1889–1940 Abd al-Hamid ibn Badis, Islamic reformer, national leader, and head of Association of Algerian Ulama

1898 Mahdist state of Sudan defeated by British; Rashid Ridda begins publishing *al-Manar* in Egypt; journal serves as leading mouthpiece of Islamic reformist ideas

1899–1992 Abol-Qasem Kho'i, major Shii mujtahid

1902–89 Ayatollah Ruhollah Khomeini, Iranian Shii cleric, leader of Islamic Revolution, and author of doctrine of "rule of the jurist" (*velayat-i faqih*)

1903–79 Mawlana Abul Ala Mawdudi, founder of Jamaat-i-Islami in Pakistan

1905–11 Constitutional revolt in Iran places limits on Shah's power; local religious leaders play key role in opposition to Shah

1906–49 Hasan al-Banna, founder of Muslim Brotherhood in Egypt

1906–66 Sayyid Qutb, Egyptian scholar, political activist, and ideologue for the Muslim Brotherhood; writings have inspired contemporary jihadism

1906–73 Muhammad Allal al-Fasi, Moroccan intellectual, historian, and founder of Istiqlal Party

1908–81 Hamka (Hajji Abdul Malik Karim Amrullah), Indonesian religious scholar and writer

1908–93 Mohammad Natsir, Indonesian intellectual, journalist, and politician

1911 Society of Call and Guidance (Jam'iyat al-Da'wah wa-al-Irshad) founded in Egypt by Muhammad Rashid Rida as cornerstone for Ottoman Pan-Islamic activities

1912 Muhammadiyah founded in Southeast Asia to promote educational and social reform

1913–98 A'ishah Abd al-Rahman (Bint al-Shati), Egyptian writer and professor of Quranic studies and Arabic language and literature

1917–96 Shaykh Muhammad al-Ghazali, Egyptian religious scholar and leading member of the Muslim Brotherhood

1917–2005 Zaynab al-Ghazali, prominent writer and teacher of Muslim Brotherhood and founder of the Muslim Women's Association in Egypt

1919 Jam'iyatul Ulama-i Hind established as organization of Muslim religious scholars of India to participate in Khilafat movement

1919–25 Khilafat movement in India in support of caliphate

1919–1980 Muhammad Reza Shah Pahlavi, last ruling monarch of the Pahlavi Dynasty of Iran

1920–79 Murtaza Mutahhari, Iranian religious scholar and writer and close associate of Ayatollah Khomeini

1925–65 Malcolm X (Malcolm Little, El-Hajj Malik El-Shabazz), powerful voice and visionary of Nation of Islam, Pan-Africanist, Pan-Islamist, and civil and human rights advocate

1925–79 Pahlavi Dynasty in Iran

1922 Partitioning of the Ottoman empire and collapse of the caliphate

1925 Kemal Ataturk abolishes Sufi orders, closes sacred tombs and shrines, and bans wearing fez in Turkey; Ali Abd al-Raziq publishes controversial book denying the connection between Islam and politics, sparking firestorm of debate and creating context for foundation of the Muslim Brotherhood in Egypt; Nahdatul Ulama established in Indonesia as social organization; Tablighi Jama'at founded on Indo-Pakistani subcontinent as grassroots Islamic movement

1928 Muslim Brotherhood founded in Egypt by Hasan al-Banna; reference to Islam as religion of state eliminated in Turkey

1928–78 Musa Al-Sadr, Iranian-born Shii cleric, Lebanese politician, and founder of Amal, whose disappearance made him a contemporary symbol of the Hidden Imam

1932 Kingdom of Saudi Arabia founded on basis of alliance between religion and politics with Sharia as law

1933 Transformation of Muslim Brotherhood from religious association to political movement

1933–77 Ali Shariati, ideologue of Iranian Revolution of 1979

1933–80 Muhammad Baqir al-Sadr, Shii religious authority, Islamic economist, and founder of Hizb al-Dawah al-Islamiyah in Iraq in opposition to Saddam Hussein regime, grandfather of Muqtada al-Sadr

1935–present Muhammad Husayn Fadlallah, Lebanese Shii religious scholar and ideologue of Hizbullah

1941 Jamaat-i-Islami founded in India/Pakistan by Mawlana Abul Ala Mawdudi; religious instruction banned in schools in Iran

1941–79 Reign of Muhammad Reza Shah Pahlavi, last shah of Iran

1947 Pakistan founded as state for Muslims of India; state of Jammu and Kashmir becomes disputed territory between India and Pakistan; UN Resolution 181 passed, recommending partition of Palestine into two states, one Arab and one Jewish; prison conversion of Malcolm X to Nation of Islam

1948 State of Israel declared; Jordan claims mandate for Jerusalem; Jami'yatul Ulama-i Pakistan established as largest Barelwi ulama party in Pakistan

1954 Muslim Brotherhood founded in Sudan, advocating Islamic political and social order via adoption of Islamic constitution based on the Quran and introduction of Islamic law; Muslim Brotherhood disbanded by Nasser regime in Egypt following purported assassination attempt against Nasser; Federation of Islamic Associations of Canada and the United States (formerly International Muslim Society) founded to maintain ties between scattered Muslim communities

1956 Pakistan adopts constitution declaring itself an Islamic Republic with a Muslim head of state and based on Islamic principles

1957 Hizb al-Da'wah al-Islamiyah, one of most important activist Shii organizations opposing Saddam Hussein regime, founded in Iraq; Tunisia adopts Law of Personal Status, abolishing polygamy, and grants women right to vote

1962 Algeria wins independence from France and grants women right to vote; Muslim World League founded in Saudi Arabia; al-Azhar University in Cairo opens college for girls to expand women's access to advanced religious studies; end of Zaydi imamate in Yemen

1965 Crackdown on Muslim Brotherhood in Egypt after Nasser accuses them of plotting to assassinate him; foundation of Islamic Pact in Saudi Arabia; assassination of Malcolm X by members of Nation of Islam

1966 Execution of Sayyid Qutb, prominent writer for Muslim Brotherhood, who gave movement radical, militant tone, by Nasser in Egypt; International Islamic Federation of Student Organizations founded as world federation of Muslim student organizations

1967 Six Day or June War between Arabs and Israelis: Israel captures Jerusalem, occupies remaining 20 percent of Palestinian lands, Sinai Peninsula, and Golan Heights and routs Arab forces, leading to Arab disillusionment with secular policies like nationalism and socialism and sparking Islamic revival

1968 Dar Ul Arqam founded in Malaysia as voluntary, nongovernmental, grassroots Islamic da'wah movement

1969 Muammar Qaddafi seizes power in Libya, later implementing his own version of Islamic state as "Third Universal Alternative"; Jafar al-Numayri seizes power in the Sudan; minbar in al-Aqsa Mosque in Jerusalem burned, leading King Faisal of Saudi Arabia to call for jihad against Israel and to organize an Islamic summit conference combining pan-Islamism with Arabism; Moro National Liberation Front founded in the Philippines; ethnic riots in Malaysia; Ayatollah Khomeini introduces concept of *velayat-i faqih* (rule of the jurist) on which the Islamic Republic of Iran is later founded

1971 Organization of the Islamic Conference founded: first official pan-Islamic institution for cooperation among Islamic governments; Libya adopts Sharia

1972 National Salvation Party founded in Turkey by Necmettin Erbakan with goal of Islamic state and Islamization of Turkish life; ABIM (Angkatan Belia Islam Malaysia, or Malaysian League of Muslim Youth) founded in Malaysia as mission movement and political party, rejecting capitalism and socialism and promoting Islam as an alternative political and economic system; Council of Muslims Communities founded in Canada; World Assembly of Muslim Youth (WAMY) established in Saudi Arabia

1973 "Operation Badr" or October War: Second Arab–Israeli war, with Egypt recovering some of the territory lost to Israel in 1967 war; Arab oil embargo against West renders Arabs world economic power; Islamic Development Bank founded; Islamic Council of Europe established to address status of Muslim minorities

1974 Musa al-Sadr founds Movement of the Disinherited, a populist movement for social and political reform in Lebanon favoring redistribution of power and resources to include Shii majority of Lebanon otherwise excluded; militant wing develops into AMAL; Islamic Solidarity Fund established; Belgium officially recognizes Islam, opening door to Islamic religious activities receiving financial aid

1975 Outbreak of civil war in Lebanon, resulting in radicalization of Shii population; foundation of AMAL as Lebanese Shii populist movement; Muammar Qaddafi of Libya publishes *The Green Book*, outlining his interpretation of Islam and the world; death of Elijah Muhammad and rise to power of Imam Warith Deen Muhammad (Wallace Deen Muhammad) leads to Nation of Islam being transformed into more normative Islamic movement; Louis Farrakhan breaks off to continue hard-core black nationalist tendencies and retaining name Nation of Islam; foundation of Islamic Development Bank by the Organization of the Islamic Conference

1975–90 Lebanese civil war

1976 King Faisal Foundation established to promote charitable work, research, and Islamic studies

1977 Zulfikar Ali Bhutto's government in Pakistan ousted by General Zia ul-Haq, who introduces Islamization

1978 Disappearance of Musa al-Sadr during trip to Libya, giving him popular "hidden imam" status among Shiis of Lebanon; Israel invades Lebanon; Pakistan announces creation of Sharia Courts; Council of Masajid of the United States established by representatives of the Muslim World League

1979 Iranian Revolution: Islamic Republic of Iran founded; Shah abdicates and goes into exile; seizure of Grand Mosque of Mecca by militants led by Juhayman al-Utaybi and Muhammad al-Qahtani (declared the Mahdi) in Saudi Arabia; Shii riots in Eastern Province of Saudi Arabia, calling for fairer distribution of oil wealth and services; Soviet Union invades Afghanistan, sparking ten-year war resulting in collapse of Afghan society and bringing *mujahidin* to power; Pakistani Abdus-Salam becomes first Muslim to win the Nobel Prize for science in shared award for physics; Federation of Islamic Associations of New Zealand (FIANZ) founded to coordinate and provide both domestic and international services for Muslims; foundation of Bahrain Islamic Bank; Islamic Jihad formed in Egypt by Muhammad Abd al-Salam Faraj

1980 Hizbullah founded in Lebanon; Islamic Jihad founded in Palestine by Muslim Brotherhood; Regional Islamic Da'wah Council of Southeast Asia and the Pacific (RISEAP) formed

1980–8 Bloody Iran–Iraq War, which ends in stalemate

1981 October 4: Anwar al-Sadat of Egypt assassinated by militant Tanzim al-Jihad; Women's Action Forum founded in Pakistan in response to implementation of Islamic penal code

1982 Hafiz al-Asad of Syria levels city of Hama to put down opposition movement led by Muslim Brotherhood; Israel invades southern Lebanon for second time; massacre of inhabitants of Sabra and Shatilla in Lebanon; Islamic Society of North America (ISNA) formed as umbrella organization for Muslim professional groups; Organization of the Islamic Jihad founded in Lebanon out of Hizbullah

1984 Women Living Under Muslim Laws (WLML) founded as network to facilitate contacts between women internationally; Muslim Brotherhood permitted to participate in Egyptian elections; Hamas founded at beginning of Palestinian *intifada* as organizational expression of Muslim Brotherhood participation in anti-Israeli resistance; Islamic Jihad movement formed in Palestine in response to intifada

1988 MTI (Mouvement de la Tendance Islamique) becomes Tunisia's leading opposition group, performing impressively in national elections and changes name to Hizb al-Nahdah (Renaissance Party); Naguib Mahfouz becomes first Muslim and first Arab to win the Nobel Prize for Literature

1989 Death *fatwa* issued by Khomeini against Salman Rushdie and his publishers, who were aware of the book's content, for committing blasphemy and apostasy in *The Satanic Verses*; death of Ayatollah Ruhollah Khomeini, first ruler of Islamic Republic of Iran and author of doctrine of *velayat-i faqih*

1990–1991 First Persian Gulf War results from Iraq's invasion of Kuwait in August 1990

1990 Islamists win thirty-two out of eighty seats in Jordanian Parliament and member of Muslim Brotherhood is elected Speaker of national parliament; Islamic Salvation Front (FIS) wins municipal and communal elections in Algeria, coming to power through democratic process, rather than revolution

1991 FIS wins parliamentary elections in Algeria and is poised to take leadership of country; Khaleda Zia becomes first female prime minister of Bangladesh

1992 Slobodan Milošević begins ethnic cleansing of Bosnian Muslims

1992 Iranian elections place conservatives in control of parliament, marginalizing hard-liners and paving way for limited liberalization of political participation and dissent; all mosques in Egypt placed under government control via anti-terrorism law; military prevents FIS from coming to power in Algeria, canceling results of democratic parliamentary elections; Algerian government crackdown on FIS, leading to civil war that claimed more than 100,000 lives

1993 Bombing of World Trade Center in New York City, tied to Shaykh Umar Abd al-Rahman and Ramzi Yousef; Anwar Ibrahim becomes deputy prime minister of Malaysia; Oslo Accords agreed on as first step to resolution of Israeli–Palestinian conflict

1994 Baruch Goldstein (Jewish settler) kills twenty-nine worshippers at Mosque of the Patriarch in Hebron, provoking suicide bombings by Qassam Brigade (military wing of Hamas); Taliban, composed of religious leaders and students, appears in Afghanistan, claiming mantle of moral leadership and ending civil war

1995 Refah (Welfare) Party wins enough seats in National Assembly to make its leader, Necmettin Erbakan, Turkey's first Islamist prime minister

1996 Chechnya wins (temporary) *de facto* independence from Russia

1997 Mohammad Khatami elected president of Iran, opening door to United States for cultural, scholarly, and economic exchanges

1998 *Reformasi* pro-Democracy era follows Suharto's resignation in Indonesia

2001 September 11 attacks on New York City and Washington, DC, inspired by al-Qaeda and planned by Khalid Shaykh Muhammad

2002 Terrorist attack on nightclub in Bali, Indonesia, attributed to Abu Sayyaf movement

2003 United States invades Iraq and overthrows Saddam Hussein regime

2004 Terrorist attack in Madrid, Spain, by al-Qaeda affiliates; the Amman Message, issued by King Abdullah II of Jordan and Islamic scholars, called for tolerance and unity in the Muslim world and emphasized that Islam's core values were compassion, mutual respect, tolerance, acceptance, and freedom of religion

2005 July 7 London bombings, also known as 7/7

2006 Muhammad Yunus, founder of microcredit Grameen Bank, wins Nobel Prize for Peace; Israeli–Hizbullah war results in Israeli withdrawal and ideological victory for Hizbullah; Hamas comes to power over Palestinian territories following election victory, resulting in cutting of financial aid to Palestinians from Europe and the United States; Keith Ellison becomes first Muslim American to be elected to U.S. House of Representatives.

2007 "A Common Word Between Us and You," letter originally signed by 138 (now 300) prominent academics, politicians, writers, and muftis representing a broad range of viewpoints from the Muslim world, was sent to the heads of the world's major Christian churches, emphasizing the foundational principles of both faiths (love of the One God, and love of the neighbor) as the common ground for joint efforts to bring peace to the world

Nov. 4–6, 2008 Representatives of the Vatican and of the original 138 Muslim signers of a Common Word meet with Pope Benedict XVI and hold meetings to establish a Catholic–Muslim Forum

2009 Death of Abdurrahman Wahid, popularly known as Gus Dur, first president of a democratic Indonesia after the resignation of President Suharto in 1998 and former president of the Nahdatul Ulama, the largest Islamic organization/movement in the Muslim world

2011 Reelection of Erdogan in Turkey; beginning of the "Arab Spring," sparked in Tunisia and Egypt, as series of nonviolent protests demanding an end of authoritarian rule, freedom, dignity, democracy, and an end to government corruption.

2011 Osama bin Laden, the founder and head of the Islamist militant group al-Qaeda, killed in Pakistan by American military

2011 Ennahda (the Renaissance Party), in Tunisia's first democratic election, wins a plurality of votes in the Constituent Assembly

2012 In first open democratic elections in Egypt, the Muslim Brotherhood wins a majority of the vote in the parliamentary election to the People's Assembly, and the Brotherhood's Mohammed Morsi is elected president

July 3, 2013 Egypt's first democratically elected president, Mohammed Morsi, after widespread anti-government demonstrations on July 30, overthrown in a military backed coup.

August 14, 2014 Egyptian security forces raid and use lethal force against Morsi supporter sit-in at two camps, al-Nahda Square and a larger one at Rabaa al-Adawiya Square, in Cairo, killing more than one thousand and injuring thousands; interim government moved quickly to declare the Muslim Brotherhood a terrorist organization and attempted to totally suppress it, using mass arrests and military trials that drew sharp criticism from major international human rights organizations; government cracked down and arrested foreign journalists and Egyptian critics and democracy activists

Dec. 25, 2014 Egypt's interim government officially declared the Muslim Brotherhood a terrorist organization.

Jan. 27, 2014 Tunisian Assembly passes new constitution

March 24, 2014 An Egyptian court sentences 529 members of the outlawed Muslim Brotherhood to death, the largest mass death sentence in modern Egyptian history

Oct. 26, 2014 Nidaa Tounes, a coalition of secular parties including former members of the Ben Ali regime, wins 85 seats in the 217-member assembly (parliament), ahead of 69 secured by Ennahda

Dec. 21, 2014 Ennahda's loss of political power finalized with the victory of Nidaa Tounes' Essebsi in the presidential elections

Jan 22, 2015 Yemen's president Abed Rabbo Mansour Hadi resigns under pressure from Shiite rebels, known as Houthis, who had seized Sanaa, the capital, in September 2014

Glossary

A Common Word Between Us and You 2007 document issued by prominent
Muslims theologians in response to Pope Benedict XII's inflammatory 2006
Regensburg remarks about Islam; it asserts that Islam and Christianity both
reduce to love of God and neighbor

Ali (c. 605–61) First-cousin and son-in-law of the Prophet Muhammad. After the
Prophet's death, he would become the fourth and last of the Rightly-Guided
Caliphs and, according to Shiites, the first of the Imams; disagreement over Ali's
authoritative status would later be considered one of the major dividing factors
between Shiites and Sunnis

Allah Arabic for "God"

Allahu Akbar "God is greater," a declaration used as a preface to the call to prayer or
as a traditional battle cry of God's fighters

Ashura the 10th day of the Islamic month of Muharram, commemorated by many
Muslims as the anniversary of the martyrdom of the Prophet's grandson Husayn

ayatollah (*ayat Allah*) "sign of God," title of a high-ranking Shii religious leader

baqa to rest or abide in God; Sufi experience that follows the annihilation (*fana*) of
the ego-self

bida innovation; deviation from Islamic tradition

chador traditional garment, worn in public, covering a woman from head to foot

Children of Abraham Jews, Christians, and Muslims who all belong to different
branches of the same family—Jews (genealogically) and Christians (spiritually)
as descendants of Abraham and Sarah and Muslims as descendants of Abraham
and Hagar

dar al-harb "abode of war"; non-Islamic territory

dar al-Islam "abode of peace"; Islamic territory, i.e., where Islamic law is in force

dawa "the call;" a term for missionary spreading of the Islamic faith

dhikr "remembrance," Sufi practice of repeating or remembering God's name to
become more conscious of God's presence

dhimmi a "protected" person or people, specifically meaning non-Muslim monotheists who live in Islamic lands; usually including Jews and Christians, *dhimmis*
are technically required to pay a poll tax (*jizya*, q.v.) in exchange for security;

treatment of *dhimmi*s has varied across history from toleration to violent oppression

din religion

fana annihilation or extinction of the ego-centered self in Sufism to experience unity of God

faqih (**pl. *fuqaha***) an Islamic jurist

faqir "poor" or mendicant; a follower of Sufism who has embraced poverty or detachment from worldly goods

fatwa legal pronouncement by an Islamic jurist binding only on those who choose to accept it

fiqh understanding, the interpretation and application of God's path (Sharia, q.v.) as found in the Quran and the Prophet's example; this jurisprudence is relevant to all aspects of life

Gamaa Islamiyya (Islamic Group), Jund Allah (God's Army) insurgent Islamist group against the Egyptian government of Mohamed Morsi. After the fall of Morsi during the Egyptian Arab Spring revolution of 2011, Gamaa Islamiyya founded the "Construction and Development" political party

hadd (**pl. *hudud***) "limits"; Quranically prescribed penalty or punishment for theft, adultery, fornication, false witness, drinking intoxicants

hadith authoritative traditions of the Prophet that supplement the Quran in the Islamic canon; Sunnis have six accepted collections, while Twelver Shiites have four; the two most important Sunnī collections are those of Ismail al-Bukhari (d. 870) and Muslim ibn al-Hajjaj (d. 875)

hajj annual pilgrimage to Mecca in modern-day Saudi Arabia that each financially and physically able Muslim is expected to perform at least once in his or her lifetime

halal permitted, lawful activities

Hamas (Islamic Resistance Movement) Palestinian Islamist movement that broke off from the Egyptian Muslim Brotherhood in 1987 following the First Intifada; grounded in the hopes of a politically independent Palestine, Hamas also functions as a major political party in the Palestinian Parliament

hanif Quranic term for a pure or true monotheist; used for Abraham and for those in pre-Islamic Arabia who before the revelation of the Quran remained monotheists despite the paganism and polytheism of their times

haram prohibited, unlawful activities

harem see purdah

Hasan al-Banna (1906–49) founder of Egypt's Muslim Brotherhood

hijab a "partition" or "veil" that keeps something unseen. In the formative period of Islam, the hijab referred to a curtain that kept the apartments of the Prophet's family out of public view; generally the term refers to the various forms of headscarves worn by many Muslim women as acts of piety, modesty, or as part of local customs

hijra migration of Muhammad and his followers from Mecca to Yathrib (Medina) in 622 as a nonviolent response to Qurayshi persecution

Hizbollah "party of God," a Shiite movement in Lebanon with a paramilitary wing

ibadat "worship"; regulations in Islamic law governing religious observances

Id al-Adha "festival of sacrifice," the last day of the *hajj*

Id al-Fitra "festival of the breaking of the fast," the end of Ramadan

ijma "consensus," a category by which many jurists use widely held beliefs to be a legitimate basis for issuing legal proclamations

ijtihad independent juristic reasoning; forbidden for most Sunnis after the ninth century but permissible for sufficiently accredited Shiite scholars

ikhwan brotherhood

imam for Sunnis, a prayer leader or prominent juridical authority; for Shiites, an heir to the Prophet's spiritual leadership/divine light; Shiite imams consist of Ali and several lines of his male descendants through Fatima

iman "faith," meaning the substance of one's beliefs in Islam, such as the belief in the unity of God, the prophecy of Muhammad, the truth of revealed words and knowledge, and the coming of final rewards and punishments; often considered the intermediate stage between *islam* (submission, q.v.) and *ihsan* ([moral/spiritual] excellence)

islah "reform," used in the modern period in reference to any religious reform of Islamic law and thought as well as political reform of Islamic governing bodies

islam submission or surrender to the will of God

Islamic revivalism or resurgence increased importance of religious identity and practice in individual and corporate life, which led to a greater role of Islam in Muslim politics and society

Islamophobia anti-Islamic or anti-Muslim discrimination based on religion, race, or culture

jahiliyya period of ignorance, i.e., pre-Islamic Arabia; used by contemporary revivalists to refer to un-Islamic behavior in society

jihad to strive or struggle; the two broad meanings of jihad, nonviolent and violent, are described in Muhammad's oft-cited "We return from the lesser jihad (warfare) to the greater jihad (community and self-improvement)."

jinn intelligent beings, usually invisible spirits, who can sin as well as be sacred; the Western word "genie" is derived from this term

jizya tax levied by an Islamic political power on its non-Muslim subjects; in lieu of paying the Muslim tax (*zakat*, q.v.) or serving in the military, non-Muslims paid various amounts of their income to the state; mostly unpracticed in the modern period, some recent Islamist groups and political entities have attempted to reinstate the tax

Kaba cube-shaped "House of God," believed to have been built by Abraham and Ismail, containing the sacred black stone (*al-hajar al-aswad*) given to Abraham by the angel Gabriel as a symbol of God's covenant with Ismail and the Muslim Community

kafir an "unbeliever;" for most Muslims, one who purposefully rejects Islam in both faith and practice; a minority of jurists historically have declared that a person can be considered a *kafir* for holding a heterodox opinion, even if the individual in question considers her/himself a Muslim

kalam literally "speech," generally referring to the science of Islamic theology

khalifa **(caliph)** "deputy" or "successor," referring to the heirs to Muhammad's as political leadership of the Muslim community

khutba sermon delivered in a mosque at the Friday congregational prayer

madrasa generally just any "school," the term is usually used in reference to a center for Islamic education grounded in Quranic memorization, legal sciences, and other Islamic literatures

Mahdi the "guided one" who many Muslims believe will appear along with Jesus toward the end of time to bring justice to the world

marja-i-taqlid "source of emulation"; supreme authority on law in Shii Islam whose interpretation should be followed; title is conferred by the people on the most distinguished clergymen of the period

masjid "place of prostration," mosque, center for Muslim worship

mihrab "niche" in the wall of a mosque, indicating the direction of Mecca, which Muslims face when performing their daily prayers (*salat*)

millet system non-Muslim religious communities living within the Islamic domain; distinctive system used by Ottoman rulers to recognize and regulate the rights and duties of non-Muslims

minbar pulpit from which a sermon is delivered at the Friday prayer

mosque *see masjid*

muamalat human relationships; Islamic laws (e.g., civil, criminal, family) governing social relations

mufti a member of the *ulama* (q.v.) who has the authority and training to provide legal opinions on controversial or new questions; in modern times, the mufti has often wielded a certain amount of political authority, or through the backing of a political body can have his opinions affirmed widely

muhtasib originally an inspector of markets who supervised or policed business transactions and practices; the office was later expanded to include the monitoring of public morality in general

mujaddid a preordained "reviver" of Islam; according to a famous report of the Prophet, such a figure will come once every century to renew the Islamic community

mujahid (**pl.** ***mujahidin***) soldier of God

mujtahid one who practices *ijtihad* or interprets Islamic law

mullah a local religious leader

mumin believer, one who possesses faith (*iman*)

Muslim an adherent to Islam, literally "one who submits" or "surrenders" to God

Nahdatul Ulama (Renaissance of Religious Scholars) the largest Islamic organization in the world's largest Muslim country, comprising 40 million members

nizam system, e.g., nizam al-Islam, Islamic system of government

people of the Book (***ahl al-kitab***) Jews and Christians whose prophets (Moses and Jesus) received God's revelations in the form of the Torah and the Gospels, respectively

pir *see* shaykh

purdah, **harem** the inner, "forbidden" section of a house that outsiders are typically not allowed to enter; despite fanciful, highly sexualized depictions by non-Muslims, the harem was overwhelmingly just the private areas of the home where women and children resided *qadi* a "judge," a legal scholar of Islamic law with the political power to enforce legal decisions

qibla direction of the Kaba at Mecca that Muslims face when performing their daily prayers (*salat*)

qiyas juristic reasoning by analogy, source of Islamic law

Quran literally "reading" or "recitation;" it is the holy book of Islam which Muhammad received as revelation between 610 and 632

Ramadan month-long fast, from dawn to dusk, observed by all adult Muslims; a time for prayer, reflection, and community

ray personal opinion or judgment in interpreting Islamic law

riba usury

salafiyya "pious ancestors" comprising the first three generations of Muslims; their thoughts and lifestyles are emulated by many contemporary believers

salat **(Persian, *namaz*)** prayer or worship prescribed to be performed five times each day

sawm fasting, the fourth pillar of Islam, which requires abstention from food and drink from dawn to sunset during the month of Ramadan

Sayyid Qutb (1906–66) Member of the Egyptian Muslim Brotherhood and author of "Milestones" and a major Quranic commentary; a major intellectual architect of Islamism, condemning both the Muslim World and the West as decadent and requiring replacement, he was hanged in 1966 as part of a plot to assassinate President Gamal Abd al-Nasser

shahada confession or profession of faith: "there is no god but Allah and Muhammad is His Prophet/Messenger"

shahid martyr ("witness" to faith)

Sharia "path"; Islamic law

shaykh or *pir* generally any older man in a position of tribal or family authority; in the political sense, a shaykh refers to the master of a powerful family; in the Sufi orders, a shaykh (or the Persian, *pir*) is a spiritual master who guides the novices

Shiites "partisans [of Ali]" who comprise roughly 15 percent of the world's Muslim population

shirk polytheism or idolatry, the association of anything with God, considered the worst of sins

shura consultation or decision by consensus

Sufism the umbrella term for the broad phenomenon of Islamic mysticism and supererogatory practices

sultan literally someone in "authority;" refers to many kinds of Islamic rulers, but typically not those who claim the caliphate

Sunna "trodden path," sayings and example of Muhammad handed down from previous generations that became the norm for community life

Sunnis largest branch of Islam (85 percent of the world's Muslim population)

tajdid religious revivalism and renewal; according to a famous tradition of the Prophet, there is to be a period of *tajdid* at the beginning of each new Islamic century, led by a *mujaddid* ("reviver")

talaq pronouncement of divorce or repudiation by husband

taqiyya the act of purposely hiding one's own Shiism in times of crisis; if a Shiite feels persecuted to the point of direct harm because of her/his religious identity, Shiite law stipulates that she/he may conceal her/his Shiism or even commit forbidden acts to save her/his own life, honor, or property

taqlid the act of following a religious opinion or practice because it has been dictated on the authority of another person; a blind deferral to authority, the opposite of *ijtihad* (q.v.)

tariqa a Sufi order or "path;" one of the many communities of Sufi thought and practice that gather around particular shaykhs and their teachings

tawhid the unity or oneness of God (Arabic: Allah, q.v.); monotheism

taziyya Shii passion play depicting the martyrdom of Husayn

ulama (**sing.** *alim*) scholars who have largely been the arbiters of Islamic jurisprudence since the ninth century

umma the global Muslim community

umra "visitation," lesser pilgrimage to Mecca, which can be performed any time of the year

usul al-fiqh principles of Islamic jurisprudence, sources of Islamic law (for Sunnis, the Quran, the Sunna of the Prophet, consensus [*ijma*], analogical reasoning [*qiyas*])

vilayat-i-faqih guardianship or government by an expert in Islamic law

wali friend or protégé of God, Sufi saint

waqf (**pl.** *awqaf*) a religious endowment of private property given in perpetuity, generally in the form of a charity, building, or public service

wisaya "testament," designation of Ali as executor of Muhammad's will and testament

zakat contributions (alms tax) for the poor and needy to redress economic inequalities; for Sunnis this is traditionally a 2.5 percent tithe

zawiyya Sufi residence or center

zina illegal sexual intercourse, includes both adultery and fornication

zulm oppression; sin

Select Bibliography

Reference Works

Cesari, Jocelyn. Ed. *Encyclopedia of Islam in the United States* (Westport, CT: Greenwood Press, 2007).

DeLong-Bas. Natana, ed. *The Oxford Encyclopedia of Islam and Women* (New York: Oxford University Press, 2014).

Esposito, John, ed. *The Islamic World: Past and Present* (New York: Oxford University Press, 2004).

Esposito, John, ed. *The Oxford Dictionary of Islam* (New York: Oxford University Press, 2003).

Esposito, John, ed. *The Oxford Encyclopedia of the Islamic World* (New York: Oxford University Press, 2009).

Espostito, John, ed. *The Oxford Encyclopedia of the Modern Islamic World* (New York: Oxford University Press, 1995).

Hodgson, Marshall G. S. *The Venture of Islam: Conscience and History in a World Civilization*, 3 vols. (Chicago: University of Chicago Press, 1974).

Khan, Muhammad Muhsin. *The Translation of the Meanings of Sahih al-Bukhari*, 9 vols., 3rd rev. ed. (Chicago: Kazi Publications, 1979).

Khan, Muhammad Muhsin. *The Islamic Near East and North Africa: An Annotated Mishkat al-Masabih*, 4 vols. James Robson, trans. (Lahore, Pakistan: Sh. Muhammad Ashraf, 1964–1966).

Sahih Muslim. Abdul Hamid Siddiqi, trans. (Lahore, Pakistan: Sh. Muhammad Ashraf, 1971–1973).

History of Islam

Afsaruddin, Asma. *The First Muslims: History and Memory* (Oxford, UK: Oneworld, 2008).

Armstrong, Karen. *Islam: A Short History* (New York: Modern Library, 2002).

Asad, Muhammad. *Islam at the Crossroads* (New Delhi, India: Kitab Bhavan, 2003).

Brown, Jonathan A. C. *Muhammad: A Short History* (Oxford: UK: Oneworld, 2011).

Brown, Jonathan A. C. *Misquoting Muhammad* (Oxford: UK: Oneworld, 2014).

Brown, Jonathan A. C. *Hadith, Muhammad's Legacy in the Medieval and Modern World* (Oxford: UK: Oneworld, 2009).

Donner, Fred McGraw. *The Early Islamic Conquests.* (Princeton, NJ: Princeton University Press, 1981).

Donner, Fred McGraw. *The Expansion of the Early Islamic State.* (Burlington, VT: Ashgate, 2008).

Donohue, John J., and John L. Esposito, eds. *Islam in Transition: Muslim Perspectives*, 2nd ed. (New York: Oxford University Press, 2007).

Esposito, John L., ed. *The Oxford History of Islam*, 2nd ed (New York: Oxford University Press, 2015).

Lapidus, Ira. *A History of Islamic Societies*, 2nd ed. (New York: Cambridge University Press, 2014).

Lowney, Chris. *A Vanished World: Medieval Spain's Golden Age of Enlightenment* (New York: Free Press, 2005).

Nasr, Sayyed Hossein. *Islam: Religion, History, and Civilization* (San Francisco, CA: Harper SanFrancisco, 2003).

Peters, F. E. *Muhammad and the Origins of Islam* (Albany, NY: State University of New York Press, 1994).

Peters, F. E. *A Reader on Classical Islam* (Princeton, NJ: Princeton University Press, 1994).

Sonn, Tamara. *A Brief History of Islam* (Malden, MA: Blackwell, 2004).

Voll, John Obert. *Islam, Continuity and Change in the Modern World*, 2nd ed. (Syracuse, NY: Syracuse University Press, 1994).

Watt, W. Montgomery. *Muhammad at Mecca* (New York: Oxford University Press, 1980).

Watt, W. *Muhammad at Medina* (New York: Oxford University Press, 1984).

Translations of the Quran

Ali, A. Yusuf. *The Koran: Text, Translation and Commentary* (Washington, DC: American International Printing Company, 1946).

Ali, Ahmed. *Al-Quran: A Contemporary Translation* (Princeton, NJ: Princeton University Press, 2001).

Asad, Muhammad. *The Message of the Quran* (Chicago: Kazi Publications, 1996).

Bakhtiar, Leila. *The Sublime Quran: Based on the Hanafi, Maliki, and Shafii Schools of Law* (Chicago: Kazi Publications, 2007).

Bell, Richard. *The Quran, Translated with a Critical Rearrangement of the Surahs*, 2 vols (Edinburgh, United Kingdom: T. T. Clark, 1937–1939).

Fakhry, Majid. *An Interpretation of the Qur'an* (New York: New York University Press, 2002).

Haleem, M. A. S. Abdul. *The Qur'an* (Oxford: Oxford University Press, 2008).

Helminski, Kabir. *The Book of Revelations: A Sourcebook of Themes from the Holy Qur'an* (Watsonville, CA: The Book Foundation, 2005).

Pickthall, Mohammed Marmaduke. *The Meaning of the Glorious Koran* (Elmhurst, NY: Tahrike Tarsile Quran, 2001).

Quranic Studies

Bakhtiar, Laleh. *Concordance of the Sublime Quran* (Chicago: Kazi, 2011).

Cragg, Kenneth. *Muhammad in the Qur'an: The Task and the Text* (London: Melisende, 2001).

Cragg, Kenneth. *The Qur'an and the West* (Washington, DC: Georgetown University Press, 2006).

Cragg, Kenneth. *The Pen and the Faith: Eight Modern Muslim Writers and the Qur'an* (New York: Routledge, 2008).

Esack, Farid. *The Qur'an: A Short Introduction* (Oxford, UK: Oneworld, 2002).

Esack, Farid. *The Qur'an: A User's Guide.* (Oxford, UK: Oneworld, 2005).

Kassis, Hanna E., ed. *A Concordance of the Qur'an* (Berkeley, CA: University of California Press, 1983).

Lawrence, Bruce B. *The Qur'an: A Biography* (New York: Atlantic Monthly Press, 2007).

McAuliffe, Jane Dammen, ed. *The Cambridge Companion to the Qur'an* (Cambridge: Cambridge University Press, 2006).

Rahman, Falzlur. *Major Themes of the Qur'an*, 2nd ed. (Chicago: Bibliotheca Islamica, 1989).

Rippin, Andrew, ed. *Blackwell Companion to the Qur'an* (Oxford, UK: Wiley-Blackwell, 2006).

Sachedina, Abdulaziz Abdulhussein. *The Qur'an on Religious Pluralism* (Washington, DC: Georgetown University Press, 1999).

Sells, Michael. *Approaching the Qur'an.* Ashland, OR: White Cloud Press, 1999).

Stowasser, Barbara Freyer. *Women in the Qur'an, Traditions and Interpretations* (New York: Oxford University Press, 1996).

Wadud, Amina. *Quran and Woman* (New York: Oxford University Press, 1999).

Religion and Theology

Abduh, Muhammad. *The Theology of Unity.* Kenneth Cragg and Ishaq Musa'ad, trans. (London: Allen and Unwin, 1966).

Armstrong, Karen. *Muhammad: A Biography of the Prophet* (San Francisco, CA: Harper SanFrancisco, 1992).

Armstrong, Karen. *Muhammad: A Prophet for Our Time* (New York: Atlas Books, 2006).

Azami, Muhammad Mustafa. *Studies in Early Hadith Literature,* 2nd ed. (Indianapolis, IN: American Trust Publications, 1978).

Bell, Richard. *Bell's Introduction to the Qur'an,* rev. ed., revised and edited by W. Montgomery Watt (Edinburgh, United Kingdom: Edinburgh University Press, 1994).

Caspar, Robert. *A Historical Introduction to Islamic Theology: Muhammad and the Classical Period* (Rome: Pontifical Institute for Arabic and Islamic Studies, 1998).

Cragg, Kenneth. *Jesus and the Muslim: An Exploration* (Boston: Oneworld, 1999).

Guillaume, Alfred, ed. and trans. *The Life of Muhammad: A Translation of Ibn Ishaq's Sirat Rasul Allah* (New York: Oxford University Press, 1997).

Iqbal, Sir Muhammad. *The Reconstruction of Religious Thought in Islam* (Chicago: Kazi Publications, 1999).

Lings, Martin. *Muhammad: His Life Based on the Earliest Sources* (London: Allen & Unwin, 1983).

Mawdudi, Abdul A'la. *Towards Understanding Islam* (Chicago: Kazi Publications, 1992).

Ramadan, Tariq. *What I Believe* (New York: Oxford University Press, 2010).

Ramadan, Tariq. *In the Footsteps of the Prophet: Lessons from the Life of Muhammad* (New York: Oxford University Press, 2007).

Ramadan, Tariq. *The Messenger: The Meanings of the Life of Muhammad* (London: Allen Lane, 2007).

Renard, John. *Understanding the Islamic Experience* (Mahwah, NJ: Paulist Press, 2002).

Renard, John, ed. *Windows on the House of Islam* (Berkeley, CA: University of California, 1998).

Sadri, Mahmoud, and Ahmad Sadri, trans. and eds. *Reason, Freedom, and Democracy in Islam: Essential Writings of Abdolkarim Soroush* (New York: Oxford University Press, 2000).

Schimmel, Annemarie. *And Muhammad Is His Messenger* (Chapel Hill, NC: University of North Carolina Press, 1985).

Watt, W. Montgomery. *Free Will and Predestination in Early Islam* (Ann Arbor, MI: University Microfilms International, 1978).

Watt, W. Montgomery. *Islamic Philosophy and Theology* (Edinburgh, United Kingdom: Edinburgh University Press, 1996).

Wolfe, Michael. *Hadj: An American's Pilgrimage to Mecca* (New York: Grove Press, 1993).

Wolfe, Michael, ed. *One Thousand Roads to Mecca: Ten Centuries of Travelers Writing About the Muslim Pilgrimage* (New York: Grove Press, 1999).

Introductions to Islam

Aslan, Reza. *There Is No God but God: The Origins, Evolution, and Future of Islam* (New York: Random House, 2005).

Bloom, Jonathan, and Sheila Blair. *Islam: A Thousand Years of Faith and Power* (New Haven, CT: Yale University Press, 2002).

Denny, Frederick M. *An Introduction to Islam,* 4th ed. (Upper Saddle River, NJ: Pearson Prentice Hall, 2011).

Esposito, John L. *The Future of Islam* (New York: Oxford University Press, 2010).

Esposito, John L. *What Everyone Needs to Know About Islam*, 2nd ed. New York: Oxford University Press, 2011.

Nasr, Sayyed Hossein. *The Heart of Islam: Enduring Values for Humanity* (San Francisco, CA: Harper San Francisco, 2002).

Nasr, Sayyed Hossein. *Ideals and Realities of Islam*, new rev. ed. (Chicago: Kazi Publications, 2000).

Nasr, Sayyed Hossein. *Traditional Islam in the Modern World* (London: KPI Limited, 1987).

Peters, F. E. *Muhammad and the Origins of Islam* (Albany, NY: State University of New York Press, 1994).

Rahman, Fazlur. *Islam*, 2nd ed. (Chicago: University of Chicago Press, 1979).

Renard, John. *Responses to 101 Questions on Islam* (New York: Gramercy Books, 2002).

Rippin, Andrew, and Jan Knappert. *Textual Sources for the Study of Islam* (Chicago: University of Chicago Press, 1990).

Shiism

Chittick, William C., ed. and trans. *A Shiite Anthology* (Albany, NY: State University of New York Press, 1981).

Cole, Juan. *Sacred Space and Holy War: The Politics, Culture and History of Shi'ite Islam* (New York: I. B. Tauris, 2002).

Dakake, Maria Massi. *The Charismatic Community: Shi'ite Identity in Early Islam* (Albany, NY: State University of New York Press, 2007).

DeGroot, Joanna. *Religion, Culture and Politics in Iran: From the Qajars to Khomeini* (New York: I.B. Tauris, 2007).

Halm, Heinz. *The Shi'ites: A Short History*, 2nd ed. (Princeton, NJ: Marcus Wiener Publishers, 2007).

Kohlberg, Etan, ed. *Shi'ism* (Burlington, VT: Ashgate, 2003).

Momen, Moojan. *An Introduction to Shii Islam* (New Haven, CT: Yale University Press, 1985).

Rogerson, Barnaby. *The Heirs of the Prophet Muhammad and the Roots of the Sunni-Shia Schism* (London: Little, Brown, 2006).

Takim, Liyakat N. *Heirs of the Prophet: Charisma and Religious Authority in Shi'ite Islam* (Albany, NY: State University of New York Press, 2007).

Thurlkill, Mary F. *Chosen among Women: Mary and Fatima in Medieval Christianity and Shi'ite Islam* (Notre Dame, IN: Notre Dame University Press, 2008).

Sufism

Abou El Fadl, Khaled. *The Search for Beauty in Islam: A Conference of the Books* (Lanham, MD: Rowman and Littlefield, 2005).

Abun-Nasr, Jamil M. *Muslim Communities of Grace: Sufi Brotherhoods in Islamic Religious Life* (New York: Columbia University Press, 2007).

Arberry, A. J. *An Introduction to the History of Sufism* (London: Longman, 1942).

Arberry, A. J. *Sufism: An Account of the Mystics of Islam* (Mineola, NY: Courier Dover Publications, 2002).

Chittick, William C. *Ibn Arabi: Heir to the Prophet* (Oxford, UK: Oneworld, 2005).

Chittick, William C. *Science of the Cosmos, Science of the Soul: The Pertinence of Islamic Cosmology in the Modern World* (Oxford, UK: Oneworld, 2007).

Chittick, William C. *Sufism: A Beginner's Guide* (Oxford, UK: Oneworld, 2007).

Chittick, William C., ed. *The Inner Journey: Views from the Islamic Tradition* (Sandpoint, IN: Morning Light Press, 2007).

Frembgen, Jürgen Wasim. *Journey to God: Sufis and Dervishes in Islam* (Oxford: Oxford University Press, 2009).

Lings, Martin. *A Sufi Saint of the Twentieth Century* (Cambridge, UK: Islamic Texts Society, 1993).

Lings, Martin. *What Is Sufism?*, 2nd ed. (Berkeley, CA: University of California Press, 1999).

Nasr, Seyyed Hossein. *The Garden of Truth: The Vision and Promise of Sufism, Islam's Mystical Tradition* (New York: HarperOne, 2007).

Nasr, Seyyed Hossein. *Sufi Essays*, 2nd ed. (Albany, NY: State University of New York Press, 1991).

Nasr, Seyyed Hossein. *Three Muslim Sages: Avicenna, Suhrawardi, Ibn 'Arabi* (Cambridge, MA: Harvard University Press, 1964).

Nasr, Seyyed Hossein, ed. *Islamic Spirituality: Foundations* (New York: Crossroads, 1997).

Nicholson, Reynold A. *The Mystics of Islam* (Sacramento, CA: Murine Press, 2007).

Nicholson, Reynold A. *Rumi: Poet and Mystic* (Oxford, UK: Oneworld, 1995).

Schimmel, Annemarie. *Mystical Dimensions of Islam* (Chapel Hill, NC: University of North Carolina Press, 1975).

Schimmel, Annemarie. *The Triumphal Sun: A Study of the Works of Jalaluddin Rumi* (Albany, NY: State University Press of New York, 1993).

Sedgwick, Mark J. *Sufism: The Essentials* (Cairo, Egypt: The American University in Cairo Press, 2000).

Trimingham, J. Spencer. *The Sufi Orders in Islam*, 2nd ed. (Oxford: Oxford University Press, 1998).

Van Bruinessen, Martin. *Sufism and the "Modern" in Islam* (New York: I.B. Tauris, 2007).

Watt, W. Montgomery. *The Faith and Practice of al-Ghazali* (Oxford, UK: Oneworld, 2000).

Law and Society

Abdo, Geneive. *No God but God: Egypt and the Triumph of Islam* (New York: Oxford University Press, 2000).

Abou El Fadl, Khaled, Joshua Cohen, and Deborah Chasman. *Islam and the Challenge of Democracy* (Princeton, NJ: Princeton University Press, 2004).

Abou El Fadl, Khaled, et al. *Speaking in God's Name: Islamic Law, Authority, and Women* (Oxford, UK: Oneworld, 2001).

Afsaruddin, Asma, ed. *Hermeneutics and Honor: Negotiating Female "Public" Space in Islamic/ate Societies* (Cambridge, MA: Distributed for the Center for Harvard University by Harvard University Press, 1999).

Ahmed, Leila. *Women and Gender in Islam* (New Haven, CT: Yale University Press, 1993).

Armstrong, Karen. *Jerusalem: One City, Three Faiths* (New York: Alfred A. Knopf, 1996).

Coulson, Noel J. *A History of Islamic Law* (Edinburgh, United Kingdom: Edinburgh University Press, 1994).

Esposito, John L. *Islam and Politics*, 4th ed. (Syracuse, NY: Syracuse University Press, 1998).

Esposito, John L., and Dalia Mogahed. *Who Speaks for Islam?* (New York: Gallup Press, 2007).

Esposito, John L., and Natana J. Delong-Bas. *Women in Muslim Family Law*, 2nd ed. (Syracuse, NY: Syracuse University Press, 2001).

Esposito, John L., and Emad Shahin, eds. *The Oxford Handbook of Islam ad Politics* (New York: Oxford University Press, 2013).

Haddad, Yvonne Yazbeck, and John L. Esposito, eds. *Islam: Gender and Social Change* (New York: Oxford University Press, 1998).

Hallaq, Wael. *A History of Islamic Legal Theories: An Introduction to Sunni Usul Al-Fiqh* (Cambridge: Cambridge University Press, 1997).

Klausen, Jytte. *The Cartoons That Shook the World* (New Haven, CT: Yale University Press, 2009).

Mernissi, Fatima. *The Veil and the Male Elite: A Feminist Interpretation of Women's Rights in Islam*. Mary Jo Lakeland, trans. (New York: Addison-Wesley, 1991).

Qaradawi, Yusuf al. *The Lawful and the Prohibited in Islam* (Qum, Iran: Islamic Culture and Relations Organization, 1998).

Rahman, Fazlur. *Islam and Modernity: The Transformation of an Intellectual Tradition* (Chicago: University of Chicago Press, 1982).

Rahman, Fazlur. *Radical Reform: Islamic Ethics and Liberation* (New York: Oxford University Press, 2009).

Ramadan, Tariq. *Radical Reform: Islamic Ethics and Liberation* (New York: Oxford University Press, 2008).

Islam in the West

Cesari, Jocelyne. *Muslims in the West after 9/11: Religions, Politics and Law* (London: Routledge, 2008).

Cesari, Jocelyne. *When Islam and Democracy Meet: Muslims in Europe and in the United States* (New York: Palgrave Macmillian, 2004).

Cesari, Jocelyne, and Sean McLoughlin, eds. *European Muslims and the Secular State* (Burlington, VT: Ashgate, 2005).

Daniel, Norman. *Islam and the West: The Making of an Image*, rev. ed. (Oxford, UK: Oneworld, 1993).

Ebrahimji, Maria & Zahra Suratwala, *I Speak for Myself; American Women on Being Muslim* (Ashland, OR: White Cloud Press, 2011).

Esposito, John L., Yvonne Haddad, and Jane Smith. *Immigrant Faiths: Christians, Jews, and Muslims Becoming Americans* (Walnut Creek, CA: Alta Mira Press, 2002).

Haddad, Yvonne Yazbeck, ed. *Muslims in the West: From Sojourners to Citizens* (New York: Oxford University Press, 2002).

Haddad, Yvonne Yazbeck, and John L. Esposito, eds. *Muslims on the Americanization Path* (New York: Oxford University Press, 2000).

Haddad, Yvonne Yazbeck, and Jane I. Smith. *Muslim Minorities in the West: Visible and Invisible* (Walnut Creek, CA: AltaMira Press, 2002).

Haddad, Yvone Yazbeck, and Kathleen M. Moore. *Muslim Women in America: The Challenge of Islamic Identity* (New York: Oxford University Press, 2006).

Haddad, Yvonne Yazbeck, and Jane I. Smith, eds. *The Oxford Handbook of American Islam* (New York: Oxford University Press, 2014).

Hunter, Shireen. *Islam: Europe's Second Religion* (Westport, CT: Praeger, 2002).

Jenkins, Philip. *God's Continent: Christianity, Islam and Europe's Religious Crisis* (New York: Oxford University Press, 2007).

Klausen, Jytte. *The Islamic Challenge: Politics and Religion in Western Europe* (New York: Oxford University Press, 2005).

Lewis, Philip. *Islamic Britain: Religion, Politics, and Identity among British Muslims* (London: I. B. Tauris, 1994).

Nielsen, Jorgen. *Muslims in Western Europe*, 3rd ed. (Edinburgh, UK: Edinburgh University Press, 2005).

Nielsen, Jorgen. *Towards a European Islam* (London: St. Martin's Press, 1999).

Nyang, Sulayman S. *Islam in the United States of America* (Chicago: ABC International Group, Inc. 1999).

Nyang, Sulayman S. *Muslims in Western Europe,* 3rd ed. (Edinburgh, UK: Edinburgh University, 2004).

Ramadan, Tariq. *To Be a European Muslim* (Leicester, UK: The Islamic Foundation, 2003).

Ramadan, Tariq. *Western Muslims and the Future of Islam* (New York: Oxford University Press, 2004).

Said, Edward W. *Covering Islam: How the Media and the Experts Determine How We See the Rest of the World* (New York: Pantheon Books, 1981).

Said, Edward W. *Culture and Imperialism* (New York: Vintage Books, 1994).

Smith, Jane I. *Islam in America* (New York: Columbia University Press, 1999).

Muslim Politics

Abou El Fadl, Khaled. *The Great Theft: Wrestling Islam from the Extremists* (New York: Harper SanFranscico, 2005).

Abou El Fadl, Khaled, Joshua Cohen, and Ian Lague. *The Place of Tolerance in Islam* (Boston: Beacon Press, 2002).

Ahmed, Akbar S. *After Terror: Promoting Dialogue among Civilizations* (Malden, MA: Polity Press, 2005).

Ahmed, Akbar S. *Islam under Siege: Living Dangerously in a Post-Honor World* (Malden, MA: Polity Press, 2003).

Bunt, Gary R. *Islam in the Digital Age: E-Jihad, On-Line Fatwas and Cyber Islamic Environments* (London: Pluto Press, 2003).

Bunt, Gary R. *iMuslims: Rewiring the House of Islam* (Chapel Hill, NC: University of North Carolina Press, 2009).

Caridi, Paola. *HAMAS: From resistance to Government* (New York: Seven Stories Pres, 2012)

Esposito, John L. *The Islamic Threat: Myth or Reality?*, 2nd ed. ed. (New York: Oxford University Press, 1999).

Esposito, John. *Unholy War: Terror in the Name of Islam* (New York: Oxford University Press, 2002).

Esposito, John, ed. *Voices of Resurgent Islam* (New York: Oxford University Press, 1983).

Esposito, John, and John O. Voll. *Islam and Democracy* (New York: Oxford University Press, 1996).

Esposito, John, and John O. Voll. *Makers of Contemporary Islam* (New York: Oxford University Press, 2001).

Esposito, John, John Voll, and Osman Bakar, eds. *Asian Islam in the 21st Century* (New York: Oxford University Press, 2007).

Fuller, Graham E. *The Future of Political Islam* (New York: Palgrave Macmillian, 2004).

Hamid, Shadi. *Temptations of Power: Islamists and Illiberal Democracy in the Middle East.* (New York: Oxford University Press, 2014).

Jansen, Johannes J. G. *The Neglected Duty: The Creed of Sadat's Assassins and Islamic Resurgence in the Middle East* (New York: The Free Press, 1988).

Kimball, Charles. *When Religion Becomes Evil* (New York: HarperCollins, 2002).

Laden, Osama bin. *Messages to the World: The Statements of Osama bin Laden*, annotated ed., Bruce Lawrence, ed. (New York: Verso, 2005).

Lewis, Bernard. *The Crisis of Islam: Holy War and Unholy Terror* (New York: Modern Library, 2003).

Lewis, Bernard. *What Went Wrong? Western Impact and Middle Eastern Response*, 4th ed. (New York: Oxford University Press, 2002).

Mandaville, Peter. *Islam and Politics* (London: Routledge, 2014).

Nasr, Vali. *The Shia Revival: How Conflicts Within Islam Will Shape the Future* (New York: Norton, 2006).

Peters, Rudolph. *Jihad in Classical and Modern Islam* (Princeton, NJ: Markus Wiener Publishers, 1996).

Qutb, Sayyid. *Milestones*, rev. ed. (Boll Ridge, IN: American Trust Publications, 1991).

Rashid, Ahmed. *Taliban: Militant Islam, Oil, and Fundamentalism in Central Asia* (New Haven, CT: Yale University Press, 2000).

Roy, Olivier. *Globalized Islam: The Search for a New Ummah* (New York: Columbia University Press, 2004).

Saad-Ghorayeb, Amal. *Hizbu'llah: Politics and Religion* (London: Pluto Press, 2002).

Sachedina, Abdulaziz Abdulhussein. *The Islamic Roots of Democratic Pluralism* (New York: Oxford University Press, 2001).

Tamimi, Azzam. *Hamas: A History from Within* (Fowlerville, MI: Olive Branch Press, 2007).

Muslim–Christian Relations

Al-Faruqi, Isma'il R. *Islam and Other Faiths.* Ataullah Siddiqui, ed. (Leicester, UK: Islamic Foundation and International Institute of Islamic Thought, 1998).

Armour, Rollin. *Islam, Christianity, and the West: A Troubled History* (Maryknoll, NY: Orbis, 2002).

Armstrong, Karen. *The Battle for God: Fundamentalism in Judaism, Christianity, and Islam* (New York: Alfred A. Knopf, 2000).

Armstrong, Karen. *Holy War: The Crusades and Their Impact on Today's World*, 2nd ed. (New York: Anchor Books, 2001).

Ayoub, Muhammad. *A Muslim View of Christianity: Essays on Dialogue*. Irfan A. Omar, ed. (Maryknoll, NY: Orbis Books, 2007).

Bill, James A., and John Alden Williams. *Roman Catholics and Shi'i Muslims* (Chapel Hill, NC: University of North Carolina Press, 2002).

Bulliet, Richard W. *The Case for Islamo-Christian Civilization* (New York: Columbia University Press, 2004).

Catlos, Brian. *Muslims of Medieval Latin Christendom, c.1050–1614* (Cambridge: Cambridge University Press, 2014).

Cragg, Kenneth. *Muhammad and the Christian: A Question of Responses* (Boston: Oneworld, 1999).

Cragg, Kenneth. *The Call of the Minaret* (Oxford, UK: Oneworld, 2000).

Cragg, Kenneth. *Islam among the Spires: An Oxford Reverie* (London: Melisende, 2000).

Daniel, Norman. *The Arabs and Medieval Europe* (London: Longman, 1975).

Daniel, Norman. *Islam and the West: The Making of an Image* (London: Oneworld, 2000).

Dardess, George. *Meeting Islam: A Guide for Christians* (Brewster, MA: Paraclete Press, 2005).

Esposito, John. *The Future of Islam* (New York: Oxford University Press, 2010).

Fitzgerald, Michael L., and John Borelli. *Interfaith Dialogue: A Catholic View* (Maryknoll, NY: Orbis, 2006).

Goddard, Hugh. *A History of Christian-Muslim Relations* (Chicago: New Amsterdam Books, 2001).

Griffiths, Sidney. *The Beginnings of Christian Theology in Arabic: Muslim-Christian Encounters in the Early Islamic Period* (Burlington, VT: Ashgate, 2002).

Griffiths, Sidney. *The Church in the Shadow of the Mosque* (Princeton, NJ: Princeton University Press, 2008).

Haddad, Yvonne, and Wadi Z. Haddad, eds. *Christian–Muslim Encounters* (Gainesville, FL: University Press of Florida, 1995).

Hussein, Amir. *Oil and Water Two Faiths: One God* (Copper House, 2006).

Kimball, Charles. *Striving Together: A Way Forward in Christian–Muslim Relations* (Maryknoll, NY: Orbis, 1991).

Lewis, David Levering. *God's Crucible: Islam and the Making of Europe 570-1215* (New York: Norton, 2008).

Michel, Thomas. *A Christian View of Islam* (New York: Orbis, 2010).

McLaren, Brian. *Why Did Jesus, Moses, the Buddha, and Mohammed Cross the Road?: Christian Identity in a Multi-Faith World* (Nashville, NY: Jericho Books, 2012).

Menocal, Maria Rosa. *The Ornament of the World: How Muslims, Jews, and Christians Created a Culture of Tolerance in Medieval Spain* (New York: Little, Brown, 2002).

Peters, F. E. *Children of Abraham* (Princeton, NJ: Princeton University Press, 2006).

Smith, Jane I. *Muslims, Christians, and the Challenge of Interfaith Dialogue* (New York: Oxford University Press, 2007).

Southern, R. W. *Western Views of Islam in the Middle Ages* (Cambridge, MA: Harvard University Press, 1978).

Spector, Stephen. *Evangelicals and Israel: The Story of American Christian Zionism* (New York: Oxford University press, 2009).

Watt, W. Montgomery. *Muslim–Christian Encounters: Perceptions and Misperceptions* (London: Routledge, 1991).

Islamophobia

Bail, Christopher. *Terrified: How Anti-Muslim Fringe Organizations Became Mainstream* (Princeton, NJ: Princeton University Press, 2014).

Cesari, Jocelyn. *Why the West Fears Islam: An Exploration of Muslims in Liberal Democracies* (New York: Palgrave, 2013).

Ernst, Carl, ed. *Islamophobia in America* (New York: Palgrave, 2013).

Esposito, John L., ed., *Islamophobia: The Challenge of Pluralism in the 21st Century* (Oxford: Oxford University Press, 2011).

Fekete, Liz. *A Suitable Enemy: Racism, Migration, and Islamophobia in Europe* (London: Pluto Press, 2009).

Gottschalk, Peter, and Gabriel Greenfield, eds. *Islamophobia: Making Muslims the Enemy* (Lanham, MD: Rowman and Littlefield, 2007).

Hafez, Farid, and Humayan Ansari, eds. *From the Far Right to the Mainstream: Islamophobia in Party Politics* (Frankfurt: Campus-Verlag, 2012).

Kumar, Deepa. *Islamophobia and the Politics of Empire* (Chicago: Haymarket Books, 2012).

Kundnani, Arun. *The Muslims Are Coming! Islamophobia, Extremism, and the Domestic War on Terror* (London: Verso Books, 2014).

Lean, Nathan. *The Islamophobia Industry: How the Right Manufactures Fear of Muslims* (London: Pluto Press, 2012).

Norton, Ann. *On the Muslim Question* (Princeton, NJ: Princeton University Press, 2013).

Saunders, Doug. *The Myth of the Muslim Tide: Do Immigrants Threaten the West?* (New York: Vintage Books, 2012).

Tyrer, David. *The Politics of Islamophobia: Race, Power, and Fantasy* (London: Pluto Press, 2013).

Photo Credits

INDEX

Figures are indicated by italic page numbers.